Introducing Machine Learning

Dino Esposito
Francesco Esposito

Introducing Machine Learning

Published with the authorization of Microsoft Corporation by:

Pearson Education, Inc.

ISBN-13: 978-0-13-556566-7

ISBN-10: 0-13-556566-9

Library of Congress Control Number: 2019954810

1 2020

Trademarks

Microsoft and the trademarks listed at http://www.microsoft.com on the "Trademarks" webpage are trademarks of the Microsoft group of companies. All other marks are property of their respective owners.

Warning and Disclaimer

Special Sales

For information about buying this title in bulk quantities, or for special sales opportunities (which may include electronic versions; custom cover designs; and content particular to your business, training goals, marketing focus, or branding interests), please contact our corporate sales department at corpsales@pearsoned.com or (800) 382-3419.

For government sales inquiries, please contact governmentsales@pearsoned.com.

For questions about sales outside the U.S., please contact intlcs@pearson.com.

Editor-in-Chief
Brett Bartow

Executive Editor
Loretta Yates

Development Editor
Mark Renfrow

Assistant Sponsoring Editor
Charvi Arora

Managing Editor
Sandra Schroeder

Senior Project Editor
Tonya Simpson

Copy Editor
Chuck Hutchinson

Indexer
Cheryl Ann Lenser

Proofreader
Abigail Manheim

Technical Editor
Cesar De la Torre Llorente

Editorial Assistant
Cindy Teeters

Cover Designer
Twist Creative, Seattle

Cover Image
IMOGI graphics

Compositor
codeMantra

Dedications

To Michela and her dreams
To my loved ones, to whom I couldn't help but dedicate a book

Contents at a Glance

Contents

PART I LAYING THE GROUNDWORK OF MACHINE LEARNING

Chapter 1 How Humans Learn 3

Chapter 2 Intelligent Software 23

Chapter 3   Mapping Problems and Algorithms   33

Chapter 4   General Steps for a Machine Learning Solution   49

Chapter 5   The Data Factor   67

PART II   MACHINE LEARNING IN .NET

Chapter 6   The .NET Way   77

PART III   FUNDAMENTALS OF SHALLOW LEARNING

Chapter 9   Math Foundations of Machine Learning   135

Chapter 10   Metrics of Machine Learning   151

Chapter 11   How to Make Simple Predictions: Linear Regression   165

Chapter 12   How to Make Complex Predictions and Decisions: Trees   181

Chapter 15 How to Group Data: Classification and Clustering   229

Chapter 16 Feed-Forward Neural Networks   255

Chapter 17 Design of a Neural Network   273

Chapter 18 Other Types of Neural Networks   291

Chapter 21 The Business Perception of AI   339

Acknowledgments

Writing a book with your son is a special experience even when it's the umpteenth book you write. For this one, I just put down in (hopefully clear) words Francesco's thoughts, vision, and his deep, and largely unexplained, understanding of machine learning. I definitely learned a lot from writing as much as I hope you will learn from reading.

If I learned a lot, well, that was mostly because of two people.

It's not the first time I have done some writing under the technical supervision of Cesar De la Torre Llorente, and it's always been a heavenly experience. I love his pragmatism and accuracy in devising, before designing, software products. He's currently principal program manager on the .NET product group at Microsoft and is in charge of the development of ML.NET. This is not specifically a book on ML.NET, but if the parts of the book that illustrate the .NET way to machine learning are accurate, well, that's because of the great help we received from Cesar.

There's an aspect in renewable energy that is little known: you need intelligent software to make it happen. At least on a functional level, it is vital to make accurate production, outage, fault, and price forecasts. Now, I don't think there are many people on this planet with a decade's worth of experience in this area that only recently was appointed the label *artificial intelligence*. Tiago Santos has been our guide in the random forest of machine learning and real-world artificial intelligence. "AI is just software" is now our shared motto.

If I've been able to give my career yet another turn (from Windows to web development and from software architecture to machine learning), it's also because two other people keep my creativity constantly stimulated. Giorgio Garcia-Agreda of Crionet made real my dreams as a tennis fanatic come true, up to singing "Easy like Sunday morning" in front of the tennis bigwigs. Simone Massaro of BaxEnergy discovered a fascinating new space where my renewable energy as a thinker can be freely expressed, sometimes even in front of top managers.

Any book is the result of teamwork, and it is our pleasure to call out the names of those who ultimately made it possible: Loretta Yates, as the acquisition editor; Charvi Arora, the managing editor, and Tonya Simpson, production editor.

—Dino

I finished high school one year early, and all I wanted was some money to practice as a professional investor. I had the wrong parents, though, and that approach didn't work. So, I asked my dad how to make money. "That's your problem," he said. "I can only teach you all I know." So, he taught me how to do things right and forgot to teach me how to do it wrong. As a result, today, we make the same mistakes in software. At this point, with some money in my hands, I was blissfully neglecting college when, on a hot summer afternoon, my dad told me, "Be honest: if you don't want to train your brain further, resign from college." As a result, a month later, I was back in class with a radically different mindset. I love mathematics, and I can't live doing anything different from it.

Then I met Gianfranco—friend, business partner, father, grandfather. He's a real professional investor, and he too taught me how to do things right and forgot to teach me how to do it wrong. As a result, today, we make the same mistakes in finance.

At school, at work, in the stock market, I study and try things. Sometimes they work, sometimes they don't, and whenever they don't, I learn something. It's the stick and carrot principle: the essence of learning for humans and machines. This book stems from my obsession for mathematical rigor and my dad's obsession for clarity. We used the stick on ourselves during the writing to ensure that carrots would be available during the reading.

This book is for you, Mom, because you'd love me anyway, regardless of triumph, disaster, or other impostors. This is for you, Maicol, because you'd love me even more if I stopped making noise on Sunday mornings.

This is for you, Alessandro, because you remind me when it's time to stop, and for you, Antonino, because you remind me of when I was too much of a smartass to be nice. This is for you, Sara, because you always give me a place to go the day before Christmas. And for you, Giorgio, because I'll always be a junior in front of you. This is for you, Grandma Concetta and Grandpa Salvatore, for the sausages, and for you, Grandma Leda, for your being as lively as any of us youngsters.

This is for you, Tiago, because we met only once to date, but enough to learn how much I have to learn from you.

This is also for all those I couldn't mention, including any of my present and future loves, so very complicated that would deserve a book of its own! And this is for me too, to help understand what I want to be.

—Francesco

About the Authors

DINO ESPOSITO

If I look back, I count more 20 books authored and 1000+ articles in a 25-year-long career. I've been writing the "Cutting Edge" column for *MSDN Magazine* month after month for 22 consecutive years. It is commonly recognized that such books and articles have helped the professional growth of thousands of .NET and ASP.NET developers and software architects worldwide.

After I escaped a dreadful COBOL project, in 1992 I started as a C developer, and since then, I have witnessed MFC and ATL, COM and DCOM, the debut of .NET, the rise and fall of Silverlight, and the ups and downs of various architectural patterns. In 1995 I led a team of five dreamers who actually deployed things that today we would call Google Photos and Shuttershock—desktop applications capable of dealing with photos stored in a virtual place that nobody had called the cloud yet. Since 2003 I have written Microsoft Press books about ASP.NET and also authored the bestseller *Microsoft .NET: Architecting Applications for the Enterprise*. I have a few successful Pluralsight courses on .NET architecture, ASP.NET MVC UI, and, recently, ML.NET. As architect of most of the backoffice applications that keep the professional tennis world tour running, I've been focusing on renewable energy, IoT, and artificial intelligence for the past two years as the corporate digital strategist at BaxEnergy.

You can get in touch with me through https://youbiquitous.net or twitter.com/despos, or you can connect to my LinkedIn network.

FRANCESCO ESPOSITO

I was 12 or so in the early days of the Windows Phone launch, and I absolutely wanted one of those devices in my hands. I could have asked Dad or Mom to buy it, but I didn't know how they would react. As a normal teenager, I had exactly zero chance of having someone buy it for me. So, I found out I was quite good at making sense of programming languages and impressed some folks at Microsoft enough to have a device to test. A Windows Phone was only the beginning; then came my insane passion for iOS and, later, the shortcuts of C#.

The current part of my life began when I graduated from high school, one year earlier than expected. By the way, only 0.006 percent of students do that in Italy. I felt as powerful as a semi-god and enrolled in mathematics. I failed my first exams, and the shock put me at work day and night on ASP.NET as a self punishment. I founded my small software company, Youbiquitous, and began living on my own money. In 2017, my innate love for mathematics was resurrected and put me back on track with studies and led me to take the plunge in financial investments and machine learning.

This book, then, is the natural consequence of the end of my childhood. I wanted to give something back to my dad and help him make sense of the deep mathematics behind neural networks and algorithms. By the way, I have a dream: developing a super-theory of intelligence that would mathematically explore why the artificial intelligence of today works and where we can go further.

You can get in touch with me at https://youbiquitous.net.

Introduction

We need men who can dream of things that never were, and ask why not.

—John F. Kennedy, Speech to the Irish Parliament, June 1963

There are two views of artificial intelligence that people face today, and they are nonexclusive. One is the view pushed and pursued by the vast majority of media; the other is the view pushed and pursued by the IT community. In both camps, there are some true experts and some true pundits.

The view pushed by media focuses on the impact that artificial intelligence as a whole, in known and yet-to-know forms, may possibly have on our lives in some unfathomable future. The view pushed by the IT community (where software and data science experts belong) presents machine learning as the foundation of a new generation of software services that are just more intelligent than current services.

In the middle ground between the mass of people that the media reach and the much smaller IT community sits the patrol of cloud giants. They're the ones who conduct research and move the state of the art one step further every day, releasing new services for everyone to potentially add intelligence to new and existing applications.

At the base of the artificial intelligence pyramid sit managers and executives. On one hand, they're eager to apply to business those stunning services they hear from the tech news to edge out their competitors. On the other hand, they face the staggering bills of the projects they embarked on with the best of hopes.

- Artificial intelligence is not a magic wand.

- Artificial intelligence is not a service to pay per use. Worse yet, it's neither a capital nor operating expenditure.

- Artificial intelligence is just software.

Any business decision about artificial intelligence is better if made through the lens of software development: set requirements, get a reliable partner, put a budget on the table, work, start again in full respect of agility.

Is it that easy, then?

While artificial intelligence is about software development, it's not exactly the same as building an e-commerce website or a booking platform.

- Don't embark on artificial intelligence projects if you don't have a clear idea of the problem to solve, the context of it, and the point(s) to make.

- Don't embark on ambitious and adventurous projects by following the sole example of your closest competitor.

- Don't embark on such projects if you're not ready to lose some good money.

Just address one pain point at a time, build a cross-functional team, and provide full access to data.

Who Should Read This Book?

In the preparation of this book, we received a lot of feedback about the structure and elaborated on it quite a few times. We radically changed the table of contents at least three times. The hard part is that we devised this book to be unique and innovative, pursuing an idea of machine learning and software development a bit far away from the reality we see. Hopefully, our vision is the vision of machine learning that comes from the near future!

We see machine learning bounded within the fences of data science, as an artifact to be delivered to developers to embed it into some web service or desktop application. This is waterfall—no more no less. Where is all the agile that companies and enterprises constantly talk about? Agile ML means that data scientists and developers work together, and business analysts and domain experts join the team. And data stakeholders— whether it's IT or DevOps or whatever else—also join to facilitate data access and manipulation. This is agile teamwork—no more, no less.

We see the (business) need of a convergence of skills—from data science to software development and from software development to data science. This entry-level book is good for both sides of the pipeline. It talks to developers and shows ML.NET in action (over Python and along with Python) before getting into the analysis of the mechanics of machine learning algorithms. It also talks to data scientists who need to learn more about software needs.

This book is ideal if you're a software developer willing to add data science and machine learning skills to your arsenal. It's also ideal if you're a data scientist willing to learn more about software. Both categories, though, need to learn more and more about the other.

This is the bet of this book. We've classified it as "introductory" because it expands in width instead of going deep. It provides .NET examples because we think that, while the Python ecosystem is rich and thriving, there's no reason not to look around for platforms that allow you to do some machine learning closer to the bare metal of software applications, software services, and microservices—where ultimately any learning pipeline (including TensorFlow, PyTorch, handcrafted Python code) ends up being used.

Who Should Not Read This Book?

This is an introductory-level book specifically devised to give a broad but clear and accurate overview of machine learning using the ML.NET platform for experimenting. If you're looking for tons of Python examples, this book is not ideal. If you're looking for how-to examples to copy and paste in your solutions, whether Python or ML.NET, we're not sure this book is ideal. If you're looking for the nitty-gritty details of the mathematics behind algorithms or for an annotated overview of some implementations of algorithms, again, this book may not be ideal. (We do include some mathematics, but we still only scratch the surface.)

Organization of This Book

This book is divided into five sections. Part I, "Laying the Groundwork of Machine Learning," provides a quick overview of the foundation of artificial intelligence, intelligent software, and the basic steps of any machine learning project within end-to-end solutions. Part II, "Machine Learning in .NET," focuses on the ML.NET library and outlines its core parts, such as tasks for data processing, training, and evaluation in the context of common problems such as regression and classification. Part III, "Fundamentals of Shallow Learning," touches on the mathematical details of families of algorithms commonly trained to solve real-life problems: regressors, decision trees, ensemble methods, Bayesian classifiers, support vector machines, K-means, online gradients. Part IV, "Fundamentals of Deep Learning," is dedicated to neural networks that may come into play when none of the previous algorithms are found suitable. Finally, Part V, "Final Thoughts," is about the business vision of artificial intelligence in general and machine learning in particular, and it provides a cursory review of the runtime services for data processing and computation made available by cloud platforms, specifically the Azure platform.

Code Samples

All the code illustrated in the book, including possible errata and extensions, can be found at *MicrosoftPressStore.com/IntroMachineLearning/downloads*.

Errata and Book Support

We've made every effort to ensure the accuracy of this book and its companion content. You can access updates to this book—in the form of a list of submitted errata and their related corrections—at

MicrosoftPressStore.com/IntroMachineLearning/errata

If you discover an error that is not already listed, please submit it to us at the same page.

For additional book support and information, please visit *http://www.MicrosoftPressStore.com/Support*.

Please note that product support for Microsoft software and hardware is not offered through the previous addresses. For help with Microsoft software or hardware, go to *http://support.microsoft.com*.

Stay in Touch

Let's keep the conversation going! We're on Twitter: *http://twitter.com/MicrosoftPress*

## PART I

Laying the Groundwork of Machine Learning

CHAPTER 1

How Humans Learn

Computers can, in theory, emulate human intelligence, and exceed it.
—Stephen Hawking, 2014

Modern fiction is full of supercomputers capable of generically crunching any sort of data to produce human-intelligible results. An extremely popular example is HAL 9000—the computer that governs the spaceship Discovery in the movie *2001: A Space Odyssey* (1968). Another famous one is JARVIS (Just A Rather Very Intelligent System), the computer that, much like today's Alexa or Cortana, serves as the home assistant for Tony Stark in the Marvel Comics and related movies. Yet another example, though not as widely popular as HAL 9000 or JARVIS, is Max—the supercomputer operated by Hiram Yeager in many of Clive Cussler's fictional NUMA stories (1984).

All these machines are extremely advanced computer systems capable of processing every piece of information, regardless of storage, format, and structure. Often, all that the human characters in such books and movies do is generically "load data into the machine," whether paper documents, digital files, or media content. Next, the machine autonomously figures out the content, learns from it, and communicates back to humans using a natural language.

At the time those supercomputers were devised by their respective authors, they were only science fiction, but today quite a few concrete implementations of software systems provide comparable results, albeit with some human assistance. For example, computer systems are capable of piloting airplanes or conducting sophisticated surgery. In just a few years, however, we will likely have computers driving cars in full autonomy without any human intervention. And that would really be fun!

This book is about the algorithms, storage, processes, and (.NET) software frameworks that can enable developers to just load data into computers and have computers communicate back usable information and perhaps solutions. This book is not about the theory of some futuristic form of artificially built intelligence. Neither is it about the technological aspects of some prebuilt set of cognitive services.

This book, instead, is all about how to use today's specific software tools for more intelligent software consulting.

The Journey Toward Thinking Machines

We humans have always dreamt of other, artificially built beings capable of reasoning and thinking better and deeper than us. Human literature is full of such fantasy characters that first appeared in ancient Greek tragedies by Aeschylus and Euripides. In the plot of those works, in fact, a device (Latins later called it *deus ex machina*) was sometimes used to simulate the intervention of the god, namely an entity able to resolve conflicts in the drama too intricate for humans to settle themselves.

The wish of a machine that irons out troubles and issues is therefore innate in human nature. On the wings of such an innate desire, many philosophers throughout the course of history have attempted to provide a theoretical formulation for the mechanics of human thought.

The Dawn of Mechanical Reasoning

A first great contribution came from Euclid (third century BC), who logically derived all theorems of geometry from five basic axioms. Euclidean geometry is an excellent example of formal reasoning. Later, in the seventeenth century, Gottfried Leibniz and other prominent thinkers conjectured that human thought could be systematized in a set of algebraic rules and postulated the existence of a general language that could reduce any human argumentation to mere machine mechanical calculation.

Leibniz's work was deeply inspired by an earlier polymath, Raymond Lull, who sowed the seeds of modern artificial intelligence research back in the thirteenth century and, in turn, inspired the successive development of mathematical logic by George Boole and, in the early twentieth century, by David Hilbert and Bertrand Russell.

In particular, back in 1900 Hilbert set a number of goals for mathematicians to prove whose leitmotif was the question "Can all mathematical statements be expressed and manipulated through a set of well-defined rules?" Hilbert's ultimate goal was finding a way to formalize all known mathematical reasoning in much the same way Euclid did for his time. Hilbert's purpose was to find a set of axioms to derive all mathematical statements.

Godel's Incompleteness Theorems

In 1931, Kurt Godel demonstrated a couple of theorems of mathematical logic that the community interpreted as a negative answer to Hilbert's fundamental question. In particular, the two theorems lay the foundation of the following statement:

> *In any formal system expressive enough to model the arithmetic of natural numbers, there is at least one undecidable statement that evidence proves true but that can't be proven true or false within the axioms of the system.*

In addition, Godel proved that even though one axiomatically assigns a value of true or false to the undecidable statement, any further reasoning will indefinitely lead to another undecidable statement.

Why are Godel's theorems crucial to formal reasoning and, following up, to artificial intelligence?

For one thing, Godel's incompleteness theory draws a line beyond which mathematical logic can't go: there are things that nobody can prove using formal reasoning. On the other hand, though, Godel's theorems demonstrate that within the limits of a consistent formal system any reasoning can always be expressed as a set of formal transformation rules and then, in some way, mechanized.

This second aspect is extremely relevant for artificial intelligence because it sets the theoretical foundation for mechanical, computer-based reasoning.

Formalization of Computing Machines

The work done by Hilbert and Godel is purely theoretical, but it gave the spark to three parallel and independent research paths that converged with the same result in a few years, around the mid-1930s.

- In 1933, Godel formulated the concept of *general recursive functions*. This computable logical function takes a finite array of natural numbers and returns a natural number.

- Later, in 1936, Alonzo Church defined a formalism called *lambda calculus* to express similar computations on natural numbers.

- At nearly the same time, in a fully independent way, Alan Turing built the theoretical model of a computing machine (the *Turing machine*) to perform calculations in terms of symbols written on an infinite tape.

Next, the Church-Turing thesis unified the three classes of computable functions, proving that a function is computable in the lambda calculus if and only if it is computable in the Turing machine if and only if it is a general recursive function. The net effect of the Church-Turing thesis was making conceivable the building of a mechanical device able to reproduce any plausible process of mathematical deduction through the manipulation of symbols.

Since the late 1930s, the thesis has been the starting point of further speculation about the possibility of having truly thinking machines one day.

Great, but how do we formalize human thought?

Toward the Formalization of Human Thought

Throughout history, there have been many great examples of calculating machines concretely built, or just devised, by polymaths and scientists. As mentioned, one was devised by Leibnitz in the seventeenth century, and a more detailed one was theorized by Charles Babbage in the nineteenth century.

In the modern era, ancestors of today's computers were the cypher and code-breaking machines employed during World War II. Examples include Enigma, its code-breaking counterpart named The Bombe (built with a great contribution from Alan Turing), the German army's Lorenz machine, and the British giant machine called Colossus, which ultimately broke the code from the Lorenz machine. ENIAC is the name of another machine built in the United States in the final days of the Second World War.

All these machines were based on the theoretical foundation laid by the Church-Turing thesis. The development of ENIAC, in particular, was led by another big name in computer science—John von Neumann. Not coincidentally, in fact, Alan Turing and John von Neumann are considered the fathers of what we today call *artificial intelligence.*

Imagine now, for a second, to be in the shoes of either of those two great men. You're in the 1950s and you know you can build machines to compute anything you can express through a consistent grammar of symbols, not just calculating numbers from numbers. You would probably feel like a god; you would probably foresee somewhere far ahead of you, but clearly identifiable, a machine that could behave in much the same way humans do. Then you would probably wonder the crucial question: *Can machines think*?

Alan Turing devised a test to determine whether machines could think. He imagined a teletype conversation between a human, a machine, and a human judge. If the machine could answer questions and convince the judge it was a human, then the machine could be said to able to think.

Over the years, many contested the effectiveness of the Turing test. In particular, John Searle (Professor Emeritus of the Philosophy of Mind and Language at Berkeley) noted that anybody with a proper dictionary and instructions written in his own language could probably provide an answer in, say, Chinese that, to a Chinese judge, could make full sense. Does that mean that the answerer (human or machine) understood Chinese?

Searle's point about thinking machines is that machines can merely process symbols according to rules, but this is not enough to reach the peaks of consciousness, cognition, perception of humans, and not even their language skills. According to Searle, language is more than plain symbol manipulation, and the "more" is just what defines human thought. Computers can just compute but can do it very carefully and fast to the point of being even better than humans in some specific tasks.

In accordance with Searle's view, today machine learning systems are just expected to operate in highly controlled scenarios under the realm of business rules and data patterns and are challenged to anticipate issues and events. Think, for example, of systems to predict hardware faults or detect financial fraud. All these modern systems may perform very well in their contexts, but our human idea of "thinking" requires (much) more computing power.

The Birth of Artificial Intelligence as a Discipline

Artificial intelligence (or AI) was officially developed in 1956, when John McCarthy organized a six-week summer research workshop at Dartmouth College in New Hampshire. He invited a dozen colleagues from different research fields including mathematics, engineering, neurology, and psychology.

The purpose of the workshop was to brainstorm around the idea of thinking machines. McCarthy coined the new name *artificial intelligence* because of its neutrality and to stay away, and ideally unify, the two souls of the ongoing academic research that he perceived to be the same entity.

At the time, in fact, the abstract theme of thinking machines was debated in two research contexts—the automata theory, directly descending from the work of Church and Turing, and cybernetics, directly descending from Babbage's theory and turned into concrete hardware by von Neumann.

The ultimate purpose of the workshop was laying the groundwork for devising an artificial brain. And this is also the ultimate purpose of artificial intelligence, as we know it today.

Important In 1943, McCulloch and Pitts proposed a computational model inspired by the known structure of the brain's neuron. Their seminal work represents the foundation of modern neural networks. Two facts are remarkable. One is that at the time McCulloch and Pitts proposed their model, there was no other concrete computational model and were no physical computers. The von Neumann architecture, on which all modern computers are based, was still in infancy. Put another way, it's fascinating to think that we could have had neuronal computers since the beginning of informatics. Second, after the success of the first physical computers in the 1960s, the research on neural networks slowed down to nearly a stop and regained strength in the late 1980s. It slowed down again in a decade blurred by the advent of the Internet and was revamped a few years ago primarily thanks to cloud computing and other factors, such as the social need for continuous connectivity.

The Biology of Learning

With slightly different wording paraphrased from various dictionaries, a broadly accepted definition of *intelligence* is the following:

> *The ability to acquire knowledge and turn that into expertise.*

In the folds of the definition, though, there's another layer of meaning that is worth bringing to the surface. Intelligence is also the ability to

- Form judgment and opinions out of the acquired knowledge

- Act based on that

- React to unknown events

In a nutshell, intelligence combines cognitive capabilities including perception, memory, language, and reasoning and uses a specific learning approach to extract, transform, and store information.

What Is Intelligent Software, Anyway?

In this section, we discuss the biology of learning as we know it works in humans. However, our final destination is still exploring a set of techniques to teach machines to learn so that any running software gets more and more intelligent in the performance of a given task.

Intelligent software is software capable of sensing the surrounding environment and reacting to detected changes. Intelligent software, however, doesn't do that in a finite and hard-coded (even high) number of cases. Truly intelligent software is able to learn so that, in the course of its life, its behavior changes autonomously without the need to be reprogrammed.

Let's look at a couple of examples of basic software intelligence.

In 2012, we built our first mobile application for a large tennis tournament hosting a number of top players. To make it easier for people to relocate within the venue to see their favorite player in action, we added a message to the live score page with an estimation of the minimum time a match on a court would last. If player X was scheduled to play on court N following the current match, and you were currently watching another game on another court, that little piece of information would be handy to let you hurry up and get to your new destination. There was no guessing and no magic behind the number of minutes our application showed. At any change of the score, the software calculated the minimum number of points necessary for the leading player to win the match and multiplied that for the average length of points played so far. It was a plain and simple mathematical operation but was perceived as a sign of intelligence. The behavior was hard-coded though.

Lately, several car manufacturers have mounted an adaptive cruise control (ACC) system. Such a system typically uses radar to monitor the car running ahead in the same lane and ensures that a minimal distance is maintained between the two vehicles. Depending on the configuration, the ACC can automatically slow down or just beep. This behavior is also commonly perceived as a sign of intelligence, but again, it is simply hard-coded. Interestingly, both the match length controller and ACC would remain hard-coded forms of software intelligence even if we made them smarter by adding to the calculation information about the average number of consecutive points statistically won by a player or traffic conditions. Asked the same question, truly intelligent software should be able to give different answers at different times if conditions (internal and/or external) are different.

Currently, computer software is not as sophisticated as the brains of humans or animals. Via software, computers can only perform deterministic operations based on provided or detected input data. If it's not written in code, it won't happen; and anything that happens is written in code. This is how computers work today, but it's not how the human brain works. The most sophisticated software we may have, functionally speaking, pales when compared to the brains of the least brain-powered animal. The reason is that modern software lacks the ability to learn.

How Neurons Work

The ability to learn is common in the animal kingdom but reaches much higher peaks in human beings than in animals. The human brain is known to contain about 90 billion densely interconnected neurons. The resulting graph is therefore unbelievably intricate because each neuron is also known to link to dozens of thousands of other neurons.

How Many Neurons Do We Have?

To form at least a faint idea about the complexity of the human brain, let's just look at the number of neurons and compare the human brain to that of other animals (see Table 1-1).

TABLE 1-1 Some Animals by Number of Neurons

Animal	Approximate Number of Neurons
Sponge	0
Jellyfish	6,000
Ant	250,000
Frog	15,000,000
Mouse	65,000,000
Pigeon	300,000,000
Octopus	500,000,000
Parrot	1,500,000,000
Dog	2,500,000,000
Lion	5,000,000,000
Bear	10,000,000,000
Dolphin	20,000,000,000
Gorilla	33,000,000,000
Elephant	250,000,000,000

A dog, which is considered a fairly intelligent animal, has a bit over 2 billion neurons, which is half as many as the lion and a quarter as many as a bear. Conversely, the elephant has nearly three times more neurons than humans, around 250 billion, but only a fraction of the actual cognitive capabilities! How is that possible?

Structure of the Cerebral Cortex

Scientists agree that, more than the total quantity, it's the distribution of neurons in the physical brain that really counts. Regardless of brain or body size, the best cognitive abilities depend on the number of neurons in the cerebral cortex. In fact, the cerebral cortex is reckoned to be the seat of thought. As humans, we also have the largest frontal lobes, and frontal lobes are associated with those typically human functions such as planning, logical analysis, and abstract thought.

Numbers in Table 1-1 are merely indicative for another reason: the surface of the cortex. The more hills and valleys the cortex has (*gyri* and *sulci*, to use the scientific language), the deeper thinking ability it may have. The surface of the human brain is quite wrinkly, whereas the brain is fairly flat and smooth in mice. (See Figure 1-1.)

Curiously, both elephants and dolphins have a level of folding on the brain surface higher than humans. This probably means that elephants and dolphins are even more intelligent than humans, but other factors (physical conformation of the body, specific devices like vocal cords) may considerably limit the expressiveness of their intelligence.

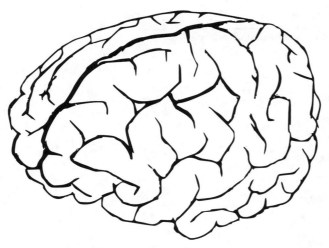

FIGURE 1-1 *Gyri* and *sulci* on the brain's cerebral cortex

The bottom line is that several parameters contribute to the power of the brain, and neurons are only the elementary processing units.

Physiology of Neurons

A neuron is a cell designed to receive, process, and transmit information to other nerve cells as well as muscles and glands. A neuron is made of a body that ends with multiple thin filaments called *dendrites*. Dendrites act as receptors of transmitted information. At the other end of the body, a nerve fiber, called the *axon*, is ultimately responsible for the electrical transmission of information toward receptors. Figure 1-2 provides a schematic view of the neuron's internal architecture and the overall network protocol (*synapse*) that multiple neurons use to communicate.

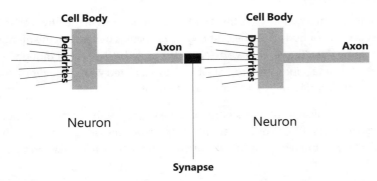

FIGURE 1-2 Schematic view of neurons and their communication

The protocol of communication between connected neurons, the synapse, is based on electrical impulses that travel along the axon to their final destination. The synapse causes electrical impulses to pass from the sender neuron to all connected ones. To be precise, Figure 1-2 describes only the most common type of synapse in mammalian nervous systems—axo-dendritic synapses—but in nature there exist other types of synapses: axon to bloodstream, axon to axon, axon to extracellular liquid, axon to cell body. It is thought that the link between two neurons results in some form of storage of information and then memory.

The Computing Power of Neurons

Although Figure 1-2 may capture the overall schematic idea of how neurons communicate, it still lacks an important trait that is critical to comprehend why the human brain is so complex and so hard to emulate with software. Have a look at Figure 1-3.

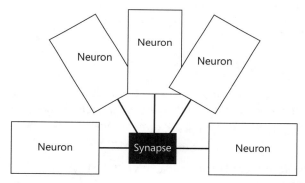

FIGURE 1-3 A synapse is not limited to connecting only a pair of neurons.

Neuron connections are not simply point-to-point. It is estimated that the human brain has up to ten billion of billion (10^{16}) synapses. This means that very rarely a synapse is made by two connected neurons, and it also means that each neuron constantly receives and processes multiple signals and transmits multiple results.

In the (unfinished) book *The Computer and the Brain* (Yale University Press, 1958), John von Neumann attempts to make a comparison between the human brain and computing machines. He notes that the brain has a very slow clock speed compared to that of a computer, even the fastest computer of the 1950s. The human brain's clock speed is estimated to be around 100 Hz. This number stems from the time it takes a neuron to light up and transmit an electrical impulse. The clock of a modern CPU flies around 3 GHz instead, meaning a frequency 10^7 larger than the neuron.

What about precision?

Given the way neurons are known to transmit data within the brain—periodic trains of pulses along the axon—it is roughly estimated that they can have a mathematical precision of 2 digits, whereas a normal computer can blissfully operate with 12-digit precision. In summary, if the brain were a computer—at least, a computer as we know it today—it would be a very slow and unreliable computer.

Yet, the human brain can do instantaneously truly amazing things such as recognizing images that would take several seconds and dedicated services to computers. It has been observed that the whole process of image recognition takes place through three consecutive synapses at the point of connection between the retina of the eye (which captures the image) and the optic nerve. In this context, the synapse is the same as a logical operation—a computer instruction. Look at the diagram in Figure 1-4 and compare its simplicity to what it takes to train software to universally recognize images.

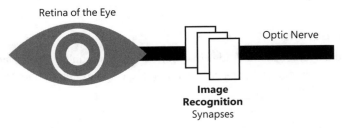

FIGURE 1-4 How the human eye recognizes images

The Architecture of the Brain

If the human brain were a computer, it would work through serial operations or, to use the same words as von Neumann, with a significant *logical depth*. But in such conditions of slow clock and poor precision, there would be no chance for a software-powered brain to perform the amazing tasks the human brain can perform.

Wait a moment, though! We said "software-powered brain," and that's just the key!

When we think of software today, we inevitably think of instructions designed for a specific computer architecture—the von Neumann serial architecture. To seriously plan an artificial brain that really behaves like the human brain, we probably need to consider an alternative computer architecture! The same von Neumann speculated that the human brain follows a different, nonserial computing model characterized by a high level of parallelism (he called it *logical amplitude*) and backed by different logical structures.

> *Whatever the system is, it cannot fail to differ considerably from what we consciously and explicitly consider as mathematics.*
>
> *John von Neumann,* The Computer and the Brain

Let's then briefly reconsider the numbers of the brain with the intent of figuring out a more accurate measure of its inherent power, still in today's computer terms. As we have seen, we won't go too far by taking the neuron as the basic processing unit of the brain. What if we take the synapse instead?

- The whole human brain counts up to 10^{16} synapses.

- Each neuron lights up 100 times per second (100 Hz).

It means that the brain has the power to execute up to 100×10^{16} operations per second, which is several orders of magnitude more than the typical computer these days.

If we could really understand and reproduce how the brain works, then we could design and build computers that work according to a new synaptic architecture. These computers might theoretically combine together the speed of hardware components and massive parallel computation from the architecture. In this scenario, we could even aim at building something that could operate several orders of magnitude faster than the human brain.

Memory in Humans and Computers

Neuroscientists repeatedly attempted to estimate the amount of data that can be stored in the human brain. The difference between estimates, however, ranges significantly and is calculated to be between 1 TB and 2,500 TB. With some realistic assumptions, the difference amounts to between 10 and 100 TB, but yet nobody has the faintest idea of how to determine how much free space there is in it. So, in the end, these remain fascinating but simplistic numbers, as the same scientists admit.

A more interesting fact is that the memory of humans works differently from the memory of computers. While a computer remembers exactly what was stored—a snapshot of the past—the human brain rebuilds a memory every time it is recalled. In other words, the brain memorizes things at a lower level of abstraction than that of remembered facts. Subsequently, every memory results from the replay of a sequence of logged events, each in the form of a sense input—whether a touch, sound, smell, taste, or sight.

The difference between computers and human memories is the same as conventional storage and *event sourcing* in software architecture. To reinforce the point, neuroscientists have found that the brain decides selectively which information needs to be saved, and the entire list of sense inputs is never fully stored for longer than a few seconds; otherwise, the brain cells would be soon overloaded. Again, this is the same thing that happens in *event sourcing* with read models and snapshots.

Note In addition to storage, another interesting value to look at is the energy required to operate the brain. It's been measured to only 12 watts, the same as a high-efficiency light bulb and about the energy burned to download, end-to-end, 2 MB of Internet data. Interestingly, a normal laptop consumes at least 20 times more.

The Carrot-and-Stick Approach

Except for genetic heritage, any newborn is a clean slate and needs guidance to learn the things of the world she needs to know. Guidance is ultimately a well-known learning algorithm that any adult human being builds in years and then, often unconsciously, transmits to children. The algorithm builds on the core findings that humans started learning in the Neolithic age with the initial development of agriculture and especially farming.

It's informally called the carrot-and-stick method.

Building a Behavior

As humans, we learn through the input we receive from senses, and senses give us instinctively the feeling that something is good or bad. Sensory inputs are then *logged* into the brain and further elaborated into a number of pieces of information (e.g., we like it, we don't like it) that, once stored, altogether contribute to the brain *database* of memories. The content of this *database* of memories will then be used further on to elaborate the next sensory input in a less instinctive, more thoughtful way.

Imagine doing this over and over and again, synapses after synapses, second after second. A humongous archive of information is built. The brain, in a way, indexes the database so that it can quickly find the set of neural commands to forward to neurons and muscles to react. Any sign of life is a matter of reacting to some stimulus.

Hence, the more you receive a given input, the more you know about the behavior you consciously want to have about it. The more you receive a given input, the more often you react in a given way—therefore, the more you morph the instinctive behavior into some more thoughtful behavior.

Changing the instinctive behavior to something smarter in terms of final results is the ultimate purpose of training—for animals, for humans, as well as for algorithms.

Reward and Punishment

The purpose of training is changing the frequency of certain behaviors so that an undesirable behavior is observed less often and a desirable behavior, instead, is observed more often. To build any form of training, you must use consequences and fine-tune your actions to trigger just the expected reactions as often as possible.

One of the core principles of training is offering the trainee a positive experience—a reward—in response to a desirable action. Another core principle of training is specular and consists of offering the trainee an aversive experience—a punishment—in return for an unwanted action. All trainers, therefore, use consequences because all trainees instinctively tend to orient their behavior toward rewards (the carrot) and to avoid punishment (the stick).

The carrot-and-stick approach is the pattern that animals and humans use to learn. What about algorithms? If the carrot exists to please the trainee and the stick serves to punish the trainee, how do you please, or punish, an algorithm? Of course, you don't. Or, at least, you don't do it in the common sense.

For a trained algorithm, the reward or the punishment results from the position of the computed result, over or under an acceptable threshold.

And Once the Behavior Is Learned?

Once a behavior is learned, should you remove any rewards from the equation and expect that the human, or the animal, behaves the desirable way only for the joy of performing? Professional dog trainers, for example, agree that you can reduce the food reward but never phase it out entirely. The reason is that dogs (the same holds true for other animals and, even more, humans) are living beings and use their behavior as a tool to trigger events and produce consequences.

The carrot (or stick) stimulus should remain even when the behavior is learned, but the strength of the stimulus should be modulated over time to maintain the likelihood of desirable behavior high enough. What about algorithms? It's just the same.

A trained algorithm, more than animals and humans, can effectively be thought of as a fountain from which desirable behaviors flow. The issue is that the landscape and the context around the fountain may continuously change. Hence, the algorithm, like animals and humans do, must adapt. Adapting the algorithm to a changed context requires a new session training and probably also fine-tuning the threshold that sets what's good and what's bad.

> **Note** Overall, the carrot-and-stick approach is a technique aimed first at teaching how to perform a desired behavior and then at internalizing it so that it becomes natural regardless of the actual conditions it was initially taught in. Thinking of carrots and sticks with an eye on machine learning, the words pronounced by Sir Winston Churchill right before the beginning of the Second World War resound evocatively: "Thus, by every device from the stick to the carrot, the emaciated Austrian donkey is made to pull the Nazi barrow up an ever-steepening hill."

Adaptability to Changes

Overall, intelligence is the summation of the results produced by a number of built-in capabilities, including cognition, perception, inference, consciousness, and analysis. In these terms, it is hard to imagine how intelligence can be adapted to unanimated things such as computers and algorithms.

In software, instead, the term *intelligent* is usually associated with the ability of code to infer information from the context and make the most appropriate decision out of it. In the 1990s, specifically during the Gulf War, the adjective *intelligent* was used to informally describe precision-guided bombs dropped against armored vehicles, with the nonfunctional requirement of minimizing collateral damage and the number of attack missions necessary to declared goals.

Can we call a bomb *intelligent*? In pure software terms, yes, we can.

An intelligent bomb is an ordinary bomb equipped with an onboard cruise control system, some electronic sensors, and a set of flight fins. Altogether, the additional equipment steers the bomb to the target. Types of intelligent bombs differ just based on the technology used by the control system to identify the target: camera, laser, or GPS. Why can we define such a bomb as intelligent? Because it doesn't just fall to the ground due to the effect of gravity, but instead it adjusts its route the best the technology allows to hit the desired target exactly.

The intelligence of a bomb is limited, though. For one thing, a bomb can be used only once, and because of this, it is not allowed to learn and reuse its acquired knowledge later. A bomb can adapt to dynamic changes (moving targets, sudden change of orders, bad weather) but can't build up a persistent knowledge base for the future.

The definition of intelligence we mean when we talk about artificial intelligence is the ability to infer information in a number of ways, process it, and retain results in the form of knowledge. Acquired knowledge will then guide the software to decisions in a number of situations. This is much like when we humans learn how to recognize a dog, and then we can recognize it whether the dog is jumping in the garden, is barking in the darkness, or is shown printed on the pages of a magazine.

Artificial Forms of Intelligence

Today, AI is an umbrella term under which we can spot two macro areas: expert systems and autonomous systems. But, as minimalistic as it may sound, even a conditional statement—yes, a plain old *IF* statement—is doubtless a (rather primordial) form of software intelligence.

Primordial Intelligence

A conditional statement performs different computations based on the value of a Boolean condition:

```
if condition is true
then do this
else do that
```

At first it may sound pretty simple and primordial, but a car that autonomously brakes when it detects an object in close proximity does exactly that: it evaluates a condition and branches off depending on the outcome.

Any piece of software that makes a decision based on some input, typed by the user or inferred through sensors, is in some way intelligent. Or, if you prefer, it shows an artificial form of intelligence. In light of this vision, Figure 1-5 captures the essence of software intelligence.

Expert Systems

An expert system is one that knows how to effectively react to input suggesting or making a thoughtful decision. In a way, an expert system is the software counterpart of a human expert and a sort of decision aid system.

```
if (...)
{
    if (...)
    {
        if (...)
        {
            if (...)
            {
                if (...)
                {
                    if (...)
                    {
                        if (...)
                        {
                            :
                        }
                    }
                }
            }
        }
    }
}
```

FIGURE 1-5 A concise (and funny) way to capture the essence of software intelligence

History of Expert Systems

Expert systems were the first concrete form of artificial intelligence over the years. The first recognized system to be labeled as an expert system was DENDRAL, built in the 1960s at Stanford University by a team headed by Edward Feigenbaum and Joshua Lederberg. In particular, this system was designed to analyze the spectrographic data of chemical substances to conjecture their underlying molecular structure. Interestingly, the performance of the system was reckoned analogous to that of human experts. This finding gave the spark to similar projects in both industry and universities.

Note A (fake) ancestor of modern expert systems was *The Turk*, the automaton chess player that Wolfgang von Kempelen, a civil servant of the Austrian Empire, built in the late eighteenth century to gain the favor of Empress Maria Theresa. Apparently, the Turk was a clock-based mechanism able to intelligently move pieces on a chessboard. In reality, the whole thing was just an illusion because the machine hid a human player who could see the status of the game and could sneakily program the mechanism to make the desired move. The fact is, no one ever unveiled the trick, and the machine won a few important games against prominent personalities such as Napoleon and Benjamin Franklin.

Internal Architecture

The key aspect of an expert system, however, is that its processing power is limited to the fixed set of decisional pathways and input parameters that have been hard-coded in the supporting software.

Architecturally speaking, an expert system is the summation of two subsystems: a database of known facts (knowledge base) and an inference engine. The system works by processing input against the known list of facts and applying rules repeatedly. The typical cycle of an inference engine is based on the following pseudocode:

```
while (exists a rule to apply to current knowledge)
{
    select rule
    execute rule
    update knowledge
}
```

The method is referred to as *forward chaining*. Here's a basic example of how it works. Let's assume the following known rules are hard-coded in the inference engine of an e-commerce site:

```
If X < 14 years => X loves pets
If X > 14 years => X loves jewelry
If X loves pets => X gets a puppy dog
If X loves jewelry => X gets a necklace
If X gets a necklace and X is 18+ => X gets a gold necklace
```

To answer the question "What should I buy for Michela for her birthday?" the system needs to process some basic input facts that could trigger the first rule. In this case, to trigger the system, you need to provide Michela's age. If the age is 18, then the first iteration adds one more fact: Michela loves jewelry. The second iteration triggers rule #4 adding the information that Michela should get a necklace. On the third iteration, rule #5 triggers, and because Michela turns 18, the final recommendation is to get her a gold necklace. The third iteration is the last one because, at that point of built knowledge, the system has no more rules to trigger.

Real-World Expert Systems

A good example of an expert system is the software that implements the autopilot mode of aircrafts. However, expert systems can be generally employed with proven success in all fields where a human expert would be too expensive or simply not available. There are a few consolidated areas where expert systems can be applied. (See Table 1-2.)

TABLE 1-2 Categories of Expert Systems

Category	Purpose
Classification	Aimed at identifying an object based on known characteristics
Diagnosis	Aimed at detecting malfunction (or health issues) from observable data
Monitoring	Aimed at comparing live data from sensors to prescribe behavior
Process Control	Aimed at controlling an ongoing process based on results of monitoring
Design	Aimed at automatically configuring a system according to given specifications
Scheduling & Planning	Aimed at developing or modifying a scheduled plan based on detected conditions
Generation of Options	Aimed at generating alternative solutions to a problem

The whole field of expert systems is sometimes referred to as *Applied AI*.

Limitations of Expert Systems

Expert systems have been implemented with success in a number of business domains, including aerospace, health care, geology, quality control, network troubleshooting, financial portfolio management, and criminology. An expert system automates the retrieval of information, thus saving human effort and making it easier to duplicate and transfer knowledge.

An expert system is not a basic query system and can effectively navigate through relationships of facts and draw conclusions showing intelligent behavior. The drawback is that an expert system is limited to a very narrow range of the codified domain. It is typically unable to manage effectively a large amount of broad-ranging contextual information and can function only in the bounded context of a fixed cognitive and logical thinking process. As a result, an expert system doesn't respond reliably—or doesn't respond at all—in any situations outside its codified range of expertise.

Maintenance is another shortcoming of expert systems. Once released in production, the set of answers an expert system can give is fixed and can be extended or modified only through a new release. But any new release requires putting hands on a rather complex and intricate code.

More autonomous systems capable of being trained to learn came to the rescue, giving life to the new field of machine learning.

Autonomous Systems

Autonomous systems are systems designed and trained to automatically recognize a given number of scenarios and successively work as an expert system on data they have never seen before. Autonomous systems are the new frontier of AI, which is often referred to as *General AI* or *machine learning*.

The Learning Dimension

The software for an autonomous system doesn't hard-code a (long) list of known cases but rather hard-codes a (relatively short) list of patterns to recognize out of the input data it receives. The list of cases that an autonomous system can handle is not hard-coded up front but results from the implementation of the software and the data used to train it.

Training is crucial because through training the system processes a huge quantity of data and learns about possible patterns that it should recognize. An autonomous system is built from a huge quantity of data that dedicated experts—data scientists—work on. A data scientist knows how to extrapolate significance from data and does that primarily armed with statistical methods and machine learning algorithms.

Most of the time, though, a data scientist just cleans and filters raw business data, trying to give it a shape that allows further elaboration. The primary limit of autonomous systems, in fact, is the quality of data because incorrect results always stem from incorrect data, even with correction! For example, if house and energy prices are used together to train a real-estate system, then results may not be fully reliable. At the same time, if tightly correlated data is used (say, house prices in euros and dollars), then any result will be built out of only a slice of the provided data.

For a data scientist, much like for a software architect, domain-specific knowledge is a big plus.

Real-World Examples

A good example of an autonomous system is the fraud detection system employed by most financial companies, like banks and credit card and insurance companies. These systems look at the logged transactions, numbers, time, and geography and try to identify a "known" pattern in it. The result, though, is not produced by a specific set of IF statements or IF-based rules as in a simpler expert system.

Another great example comes from maintenance of machines in the manufacturing industry. To check the state of working parts, inspections are conducted periodically according to a predetermined schedule. Scheduled maintenance is a good-enough approach, but it has a number of drawbacks. For example, maintenance may be scheduled at a less than optimal time right before a significant workload. By contrast, condition-based maintenance uses hard-coded rules to calculate the ideal time for maintenance based on the actual wear of components as embedded sensors report it. A condition-based maintenance system is essentially an expert system from the Monitoring category of Table 1-2. The next step in the manufacturing industry is *predictive maintenance*.

Predictive maintenance aims at trying to determine what would be a really good time for technicians to intervene. Predictive maintenance requires constant monitoring of the electronics and mechanical parts, and an abundance of data in this regard comes from IoT or conventional internal sensors. The prediction should not be based exclusively on reported numbers but also should rely on environmental conditions such as weather, noise, heat, and humidity. Analytical algorithms are then required, along with an effective data model, to figure out the hidden patterns of when failures on a given type of component are more likely to happen. Once it is fully trained, all that an autonomous system does is take live data and check whether it matches any of the known patterns. To keep going with the predictive maintenance example, an autonomous system will simply answer questions like "Given the current status of the gear, what's the likelihood it will break in the next week?"

An autonomous system is not necessarily more effective than an expert system. For sure, an autonomous system is more sophisticated to design and build. However, which one is the best fit depends ultimately on the nature of the problem. Autonomous systems are divided in two categories depending on the type of training they receive: *supervised* learning and *unsupervised* learning. (We'll cover this in the next chapter.)

> **Note** Other good examples of autonomous systems are systems like the recommendation engine for curated content (i.e., Quora, StackOverflow, Facebook), advertising or purchases (i.e., Google, Amazon), natural language processing in call centers, and even power production forecasts in energy.

Artificial Forms of Sentiment

In the same speech we quoted at the beginning of the chapter, Stephen Hawking states that the rise of powerful AI will be either the best or the worst thing ever to happen to humanity but that we don't yet know which. Anyway, in the collective imagination, computers are fast and smart but insensitive.

Is this an inherent limitation of machines, or is it purely a matter of computing power?

Both von Neumann and Hawking believed that there is no deep difference between what can be achieved by a biological brain and what can be achieved by a computer. Does that mean that a day may come when physical computers reach a computing power comparable to humans? On that day will computers be able to reach the peaks of consciousness, cognition, and perception of humans?

Proponents of AI divide in two camps: strong AI and weak AI. Supporters of strong AI believe that machines can fully replicate human intelligence, including sentiments and conscience. Supporters of weak AI, instead, limit what machines can do to a mere simulation of advanced reasoning and learning. As weird as it may sound, this has ethical implications too and is a line of thought that can take us really far ahead.

The vision behind strong AI is tightly connected to determinism; therefore, the idea is that any behavior is the result of some preceding behavior and the cause of any successive behavior. Ultimately, these are nearly the same words written by Pierre Simon de Laplace in his seminal work *A Philosophical Essay on Probabilities* in 1814. For an intellect with enough knowledge and processing power, Laplace writes, "nothing would be uncertain and the future just like the past would be present before its eyes." In this piece, this intellect is named *Laplace's demon*.

Important By the way, if you think that the words and the points made by Laplace's demon are pure sci-fi speculation only good for catastrophe literature, consider that those are just the points that String Theory—one of the most recent and advanced implementations of the Theory of Everything in physics and cosmology—is currently delineating.

In light of strong AI, assuming that machines can duplicate humans takes us straight to the conclusion that humans act deterministically and make their decisions based on some built-in software hardcoded in the brain that triggers behavior and only after that notifies the conscience.

What is right then? And what is wrong? And who's really liable for what? Who are we?

The pillars of human life (ontology, anthropology, ethics) are at risk of being rephrased.

Note Let's end the chapter with another borderline thought about the deep future of software machines. As you may know, a few companies are developing the so-called total artificial heart (TAH). Early TAH projects date back to the 1960s, but today there's a lot more excitement and are more capital ventures. A TAH is an implantable device that fully replaces the functions of the human heart. More precisely, the TAH occupies the same physical space as the human heart. A patient with a TAH is therefore heartless. (By the way, you can read stories [https://bit.ly/2AFBdue] of patients who returned to active lives with their loved ones.)

Heartless? What about sentiments then? Can a machine simulate sentiments? Ultimately, sentiments are electrical impulses, but they belong to the physical brains rather than the physical heart.

Summary

Although with some deviation toward the end, in this first chapter we essentially tried to clean the road ahead from all the debris of science and fiction, biology and behavior, and built the foundation for upcoming technical coverage of learning techniques as we can code them today with programming languages. We first approached the mathematical foundation of AI and then explored the biology of learning to finish with a taxonomy of AI-related software approaches.

Artificial intelligence is an old concept that's been around for nearly the same amount of time as computers. For some reason, though, the interest around AI has never been constant.

We, the authors, are father and son, and the time lapse of a generation passes between us. AI was hot, at least in academic environments, when Dino was getting his computer science degree in the late 1980s, and it is hot in the industry today as Francesco is studying mathematics at university. For some reason, AI has been nearly neglected in the 30 years in between.

The father's generation has grown up with a fictional idea of AI in which "loading data into the machine" was expressive enough, albeit highly impractical. The son's generation is giving substance and significance to the same expression by making automated learning deeper than ever. The effort today is concentrated in giving a concrete implementation to the otherwise evanescent commitment of "loading data into the machine."

In doing so, the community can't simply ignore some amount of randomness, and looking ahead, it can't avoid delving deep into some advanced mathematics such as feedback systems and chaos and complexity theory. In the end, being smart is much more about how well we learn from mistakes than the (low) number of mistakes we make.

Smart systems, like humans, are not going to be infallible.

## CHAPTER 2

Intelligent Software

Of course, machines can't think as people do. A machine is different from a person.
Hence, they think differently. The interesting question is, just because something
thinks differently from you, does that mean it's not thinking?

—*Benedict Cumberbatch as Alan Turing,* The Imitation Game, *2014*

The truth is, no one knows how to build the software counterpart of the human brain. One reason is the current, effective lack of knowledge about the internal functioning of the brain. Another reason is the recognizably different architecture of the biological brain compared to the architecture of today's computers.

As long as neuroscientists learn more and in more depth about the behavior of the brain, mathematicians have a better chance to devise an abstract model that could reproduce it. To be implemented, any abstract model devised so far requires a computing architecture radically different from that of modern computers. Remarkably, the computational model in use today is still the model that John von Neumann figured out in the 1950s from the theoretical works by Alan Turing.

In a nutshell, we face a form of brain/computer impedance mismatch, as if a logical gap existed between two distinct entities we want to forcibly relate together. The effective intelligence we can build today depends on the actual level of impedance matching between the brain and the software we are able to build with the current tools and armed with the best knowledge.

So, which forms of artificial intelligence (AI) are concretely actionable in modern software? We can recognize two branches of software systems: applied artificial intelligence, which is our inheritance from the past, and general artificial intelligence, which adds up learning capabilities and lays the groundwork for a brilliant future.

Applied Artificial Intelligence

The idea we propose is that intelligence is only an attribute of software. Therefore, you can have more intelligent software and less intelligent software, but making a distinction between regular software and artificial intelligence is the wrong perspective to understand how to leverage modern tools to improve applications and solutions.

Evolution of Software Intelligence

There's a lot of expectation around AI these days. And sometimes that expectation seems to be unstoppable. The substance underneath such a great level of expectation, however, is nearly the same as it was back in the 1980s.

AI in Just One Picture

We find that Figure 2-1 summarizes quite effectively the hype around artificial intelligence every day and the often-confusing use of related terms such as *machine learning* and *deep learning* we experience every day.

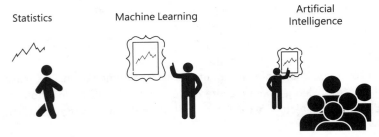

FIGURE 2-1 Different views and perspectives of artificial intelligence

Admittedly, we devised Figure 2-1 expressly to carry out a bit of geek humor. However, the leftmost part of the figure really captures the true substance of artificial intelligence today. And it is the same as it was years ago: statistics.

Statistics is about using mathematical methods to discover relationships between data points. Machine learning uses statistical methods to devise a model that can predict future events or classify existing information. This is the new part that has been in development in more recent years.

Finally, *artificial intelligence* is just a marketing term with the tremendous power of synthesizing the message and capturing C-level executives' attention.

The Root Cause of Today's AI Hype

Today, AI is commonly perceived as a form of broadly available (mostly free) software with which companies could fly into unexplored and unimagined territories—in some way close to where sci-fi authors found inspiration for super-computers and super-intelligent technologies.

AI is just software. It's optimization and data mining algorithms under a different name but applied in a broader scope than used only a few years ago. It's nothing completely new that didn't exist before, but it's perceived exactly as if it were.

We wonder why. Where does the hype come from?

There's an obvious commercial reason—the wish (or the need) to jump on any passing bandwagon—but there's also another, subtler, reason.

Most software applications today mirror an unevolved and prehistoric reality. The desire for AI is the way that consumers and business customers express the need of just having more intelligent applications. Applications with a smart user interface that deliver a thoughtful experience. Applications with embedded business logic to anticipate needs and trends and capable to speed up and automate business processes.

Expert Systems

For many years, the concrete implementation of forms of artificial intelligence focused on creating the computer counterpart of a human expert, and *expert systems* have been the cutting edge of software intelligence applied to industry fields.

An expert system is a software system applied to a given but restricted field. If competently programmed, an expert system can give nearly the same answer a human expert would give when presented with similar input data.

Expert systems (and, in general, applied AI systems) are smart and fast if the provided input lets the engine find the path to an answer. Otherwise, they fail or, like a human, just surrender, unable to provide an answer.

Unlike humans, though, expert systems are not able to learn.

Is *Expert* a Synonym of *Intelligent*?

A broadly accepted definition of an *expert* is a person (or a system) who is very knowledgeable about a particular domain. We can rephrase this as a person (or a system) who knows the answer to a great deal of possible questions.

In this regard, an expert system is not very intelligent, not at least if the intelligence is measured against the canonical human yardstick of intelligence. How would you rate an individual who is great at carrying out known and familiar tasks but who flips out whenever an unknown situation occurs?

As you saw in the preceding chapter, an expert system works by blindly and unconditionally applying a large but fixed and hard-coded set of rules with no exceptions. An expert system may be a rather sophisticated machine, but, by construction, it cannot deal with completely new and unplanned situations. Furthermore, an expert system can be extended only by releasing a new version.

The "Miracle on the Hudson" Story

In 2009, US Airways flight 1549 departed as usual from LaGuardia airport in New York on the early afternoon of January 15. Less than three minutes after takeoff, the aircraft incurred a bird strike and lost both engines. At 2,800 feet, the plane was governed by the autopilot system.

The autopilot software processes signals from a series of sensors around the aircraft in a continuous loop, many times a second. It's called a *negative* or *balancing* loop because the value of an output triggers an action whose results reduce the fluctuations between what's been measured and what's the expected output. The autopilot system checks input data like GPS position, speed, altitude, and turbulence against preset values and makes the necessary changes much more quickly and smoothly than a human pilot could.

An autopilot can do everything a human pilot can do. Or, better yet, almost everything.

In fact, the autopilot system would have kept the plane climbing as far as possible till the end, we'd say, given the shutdown of the engines. In the case of US Airways flight 1549, Capt. Sullenberger regained control of the plane while his first officer was going through the checklist for restarting the engines. The autopilot expert system was unable to deal with a similar unexpected situation, and likewise, the predefined manual procedures also were not. As a result, the captain evaluated—with the power of the human brain—that no other option was actually viable other than ditching in the Hudson River. Quite imaginatively, the press called this event the "Miracle on the Hudson."

 Note More recently, in late 2018 and early 2019, two unfortunate crashes of the same type of aircraft were attributed to one of the modules of the cruise control system. In short, driven by inaccurate measurement, the software kept changing the climbing angle to mistakenly try to prevent stalling but actually crashing the plane. Scarily enough, the software kept overriding any pilot command till the end. As of March 2019, this type of plane was banned from the skies until the software was modified.

Keeping Skills Up to Date

Today, expert systems are a valid solution in those fields where they have been used for long time and improved again and again. The flight control system of airplanes, of which the autopilot is a module, remains the canonical example of an expert system. An expert system needs regular updates, much like human experts need to refresh, refine, and extend their knowledge periodically.

Obviously, keeping expert systems up to date represents a cost. For this and other reasons, today greenfield development in the area of software intelligence is oriented more toward general artificial intelligence and systems that are designed from the ground up to learn and, in a way, to self-train.

 Important Would a different self-training AI system really be able to land a plane after a bird strike with both engines down? Tough question indeed. Without blissfully trespassing the borders of sci-fi, the human brain is still way more powerful than any known software at performing complex tasks that may not be broken down into relatively simple and repeatable steps. So no realistic chance exists today for any system to be instructed to handle such a complicated scenario in real time.

In fact, the best that AI can do is to break down complex problems into smaller chunks of the right size to be processed by machines and, at the same time, increase the power of machines and ideally their internal architecture.

General Artificial Intelligence

General AI today often goes under the more fascinating name *machine learning* (ML). In pure software terms, ML is a two-step process. First, you train the machine to recognize a model in a large dataset that simulates the real data flow. Second, you make the model available for a software application to invoke. Any client call provides input and receives an answer. If too many answers are determined not to be good enough, you have to refine the model, modify the training dataset, and retrain the machine.

In athletic terms, you set a target performance, define a set of exercises, and just train. When you're ready, you compete. If results are not in line with expectations, you go through a different set of exercises, train again, and get back to competitions. In ML, exercises are called algorithms, and ML-based systems are also known as autonomous systems.

Autonomous ML-based systems use two main classes of learning algorithms: unsupervised and supervised. Because any AI-powered system exists to solve a specific, complex problem, it is reasonable that multiple algorithms are employed and from any of the preceding classes.

The professional figure who deals with learning algorithms can be a software engineer but, more likely, it is a relatively new one—a *data scientist*.

Unsupervised Learning

Unsupervised learning groups a number of algorithms that serve the overall purpose of classifying unpolished data. The algorithms process data to discover commonalities that could help to tag and/or index the original data. Those commonalities are generically expressed in the form of clusters or labels. (See Figure 2-2.)

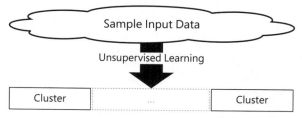

FIGURE 2-2 The core functioning of unsupervised learning

Discovering Clusters of Data

You choose an unsupervised learning algorithm whenever you don't know much about the output that is typically associated with a given input. It's up to the algorithm to identify hidden structures in the input data and, ideally, suggest correlations that could lead to further analysis. Unsupervised learning tries to identify subsets of the original data items that have something in common.

You can imagine the input of an unsupervised learning algorithm as a relational table where each column represents an attribute of the data item. Abstractly speaking, the algorithms attempt to determine an ideal way to group input data items. For the sake of (visual) simplicity, imagine that you have a table of input data with only two attributes. The dots in the chart in Figure 2-3 provide a bidimensional representation of the input.

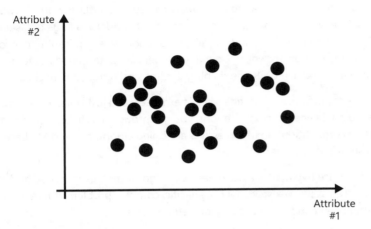

FIGURE 2-3 Bidimensional representation of the input data

The algorithm attempts to group data items by affinity, and each algorithm of unsupervised learning may have its own specific way to measure the logical distance between data items in the same cluster. Figure 2-4 shows a possible output.

Note that in Figure 2-4 not all dots (data items) belong to a cluster. The clusters identified by the algorithm may have different characteristics. The resulting set can be a partition, or it can have some redundancy if the same data item belongs to multiple clusters. More likely, though, some data items may be left out as if they were an anomaly.

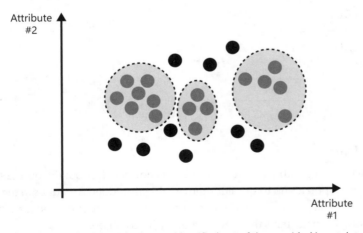

FIGURE 2-4 Three sample clusters identified out of the provided input data

Evaluating the Discovered Clusters

There might be different reasons why an input data item can be left out of the returned set of clusters. The most common reason is that it is determined to be too unlike other data items and then not relevant for the purpose of clustering. Note that not being part of any selected cluster is information that can be read in a specular way: a data item that is not part of any known groups represents an anomaly. Anomaly detection is another popular learning scheme under the umbrella of unsupervised learning.

Another reason for a data item to be left out of all clusters is that the rules the algorithm used to select data items into the cluster might not be appropriate for the problem at hand, and this may cause the clusters to lose valuable pieces of information. In this case, the algorithm has to run again with different parameters, or an entirely different algorithm has to be used for the problem.

Dimensionality reduction is another perspective you may apply to the discovered clusters to reach the most appropriate groupings for the problem at hand. Dimensionality reduction consists of replacing an entire cluster, or even only a part of it, with a single but representative data item. A common example is replacing all the items in one of the clusters with a data item that is the mean of all values. After the reduction is applied, you have an entire new input dataset on which you may iteratively apply clustering again. You can repeat the task until you end up with a set of clusters that is determined appropriate. The real world of AI is all about trial and error no matter what sales and marketing people say.

Supervised Learning

An unsupervised algorithm is left alone to explore the input dataset and discover patterns and relationships. In this regard, unsupervised learning is very close to data mining, at least in the role that statistical methods play in both contexts.

A supervised algorithm works on both an input and an output dataset with a learning path that essentially tries to figure out the correlation between input and output. In a nutshell, supervised learning means that you know the expected output and want to train the machine learning solution to guess as correctly as possible the output based on some input.

Capturing Relationships Between Input and Output

Supervised learning algorithms aim at two goals: prediction and classification. Prediction relies heavily on regression and is primarily good at forecasts, whereas classification is a more precise form of clustering where a number of labeled baskets are provided for the algorithm to place input data.

Regression builds a model that, by discovering cause-effect relationships between input and output, can forecast a value based on a given input. There are a number of regression algorithms to choose from that differ in the number of input variables they take into account and for the type of relationship between input values and known outputs.

Classification is the process of predicting the cluster to which a given data item belongs. In strict math terms, a classification algorithm is a function that maps input variables to discrete output variables. (See Figure 2-5.)

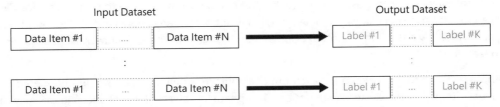

FIGURE 2-5 The core functioning of supervised learning

Labeled Data

Abstractly speaking, a supervised algorithm is a function that takes a vector of data as its input—the data item row of Figure 2-5—and returns another vector of data as its output—the label row of Figure 2-5. A call to the function can be read as follows: "The given input data row should return the given output labeled data." You expect the algorithm to return labels when the input vector is provided. Ultimately, the algorithm infers a function that it then uses to map live values to a set of known and expected results.

To prepare a dataset for supervised learning, you collect the data that typically captures the state of a system at a given time and binds it to labels that describe the expected answer. The input dataset may contain a number of attributes that, for example, capture a credit card transaction such as amount, goods purchased, date and time of purchase, IP addresses, and geographical locations. A similar set of records is referred to as a *timeline series*.

The corresponding record in the output dataset may indicate the grade of risk for further actions to be taken. (See Figure 2-6.)

During the learning phase, the algorithm explores correlations between the input fields and the expected output. Concretely, in the specific scenario, the labeled data can be as simple as 0/1, to indicate whether the sample transaction denotes a low, medium, or high risk of fraud.

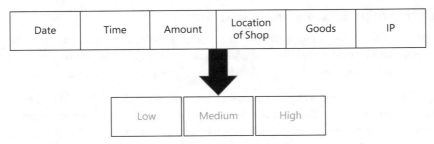

FIGURE 2-6 Actual input values generate a set of labeled data as the answer

Supervised learning mostly serves to predict the output of a given input, choosing from a set of pre-defined answers. In other words, you must know the answer you expect for a given sequence of input data and have the algorithm learn how to match new input data to any known answer. In this regard, the difference with unsupervised learning is self-evident: in unsupervised learning, there's no known list of possible answers.

The Inferred Function

The inferred function that supervised learning tries to discover is essentially a function that captures the dynamics of the sample data and therefore a function that, put at work on similar but real-world data, continues on the same trend. To form a rather simple but still effective idea of the function, look at Figure 2-7. In this case, the dataset is bidimensional (one feature and one output label), and there-fore, the function used to capture the trend is linear.

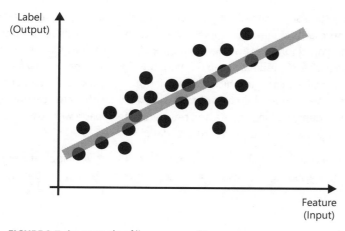

FIGURE 2-7 An example of linear regression

The line in the graph is the best-fit straight line for the given data. Quality of training data is crucial for the success of machine learning algorithms. Any dataset can reveal only the relationships it really contains, but, at the same time, it can induce you to see false or just inaccurate relationships.

Note Probably the first example of supervised learning in history is the work on The Bombe done by Alan Turing at Bletchley Park during the Second World War. This machine was used to decrypt communications between the German Navy and U-boats. Built for brute-force attack, the Bombe became successful when researchers found a fast way to rule out com-binations algorithmically. That was made possible by the knowledge that every day some ciphered characters always corresponded to the same words. In other words, the machine was supervised in its learning process by the knowledge of a few certain relationships hid-den in the training data.

Summary

Expert systems are the first concrete form of artificial intelligence put to work in a number of business domains, such as cruise control systems, along with legal, tax, finance, and health-care systems. Those intelligent software systems do the work of a human expert and are able to give the same insightful answer to a fixed number of questions. Expert systems are expensive to update, but, as a matter of fact, at some point they face obsolescence. Machine learning is the next step.

Machine learning works by creating a model that can answer questions it was never explicitly programmed to answer. In action, a machine learning model uses a previously identified mathematical function to calculate the output from a given input. Before it can be used, the model is trained on a large sample dataset, and training is aimed at discovering just that mathematical function that captures the hidden relationships between input and output.

Machine learning is articulated in two areas: supervised and unsupervised learning. In both cases, the input is a matrix of data that represents a relevant sample of the data the model will be called to process at runtime. Supervised learning algorithms also need a matrix of expected results so that for each input row there's also a number of expected results. In this way, the algorithm learns how to best match input with expected output. In all the cases in which only the input data is available, you opt for an unsupervised learning algorithm. An unsupervised algorithm mostly works with statistical methods to identify the areas with the highest density of input data and returns clusters made with just those data points. It does that by trying to guess the hidden structure of data.

In this chapter we briefly mentioned classes of algorithms. In the next chapter, we'll look at a number of specific supervised and unsupervised algorithms and analyze their behavior in more detail.

## CHAPTER 3

Mapping Problems and Algorithms

When I consider what people generally want in calculating, I found that it always is a number.

—Muḥammad ibn Mūsā al-Khwārizmī
Persian mathematician of eighth century whose name originated the word algorithm

More often than not, the user experience produced by machine learning looks like magic to users. At the end of the day, though, machine learning is only a new flavor of software—a new specialty much like web or database development—and a flavor of software that today is a real breakthrough.

A breakthrough technology is any technology that enables people to do things that weren't possible before. Behind the apparent magic of final effects, however, there is a series of cumbersome tasks and, more than everything else, there's a series of sequential and interconnected decisions along the way that are hard to make and time consuming. In a nutshell, they are critical decisions for the success of the solution.

This chapter has two purposes. First, it identifies the classes of problems that machine learning can realistically address and the algorithms known to be appropriate for each class. Second, it introduces a relatively new approach—automated machine learning or AutoML for short—that can automate the selection of the best machine learning pipeline for a given problem and a given dataset.

In this chapter, we'll describe classes of problems and classes of algorithms. We'll focus on the building blocks of a learning pipeline in the next chapter.

Fundamental Problems

As you saw in Chapter 2, "Intelligent Software," the whole area of machine-based learning can be split into supervised and unsupervised learning. It's an abstract partition of the space of algorithms, and the main discriminant for being supervised or unsupervised is whether or not the initial dataset includes valid answers. Put another way, we can reduce automated learning into the union of two learning approaches—*learning by example* (supervised) and *learning by discovery* (unsupervised).

Under these two forms of learning, we can identify a number of general problems and for each a number of general algorithms. This layout is reflected in the organization of any machine learning software development library you can find out there and use—whether it's based on Python, Java, or .NET.

> **Note** Not coincidentally, most of the topics covered in the following chapters match, to a large extent, the tasks of the newest Microsoft's ML.NET framework (covered in Part II, "Machine Learning in .NET") and algorithm cheat-sheet of scikit-learn—an extremely popular machine learning Python library. (See https://scikit-learn.org.)

Classifying Objects

The classification problem is about identifying the category an object belongs to. In this context, an object is a data item and is fully represented by an array of values (known as *features*). Each value refers to a measurable property that makes sense to consider in the scenario under analysis. It is key to note that classification can predict values only in a discrete, categorical set.

Variations of the Problem

The actual rules that govern the object-to-category mapping process lead to slightly different variations of the classification problem and subsequently different implementation tasks.

Binary Classification. The algorithm has to assign the processed object to one of only two possible categories. An example is deciding whether, based on a battery of tests for a particular disease, a patient should be placed in the "disease" or "no-disease" group.

Multiclass Classification. The algorithm has to assign the processed object to one of many possible categories. Each object can be assigned to one and only one category. For example, classifying the competency of a candidate, it can be any of poor/sufficient/good/great but not any two at the same time.

Multilabel Classification. The algorithm is expected to provide an array of categories (or labels) that the object belongs to. An example is how to classify a blog post. It can be about sports, technology, and perhaps politics at the same time.

Anomaly Detection. The algorithm aims to spot objects in the dataset whose property values are significantly different from the values of the majority of other objects. Those anomalies are also often referred to as *outliers*.

Commonly Used Algorithms

At the highest level of abstraction, classification is the process of predicting the group to which a given data item belongs. In stricter math terms, a classification algorithm is a function that maps input variables to discrete output variables. (See Figure 3-1.)

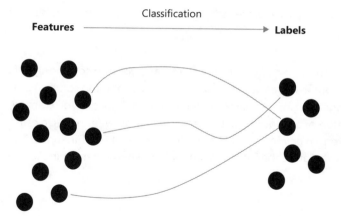

FIGURE 3-1 A graphical representation of a classification function

The classes of algorithms most commonly used for classification problems are as follows:

Decision Tree. A decision tree is a tailor-made binary tree that implements a sequence of rules to be progressively applied to each input object. Each leaf of the tree represents one of the possible output categories. Along the way, the input object is routed downward through the levels of the tree based on rules set at each node. Each rule is based on a possible value of one of the features. In other words, at each step, the key feature value of the input object (say, Age) is checked against the set value (say, 40), and the visit proceeds in the subtree that applies (say, less than or greater than or equal to 40). The number of nodes and the feature/value rules implemented are determined during the training of the algorithm.

Random Forest. This is a more specialized version of the decision tree algorithm. Instead of a single tree, the algorithm uses a forest of simpler trees trained differently and then provides a response that is some average of all the responses obtained.

Support Vector Machine. Conceptually, this algorithm represents the input values as points in an n-dimensional space and looks for a sufficiently wide gap between points. In two dimensions, you can imagine the algorithm looking for a curve that cuts the plane in two, leaving as much space as possible along the margin. In three dimensions, you can think of a plane that cuts the space in two.

Naïve Bayes. This algorithm works by computing the probability that a given object, given its values, may fall in one of the predefined categories. The algorithm is based on Bayes' theorem, which describes the likelihood of an event given some related conditions.

Logistic Regression. This algorithm calculates the probability of an object falling in a given category given its properties. The algorithm uses a sigmoid (logistic) function that, for its mathematical nature, lends itself well to be optimized to calculate a probability very close to 1 (or very close to 0). For this reason, the algorithm works well in either/or scenarios, and so it is mostly used in binary classification.

The preceding list is not exhaustive but includes the most-used classes of algorithms battle-tested for classification problems.

> **Important** In the everyday jargon of machine learning, the term *algorithm* commonly refers to an entire family of algorithms that share the same general approach to the solution but may differ on a number of minor and not-so-minor implementation details. If you want to refer to a specific implementation of an algorithm, the term *trainer* (or even the term *estimator*) is more common. The term *pipeline*, instead, refers to the overall combination of data transformations, trainers, and evaluators that form the ultimately deployed machine learning *model*.

Common Problems Addressed by Classification

A number of real-life problems can be modeled as classification problems, whether binary, multiclass, or multilabel. Again, the following list can't and won't be exhaustive, but it is enough to give a clue about where to look when a concrete business issue surfaces:

- Spam and customer churn detection
- Data ranking and sentiment analysis
- Early diagnosis of a disease from medical images
- A recommender system built for customers
- News tagging
- Fraud or fault detection

Spam detection can be seen as a binary classification problem: an email is spam or is not. The same can be said for early diagnosis solutions although in this case the nature of the input data—images instead of records of data—requires a more sophisticated pipeline and probably would be solved using a neural network rather than any of the algorithms described earlier. Customer churn detection and sentiment analysis are multiclass problems, whereas news tagging and recommenders are multilabel problems. Finally, fraud or fault detection can be catalogued as an anomaly detection problem.

Predicting Results

Many would associate artificial intelligence with the ability to make smart predictions about future events. In spite of appearances, prediction is not magic but the result of a few statistical techniques, the most relevant of which is regression analysis. Regression measures the strength of a relationship set between one output variable and a series of input variables.

Regression is a supervised technique and is used to predict a continuous value (as opposed to discrete categorical values of classification).

Variations of the Problem

Regression is about finding a mathematical function that captures the relationship between input and output values. What kind of function? Different formulations of the regression function lead to different variations of the regression problem. Here are some macro areas:

Linear Regression. The algorithm seeks a linear, straight-line function so that all values, present and future, plot around it. The linear regression algorithm is fairly simple and, to a large extent, even unrealistic because, in practice, it means that a single value guides the prediction. Any realistic predictive scenarios, instead, bring in several different input data flows.

Multilinear Regression. In this case, the regression function responsible for the actual prediction is based on a larger number of input parameters. This fits in a much smoother way into the real world because to predict the price of a house, for example, you would use not only square footage but also historical trends, neighborhood, rooms, age, and maybe more factors.

Polynomial Regression. The relationship between the input values and the predicted value is modeled as an nth degree polynomial in one of the input values. In this regard, polynomial regression is a special case of multilinear regression and is useful when data scientists have reasons to hypothesize a curvilinear relationship.

Nonlinear Regression. Any techniques that need a nonlinear curve to describe the trend of the output value given a set of input data fall under the umbrella of nonlinear regression.

Commonly Used Algorithms

The solution to a regression problem is finding the curve that best follows the trend of input data. Needless to say, the training phase of the algorithm works on training data, but the deployed model, instead, needs to perform well on similar live data. The curve that predicts the output value based on the input is the curve that minimizes a given error function. The various algorithms define the error function in different ways and measure the error in different ways.

The classes of algorithms most commonly used for regression problems are as follows:

Gradient Descent. The gradient descent algorithm is expected to return the coefficients that minimize an error function. It works iteratively by first assigning default values to the coefficient and then measuring the error. If the error is large, it then looks at the gradient of the function and moves ahead in that direction, determining new values for the coefficients. It repeats the step until some stop condition is met.

Stochastic Dual Coordinate Ascent. This algorithm takes a different approach and essentially solves a dual problem—maximizing the value calculated by the function rather than minimizing the error. It doesn't use the gradient but proceeds along each axis until it finds a maximum and then moves to the next axis.

Regression Decision Tree. This algorithm builds a decision tree, as discussed previously, for classification problems. The main differences are the type of the error function used to decide if the tree is deep enough and the way in which the feature value in each node is chosen (in this case, it is the mean of all values).

Gradient Boosting Machine. This algorithm combines multiple weaker algorithms (e.g., most commonly, a basic decision tree) and builds a unified, stronger learner. Typically, the prediction results from the weighed combination of the output of all the chained weak learners. Extremely popular algorithms in this class are XGBoost and LightGBM.

> **Important** Both regression and classification cover very large areas of real-life problems. And often the actual problems faced can't be solved with any of these algorithms. Instead, they require a deeper learning approach via some neural network.

Common Problems Addressed by Regression

Regression is the task of predicting a continuous value, whether a quantity, a price, or a temperature.

- Price prediction (houses, stocks, taxi fares, energy)
- Production prediction (food, goods, energy, availability of water)
- Income prediction
- Time series forecasting

Time series regression is interesting because it can help understand and, better yet, predict the behavior of sophisticated dynamic systems that periodically report their status. This is fairly common in industrial plants where, even thanks to Internet of Things (IoT) devices, there's plenty of observational data. Time series regression is also commonly used in the forecasts of financial, industrial, and medical systems.

Grouping Objects

In machine learning, clustering refers to the grouping of objects represented as a set of input values. A clustering algorithm will place each object point into a specific group based on the assumption that objects in the same group have similar properties and objects in different groups have quite dissimilar properties.

At first, clustering may look like classification, and in fact, both problems are about deciding the category that a given data item belongs to. There's one key difference between the two, however. A clustering algorithm receives no guidance from the training dataset about the possible target groups. In other words, clustering is a form of unsupervised learning, and the algorithm is left alone to figure out how many groups the available dataset can be split on.

A clustering algorithm processes a dataset and returns an array of subsets. Those subsets receive no labels and no clues about the content from the algorithm itself. Any further analysis is left to the data science team. (See Figure 3-2.)

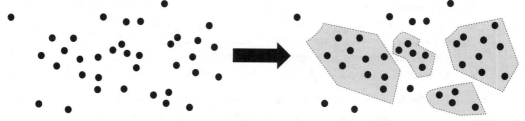

FIGURE 3-2 The final outcome of a clustering algorithm run on a dataset

Commonly Used Algorithms

The essence of clustering is analyzing data and identifying as many relevant clusters of data as it can find. While the idea of a cluster is fairly intuitive—a group of correlated data items—it still needs some formal definition of the concept of correlation to be concretely applied. In the end, a clustering algorithm looks for disjoint areas (not necessarily partitions) of the data space that contain data items with some sort of similarity.

This fact leads straight to another noticeable difference between clustering and regression or classification. You'll never deploy a clustering model in production and never run it on live data to get a label or a prediction. Instead, you may use the clustering step to make sense of the available data and plan some further supervised learning pipeline.

Clustering algorithms adopt one of the following approaches: partition-based, density-based, or hierarchy-based. Here are the most popular algorithms:

K-Means. This partition-based algorithm sets a fixed number of clusters (according to some preliminary data analysis) and randomly defines their data center. Next, it goes through the entire dataset and calculates the distance between each point and each of the data centers. The point finds its place in the cluster whose center is the nearest. The algorithm proceeds iteratively and recalculates the data center at each step.

Mean-Shift. This partition-based algorithm defines a circular sliding window (with arbitrary radius) and initially centers it at a random point. At each step, the algorithm shifts the center point of the window to the mean of the points within the radius. The method converges when no better center point is found. The process is repeated until all points fall in a window and overlapping windows are resolved, keeping only the window with the most points.

DBSCAN. This density-based algorithm starts from the first unvisited point in the dataset and includes all points located within a given range in a new cluster. If too few points are found, the point is marked as an outlier for the current iteration. Otherwise, all points within a given range of each point currently in the cluster are recursively added to the cluster. Iterations continue until there's at least one point not included in any cluster or their number is so small that it's OK to ignore them.

Agglomerative Hierarchical Clustering. This hierarchy-based algorithm initially treats each point as a cluster and proceeds iteratively, combining clusters that are close enough to a given distance metric. Technically, the algorithm would end when all the points fit in a single cluster, which would be the same as the original dataset. Needless to say, you can set a maximum number of iterations or use any other logic to decide when to stop merging clusters.

K-Means is by far the simplest and fastest algorithm, but, in some way, it violates the core principle of clustering because it sets a fixed number of groups. So, in the end, it's halfway between classification and clustering. In general, clustering algorithms have a linear complexity, with the notable exception of hierarchy-based methods. Not all algorithms, however, produce the same quality of clustering regardless of the distribution of the dataset. DBSCAN, for example, doesn't perform as well as others when the clusters are of varying density, but it's more efficient than, say, partition-based methods in the detection of outliers.

Common Problems Addressed by Clustering

Clustering is the method of many crucial business tasks in a number of different fields, including marketing, biology, insurance, and in general wherever screening of population, habits, numbers, media content, or text is relevant.

- Tagging digital content (videos, music, images, blog posts)

- Regrouping books and news based on author, topics, and other valuable information

- Discovering customer segments for marketing purposes

- Identifying suspicious fraudulent finance or insurance operations

- Performing geographical analysis for city planning or energy power plant planning

It is remarkable to consider that clustering solutions are often used in combination with a classification system. Clustering may be first used to find a reasonable number of categories for the data expected in production, and then a classification method could be employed on the identified clusters. In this case, categories will be manually labeled, looking at the content of identified clusters. In addition, the clustering method might be periodically rerun on a larger and updated dataset to see whether a better categorization of the content is possible.

More Complex Problems

Classification, regression, and clustering algorithms are sometimes referred to as *shallow learning*, in contrast to *deep learning*. Admittedly, the distinction between shallow learning and deep learning is a bit sketchy and cursory; yet, it marks the point of separating problems that can be solved with a relatively straight algorithm from those that require the introduction of some flavor of neural networks (more or less deep in terms of constituent layers) or the pipelining of multiple straight algorithms. Typically, these problems revolve around the area of cognition such as computer vision, creative work, and speech synthesis.

Image Classification

Image processing began in the late 1960s when a group of NASA scientists had the problem of converting analogic signals to digital images. The core of image processing is the simple application of mathematical functions to a matrix of pixels. A much more enhanced form of image processing is computer vision.

Computer vision isn't limited to processing data points but attempts to recognize patterns of pixels and how they match to forms (objects, animals, persons) in the real world. Computer vision is the branch of machine learning devoted to the emulation of the human eye, capable of capturing images and recognizing and classifying them based on properties such as size, color, and luminosity.

In the realm of computer vision, image classification is one of the most interesting sectors, especially for its applications to sensitive fields such as health care and security. Image classification is the process of taking a picture (or a video frame), analyzing it, and producing a response in the form of a categorical value (it's a dog) or a set of probabilistic values (70 percent, it's a dog; 20 percent, it's a wolf; 10 percent, it's a fox). In much the same way, an image classifier can guess mood, attitude, or even pain.

Even though many existing cloud services can recognize and classify images (even video frames), the problem of image classification can hardly be tackled outside a specific business context. In other words, you can hardly take a generic public cloud cognitive service and use it to process medical images (of a certain type) or monitor the live stream of a public camera. You need specific training for the algorithm tailor-made for the scenario you're facing.

An image classifier is typically a convolutional multilayer neural network. In such a software environment, each processing node receives input from the previous layers and passes processed data to the next. Depending on the number (and type) of layers, the resulting algorithm proves able (or not so able) to do certain things.

Object Detection

A side aspect of computer vision, tightly related to image classification, is object detection. With image classification, you can rely on a class of algorithms capable of looking at live streams of pictures and recognize elements in it. In other words, image classification can tell you what is in the processed picture. Object detection goes one step further and operates a sort of multiclass classification of the picture, telling about all the forms recognized and also about their relative position.

Object detection is very hot in technologies like self-driving cars and robotics. Advanced forms of object detection can also identify bounding boxes for the form to find and even draw precise boundaries around it. Object detection algorithms typically belong to either of two classes—classification-based or regression-based.

In this context, classification and regression don't refer to the straight shallow learning algorithms covered earlier in the chapter but relate to the learning approach taken by the neural network to come to a conclusion.

Text Analytics

Text analytics consists of parsing and tokenizing text, looking for patterns and trends. It is about learning relationships between named entities, performing lexical analysis, calculating and evaluating the frequency of words, and identifying sentence boundaries and lemmas. In a way, it's a statistical exercise of data mining and predictive analysis applied to text with the ultimate goal of taking software to interact with humans using the same natural language.

A typical application of text analytics is summarizing, indexing, and tagging the content of large digital free text databases and documents such as the comments (and complaints) left by customers of a public service. Text analytics often goes under the more expressive name of *natural language processing* (NLP) and is currently explored in more ambitious scenarios such as processing a live stream, performing speech recognition, and using recognized text for further parsing and information retrieval. Natural language processing applications are commonly built on top of neural networks in which the input text passes through multiple layers to be progressively parsed and tokenized until the networks produce a set of probabilistic intents.

There are quite a few applications of NLP available in the industry, buried in the folds of enterprise frameworks used in answering machine applications and call centers. However, if you just want to explore the power of the raw NLP, research a few of the existing test platforms, such as https://knowledge-studio-demo. ng.bluemix.net. The tool parses text, an excerpt of a police car accident report, and automatically extracts relevant facts, such as age of the involved people, characteristics of involved vehicles, location, and time.

Automated Machine Learning

Machine learning is a large field and is growing larger every day. As you'll see in much more detail in the next chapter, building an intelligent solution for a real-life business problem requires a *workflow* that essentially consists of a combination of different steps: data transformations, training algorithms, evaluation metrics, and, last but not least, domain knowledge, knowledge base, trial-and-error attitude, and imagination.

In this context, while the human ability to sort things out probably remains unparalleled, the community is seriously investigating the possibility of using automated, wizard-style tools to prepare a sketchy plan that could possibly represent the foundation of a true solution in a matter of minutes instead of days.

This is just the essence of the automated machine learning (AutoML) approach and consists of a framework that looks at your data and declared intent and intelligently suggests the steps to take that it determines most appropriate.

Aspects of an AutoML Platform

The typical end-to-end pipeline of any machine learning solution applied to a real-world problem most likely includes a number of steps, as outlined here:

- Preliminary analysis and cleaning of available data

- Identification of the properties (features) of the data that look most promising and relevant to solve the actual problem

- Selection of the algorithm

- Configuration of the parameters of the algorithm

- Definition of an appropriate validation model to measure the performance of the algorithm and indirectly the quality of the data it is set to use

Machine learning may not be for the faint-hearted, and even when one has a strong domain knowledge, the risk of feeling like a nonexpert newbie is fairly high.

Hence, AutoML is emerging as a solution to get people started quickly on machine learning projects and sometimes even effectively. AutoML offers the clear advantage of being fast and producing working solutions. The debatable point is not how objectively good the solution is that you can get out of an AutoML wizard, but the trade-off between what you get from AutoML and what you might be able to design by hand, especially if your team is not made up of domain and machine learning super-experts.

> **Note** To some extent, the debate about the alleged superficiality of AutoML solutions recalls past debates about the use of high-level programming languages over Assembly and the use of system-managed memory over memory cells directly allocated by the programmer. Our frank opinion is that AutoML frameworks are excellent at doing their job on simple problems. They can't do much for complex problems, however. But unfortunately, as of today, most real-world problems are quite complex.

Common Features

An AutoML framework is made of two distinct parts: a public list of supported learning scenarios and an invisible runtime service that returns a deliverable model based on some input parameters. A learning scenario is essentially an expert subsystem designed to solve specific classes of problems using data in one of a few predefined formats. The runtime is a learning pipeline in which a set of predefined data transformations are performed on selected input given the learning objective; target features are selected; and the trainer is selected, configured, trained, and tested.

An AutoML framework will perform any of the following tasks in an automated way after the user has indicated the physical source of data (tabular files, relational databases, cloud-based data warehouses) and the learning objective:

- Preprocessing and loading of data from different formats including detection of missing and skewed values

- Understanding of the type of each dataset column to figure out whether the column is, say, a Boolean, a discrete number, a categorical value, or free text

- Application of built-in forms of feature engineering and selection, namely the addition or transformation of data columns in a way that makes particular sense for the learning objective

- Detection of the type of work required by the learning objective (binary classification, regression, anomaly detection) and selection of a range of most appropriate training algorithms

- Configuration of the hyperparameters of the selected training algorithms

- Training of the model, application of appropriate evaluation metrics, and testing of the model

In addition, an AutoML framework is also often capable of visualizing data and results in a fancy way that is also helpful to better understand the underpinnings of the problem at hand.

There are a couple of popular AutoML frameworks: one is from Google and one, the newest, from Microsoft. Let's first briefly examine the Google Cloud AutoML platform, and then we'll go for a deeper live demonstration of the Microsoft AutoML framework as integrated in Visual Studio 2019.

Google Cloud AutoML

The Google Cloud AutoML platform is located at https://cloud.google.com/automl. It comes as a suite of machine learning systems specifically designed to simplify as much as possible the building of models tailor-made for specific needs. The platform works much like a UI wizard and guides the user through the steps of selecting the scenario, data, and parameters and then does the apparent magic of returning a deployable artifact out of nowhere. Internally, the Google Cloud AutoML platform relies on Google's transfer learning technology, which allows the building of neural networks as the composition of predefined existing networks.

Google Cloud AutoML supports a few learning scenarios such as computer vision, object detection in videos and still images, and natural language processing and translation. As you can see, it's a group of pretty advanced and sophisticated scenarios. It also supports a simpler one, called AutoML Tables, that works on tabular datasets and tests multiple model types at the same time (regression, feedforward neural network, decision tree, ensemble methods).

Microsoft AutoML Model Builder

An AutoML framework is also integrated in Visual Studio 2019 and comes packaged with ML.NET—the newest Microsoft .NET-based library for machine learning. The AutoML Model Builder framework has both a visual, wizard-style interface in Visual Studio (more on this in a moment) and a command-line interface (CLI) for use from within command-based environments such as PowerShell. A quick but effective summary of AutoML CLI can be found at https://bit.ly/2FaK7SP.

In Microsoft's AutoML framework, developers choose a task, provide the data source, and indicate a maximum training duration. Needless to say, the selected maximum duration is a discriminant for the quality of the final model. The shorter time you choose, the less reliable the final model can be.

 Note Compared to Google Cloud AutoML, the Microsoft AutoML solution currently focuses on simpler tasks and is available also on premise and then for shorter training cycles. The Google platform, instead, is cloud-based and suitable for longer and more realistic training cycles available through a paid subscription.

The AutoML Model Builder in Action

In Visual Studio 2019, after you install the latest version of the ML.NET Model Builder extension, you gain the ability to add a machine learning item to an existing project. When you do that, you're sent to a wizard like the one shown in Figure 3-3.

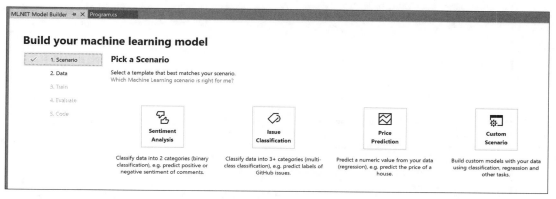

FIGURE 3-3 The main page of the Model Builder Visual Studio extension

As you can see, the wizard is articulated in five steps that broadly match the main steps of any machine learning pipeline. The first step of the builder is choosing the learning scenario—namely, the broad category of the problem for which you'd like to build a machine learning solution. In the version of the builder used for the test, the choice is not very large: Sentiment Analysis, Issue Classification, Price Prediction, and Custom Scenario. As an example, let's go for Price Prediction.

Exploring the Price Prediction Scenario

After you pick the scenario, the wizard asks you to load some data into the system. For the price prediction scenario, you can choose from a plain file or a SQL Server table. In the example shown in Figure 3-4, the loaded file is a CSV file. One key input to provide is the name of the column you want the final model to predict. In this case, the CSV file contains about one million rows, representing a taxi ride that really took place. The column to predict is the fare amount.

Training the Model

The third step is about the selection of the ideal trainer—the algorithm that is the most appropriate for the learning scenario and the data. This is where the power (and from a certain angle also the weakness) of the automated machine learning framework emerges. Some hard-coded logic, specific to the chosen scenario, tries a few training algorithms based on the allotted training time. Figure 3-5 shows an estimation of the training time necessary for a certain amount of data.

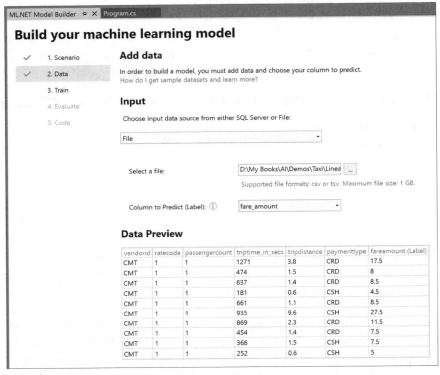

FIGURE 3-4 Loading data into the model

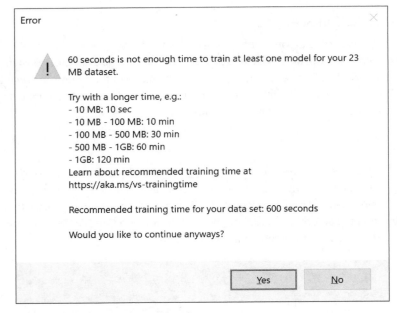

FIGURE 3-5 Estimating the training time

During the training phase, the system tries several different algorithms and uses an apt metric to evaluate its performance. (See Figure 3-6.)

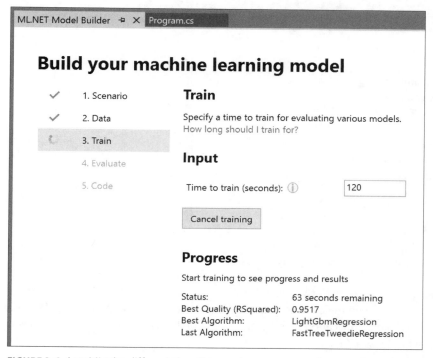

FIGURE 3-6 AutoML tries different algorithms and uses some metrics to evaluate the quality.

Evaluating the Results

At the end of the training, the AutoML system has data about a few algorithms it has tried with different hyperparameters. The metrics for evaluating the performance depend on the tasks and the algorithm. Price prediction is essentially a regression task for which the R-squared measure is the most commonly used. (We'll cover the math behind regression and R-squared in Chapter 11, "How to Make Simple Predictions: Linear Regression.") The theoretic ideal value of the R-squared metrics is 1; therefore, any value close enough to 1 is more than acceptable. Consider that in training, a resulting metric with a value of 1 (or very close to 1) is often the sign of overfitting—the model fits too much to the training data and potentially might not work effectively on live data once in production.

The AutoML process then suggests the use of the *LightGbmRegression* algorithm. If you want, you can just take the ZIP file with the final model ready for deployment. But what about looking into the actual set of data transformation and the actual code to possibly modify for further improvements?

The AutoML also offers the option to add the C# files to the current project for you to further edit them and retrain the model on a different dataset, for example. (See Figure 3-7.)

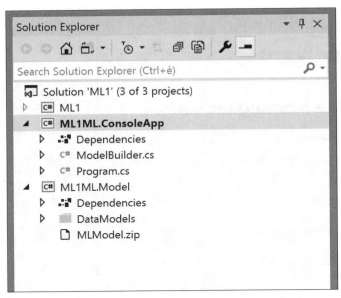

FIGURE 3-7 Autogenerated projects added by the Model Builder

As you can see, the figure contains two projects. One is a console application that contains a *ModelBuilder.cs* file packed with the code used to build the model. The other project is a class library and contains a sample client application seen as the foundation for using the model. This project also contains the actual model as a ZIP file.

Summary

Machine learning is ultimately intelligent software, but it is not the magic wand that movies and literature (and recently also sales/marketing departments) love to depict. More importantly, machine learning is not a physical black box you can pick from the shelves of a drugstore, bring home, mount, and use.

In the real world, you can't just "load data into the machine" and have the machine, in some way, just use it. In the real world, there are a few classes of approaches (mostly derived from statistics) such as regression, classification, and clustering and a bunch of concrete training algorithms. However, when to use which?

Determining which to use is a matter of experience and know-how, but it is also a matter of knowing data and how things actually work in the actual business domain. Does that mean that only experts can do machine learning? Yes, for the most part, that is just the point. However, nobody is born an expert, and everyone needs to get started in some way. This is the reason why automated tools for machine learning are emerging. In this chapter, we briefly looked at the Google Cloud AutoML and Visual Studio ML.NET Model Builder.

With the next chapter, we complete the preliminary path of machine learning, discussing the concept of a pipeline—namely, the sequence of steps that ultimately lead to the production of a deliverable model.

## CHAPTER 4

General Steps for a Machine Learning Solution

In preparing for battle I have always found that plans are useless, but planning is indispensable.

—Dwight Eisenhower
General of the US Army and 34th President of the United States

Any machine learning solution is a pipeline made of relatively tricky steps. More precisely, it is a kind of full-stack process that spans from data acquisition and preparation to training and from evaluation of the model to the actual deployment. It's a staged approach, collectively known as building a *pipeline*, that involves different skills along the way and requires, more than everything else, a clear business vision.

In this chapter, we'll discuss the bare bones of a canonical machine learning solution and the stages you go through: data collection, data preparation, selection of the model to employ, training of the model, evaluation of the results, and finally, when the obtained performance—the quality of the answers the system can provide—has become acceptable, deployment to production.

If this process sounds a bit too complicated and collides with the sense of smoothness of some marketing messages you may have seen, well, consider that as of today no better (or just shorter) way of building a machine learning solution is known and imagining a different one is even harder.

Note In some ways, the advent of machine learning is comparable to the advent of the Internet. For companies, the challenge with the Internet was designing new processes, new services, or new functions to leverage the power of connectivity. Getting basic Internet access from a provider was not enough; you had to plan and build solutions addressing problems or challenges. In much the same way, getting raw data is not enough; you have to plan and build solutions addressing problems or challenges. However, building a machine learning solution is much more complicated and business intrusive than building a web application.

Data Collection

As we described in Chapter 1, "How Humans Learn," movies and literature are full of experts who just "load data" into supercomputers and get brilliant and fast answers from the installed software. Beyond this oversimplification of the storytelling model, at the highest level of abstraction, things go more or less in the same way in the real world. Well, except for a number of nontrivial details that we will explore further.

Once the final goal to achieve with machine learning is defined, the first detail to tackle is determining if you have enough data to load in the machine. Data collection is by far the most essential first step because it addresses common challenges such as data exploration and profiling and touches on the overall level of data culture that permeates the company.

Data-Driven Culture in the Organization

If you want to build an artificial intelligence solution for your company, you need to have your own data. If you don't have your own data, you can't reasonably expect to run an effective AI solution. Period.

A Quick Proof-of-Concept Is Hardly Enough

Not having data is a common mistake that executives make these days. On the wings of enthusiasm for some exciting marketing messages, executives encourage research and authorize proof-of-concept (PoC) projects. The quantity, quality, and correlation of data are crucial for the success of any machine learning activity, and using just the data you have without further analysis leads to purely indicative PoCs that are of no concrete satisfaction to any of the involved parties.

Without data, you have exactly zero chances of running a machine learning project successfully. Just having operational data, however, is not enough. Most software in use today tracks business transactions, making a large quantity of records available. Machine learning, though, needs much more.

Depending on the business scenario, you might want to correlate operational data with other data flows such as weather forecasts, schedules, traffic information, maintenance records, social activity, and even more. It's the specific problem at hand that, fully understood in its entire web of correlations, reveals the appropriate data dependencies to explore and subsequently enables you to figure out the data you have and the data you don't have for the job.

Resistance Is Futile

A data-driven culture means that all members of the organization are involved with data collection and storage as part of their daily activity. Any single action within the normal activity should be targeted to collecting data and storing it permanently. The format of the data may not be important at first as long as it is collected. This is a key point for you, as an AI consultant, to remark or suggest.

Are you thinking that employees may not much like the extra burden of a data-driven culture? Probably that's just what's on one side of the scale. On the other side, the lack of proper data, regardless of the format, can easily jeopardize a machine learning project. Automatic collection of data (for example, through monitoring systems and event-based software architecture) is the first necessary step toward artificial intelligence.

Data Accessibility and Ownership

Sometimes companies own an acceptable quantity of data that is regularly updated and that grows at an amazing pace. But, guess what? This data is problematic to access when it is not just locked down by legal protections.

Data collection is important, but storage is not a secondary point because storage devices should be selected to make data quickly available on demand. As we'll see in a moment, maintaining the storage layer is a trade-off between the raw cost of storage and speed of access. Both points must be optimized because you must collect as much data as possible (without paying a fortune for keeping it safe) and have it back in a reasonable time when you need it. This means that if data can't be kept in a single location and is distributed across multiple data silos, you need to set up connections to gather data from multiple sources in a timely manner.

Finally, who is the real owner of the data you manage and store in servers and silos under your direct control? The General Data Protection Regulation (GDPR), for example, draws a neat distinction between data owners, data controllers, and data processors. Typically, processors are software houses that manage the software that physically stores any data. Controllers, instead, are companies (i.e., banks) that collect data and have access to it. Whether you're a processor or a controller, before you set up a machine learning project, you'd better double-check that you have the right to use any data you have stored somewhere.

Storage Options

Today most companies use a data lake as a general-purpose container for whatever data they deal with. Having a data lake, however, is only the first necessary step. The data lake is the first-level silo from which data must be extracted to be processed and prepared for machine learning pipelines.

Building a Data Lake

A *data lake* is a vast repository of raw data stored in any form as produced by line-of-business applications and utilities, including time-series, email, PDF, and Office files. The content of a data lake is fairly generic and unclassified because the purpose of the data is not defined yet. For example, on Microsoft Azure, a single instance of a data lake uses a blob storage account and can contain trillions of files and even individual files larger than one petabyte.

Typically, a data collection process distinguishes data in three categories: hot data, semi-hot data, and cold data. All of them fit in a data lake though with different storage settings and, consequently, costs. *Hot data* commonly refers to frequently used data collected in less than 24 months. *Semi-hot data* refers to data collected in less than 24 months but rarely used. *Cold data* typically can go back up to five years or even more.

Depending on the nature of the data (hot, semi-hot, or cold), a specific implementation of the data lake can also use different storage technologies such as tape and, in the future, even light-based writing technology.

Shaping a Data Warehouse

The term *data lake* is sometimes used interchangeably with the term *data warehouse*. There's a neat difference between the two, however. Unlike the data lake, a data warehouse is a repository for structured and filtered data that has already been processed for a specific goal.

Often, but not necessarily, a data warehouse is built out of an existing data lake. In terms of the performance of data access, a data warehouse provides exceptional horizontal scalability and doesn't distinguish between age and temperature (hot, cold) of the data. In most cloud providers (such as Microsoft Azure), a data warehouse instance has a significantly higher cost than a data lake in the same order of magnitude as the cost for a relational solution.

Most of the time, the data collection process feeds a data lake and lets the company gather data even without a clear, well-defined purpose. Feeding a data warehouse from a data lake is the next step that starts when a specific objective for the data has been identified. You can think of a data lake as a low-level repository of data. As is, the data is not very usable, and in particular is not usable for artificial intelligence purposes. In fact, in the real world, just loading data in a digital repository doesn't work as it does in fiction.

Making data usable for a specific purpose is the goal of data preparation—the second step of a machine learning pipeline. Data preparation is about selecting segments of data and organizing that data in a way that makes it functional.

Because a large data lake may contain an enormous number of records, it may not be obvious what is in it and what is not. Data scientists and domain experts use exploration and profiling to outline the steps to extract data to train a machine learning model.

> **Important** Working on data is crucial and much more relevant and time consuming than just training a model. Put another way, training is possible only if you have data, and often the reason for an unsatisfying training process is invalid or insufficient data. It's all about the data then.

Data Preparation

Quite a few of those marketing whitepapers abundantly sponsored over social networks assure that 40 percent and more of the world's companies are making investments to improve the quality of their data to get better analytics—whatever that means and however it is obtained.

In spite of the percentage of companies and the related hype around this reported fact, however, the pattern described is decidedly credible. Any company needs to make an investment in data to improve the quality of collected items. This is a core step in the process to get truly usable data for machine learning projects.

Improving Data Quality

The major risk for any machine learning project is ending up training the model on an insufficient and inadequate dataset. Inaccurate data, in fact, will inevitably affect the results, and a low amount of data will not be sufficient for the model. This brings up the whole problem of data quality.

Toward a Continuous Training Model

Data quality refers to a number of attributes (for example, completeness, consistency, distribution) of the collected data, and we'll address this issue in more detail in the next chapter. Data quality is addressed in one of two ways. If the data is collected in real time via some IoT acquisition platform, quality is in some way guaranteed at the source. Otherwise, data quality requires the extra step of offline data processing.

It is worth noting, however, that more and more companies are taking data science one step further and bringing data analysis capabilities right into the acquisition chain. No longer is data analysis about processing a batch of historical data to guess an underlying prediction model. Companies are now eagerly looking into models that can intelligently react to live data and turn the training step into a much more sophisticated "continuous training" step.

The Store-and-Train Model

Although most companies are still debating about the opportunity of building a data lake, industry-leading companies are organizing themselves to process data as it is streamed into the system instead of first dumping it into some data lake to clean later.

Modern monitoring systems (such as in the energy, telecom, manufacturing, and health-care industries) are practicing this sort of store-and-train model that bypasses the data lake or just uses the data lake as a cheap data store for purposely acquired data.

Cleaning Data

Having data is not enough. You must verify that the data is good for the specific machine learning task you're planning. If you assume the quality of data is acceptable and most of the missing data has been replaced and inconsistencies fixed, it's time to clean and harmonize data.

Avoiding Biased Datasets

The process of cleaning and harmonizing data for machine learning purposes means identifying trends, discovering outliers, and spotting and correcting skewed information. The ultimate goal of this step is ensuring that the data that will be used to train the model, and subsequently the data that will guide the successive model's answers, is not biased or imbalanced.

Going with a training dataset that contains too much information of a certain type and too little of another type poses serious concerns regarding the reliability of the predictions.

Harmonization of Data

The harmonization of data consists of applying a number of relatively simple transformations to format the data in a way that best fits the machine learning model:

Uniform representation of data. If data contains prices or other monetary values, you might want to ensure all values are based on the same scale and currency. The same can be said for values representing country names, dates, temperatures, measurements, and the like.

Range normalization. When numeric values fall in different ranges, you might want to normalize data by using a common scale. Normalization consists of changing numeric values in the dataset according to a common scale. Needless to say, changes should not skew the ratio between numbers in the same column.

Deduping. This operation consists of merging records that, although distinct in the dataset, are in practice recognized to refer to the same item of information. This is one of the few realistic operations in the dataset that shrinks its vertical size.

Outlier removal. Another common transformation consists of cutting off values below and beyond given thresholds. How you actually do this depends on the scenario. For example, if the dataset contains enough data, you can simply remove the rows that have outliers in at least one column. If you don't want to shrink the dataset vertically, you can simply replace outlier values with the mean of the column. That said, if you realize that values you're going to drop or flatten represent relevant business cases, it may be the evidence of an unbalanced dataset with too few relevant rows of data.

Feature Engineering

Data quality assessment and overall data harmonization are part of a preliminary preparation process that runs before any machine learning development can begin. Feature engineering, instead, is a part of the data preparation phase that has most to do with the building of an effective machine learning model.

In the pre-engineering step, data scientists remove rows and values from the dataset that domain knowledge suggests to be redundant or noisy. In the feature engineering phase, instead, data scientists focus on columns, also known as features. Ultimately, feature engineering is about adding, combining, and/or dropping columns of data to obtain a final dataset that could be used to train the model in a possibly ideal way.

Feature Generation

Feature generation is the first step of the data engineering process in which raw and unstructured data found in sources like CSV files, relational and nonrelational databases, and textual documents is organized in a tabular format made of rows and columns.

The first range of features is generated through whatever technique is easy to use given the nature of the source. A relational table or a CSV file, for example, is already in a tabular format. The same is not true for nonrelational data stores or textual documents. In this case, domain knowledge is expected to suggest what could be a reasonable representation (featurization) of the raw data. For example, a text document, like an email, could be initially split by words, perhaps skipping some that the domain expertise may identify as stop words.

After getting a first dataset, data scientists need to reduce its complexity to prevent the resulting model from receiving too much information. When this happens, during the learning phase it may generate a model too close to the training data, which may miserably fail on live data. This post-generation phase is articulated in feature selection and feature extraction. Feature selection is about keeping only the features that look more relevant. Feature extraction is about merging more columns into one or adding extra columns that better aggregate and represent the information.

Feature Selection

If it is glaringly obvious that some of the features in a dataset are irrelevant for a purpose, they can be removed manually at the source. Sometimes, though, there's no common domain knowledge that assures the limited value of some features. In this case, a number of techniques come to the rescue to evaluate the relevance of a feature algorithmically:

Heatmaps. A heatmap shows the correlation between a given feature in a dataset and the target variable that the model is expected to predict. A low correlation may indicate that the feature can be safely dropped, and the data scientist then decides about it.

Variance threshold. Variance threshold starts from the premise that a feature whose values are nearly constant and enclosed in a limited range of values is not of much use to count. Hence, a transformation algorithm based on variance threshold just drops all columns whose variance falls below a given threshold.

Correlation analysis. Two features are examined to measure their level of correlation. If they look particularly correlated, the data scientist may decide that only one of the two features is needed and may drop the other.

Sometimes, though, a deeper refactoring is necessary to further increase the value of the dataset, often by further reducing the number of columns.

Feature Extraction

The selection of the right number of features is driven by the contrasting needs of having specific summary information available while minimizing the total number of features. In doing so, data scientists often use ad hoc techniques to achieve the right content with a minimum number of features:

Grouping of sparse data. When a column has categorical content (values from a closed set of options), sometimes you want to merge some of the distinct options into a larger category. The purpose is to simplify the dataset without losing information. At the same time, this technique stimulates reasoning on the data available and leads to identifying really key information.

Computed features. When two or more features have value by themselves but knowing the result of their combination is even more useful, you might want to create an additional feature that contains the result of evaluating some rules on the features. For example, imagine you have the time that a taxi ride takes and the distance. Depending on the purpose, you can decide to add a new column that qualifies the ride as short, medium, or long range. You do that if you determine that it is more valuable for the model. When you do so, however, you then drop the original features unless you also have evidence that they're still useful.

Dummy variables. When a column has a finalized set of categorical values (e.g., short range, medium range, long range), you have to turn them into numerical values. This is required because of the way in which machine learning algorithms work. (Note that all of them are the offspring of some statistical method.) Apparently, the easiest way to turn categorical values into numerical values is to use distinct numbers in much the same way high-level programming languages like C# do with enum types. However, this approach is problematic because, in front of numeric values in a range, most algorithms tend to calculate means, and means make no sense for categorical values. For this reason, data scientists add dummy columns (0/1 binary values) to denote whether a given categorical value is found in the row. In other words, you end up with binary columns like is-short-range, is-medium-range, and is-long-range. This particular technique is also known as *one-hot encoding*.

Dimensionality reduction. This is the umbrella term for a number of data transformation techniques aimed at algorithmically compressing two or more columns into one. An extremely popular technique is Principal Component Analysis (PCA), which essentially projects the dataset originally sitting in an *N*-dimensional space to a space with a smaller number of dimensions. Note, though, that dimensionality reduction is not simply about dropping some of the least relevant columns. The projection algorithm instead tries to combine multiple columns linearly so that the same information is rendered through a smaller number of columns. It's clearly lossy transformation but hopefully does not negatively impact the prediction capabilities of the resulting model.

Finally, note that most of the featurization techniques presented here are natively built in most of the popular machine learning libraries out there, for Python as well as for C#.

Finalizing the Training Dataset

Machine learning has a lot in common with statistics, but one fundamental difference exists between the two. While statistics is mostly about a post-mortem analysis of data and aims at extracting the best-ever approximation of the model underneath the observed data, machine learning just attempts to work out a guessing engine that fits the training data as well as any other data it may face in production that is sufficiently close to the training set.

In a machine learning perspective, both training and test datasets are equally important for the final result.

Splitting Training and Test Datasets

At this point of the machine learning pipeline, you have the data to train the model and have its features arranged in a way that, although possibly not perfect, still represents a good start for a first training session. You need to have two distinct datasets available: one to teach the model the relevant things of the business and one to test if the trained model has successfully grabbed the essence of things.

A common approach consists of separating the original dataset into two subsets of different cardinality. The larger part is used for training (typically, 70 percent) and a smaller portion for testing (the remaining 30 percent). In other cases, however, you may well be using distinct (and equally large) datasets. That mostly depends on the amount of data effectively available. It is crucial to note a few things:

Statistical significance. The training dataset must be large enough to yield results of some statistical significance. Statistical significance is not a vague concept but refers instead to a specific set of formulas and can be summarized by saying that results obtained should be unlikely due to chance.

Relevance of the dataset. The training dataset must be representative of the data being used in the context of the machine learning application. Training and test datasets must have the same characteristics of data and the same distribution, and both must comply with what will be the case in production.

Based on the preceding two points, the goal of the machine learning pipeline is to create a model that, learning from training data, is able to generalize predictions well to live data. The test dataset is then merely seen as a mock for live data.

A More Advanced Splitting Technique

A neat split of the dataset, whether it is 80/20 or 70/30, may work in practice, but it is not a highly recommended strategy in terms of accuracy. At the end of the day, in fact, the model is tested only on a small fraction of the dataset. Worse yet, you can't even realistically go further from those splits; you still need enough data to train and a decent amount of it to test.

To bypass this hurdle, some more advanced splitting techniques have been introduced that, once streamlined in the overall machine learning process, give the model the chance to train and be tested on the entire spectrum of data although not at the same time.

Important You don't want to train and test the model on the same dataset. It is important that the model is tested on data it has never seen before. Not doing so would be a patent violation of the most elementary foundation of machine learning.

The aforementioned splitting technique (80/20 or whatever other numbers you use) is known as *holdout*. Another powerful technique is known as *k-fold*. The k-fold technique partitions the dataset in k subsets and iteratively trains the model on the union of the first $k-1$ subsets and trains it on the kth subset. The score of the model is the mean of the scores obtained during the iterations. A common value for the *k* parameter in the k-fold algorithm is 5.

Testing the Model for Acceptance

When there's an abundance of data, or when a customer commissions a proof of concept to a consulting company, it is common to keep the testing that has been done to validate the model distinct from the testing that has been done to see if it makes the needed cut. Using terms from software development, we could explain this as *unit testing* versus *acceptance testing*.

The machine learning team uses testing techniques like holdout or k-fold to gauge the performance of the model before shipping it. When all necessary adjustments to the training algorithm and dataset have been made and the model scores good results, it is ready to ship.

When delivered to the customer for acceptance, the model typically undergoes another testing phase. However, this extra phase is more delicate than just deploying the model to production. The test-for-acceptance phase, in fact, means that the model is presented an unknown but static dataset.

It is crucial for this unknown dataset that the aforementioned points of statistical significance and relevance are valid and that the distribution of data is in line with the data used for training and that both are in line with data expected in production.

Model Selection and Training

The most important step of a machine learning pipeline—the easiest to summarize and the most challenging to implement—is model selection and subsequent training.

It's the most important part of the pipeline because the ultimate goal of any machine learning pipeline is just the creation of a model. It is the easiest part to explain because it's all about categorizing the specific problem and selecting an appropriate algorithm or a chain of algorithms. (See Chapter 3, "Mapping Problems and Algorithms.") Finally, it's challenging because, more often than not, the algorithm to select is not obvious, and making a good choice may require a lot of troubleshooting.

Model or Algorithm: Settling the Affair

Before going any further, let's settle some fundamental questions: what is commonly intended by the word *model*, and what is meant by the word *algorithm*? In the industry (and even more in the literature), the two words are sometimes used interchangeably. In the scope of this book, we're not using the two terms as synonyms, but at the same time, considering them synonyms is not wrong per se. If you consider them synonyms, though, another term must be introduced and used accordingly: *trained model or algorithm*. This new term is set to indicate the output of the training phase.

The output of a machine learning pipeline, in fact, is a software artifact made of an algorithm (or a chain of algorithms) whose parametric parts (settings and configurable elements) have been adjusted based on the provided training data. In other words, the output of a machine learning pipeline is the instance of an algorithm that, much like the instance of an object-oriented language class, has been initialized to hold a given configuration. The configuration to use for the instance of the algorithm is discovered during the training phase.

In a nutshell, if you like to consider the terms *model* and *algorithm* as synonyms, the training gives you a *trained model* or *trained algorithm*. If you don't want to consider the two terms as synonyms (as we do in this book), the pipeline receives an algorithm and returns a model. The model in this case is a trained model. (See Figure 4-1.)

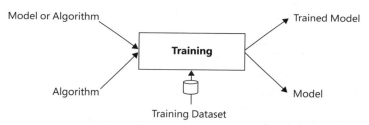

FIGURE 4-1 Clarifying the meaning of words model and algorithm in the context of the machine learning pipeline

The Algorithm Cheat Sheet

In the preceding chapter, we looked at how general problems map to machine learning solutions. We identified three main classes of problems with related algorithms. Without loss of generality, we can say that any problem can be mapped to any of the following machine learning categories: regression, classification, and clustering. Figure 4-2 presents a basic flowchart to help find the way out.

The first question to settle is whether to look for a supervised or an unsupervised algorithm. If the dataset doesn't have target output, you'd go for the unsupervised branch, as in Figure 4-2. Unsupervised algorithms are of two main families, depending on whether you want to or can indicate the desired number of clusters. If not, the main option is the DBSCAN algorithm; otherwise, you can pick up the K-means algorithm or one of its variations such as K-modes or K-prototypes if categorical data is involved.

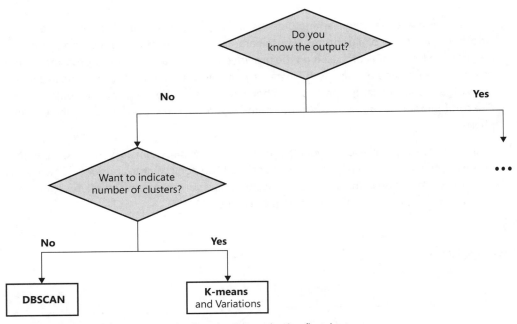

FIGURE 4-2 The unsupervised branch of an algorithm selection flowchart

Figure 4-3 expands the supervised branch of the algorithm selection flowchart.

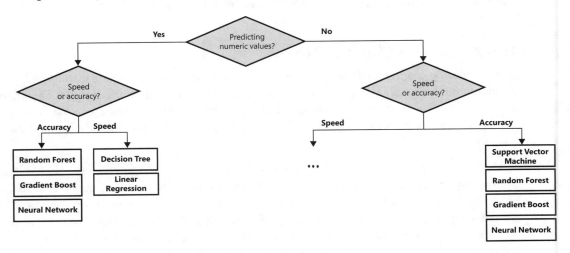

FIGURE 4-3 The supervised branch of an algorithm selection flowchart

The fundamental question to settle for any supervised learning algorithm is whether or not it is called to predict numeric values. If the target output is numeric, the choice is between speed and accuracy. It is worth noting that speed (or accuracy) refers to the performance of the algorithm in production. If speed is preferred, you go for a decision tree or linear regression; otherwise, random forest, gradient boost, and neural network are the most common options.

The set of possible choices is more ample if you enter the realm of classification algorithms. Even in this case, it's mostly about speed or accuracy. Opting for accuracy leads to picking one between kernel support vector machine, random forest, gradient boost, or a neural network. The graph of choices if opting for speed is summarized in Figure 4-4.

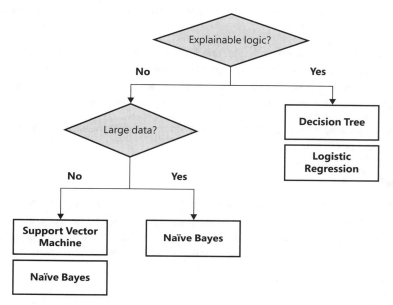

FIGURE 4-4 The graph of choices for supervised learning when prioritizing speed versus accuracy

When you are looking for a fast algorithm at the cost of accuracy, the first point to clarify is if the overall logic of the problem can be explained in a sequence of steps. If yes, it's about choosing a decision tree or perhaps logistic regression. Otherwise, in the case of hard-to-explain logic, the next question is about the overall size of the data. For large datasets, the fastest option is naïve Bayes; otherwise, a linear Support Vector Machine (SVM) is also a possibility.

The Case for Neural Networks

What if the problem at hand doesn't (easily) fall into any of the categories discussed in the preceding chapter (regression, classification, clustering) or stops at some point of the previous flowchart? This is where a neural network comes into play. A neural network is a hot option in three main scenarios.

Dealing with Time-Based Data

Modern hardware devices (such as industrial machines) produce a large quantity of data that gets captured in some way through IoT platforms or using ad hoc monitoring software that targets lower-level protocols. Any data you capture in this way consists of a sequence of data points denoting the state of the device at a specific point in time. Each data point is commonly made up of the values of multiple signals captured at regular intervals (e.g., every 10 seconds). Such a data format is known as a time series. When you have time series data, your dataset is a huge table of time-stamped records where each column refers to the value of a hardware signal at the specified time.

How would you use this information in a machine learning pipeline? Apparently, you could use time series to predict an incoming fault of the device. Most likely, in fact, one of the columns refers to the overall state of the device. Therefore, a basic classification or even regression algorithm can do the job. Well, sort of.

When you are working with time-based data, chances are that each data point is correlated to some of the previous points. How would you cope with that? Common training algorithms process data sequentially, one data point at a time without memory. This may not be acceptable with time series, or put another way, sticking to a classic algorithm may hardly produce acceptable results.

With a neural network—especially with a recurrent, memory-enabled neural network—you endow yourself with a much more powerful tool to do the job.

Doing Creative Work

Another problem that doesn't fall into any of the canonical classes of machine learning problems is doing creative work. To cut a long story short, none of the algorithms mentioned here and in the preceding chapter can do anything like creating text or an image or recognizing text or an image. This leads to fields of deep learning such as natural language processing and computational creativity.

This is work that only a neural network can do.

When Nothing Else Works

Taking the previous point one step further, we love to say that a neural network is the option left when everything else fails. You try regression or classification, and it doesn't deliver the quality you expect even after several training sessions and tons of configuration parameter changes. The solution is probably a matter of changing the approach and using a neural network.

A neural network is also an option when, even in a glaringly obvious classification problem, the target output to produce is particularly complex and made of multiple pieces. Think, for example, of a trading system in which the output to predict is not simply a Boolean answer (Buy/Don't buy), but it's a complex data object that includes the price to buy and maybe the time window.

When the problem expects multiple outputs, a neural network is always an option to consider carefully even though in simple situations you can obtain multiple predictions by using chaining models. If you do this, though, note that you're calling two models and likely doubling the response time.

Evaluation of the Model Performance

When you're done with training, you need to test the model in order to have indications about the overall quality. Because the model is a black box, you can discover its performance only by trying it out, tracking its scores, and evaluating. The training and evaluation phase should be intended as a sort of a loop where you train, test, fix, and train again. (See Figure 4-5.)

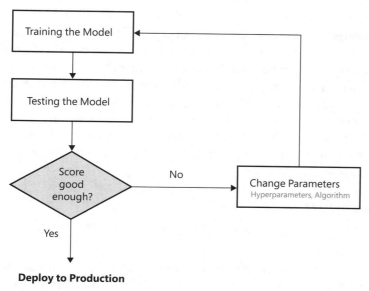

FIGURE 4-5 The development cycle of a machine learning model

Hyperparameter Tuning

In machine learning, a *hyperparameter* is a setting applied to an algorithm that controls the learning process. For example, a hyperparameter is the maximum depth of a decision that gives the actual algorithm clues on when to stop the training. If the training stops too early, the current values of all hyperparameters may produce prediction machinery that may or may not work accurately in production.

Most algorithms have default values for hyperparameters, which are good most of the time, but in case of unsatisfying performance (say, too poor predictions), trying with different hyperparameters is the first option. In case of further trouble, even changing the algorithm is an option to consider. And even the dataset!

How Long Will It Take to Train a Model?

Training a machine learning model may take time, typically ranging from just a few minutes to many hours. It's hard to come out with a basic rule of thumb to estimate the time it may take to train a model because the time depends on both the type of the algorithm—a neural network is much harder to train than a regression algorithm—and the hardware platform and the CPU power.

A rule of thumb, however, can be a couple of hours per gigabyte on a modern PC, but then, again, it is purely indicative.

Because it can take hours to train a model, clearly working out even a proof of concept may be a long process. Add this to the time (and troubleshooting) it takes to prepare the data, and you come to the conclusion that there's no magic at all in machine learning. It might look like magic, but it isn't when it comes to implementation.

Note Training is particularly expensive for deep learning neural networks, and neural networks are also particularly obscure boxes. In the case of poor performance, therefore, it may even be problematic to guess what must be fixed. Often, it's really a matter of taking a stab in the dark. To try to mitigate the problem, pretrained models are coming out. A pretrained model is a neural network already trained on a large dataset that can be used as is or as the starting point for further training. This is a technique that machine learning frameworks support and that can really cut short the time it takes to train even a complex model. At the moment, however, deep pretrained models are available mostly for image recognition.

How Much Data Do You Need?

Finally, here's the key question: how much data do you need to have available in order to train a realistically useful model?

The right amount of data needed for a successful machine learning model depends on a couple of factors: the complexity of the problem and the complexity of the algorithm. Even though it's only two factors, the point of making sense of them is nearly an intractable problem for which the only answer is empirical trial and error.

The reason is mostly due to the objective difficulty to formalize and measure the underlying complexity of both the problem and the algorithm. Intuitively, the complexity of the problem is given by the function that binds together input and output values, and the complexity of the algorithm results from the effort to identify, by example, the hidden relationship between input and output pairs.

How much data do we need? It's hard to say, and each business domain is different. More than the physical number of gigabytes, however, it's the number of rows or time series or logs that really matter and the overall period they span and the frequency of sampling.

Estimates can only come from domain experts.

Deployment of the Model

A trained model is nothing more than a software library. As such, it can be consumed in-process from within a client application or wrapped in a server-side environment (say, a web API or a container-based microservice). The complexity and the size of the model, though, pose some challenges.

Choosing the Appropriate Hosting Platform

Unless you're going to deploy a small basic model, the choice of the host platform may not be trivial. The nature of machine learning models requires that frequent updates are made. Hence, the host platform must be flexible and powerful enough to accommodate growing requirements.

It must be a DevOps-friendly infrastructure.

With few exceptions, the deployment of trained models occurs on cloud platforms (say, Microsoft Azure), preferably in an IaaS form in order to leverage hardware accelerators (that is, GPUs) and scale computing power in case of need. In this context, Docker containers and Kubernetes as the orchestrator are proving increasingly successful, and their adoption, even in machine learning, is growing.

For reasons of scale and separation, containerization and microservices are more and more often becoming the preferred way to deploy a machine learning model. Another reason that is making containers successful is the fact that a model usually needs to run in a richly configured environment equipped with specific libraries and frameworks. This is trivial to achieve with containers and also the primary reason why containers were introduced.

Exposing an API

No trained model is useful if you fail, making it easily accessible to software clients. The model is a zipped file that machine learning frameworks that are hosted in client applications allow to import and instantiate. At that point, it's all about building a façade around the model and dealing with cross-cutting concerns such as authorization and caching. Next, let's look at a couple of concrete scenarios.

Inside a Web Application

A web application is the most common and easiest way to expose an API. The web application links a specific machine learning framework through the bindings for a specific programming language or platform (for example, .NET and C# or F#) and proxies calls from the outside to the model. The model is loaded as a file, initialized, and hidden behind a REST façade.

The model can be embedded in the web solution or isolated as a distinct microservice. Having it as a standalone microservice may slow down the individual call, but it scales much better and provides a better deployment experience.

Inside a gRPC Service

Originally developed at Google for speeding up the remote procedure calls between a variety of internal applications and then open-sourced a few years ago, the gRPC framework is gaining a lot of traction lately because of the performance improvements it can guarantee over a canonical REST API.

The gRPC framework is based on a binary protocol (Google Protobuf) and uses HTTP/2 as the primary transportation layer. In ASP.NET Core 3.x, a gRPC server is natively hosted in Kestrel for even better performance. Today, gRPC is used to speed up communication between microservices and in this regard is an option to host some machine learning models.

Summary

A machine learning solution produces a deployable trained model through a sequence of steps. First, you collect data and make sure the inherent quality is good enough. This means fixing missing values, harmonizing data representation, removing exceptions, and flattening outliers. At this stage, the dataset is a collection of columns or features directly coming from the source.

Feature engineering is the first crucial step on the way to building a machine learning solution and consists of selecting the most appropriate set of features, dropping the least relevant columns, and merging similar columns. Next comes the selection of the algorithm, the training and testing of the dataset, and the evaluation of the model. If the model is not performing as expected, the entire cycle is repeated until the model is determined ready for production.

As you can see, machine learning is not about improvising and should be seen as something that needs careful planning and investment. It's about guessing, however, and in this regard it is not a classic, exact science. It's not just about guessing, though; it is about finding the best way to guess. Hence, it can actually deliver value but at the cost of a possibly long trial-and-error phase.

Realizing this fact leads investing companies to look for packaged solutions and consulting companies to try to commoditize solutions. None of the above works. Machine learning is not a service. Machine learning is just about software.

## CHAPTER 5

The Data Factor

The sculpture is already complete within the marble block before I start my work. It is already there; I just have to chisel away the superfluous material.

—*Michelangelo Buonarroti*

From incorrect (or inadequate or poorly relevant) data only stems incorrect (or inadequate or poorly relevant) answers. It's the underlying equation of machine learning, and it is not different at all from the fundamental equation that rules life and behavior of human beings.

An intelligent system learns how to achieve its declared goals from provided data. Therefore, it's data that drives the algorithm toward the expected outcome. For this reason, low relevance of content, inaccuracy, or even shortage of facts inevitably leads to little precision in the output and straight to the failure of the overall effort.

An essential condition for machine learning to work is then the availability of abundant and reliable data. Reliability of data is measured against a variety of qualitative and quantitative parameters, including relevance, significance, completeness, accuracy, and consistency.

In machine learning, effectively usable data that can facilitate reliable decisions is data with quality and integrity.

Data Quality

Data quality expresses the relevance and significance that some information may have in the context of some specific real-world circumstances. Data quality measures the usability of information to address the specific needs and implications of a decision-making process. Data quality is necessary to create the ideal environment for reliable decisions and avoid bias and distortion.

Data quality is primarily data with validity in the context and physical integrity for the context. Validity and integrity depend on the data collection process and, more specifically in machine learning, also on the data sampling process.

Data Validity

Data validity is the measure of conformity to the specific business requirements. It measures the significance carried by the information in the context of the specific problem and the extent to which that information really matters. In addition, data validity measures the relevance of the information, namely how much it is directly related and pertinent.

The validity of data also encompasses the relationships between data items.

To get a grasp of this point, let's look an example taken from one of the today's hottest topics in the manufacturing industry: predictive maintenance.

A Case Study for Maintenance of Hardware Components

For years, the industry checked hardware components periodically according to a predetermined schedule that didn't necessarily take into account the actual state of the component and ongoing situations. Maintenance could be easily scheduled at the wrong time given the workload of the machine. For example, stopping a working wind turbine in windy days definitely results in loss of money.

Condition-based maintenance, instead, uses fixed rules to calculate the ideal time for maintenance based on the actual wear of components as reported by embedded sensors. The good news is that no unnecessary maintenance is carried out, and by fine-tuning alarms, one can reserve a margin to postpone or anticipate maintenance according to volatile conditions such as bad or good weather. The weak point of condition-based maintenance is that alarm parameters must be set by the rule of thumb and are subject to the highly variable human ability to learn from numbers and mistakes.

So, the frontier is predictive maintenance, where machine learning is used to determine the ideal time to intervene.

Valid Data for Intelligent Maintenance

For predictive maintenance to be effective, first and foremost you need all the data captured through the constant monitoring of the internal components. In addition, you certainly also need data from special sensors measuring noise, heat, and humidity and cameras to record live action.

All these numbers alone aren't sufficient though.

The reason is that these numbers tell only the (detailed) story of how some damage developed that put the component in an offline state. You still lack the connection between monitored conditions and actual facts. In this scenario, data validity is achieved by also adding to the dataset records of the actual repairs performed by field technicians.

Today just this aspect is a serious showstopper for predictive maintenance to ramp up. Records of past repairs, in fact, are mostly paper-based and hard to turn into a digital form that matches the requirements of data integrity.

Data Collection

A high-quality dataset is the product of an effective data collection and storage process. In a machine learning context, data quality refers to the techniques employed in the selection and preprocessing of the sample dataset that will help training and testing the model.

Time Series Data

In many machine learning cases, data is made of time series. A time series is a sequence of data points taken at successive, equally spaced, points in time. Good examples of a time series are the daily closing values of a traded stock or the fluctuations of the same traded stock during the day. By the same token, archetypal time series are the reported states of some electronic equipment (levels, pressure, temperatures) in a wind turbine or an industrial robot.

A time series is a discrete-time data series collected automatically. In this context, data quality refers to having collected data cover the broadest range of situations with no missing pieces.

Data Availability

Effective data collection also depends on data availability, namely the ability to physically access the data at the source. Time series data, for example, often comes from automatic monitoring systems, and a sudden and unrecovered downtime of the collecting devices may generate a large loss of valuable data.

In an industrial context, data availability less than 90 percent of the time is considered likely insufficient to build valid predictive solutions and also to measure the quality of the monitoring system and underlying network infrastructure. An ideal data availability rate for data collection is not below 95 percent.

Document Data

Another common source of relevant information is documents, including Office files, PDF files, emails, IoT sensor data, and saved Skype conversations. This information is commonly offloaded to a data lake and then reorganized in a way that makes sense for the specific task.

It is useful to briefly recall the difference between two terms sometimes (wrongly) used interchangeably: *data lake* and *data warehouse*. Both are vast repositories of data, but the information stored in a data lake is largely unstructured and unclassified because the purpose of the data is not defined yet. On the contrary, the content of a data warehouse is made of structured and carefully filtered data already preprocessed for a specific goal.

Data Sampling

Statistics plays a key role in machine learning. The long shadow of statistics reaches the world of data collection too. Typically, a company data lake contains several gigabytes of unstructured and also partially unrelated data. To make machine learning effective, though, this data must be manipulated to form a valid and consistent repository.

It's about purely statistical sampling, but it is also about adding the right set of attributes to build the broadest possible vision of the data available while keeping it to an acceptable size.

The concept of "acceptable size" is relative and not simply quantitative.

If you're building a solution to detect fraud, then not just the quantity of samples is crucial but also the number of details you can provide. The broader is the vision the data delivers, the higher are the chances to have the anomaly (read: the fraud) detected. The amplitude of data samples is relevant also when plain text is being examined—for example, in a natural language processing scenario.

The whole set of official documents issued by the European Union (EU), translated in a number of different languages, is a great example of a comprehensive dataset for EU-related topics and represents the ideal database to sift for extracting specific pieces of information that might be needed by an answering machine or any other AI-based solution.

Similarly, large datasets of leaked passwords form a crucial sample of data for evaluating the strength of any new password accepted by a high-security system.

Data Integrity

Data integrity refers to the physical characteristics of collected data that determine the reliability of the information. Data integrity is based on parameters such as completeness, uniqueness, timeliness, accuracy, and consistency.

Completeness

Data completeness refers to collecting all items necessary to the full description of the states of a considered object or process. A data item is considered complete if its digital description contains all attributes that are strictly required for human or machine comprehension. In other words, it may be acceptable to have missing pieces in the expected records (i.e., no contact information) as long as the remaining data is comprehensive enough for the domain.

For example, when a sensor (e.g., an IoT sensor) is involved, you might want it to sample data at a frequency of 10 minutes or even less if required or appropriate for the scenario. At the same time, you might want to be sure that the timeline is continuous with no gaps in between. If you plan to use that data to predict possible hardware failures, then you need be sure you can keep an eye close enough to the target event and not miss anything along the way.

Completeness results from having no gaps in the data from what was supposed to be collected and what is actually collected. In automatic data collection (i.e., IoT sensors), this aspect is also related to physical connectivity and data availability.

Uniqueness

When large chunks of data are collected and sampled for further use, there's the concrete risk that some data items are duplicated. Depending on the business requirements, duplicates may or may not be an issue. Poor data uniqueness is an issue if, for example, it could lead to skewed results and inaccuracies.

Uniqueness is fairly easy to define mathematically. It is 100 percent if there are no duplicates. The definition of duplicates, however, depends on the context. For example, two records about Joseph Doe and Joe Doe are apparently unique but may refer to the same individual and then be duplicates that must be cleaned.

Timeliness

Data timeliness refers to the distribution of data records within an acceptable time frame. The definition of an acceptable time frame is also context-specific. It refers to the duration of the time frame and the appropriate timeline.

In predictive maintenance, for example, the timeline varies depending on the industry. Usually, a 10-minute timeline is more than acceptable but not for reliable fault predictions in wind turbines. In this case, a 5-minute interval is debated, and some experts suggest an even shorter rate of data collection.

Duration is the overall time interval for which data collection should occur to ensure reliable analysis of data and satisfactory results. In predictive maintenance, an acceptable duration is on the order of two years' worth of data.

Accuracy

Data accuracy measures the degree to which the record correctly describes the observed real-world item. Accuracy is primarily about the correctness of the data acquired. The business requirements set the specifications of what would be a valid range of values for any expected data item.

When inaccuracies are detected, some policies should be applied to minimize the impact on decisions. Common practices are to replace out-of-range values with a default value or with the arithmetic mean of values detected in a realistic interval.

Consistency

Data consistency measures the difference between the values reported by data items that represent the same object. An example of inconsistency is a negative value of output when no other value reports failures of any kind. Definitions of data consistency are, however, also highly influenced by business requirements.

What's a Data Scientist, Anyway?

So far, we have successfully formalized the concepts behind data quality and integrity. But who is in charge of ensuring and verifying data quality and data integrity?

An extremely popular term (and profession) these days is *data scientist*. Data science is a new discipline that builds on the foundation of statistics, data analysis, and a bunch of mathematical skills. The purpose of data science is understanding—in a possibly mechanical way—the hidden structure of data and extracting valuable information and insights from it.

The physical format of the data—structured or unstructured—doesn't matter, and in fact, one of the aspects of a data science job is figuring out the most appropriate shape the data should have for the business scenario. Preparing the data is only one aspect; another is extracting just the information required and validating it against requirements. In doing so, machine learning algorithms may come handy.

The Data Scientist at Work

The hype around machine learning is hot these days, but most machine learning projects experience a cold start. The reasons for the cold start are multiple and heterogeneous. The metaphor of *just loading data in the computer*, borrowed from literature, doesn't work at all in real life. The primary problem is the frequent lack of a suitable infrastructure that could allow experts to squeeze out value from available data. Even the smartest and most expert data scientist struggles to extract insights from data if she has no actionable data to work on.

The Job Description

The job description of a data scientist is fairly clear, in the end. It's the surrounding environment of the employer company, instead, that often doesn't seem aware of the preliminary work necessary for any serious machine learning attempt.

The general hype about artificial intelligence and the intensive advertising about its alleged superpowers amplify the expectations of companies often well beyond any realistic boundaries. Artificial intelligence (and machine learning) is not a magic wand and is not free.

The data scientist is sometimes faced with the urgent need for monetizable results or, at least, dazzling charts to show off in weekly board meetings. Too often those charts are perceived as a clear sign that the company is doing artificial intelligence well, maybe even better than competitors.

Every Day Tasks

The data scientist is hired to write magical machine learning algorithms to cut costs, recapture production losses, and increase profitability. The first thing to do, however, is sort out the data infrastructure, and this task takes the lion's share of the overall effort.

As a result, the management doesn't see any concrete value being delivered, gets frustrated, and redirects frustration to the data science team. In the end, the data scientist role is too many things, and none that is really directly connected to the original point. The data science team ends up being the collector of any analytics demands, the main contact for reporting tweaks, and in small companies, also the database owner.

Another remarkable point is the effective experience of data scientists—in general and in the specific business domain.

It takes time, even for individuals with a solid educational foundation, to build the knowledge base that really makes a difference. It's never as simple as pushing a button or asking a question to a software assistant with a professional voice. Often data science is only going to provide small incremental gains over time. But, even if worldly wisdom reminds us that any long journey is made up of small steps, this way of thinking is often against many executives' expectations.

The Data Scientist Tool Chest

Today, a number of development environments are available for data scientists to work. The tool chest of a data scientist has the same variegated conformation as that of a software developer.

This tool chest contains special database tools such as plain relational products including Spark, Apache Hadoop, and Apache Hive. It contains scripting languages such as Pig or plain SQL. You may also find more sophisticated graph databases such as Neo4j and programming languages such as Python or R.

For sure, in the data scientist tool chest, there must be one or more numerical computation libraries such as Tensorflow, Pytorch, or CNTK and perhaps an integrated environment such as Matlab. Finally, a data scientist will have familiarity with tools and concepts of statistical analysis such as A/B testing.

More in general, while the everyday job of a data scientist revolves around algorithms for machine learning, it can't disregard fundamental programming concepts such as conditions and control flow and common tasks with data such as loading, parsing, aggregating, filtering, and sorting. For most of these tasks, the data scientist ends up using one or more ad hoc packages.

Data Scientists and Software Developers

More often than not, the results of intelligent learning algorithms must be incorporated into comprehensive solutions that include an API and some form of website or mobile application. While data scientists and developers clearly perceive this separation of concerns, it may sometimes be hard to explain to management.

The separation of concerns results in two distinct sets of resources to build respective modules (see Figure 5-1).

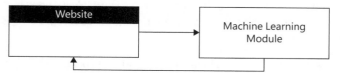

FIGURE 5-1 Separation of concerns between general software and machine learning modules

On the pure software side, you find front-end and back-end frameworks for application development and related languages such as C# and Java/Kotlin. On the AI side, instead, it's all about algorithms for learning, such as regression, random forest, simple, and less simple neural networks. The machine learning module is often a combination of algorithms as the specific problem demands and the expertise of the data scientist envisions. Furthermore, data scientists often resort to optimization tools, like genetic algorithms and particle swarm optimization.

The boundary between pure data manipulation and pure solution development gets thinner every day. You can see a clear convergence: data science toward software development and software development toward data science. The path to machine learning can start from any of the two ends, but the final destination will be the same.

Most of the time, a machine learning development environment is made of a programming language (Python, R, and functional languages are commonly used), a framework specialized in numerical calculation and/or deep learning (Tensorflow, Pytorch, Matlab, CNTK) and a platform for data storage and processing commonly based on Apache Hadoop, Spark, or cloud-centered ecosystems such as Azure Databricks.

As discussed in past chapters, however, there's no reason for only using a Python-based development platform, though a Python-based development platform is today the one with the richest and most consolidated set of tools. Earlier, we introduced ML.NET—the newest .NET-based development platform that promises to grow big and reach the same programming power as today in the Python ecosystem. ML.NET is not (yet) a full replacement for the Python ecosystem, but it for sure empowers software developers to do good machine learning at least for a subset of real-life scenarios. This is an example of convergence from software to data science.

Summary

Data is the lifeblood of machine learning. Data is considered of good quality if it serves the purpose it was collected for and this happens if data accurately represents the real-world segment it refers to.

There are a few attributes that ensure data quality and integrity. They are primarily validity, completeness, timeliness, and accuracy. These attributes should emerge across the entire supply chain of data and along the entire time frame of collection. Failing on any will likely put at risk the overall quality of data.

In addition, it is imperative that everyone who manages the data has a good understanding of what the data represents. It should be clear, in fact, that no serious machine learning is possible without a deep comprehension of the domain and the mechanics of the problem to solve. Only in this way, in fact, can the data team collect information in a proper way and then prepare the data to be processed effectively.

High-quality data is essential to the success of any machine learning initiatives because it makes decisions based on (automatically) analyzed facts rather than pure (and largely random) human intuition.

Machine Learning in .NET

## CHAPTER 6

The .NET Way

"Artificial intelligence would be the ultimate version of Google. It would understand exactly what you wanted, and it would give you the right thing. We're nowhere near doing that now."

—Larry Page, Google cofounder

In the first part of the book we analyzed the general steps it takes to build a machine learning solution. Any solution consists of a deliverable model that results from training an algorithm on a sufficiently large dataset. The process of selecting and adapting the dataset is by far the most time-consuming step and the one with the greatest impact on the final solution. It is estimated that data preparation in a real-life scenario can consume up to 80 percent of the whole project budget. In fact, data preparation is related to actual problems at hand, to the business vision, and, last but not least, to the availability of data. Note that in some cases companies willing to set up a machine learning solution don't even have the infrastructure necessary to collect the data they need for the project. However, once data is available, whether in a raw format such a CSV file or a relational database, the machine learning pipeline may require a feature engineering step in which the dataset is manipulated to more effectively pursue a specific machine learning goal.

Then comes the selection of the algorithm and the training phase.

The training phase is time-consuming, but it takes hours or days at most—so nothing compared to the time it may take to collect data when it is not already available. In general terms, training consists of finding the set of values that would let the selected algorithm work effectively in the considered scenario. Values are determined by looking at the content of the training dataset. After that, if the discovered values produce an acceptable output, you're pretty much done. You save the model to a .zip file and move on to consider the most appropriate way to make it available to client applications. Getting acceptable output, though, is a cyclic process. If you get new data, or if you get data that doesn't match closely with real-world data, you need to train the model again. In the end, the entire cycle of machine learning development is close to a classic DevOps cycle.

At the end of the day, in fact, customers need an end-to-end solution that internally implements intelligent prediction and classification, which is best achieved today through machine learning solutions. This means not just building and training a model but also exposing it as an in-process or out-of-process service. In the context of an application architecture, a machine learning solution is nothing but a domain service that is invoked by the business logic in order to produce results for both the presentation and the infrastructure layer.

Most machine learning solutions today are built in the Python ecosystem. It's a matter of convenience, however, rather than a matter of technological merit. In this chapter, we'll introduce the ML.NET platform—the .NET way to machine learning.

Why (Not) Python?

Let's say it up front: there's no strict business reason why machine learning shouldn't be also implemented in .NET, and nothing in the .NET platform prevents the processing of datasets and the writing of training algorithms for business problems.

Yet, when it comes to implementing machine learning, Python is at the forefront, along with its impressive ecosystem of dedicated tools and libraries.

Why Is Python So Popular in Machine Learning?

Python, R, and C++ are the prevalent languages in machine learning, but the actual reasons for their popularity are probably hard to investigate. However, despite whatever reasons make Python, R, and C/C++ platforms widespread in machine learning, there's no technical argument that prevents .NET and related languages (C# and F# primarily) from being used to train machine learning models.

Python at a Glance

Python is an interpreted and object-oriented programming language created by Guido van Rossum in the late 1980s at the National Research Institute for Mathematics and Computer Science in Amsterdam.

First released in 1991, the language went through many improvements without losing its focus on syntax minimalism and readability. The vision of Python as a programming language is that of a small core language engine with a large standard library and an easily extensible interpreter.

Speaking of Python, it is worth noting that being interpreted is not necessarily a sign of poor performance. However, when performance really matters, Python code needs to be translated into C, just-in-time compiled, or simply be extended with modules written in C. But C development is a lot more low level and costly than developing in a .NET language or Python itself.

> **Note** Python is not truly multithreaded like any of the .NET languages. In fact, even when threading is allowed, the Global Interpreter Lock (GIL) will make sure that just one thread is executing Python code at a time. GIL prevents use of more than one CPU core (or separate CPUs) to run threads in parallel. This applies only to raw Python code because C extensions being written usually release the GIL to allow multiple threads of C code.

The Perfect Tool for Scientists

In light of the huge adoption in the machine learning field, we dare say that Python owes its success primarily to its nature as an *interpreted* (no compile step ever needed) and *interactive* (sit at prompt and type instructions) language with a syntax that looks more descriptive to the human eyes than the more structured and well-formed syntax of Java and C#, not to mention trickier languages such as C and C++.

Born in a scientific environment, Python has become the de facto standard programming language for scientists to practice, explore, and experiment with numbers. In a way, it took the place that Fortran held in the 1960s and 1970s.

In the beginning, using Python in a hot new scientific field such as machine learning was a natural choice, and over time—given the natural extensibility of the language—it led to the creation of a vast ecosystem of dedicated libraries and tools. This, in turn, reinforced the belief that using Python for building computational models was the best option.

Today, most data scientists find Python comfortable to use for machine learning projects, and that is probably due to the combination of simplicity of the language, available tools, and plenty of examples.

But, then again, why choose Python over Java and more modern languages including C#?

Complex Is Better Than Complicated

Why? Because data scientists are rarely software developers, though they often have the skills to use programming languages effectively. Data scientists tend to find more formally elegant and terser languages such as C# and Java uselessly complicated, not to mention the burden they face when dealing with additional steps such as compiling, building, and deployment.

The *Zen of Python*—a collection of principles that summarize the core philosophy of the language—has crystal-clear points like these:

- Simple is better than complex.

- Complex is better than complicated.

- Flat is better than nested.

- Readability counts.

- If the implementation is easy to explain, it may be a good idea.

If interested, you can read the full set of these principles at www.python.org/dev/peps/pep-0020.

All this said, though, from a purely functional perspective, there's no reason for not considering C# and the .NET Framework a valid alternative for building and training machine learning models.

If only one could achieve in C# and .NET the same level of machine learning proficiency that is possible today in Python! In the end, it's a matter of tools and ecosystem.

Taxonomy of Python Machine Learning Libraries

The ecosystem of tools and libraries available in Python can be divided into five main areas: data manipulation, data visualization, numeric computing, model training, and neural networks. This is probably not an exhaustive list because many other existing libraries perform more specific tasks and focus on some specific areas of machine learning, such as natural language processing and image recognition.

In Python, the steps to build a machine learning pipeline are typically performed within the boundaries of a notebook. A notebook is a document created in a specific web or local interactive environment called Jupyter Notebook (see https://jupyter.org). Each notebook contains a combination of executable Python code, richly formatted text, data grids, charts, and pictures through which you build and share your development story.

In a notebook, you perform tasks such as data manipulation, plotting, and training, for which you can rely on a number of predefined and battle-tested libraries.

Data Manipulation and Analysis

Pandas (https://pandas.pydata.org) is a library centered around the *DataFrame* object through which developers can load and manipulate in-memory tabular data. The object can import content from CSV and text files as well as SQL databases; it provides core capabilities such as conditional searching, filtering, indexing and sorting, data slicing, and grouping, along with column operations like adding, removing, and renaming. The *DataFrame* has the built-in capability to flexibly reshape and pivot data as well as merge multiple frames together. It also works well with time-series data.

The Pandas library is ideal for data preparation operations, and its integration with interactive notebooks allows you to test different configurations and groupings of the data on the fly.

There's a downside too. In particular, Pandas doesn't support data streaming, which means that if the dataset is huge (that is, many gigabytes), you probably won't be able to fit everything in memory in your training machine.

> **Important** Later in the chapter, we'll introduce the ML.NET library. In particular, the library features an interface—the *IDataView* interface—that just supports data streaming. So, for example, you could have a 1 TB dataset file and you could train with it on any computer because the training process reads (actually, streams) data as needed, without the need to load everything into memory.

Data Visualization

Matplotlib (https://matplotlib.org) is a helper library that, although not directly related to any of the common tasks of a machine learning pipeline, comes in very handy to visually represent data during the various phases of the data preparation step or metrics obtained after evaluating trained models.

In general terms, it's a mere data visualization library built for Python code. It includes a 2D rendering engine and supports common types of graphs such as histograms, pie charts, and bar charts. Graphs are fully customizable in terms of line styles, font properties, axes, legends, and the like.

Numeric Computing

As a language largely used in scientific environments, Python can't miss a bunch of extensions specifically designed for numeric computation. In this area, popular libraries, although with slightly different capabilities, are NumPy and SciPy.

NumPy (www.numpy.org) focuses on array operations and provides facilities to create, manipulate, and reshape one- and multidimensional arrays. The library also supplies linear algebra, Fourier transform, and random number operations.

SciPy (https://scipy.org) extends NumPy with polynomials, file I/O, image and signal processing, and more advanced features such as integration, interpolation, optimization, and statistics.

In the area of scientific computation, another Python library that is worth mentioning is Theano (http://deeplearning.net/software/theano). Theano evaluates mathematical expressions based on multidimensional arrays very efficiently, making transparent use of the GPU. It also does symbolic differentiation for functions with one or more inputs.

Model Training

Originally designed for data mining, today scikit-learn (https://scikit-learn.org) is a library mainly focused on model training. It provides implementations of popular algorithms for regression, classification, and clustering and also methods for data preprocessing such as dimensionality reduction, feature extraction, and normalization.

Most data scientists use the scikit package, which includes scikit-learn for algorithms, and SciPy and NumPy for calculation. For pure machine learning pipelines, though, Pandas is also a common element for its capability to recombine data and explore content to help decide the most appropriate algorithm. It is also worth noting that scikit-learn has model selection methods and built-in tools to evaluate the performance of trained models against metrics.

In a nutshell, scikit-learn is the Python foundation for shallow learning.

Neural Networks

Shallow learning is an area of machine learning that covers a broad section of fundamental problems such as regression and classification. Outside the realm of shallow learning, there's deep learning and neural networks. For building neural networks in Python, more specialized libraries exist.

TensorFlow (www.tensorflow.org) is probably the most popular for training deep neural networks. It is part of a comprehensive framework that can be programmed at various levels. For example, you can use the high-level Keras API to build neural networks, or you can manually build the desired topology that specifies forward and activation steps through code, custom layers, and training loops. Overall, TensorFlow is an end-to-end machine learning platform providing facilities to train and deploy. Note, though, that TensorFlow shouldn't be devised exclusively as part of the Python ecosystem. TensorFlow is a native library, created in C, and it has binding for Python and other languages, including .NET via TensorFlow.NET and ML.NET.

Keras (https://keras.io) is probably the easiest way to get into the dazzling world of deep learning in Python. It offers a very straightforward programming interface that at least comes in handy for quick prototyping. As mentioned, Keras can be used from within TensorFlow.

Yet another option is PyTorch, available at https://pytorch.org. PyTorch is the Python adaptation of an existing C-based library specialized in natural language processing and computer vision. Of the three neural network options, Keras is by far the ideal entry point and the tool of choice as long as it can deliver what you're looking for. PyTorch and TensorFlow do the same job of enabling the building of sophisticated neural networks but use different approaches to the task. TensorFlow requires you to define the entire topology of the network before you can train it, whereas PyTorch follows a more agile approach and allows you to make changes to the graph more dynamically. Their difference can be summarized in some way as "Waterfall versus Agile." PyTorch is younger and doesn't have the same huge community behind it as TensorFlow has.

End-to-End Solutions on Top of Python Models

With Python, you can easily find a way to build and train a machine learning model. A model is a binary file that must be loaded into some client application and in some way invoked. Most of the time, the client application for a Python model is a Java or .NET application. There are three main ways to consume a trained model from outside Python, and none is perfect:

- Hosting the trained model in a service and exposing its logic via a REST or gRPC API.

- Letting the client application import the trained model as a serialized file and interact with it through the programming interface provided by the infrastructure the model is built upon. This is possible only if the founding infrastructure provides bindings for the language the client application is written to.

- Exposing the trained model via the new universal ONNX format so that the client application incorporates a wrapper for consuming ONNX binaries. Note, though, that often ONNX lacks support for certain areas of each original framework.

The most common option is hosting the model in an environment that makes it accessible via a REST or gRPC API. This is the case of TensorFlow and its TensorFlow Serving infrastructure and also the case of scikit-learn and the Flask framework. It should be noted that an HTTP service has an impact on the application architecture (even bigger because the model was created in Python); anyway, it introduces latency in the system. This is one of the reasons that companies are intrigued by ML.NET models because they can run them directly as part of their existing .NET applications.

As mentioned, TensorFlow supports a number of direct language bindings, and thanks to language bindings, the development team of a client application can call the model without the intermediation of a web API. Using a direct API specific for the client language of choice may seem the fastest way to consume a trained model. There are a couple of aspects to review, however:

- Using a direct API may prevent you from taking advantage of hardware acceleration and network distribution. If the API is hosted locally, in fact, any dedicated hardware (e.g., GPU) is up to you. For this reason, if you want to invoke a graph at a very high rate in real time, you should consider using some ad hoc, hardware-accelerated cloud host. Note also that a GPU is beneficial only in deep learning, such as when using TensorFlow or PyTorch. With regular machine learning algorithms (e.g., scikit-learn), a GPU won't offer any benefits.

- A binding for the specific trained model might not exist for the language (or the framework) of your choice. For example, TensorFlow natively supports Python and C as well as C++, Go, Swift, and Java. By contrast, scikit-learn can only be used through Python or embedded in an HTTP service.

Note that using TensorFlow from a .NET application is possible too. One sort of low-level way to do it is via the third-party TensorFlow.NET library, which ultimately covers the entire low-level TensorFlow API in the same way that other language bindings do (e.g., Java). Another other way is passing through the newest ML.NET framework, which we'll introduce in a moment. Interestingly, the ML.NET framework allows both direct calls to a TensorFlow model and importing the trained model via the ONNX format.

Invoking a Python or C++ library from within .NET code is not an unsurmountable technical issue. However, invoking a specific library such as a trained machine learning model is usually harder than calling some plain Python or C++ class. The fact is, machine learning doesn't live on its own and must be framed in the context of an end-to-end business solution. And a lot of business solutions out there are based on the .NET stack.

So what about some .NET native machine learning capabilities? Enter ML.NET.

Introducing ML.NET

Generally available since the spring of 2019, ML.NET is a free, cross-platform, and open-source framework designed to build and train learning models and host them within .NET Core and .NET Framework applications and .NET-standard libraries. The home page is at https://dotnet.microsoft.com/apps/machinelearning-ai/ml-dotnet.

Although relatively young and in progress, ML.NET aims at democratizing machine learning for developers, thus trying to simplify it to levels that are easy enough for developers. It doesn't specifically target data scientists, which means there might be data science approaches that ML.NET doesn't cover.

The most interesting aspect of ML.NET is that it just offers a pragmatic programming platform arranged around the idea of predefined *learning tasks*. The library comes equipped to make it relatively easy, even for machine learning newbies, to tackle common machine learning scenarios such as sentiment analysis, fraud detection, and price prediction as if it were just plain programming. The number of built-in tasks will likely increase over time.

Compared to the pillars of the Python ecosystem presented previously, ML.NET can be seen primarily as the counterpart of the *scikit-learn* model building library. The framework, however, also includes some basic facilities for data preparation and analysis that you can find in Pandas or NumPy. It is remarkable, though, that the whole ML.NET library builds atop the tremendous power of the whole .NET Core and .NET Framework.

To start with the ML.NET framework, you need to install ML.NET package and start creating models with plain C# using any editor on Windows, Mac, or Linux. A specific extension—the Model Builder—is available for Visual Studio 2019.

Creating and Consuming Models in ML.NET

Any machine learning solution is articulated in two projects. One is typically a console application, and it scripts the various steps of the machine learning pipeline: data collection, feature engineering, model selection, training, evaluation, and storage of the trained model. The other is typically a class library, and it contains the data types necessary to have the deployed model make a prediction once hosted in a client application.

Needless to say, there will also be a client application project—most likely an ASP.NET Core application or service.

Getting Started

In an ML.NET solution, you can create the builder and the model projects manually and configure each with the appropriate Nuget packages, or you can opt for the Model Builder wizard in Visual Studio that we briefly introduced in Chapter 3, "Mapping Problems and Algorithms." The primary Nuget package to add is Microsoft.ML. More packages might be required as long as you reference more specific functionalities or algorithms. To go through a Model Builder session, instead, you use the Add menu of the Visual Studio solution and select Machine Learning. (See Figure 6-1.)

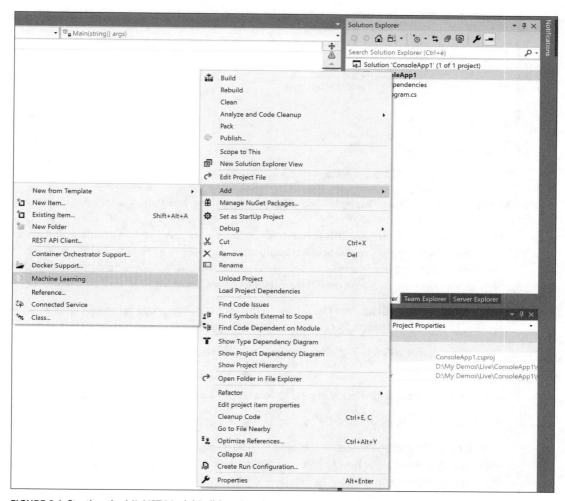

FIGURE 6-1 Starting the ML.NET Model Builder wizard in Visual Studio 2019

The wizard will guide you through the minimally necessary steps—the same programming steps that you would manually code in the host application (say, a console application) if you opt for a manual approach.

Scenario-based Shallow Learning

The Model Builder is a wizard that lets you pick one of a few predefined scenarios, such as classification, sentiment analysis, or price prediction. (See Figure 6-2.)

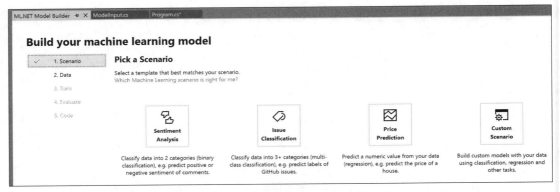

FIGURE 6-2 The Model Builder wizard lets you choose a sample scenario to show how to build a model

In general, the Sentiment Analysis scenario refers to a binary classification problem. The Issue Classification scenario refers to multiclass classification, and the Price Prediction scenario is about numeric regression and prediction of a continuous value. The Custom Scenario option is slightly more generic and allows you to choose one of the previous core algorithms.

In the future, additional tasks will be added to the Model Builder in Visual Studio, such as Anomaly Detection, Time Series Forecast, Recommendations, Image Classification, and Object Detection.

The wizard shown in Figure 6-2 is far from covering all possible learning scenarios, but it has two main merits:

- It makes it incredibly quick and easy to form an idea of how machine learning could work.

- It delivers, in the end, some C# code to build the sample model.

Even though the model the wizard has built for you is only a toy, the structure of the source it provides is a valid example of how to plan and build an ML.NET pipeline for any other task you may want to further implement.

A useful exercise is picking one of the sample scenarios and taking it to the end, and we'll do just that in a moment.

Deep Learning in ML.NET

At the time of its first version, ML.NET focuses only on shallow learning algorithms, and only a few of them are backed into the core Nuget package *Microsoft.ML*. A growing number of algorithms and functions, though, are being added through additional packages.

In particular, in ML.NET you can't directly create neural networks in the same way you do, say, with Keras, but ML.NET provides the remarkable capability to invoke pretrained TensorFlow neural networks natively from within .NET. In addition, ML.NET provides deep learning capabilities in the form of tasks, through high-level APIs such as ImageClassification and ObjectDetection.

This means that if you have, for example, a TensorFlow solution up and running and want to use it from within a .NET client, you can have ML.NET in the middle to do the job. At the same time, if you have a team of data scientists familiar with TensorFlow, you can have them doing the work in the way they prefer and still be able to consume it from within a .NET client application.

This said, to avoid further confusion in ML.NET (and related packages), you can find most of the algorithms available in scikit-learn, but none of the programming objects in Keras, TensorFlow, or PyTorch. At the same time, if you have something already built with any of those (or some other libraries such as CNTK), you can easily import them in ML.NET.

Elements of the Learning Context

Let's see what it takes to interact with the ML.NET library and how to plan and build a basic machine learning pipeline without the help of Model Builder wizard but close to the actual code it would generate for us. (The Model Builder wizard is authored by the same team that delivered the ML.NET library, so it shows the appropriate way of using the library.)

The Root Object

The entry point in the ML.NET world is the *MLContext* object. You use it in much the same way you use the Entity Framework context object or the connection object to a database. It represents the root node of the machine learning pipeline you're building:

```
var mlContext = new MLContext();
```

You need to have an instance of this class shared across the various objects that participate in the model building workflow. During a single run of the model building code, all objects must refer to the same pipeline object. Figure 6-3 summarizes the model building lifecycle in a diagram using ML.NET C# code to express the steps instead of the canonical flowchart blocks.

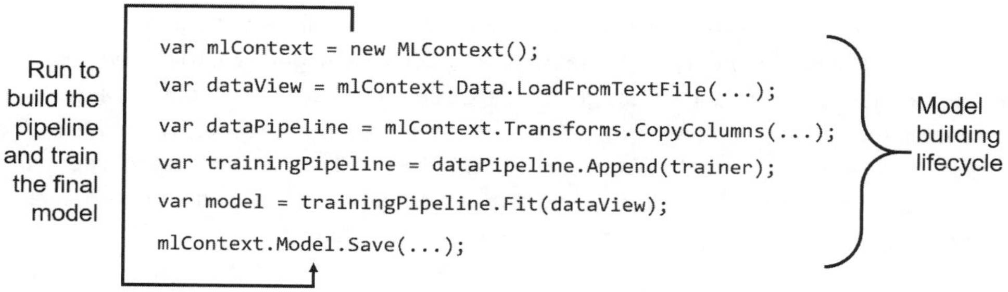

```
var mlContext = new MLContext();
var dataView = mlContext.Data.LoadFromTextFile(...);
var dataPipeline = mlContext.Transforms.CopyColumns(...);
var trainingPipeline = dataPipeline.Append(trainer);
var model = trainingPipeline.Fit(dataView);
mlContext.Model.Save(...);
```

Run to build the pipeline and train the final model

Model building lifecycle

FIGURE 6-3 The model building lifecycle in ML.NET

You can run the code that builds the model anytime you need to refresh the model because you have new data or want to try to improve using a different set of features or a different algorithm.

You also need an instance of the *MLContext* object to load a pretrained model and use it in production. For whatever task you need to perform in ML.NET, a context object is required because it acts as the central repository of references for any machine learning pipeline operations, whether data transformation, feature engineering, model selection, training, evaluation, or persistence.

Data Preparation

The ML.NET library defines its own interface to manipulate data—the *IDataView* interface. You can see it as a cursor-based accessor to a possibly huge collection of data made of millions of rows or even terabytes of data.

The ML.NET framework provides some predefined loaders to populate a data view, for example, from a CSV-style text file, a binary file, any *IEnumerable*-based source wrapper, or the very easy-to-use *DatabaseLoader* object. The interface supplies methods to move around the data set at any acceptable pace. The *SkipRows* method jumps ahead, and the *TakeRows* method selects a subset. The data view also provides an in-memory cache and methods to write the modified content back to disk.

All methods to load and modify the data source are exposed through a *DataOperationsCatalog* object, which the *Data* property references on the pipeline root:

```
var mlContext = new MLContext();

// Load data into the pipeline
var dataView = mlContext.Data.LoadFromTextFile<ModelInput>(INPUT_FILE);
```

The sample code loads training data from the specified file and manages it as a collection of *ModelInput* types. Needless to say, the *ModelInput* type is a custom class that reflects the rows of data loaded from the text file.

Note that in this code snippet, we assume that the loaded data is already in a format that is acceptable for machine learning. Typical data transformations you might want to perform are converting categorical values (and strings) to numbers, adding ad hoc feature columns, and—if it makes sense in the context—removing rows that are too far away from expectations. In ML.NET, you can do that precisely as part of a *pipeline*. In ML.NET, the pipeline is an informal concept that corresponds to a chain of estimator objects for transforming data and finally adding the trainer (algorithm). Here's how to transform the dataset adding a new column.

```
mlContext.Transforms.CopyColumns("Label", "FareAmount");
```

Those transformations can be performed offline on the persisted file so that the Model Builder gets the file ready for training, or the file can be maintained in a raw format (as it is being acquired) and transformations are applied every time the model is built. It's a pure speed versus flexibility trade-off.

Trainers and Their Categorization

The crucial phase of a machine learning pipeline is the training. The training consists of picking an algorithm, setting in some way its configuration parameters, and running it repeatedly on a given (training) dataset. The output of the training phase is the set of parameters that lead the algorithm to generate the best results. In the ML.NET jargon, the algorithm is called the *trainer*. Some supported trainers are grouped in a few tasks, as in Table 6-1.

TABLE 6-1 ML.NET Tasks Related to Training

Task	Description
AnomalyDetection	Aims at detecting unexpected or unusual events or behaviors compared to the received training
BinaryClassification	Aims at classifying data in one of two categories
Clustering	Aims at splitting data in a number of possibly correlated groups without knowing which aspects could possibly make data items related
Forecasting	Aims at time series forecasting and spike detection
ImageClassification	Aims at classifying images
MulticlassClassification	Aims at classifying data in three or more categories
Ranking	Aims at building recommendation systems
Regression	Aims at predicting the value of a data item

We'll return to ML.NET tasks in the next chapter and take a closer look at the related programming interface.

Each of the task properties in Table 6-1 has a *Trainers* property with the predefined algorithms considered good for the job. For example, for a regression task, a good algorithm is the Online Gradient Descent algorithm. Note, though, that it's not the only one, and it may not even be the best ever. The ML.NET framework, in fact, also supports the Poisson Regression and the Stochastic Dual Coordinate Ascent algorithms out of the box, and other algorithms can be added to the project at any time through new Nuget packages. Here's some sample code to set a trainer and train the model on a sample data view:

```
var dataPipeline = mlContext.Transforms.CopyColumns("Label", "FareAmount");
var trainer = mlContext.Regression.Trainers.OnlineGradientDescent("FareAmount", "Features");
var trainingPipeline = dataPipeline.Append(trainer);
var model = trainingPipeline.Fit(dataView);
```

The ultimate goal of the "training-the-trainer" step (the *Fit* method shown here) is running the algorithm on the training dataset to discover the content to save in the model so that the model, running in production, will produce the best result.

Evaluators

The end of the training phase doesn't mean at all that you've got the model you were looking for. In this context, the model is an "algorithm and the best configuration found for all of its parameters." As the discovery of the ideal set of parameters is made by testing the algorithm on a given dataset, a few things could possibly turn bad:

- The selected algorithm may not be the most appropriate to explore the given dataset.

- The original dataset needs more (or less) column transformation.

- The original dataset is too small (or too large) for the intended purpose.

For this reason, you might want to resort to some additional metrics—mostly specific to the task but sometimes even specific to the algorithm—to evaluate or just review the performance of the algorithm. Let's look at Figure 6-4. Note that the figure has been taken from the Visual Studio Model Builder extension, which uses the AutoML.NET command-line tools under the covers. The ML.NET API simply trains on a single specific algorithm (trainer) using a single configuration of parameters.

ML.NET Model Builder

Top 4 models explored

Rank	Trainer	RSquared	Absolute-loss	Squared-loss	RMS-loss	Duration
1	LightGbmRegression	0.9513	0.42	4.49	2.12	5.6
2	FastTreeTweedieRegression	0.9491	0.44	4.70	2.17	9.6
3	FastTreeRegression	0.9486	0.43	4.74	2.18	6.8
4	SdcaRegression	0.8833	0.90	10.76	3.28	3.7

FIGURE 6-4 Multiple algorithms for a regression task

The figure presents the output of the Model Builder wizard after configuring a sample price prediction scenario. The internals of the wizard give an idea of the whole training workflow. All the featured algorithms ended their training phase with good marks, but trying a better algorithm can lead to better results. Look in particular at the RSquared column. As you'll see in Part III, the RSquared metric (fairly common in regression tasks) is acceptably high for all algorithms, but its ideal value is 1. So, 0.88 is high, but 0.95 is much more. The point of the evaluation phase is finding the best possible.

Note Another aspect to consider is that once the model goes to production—even with the best metrics—there might still be a chance that things will go wrong and the predictions are not in line with business expectations. This might be due to an inadequate set of data rows used for training.

Hosting Scenarios

At the end of the training phase, you have a model that contains instructions on which algorithm to run in production and using which configuration. The model file is a zipped file in some serialization format.

In production, the client application will be making calls to a façade API offered by the ML.NET framework, as follows:

```
var mlContext = new MLContext();
var model = mlContext.Model.Load("model.zip", out var schema);
var predictionEngine = mlContext.Model.CreatePredictionEngine<ModelInput, ModelOutput>(model);
var result = predictionEngine.Predict(input);
```

As you can guess, in production the model is only a black box that accepts a *ModelInput* class and returns a *ModelOutput* class. Needless to say, those classes are defined during the training phase and depend on the dataset and the problem.

Note Each machine learning library has its own serialization format and uses its own schema to save information to be used in production. A universal, interoperable format also exists: the ONNX format. ML.NET supports it. It should be noted, though, that ONNX is a sort of common denominator across machine learning frameworks and may not support certain features of certain frameworks.

Summary

This chapter offered a condensed, but hopefully juicy, summary of the pillars of the ML.NET library slated to become the reference platform for machine learning in the .NET space. Version 1.0 was released in the spring of 2019, and the library is growing at a rapid pace. For example, it already supports deep learning training via TensorFlow models for image classification.

Although Python is popular among data scientists, there's no strict reason why machine learning models can't be developed and tested in .NET or other languages, including Java and Go. It's all about the ecosystem and ease of use. ML.NET relies on the .NET Core infrastructure and Visual Studio 2019. The main points leading to ML.NET are as follows:

- Many enterprise .NET and .NET Core applications want to directly deploy and consume machine learning models natively instead of having to install some additional Python environment in production. In addition, in many enterprise production environments, Python might be hard to get approved and, even if it is, it would require adding additional HTTP services. ML.NET allows precisely that: training natively in .NET and deploying natively into the .NET application.

- Many .NET developers don't want to have to learn Python to be able to create custom machine learning models and infuse them into their .NET applications.

Finally, there is NimbusML, namely ML.NET bindings for Python. NimbusML is a Python module—fully interoperable with scikit-learn, NumPy, and Pandas—that allows data scientists or developers familiar with Python to code and then have the model saved as a .zip file fully compatible with the ML.NET library and then natively hostable in .NET applications.

Let's now go with a simple but not-so-trivial and complete example: taxi fare prediction. In the next chapter, we'll see a bit of feature engineering, feature selection, and more importantly, an ASP.NET client application.

## CHAPTER 7

Implementing the ML.NET Pipeline

You are not thinking; you are just being logical.
—Niels Bohr, Nobel Prize in Physics in 1922 and father of quantum mechanics

Since the early days of software, humans have dreamed of it as a tool capable of looking into the future and reporting bits and pieces of what is to come. Price prediction is a canonical example, whether it is in regard to the stock exchange, real estate, the supply chain, energy, or individual services such as taxi rides.

We looked deep into statistics to try to make sense of the future fluctuations of prices but found out that statistics is great only at post-mortem analysis of gathered data. Statistics excels at dissecting data to extract models; it is great to understand with 100 percent accuracy what led to those numbers and why. However, there's not much that statistics can tell about the future with sufficient reliability and credibility.

Looking into the future is the job of machine learning. Machine learning builds on statistics but elaborates on a model that starts from gathered data to try to guess what will happen. The elaborated model is never 100 percent accurate with regard to gathered data but is expected to provide some higher reliability (ideally over 90 percent) with any data in line with those it was trained on.

Let's look at a full example of price prediction in ML.NET.

The Data to Start From

The example we consider here is based on a sample dataset available from the Github website of the ML.NET library. It refers to over one million taxi rides logged in New York City. The ultimate purpose of the example is predicting the price of a taxi ride in New York.

Note that it is reasonable to expect that the prediction made by a model trained on that dataset would work also for any city whose dynamics of taxi rides and prices is comparable to the one that emerges from the file, regardless of geography.

Exploring the Dataset

The sample file is a CSV file made of seven columns: the ID of the taxi company, the code of the rate, the number of passengers, the time it took to complete the ride, the distance, the type of payment (cash or card), and fare paid. Before embarking on a deeper analysis of the actual information contained by the CSV file, let's figure out how to use it.

The rows of the dataset should be turned into a C# class to make it easier to build and consume the final model. The following class represents one row of the raw file:

```
public class TaxiTrip
{
    [LoadColumn(0)]
    public string VendorId;

    [LoadColumn(1)]
    public string RateCode;

    [LoadColumn(2)]
    public float PassengerCount;

    [LoadColumn(3)]
    public float TripTime;

    [LoadColumn(4)]
    public float TripDistance;

    [LoadColumn(5)]
    public string PaymentType;

    [LoadColumn(6)]
    public float FareAmount;
}
```

The *LoadColumn* attribute establishes a static binding between the specific property and corresponding column—indicated by name or position—in the dataset. This class needs to be placed in a separate assembly because it must be also referenced by any .NET client applications entitled to use the model.

Applying Common Data Transformations

Any machine learning algorithm requires numbers to work nicely. In the sample dataset, instead, a few columns are made of text—the vendor ID, rate code, and payment type. The values in those columns must be turned into numbers in some way that doesn't alter the distribution and relevance of individual values:

```
var vendor = mlContext.Transforms.Categorical.OneHotEncoding(V_Id, "VendorId");
var rate = mlContext.Transforms.Categorical.OneHotEncoding(Rate_Code, "RateCode");
var payment = mlContext.Transforms.Categorical.OneHotEncoding(Payment_Type, "PaymentType");
mlContext.Append(vendor)
        .Append(rate)
        .Append(payment);
```

The *OneHotEncoding* object applies a common data transformation algorithm to categorical values. The algorithm consists of adding one binary (0/1) column for each distinct categorical value found in the specified column. The first parameter of the method is the prefix to name new columns.

Another transformation that might make sense to apply is the normalization of mean variance on numeric columns:

```
mlContext.Append(mlContext.Transforms.NormalizeMeanVariance("PassengerCount"));
```

In addition, you might want to remove outliers, namely values that are too far away from the mean. This step may not be necessary all the time, but if you have reason to believe that outliers affect results, by all means you should do so. You remove outliers by simply filtering the loaded dataset. For the example, remove from the dataset all rows that have a value of the *FareAmount* column lower than 1 and higher than 150:

```
mlContext.Data.FilterRowsByColumn(rawData, "FareAmount", 1, 150);
```

Finally, a couple of further transformations are required because of the internal mechanics of the ML.NET library. You need to have a column named *Label* that represents the target of the prediction and a column named *Features* that contains all values of the row serialized in an array:

```
mlContext.Transforms.CopyColumns("Label", "FareAmount");
mlContext.Transforms.Concatenate("Features", ...);
```

In this way, you tell the training algorithm to target the values of the original FareAmount column (now duplicated in the Label column) and to process the input values in the Features column made by the concatenation of all other values in the row.

Considerations on the Dataset

Any machine learning model is essentially a transformer that works on whatever you pass to produce whatever it can figure out. If the input data is inadequate or insufficient or in some way unbalanced, you will get inadequate or insufficient or unbalanced answers.

It is therefore particularly important that the training dataset contains information about all possible factors that could influence the prediction. Sometimes, if two or more individual values assume a particular relevance when combined, you might want to add an ad hoc column. This is ultimately the realm of feature engineering.

Is there anything about the sample dataset that you can argue is wrong?

For one thing, it completely misses the traffic factor. The traffic factor can be expressed as a normalized value in the 0–1 range to indicate the level or even a categorical value. It depends on the desired accuracy and also on the data feed available. If no feed is available, you can even think of adding some traffic context information to calculate the categorical value by looking at the time of the day the ride took place. And here's another one! The time of the day is not in the sample dataset.

Even in such a simple scenario, we have found a couple of arguable points to dissect and to test on. Just imagine how many and how deep they could be in a much more complex and sophisticated prediction scenario!

The Training Step

When it comes to predicting a numeric value like the price of a service, the class of algorithms that works most of the time is regression. (We'll tackle the internals of the most common classes of machine learning algorithms in Part III, "Fundamentals of Shallow Learning.") A number of different specific algorithms fall under the umbrella of regression, and choosing the one to try first is a matter of experience, knowledge of the domain, and sometimes even a gut feeling.

Whatever algorithm you choose for the first run of training needs to survive the metrics of the post-training test. If numbers don't support the choice, you might consider trying a different algorithm or shape the training set differently. Machine learning is almost always a matter of trial and error.

Picking an Algorithm

Conceptually, price prediction is a (relatively) easy regression problem to solve. If you have good and detailed data, prediction should be essentially a matter of choosing the fastest algorithm. In ML.NET, the trainers available for the regression task are grouped under the Regression property of the context. Here's how to add a regression trainer to the pipeline:

```
// Identify the training algorithm
var trainer = mlContext
        .Regression
        .Trainers
        .OnlineGradientDescent("Label", "Features", new SquaredLoss());

// Add it to the current ML pipeline
mlContext.Append(trainer);

// Start training of the model
var trainedModel = mlContext.Fit(dataView);
```

The selected algorithm—the online gradient descent algorithm—is generally a good choice, but faster and more precise algorithms exist, such as the *LightGbmRegression* algorithm. You can use any of those more sophisticated algorithms by referencing additional Nuget packages. With the default configuration of ML.NET, the online gradient descent is commonly a good option.

The algorithm takes two string parameters to denote the names of the input and output columns (or features) in the dataset. The output column is the column to predict. The third parameter indicates the error function that will be used during the testing phase to measure the distance between the predicted value and the expected value. The *SquaredLoss* object refers to the R-squared metric—a fairly common metric for regression problems. When all is ready, you just call the *Fit* method to start the training of the model.

Measuring the Actual Value of an Algorithm

The value of a machine learning algorithm results from a combination of factors. One is certainly the speed, measured through the formula of computational complexity, namely the number of steps and resources required for running it. Another aspect is how the specific algorithm—given its internal steps—reacts to the actual data it is presented. The same algorithm, in fact, can produce more (or less) accurate results working on different shapes of the same raw data. This is not surprising at all, if you know at least a bit of the theory of computational complexity.

Because the complexity of an algorithm may significantly vary for different shapes of the same input, the complexity is, in fact, calculated for the best, average, and worst-case scenarios. The complexity calculated for the worst-case scenario indicates the longest it may take whatever is the input. The complexity is usually expressed as a function in the size of the input, and only its asymptotic behavior is taken into account when the size of the input grows indefinitely.

As an interesting example of how the shape of the data may affect the performance of algorithms, let's consider the Quicksort algorithm. Written in the early 1960s by Tony Hoare, Quicksort is still one of the fastest sorting algorithms today and one of the most commonly used in libraries and frameworks. On average, it has a complexity of, where n is the size of the input. This is also known to be the fastest asymptotic complexity for any sorting algorithm. In the early implementations of Quicksort, researchers and developers observed an interesting relationship between the algorithm and the input data. In particular, if the data was presorted (ascending or descending), or if all elements in the input dataset were the same, the complexity of the algorithm grew an unacceptable n^2.

In more recent real-life implementations of the algorithm, those cases have been easily ruled out. Today, when properly coded (e.g., when hyperparameters are selected in a close-to-ideal way), the Quicksort algorithm can run a few times faster than any other sorting algorithms showing the same (optimal) asymptotic behavior.

Now let's shift our attention back to machine learning: the weird behavior of the originally proposed flavor of the Quicksort algorithm reminds us that a given representation of the training dataset can make an otherwise superfast algorithm perform worse than another. Hence, you need to be careful with testing the model and aim for the best possible metrics you're able to achieve.

Planning the Testing Phase

In any machine learning project, you have a unique heap of data to work with. Most of this data should be used for training the model; the remaining part should be used for testing the trained model and grabbing some metrics to evaluate.

A reasonable split of the dataset between training and testing subsets is 80/20. However, the point is leaving enough data for the trainer to understand and enough for the evaluator to test. An 80/20 split is generally good, but only if the data is evenly distributed so that the "inner nature" of the data items in the training set matches the "inner nature" of the data in the testing set.

Note that a plain 80/20 split (or any other that uses similar numbers) refers to a technique called *holdout*. Holdout is quick and easy to code but works effectively only if data is balanced and the split keeps both subsets balanced as well. At any rate, though, you're testing the model on only 20 percent of the data. Cross-validation is another technique; it is longer to run but more accurate. We'll discuss more about cross-validation in Chapter 10, "Metrics of Machine Learning."

A Look at the Metrics

After you have a trained model, ML.NET provides a number of predefined services for evaluating the quality of the resulting model. Here's how you can run a test and grab metrics:

```
// Run the trained model on the testing dataset
IDataView predictions = trainedModel.Transform(testDataView);
var metrics = mlContext.Regression.Evaluate(predictions, "Label", "FareAmount");
```

The *Evaluate* method on the *Regression* object gets the testing dataset and goes through all the contained items looking at the input values in the *Label* column and the expected values, such as in the *FareAmount* column. In ML.NET, the *Evaluate* method returns a *RegressionMetrics* object. Table 7-1 shows the information you get from it.

TABLE 7-1 Properties of the *RegressionMetrics* Type

Name of Metric	Description
LossFunction	Double value; it indicates the average of values returned by the loss function passed to the trainer. In the example, it is a *SquaredLoss* object.
MeanAbsoluteError	Double value; it indicates the average of the absolute errors found between the predicted and the expected values.
MeanSquaredError	Double value; it indicates the average of the squares of the errors found between the predicted and the expected values.
RootMeanSquaredError	Double value; it refers to the square root of the average of squared errors found between the predicted and the expected values.
RSquared	Double value; RSquared indicates the coefficient of determination of the model. It is given by the ratio of the mean squared error of the model and the variance of the predicted feature.

Of all these metrics, the most relevant for a regression algorithm is *RSquared* because it tells how good the algorithm to capture the variance of the predicted feature is. The optimal value of the *RSquared* metric is as close as possible to 1. (We'll address this issue more in Chapter 11, "How to Make Simple Predictions: Linear Regression.")

Price Prediction from Within a Client Application

A trained model is only a binary file that stored some information for some host environment to expose in a rigorous schema. In ML.NET, as well as in other machine learning frameworks, the model itself is not running code. It needs to be deployed as a project file and loaded into a new instance of *MLContext* to become usable from .NET code.

Let's see what it takes to create a sample ASP.NET Core application to utilize the taxi fare prediction model.

Getting the Model File

Typically, an ML.NET project consists of a console application that loads data from some local or remote source, applies transformations, picks a trainer, trains, evaluates, and persists the model. The typical output is

- A .zip file with a serialized trained model

- A class library that contains the C# classes used to map the training dataset

In this example, the *TaxiTrip* class presented earlier goes into the class library because it needs to be accessible from any .NET client application. The following code saves the trained model to a disk file:

```
// Saves the trained model to the given file name.
mlContext.Model.Save(trainedModel, trainingDataView.Schema, "model.zip");
```

The schema parameter describes the schema of the data used to train the model. This information is necessary to any newly created *MLContext* instances that will later load the model.

Setting Up the ASP.NET Application

Suppose you have a ready-made template for an ASP.NET Core application. Figure 7-1 shows the project open in Visual Studio. Note the list of dependencies. Beyond some ASP.NET and project-specific references, you can see the core *Microsoft.ML* package and the *LinearRegression* class library. In the *ML* folder, you see the .zip file that is a serialized copy of the trained model.

The *Application* folder contains a helper class to decouple the controller class invoked from the user interface from the ML.NET wrapper that will run the model in production. In an end-to-end scenario, you should see any trained machine learning model as a domain service, part of the business layer of your solution.

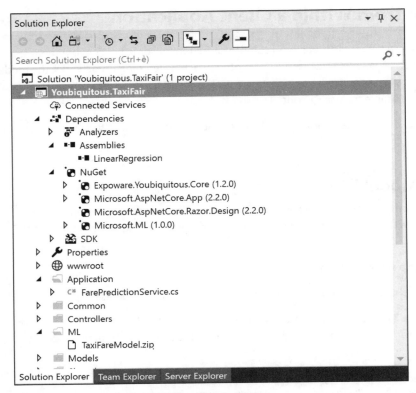

FIGURE 7-1 The sample project in Visual Studio 2019

The application sets up an HTML view where it collects some input data (more on how to do this in a moment) and invokes a controller endpoint. In turn, the controller endpoint calls the *FarePredictionEngine* class shown in the figure. The whole interaction between the machine learning model and the client application happens through this class.

Making a Taxi Fare Prediction

Even though the example is written for ASP.NET Core, you can use the ML.NET library with .NET Framework applications as well, including classic ASP.NET MVC applications. Here's the controller class that in the sample application deals with the prediction service that, in turn, encapsulates the machine learning model:

```
public class FareController : Controller
{
    private readonly FarePredictionService _service;
    public FareController(IHostingEnvironment environment)
    {
        _service = new FarePredictionService(environment.ContentRootPath);
    }
```

```
    public IActionResult Suggest(TaxiTripEstimation input)
    {
        var response = _service.Predict(input);
        return Json(response);
    }
}
```

Note that the *FarePredictionService* class is not injected in the controller through the ASP.NET Core Dependency Injection layer to maintain the controller class as neutral as possible. The prediction service receives the content root path that it will use to locate the ZIP file with the trained model to load. Here's the code necessary to invoke the model:

```
public TaxiTripEstimation Predict(TaxiTripEstimation input)
{
    // Map the input received from the UI to the input required by the model
    var trip = FillTaxiTripFromInput(input);

    // Predict the amount of the fare given the input parameters
    var ml = new MLContext();
    var fare = MakePrediction(trip, ml, _mlFareModelPath);

    // Copy prediction to the input object
    input.EstimatedFare = fare;
    input.EstimatedFareForDisplay = TaxiTripEstimation.FareForDisplay(fare);
    return input;
}
```

The key thing that's going on here, more than the actual prediction, is the mapping between the input data coming from the user interface and the data required by the model—the *TaxiTrip* class imported from the referenced model library. Note that *TaxiTripEstimation* belongs to the client application, and it is a helper class that the ASP.NET MVC layer populates from the HTTP context using ASP.NET MVC model binding. The details—a mere copy of fields—are hidden in the *FillTaxiTripFromInput* method.

The actual prediction takes place in the *MakePrediction* method, as follows:

```
float MakePrediction(TaxiTrip trip, MLContext mlContext, string modelPath)
{
    // Load the trained model
    var trainedModel = mlContext.Model.Load(modelPath, out var modelInputSchema);

    // Create prediction engine related to the loaded trained model
    var predEngine = mlContext
        .Model
        .CreatePredictionEngine<TaxiTrip, TaxiTripFarePrediction>(trainedModel);

    // Predict
    var prediction = predEngine.Predict(trip);
    return prediction.FareAmount;
}
```

In a real-life scenario, you might want to load the model and build the ML.NET prediction engine once and reuse it across multiple calls. The actual invocation of the trained model takes place in the *Predict* method call.

Devising an Adequate User Interface

In spite of its overall simplicity, the example still raises a number of practical questions about the trained model, the client application, and the whole feedback cycle for the project.

One issue is that the model needs to know the distance of the ride in order to make a price prediction. (See the definition of the *TaxiTrip* class, derived from the considered dataset.) It's reasonable, but how would you devise the user interface around it? Should you ask end users to type the distance they want to go through?

More realistically, the user interface on top of this sample taxi service will let users enter two addresses and will calculate the distance using some third-party geographical information system. In addition, how would you render the response to the user? Should you go with a plain float number or is a calculated range preferable? (See Figure 7-2.)

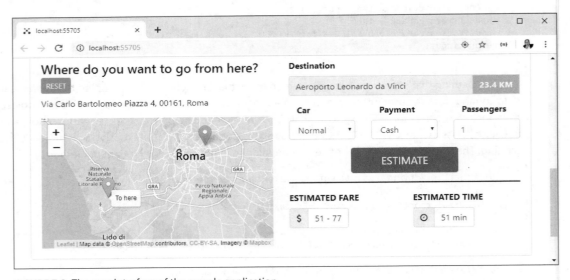

FIGURE 7-2 The user interface of the sample application

As you can see in the figure, type of car, payment, and number of passengers are collected from the user interface and passed to the controller via HTTP. Those values are mapped to corresponding properties of the model-specific *TaxiTrip* class. The addresses, instead, must be programmatically converted into a distance. (The JavaScript API of the GIS service does it in the example.) The Estimate button posts the form back to the ASP.NET Core application and receives the text to display as the estimated range for fare and time.

The demo is live at https://youbiquitous-taxifare.azurewebsites.net/.

> **Note** Although the model was built based on New York City taxi rides, the predictions it made in Figure 7-2 are not very far from what it would really take to go from the city center in Rome to the airport! This also means that machine learning is only about guessing and, in spite of metrics and evaluators, it's the business scenario that determines when a guess is acceptable.

Questioning Data and Approach to the Problem

There's another, and probably deeper, issue, however. The training dataset contains a feature that represents the time it took to go a given distance at a given cost. Therefore, to invoke the model, you should also indicate the time. Where do you, as an end user of this sample taxi-booking application, get this information or at least an estimation of it? More realistically, the taxi-booking application—the client of the machine learning model—could return both the fare and the time prediction to the end user, as in Figure 7-2.

When it comes to this, though, an entire new dimension of data kicks in, and the whole approach to the problem is under discussion.

The time it may take depends on traffic conditions, time of the day, day of the week, and maybe even time of the year. Should you then also have a second model trained to predict the time it may take to run a certain distance in New York by taxi? And how could you train this model? Using the same dataset that you have used for fare prediction? How reliable is a dataset devised for fare prediction to also make time prediction? And further on, have you really used the right approach for the specific problem you intended to solve?

The bottom line is that *this* demo started from the model—to see what it may take to build a price prediction engine. In the real world, instead, you should start from the problem and review all aspects of it before you commit to building a machine learning model.

Summary

This chapter covered the canonical steps of machine learning projects as the ML.NET library implements them and provided an end-to-end, full .NET example of a sample model in action. In spite of the language (and the libraries) employed, the steps are the same, and data preparation is by far the most time-consuming and expensive part of the process.

On the other hand, data preparation is often neglected in demos because most demos start from readymade data. We'll return to the costs of data preparation in Chapter 19, "Sentiment Analysis: An End-to-End Solution," when discussing a larger example involving a Python-based neural network. Just data preparation, however, suggests that sticking to one language and platform may not always be a great idea. In Python, for example, you tend to work with CSV files, whereas sometimes a plain relational database (and some Java or C# code to populate it) would make it cheaper and faster.

Beyond data preparation, this chapter focused on regression problems. In the next chapter, we'll review the whole set of machine learning tasks that the ML.NET library supports.

## CHAPTER 8

ML.NET Tasks and Algorithms

Artificial intelligence is obviously an intelligence transmitted by conscious subjects and placed in equipment. It has a clear origin, in fact, in the intelligence of the human creators of such equipment.

—*Pope Benedict XVI*

In the preceding chapter, you got your first exposure to the new ML.NET framework aimed at making the .NET Core platform viable for machine learning projects. We explored the foundation of the library and its core pieces, and we went through the software elements that enable you to build the canonical pipeline of machine learning projects. We also discussed a linear regression example.

Linear regression, even in its more sophisticated multilinear version with multiple features involved, is hardly the ideal approach to most real-world problems. This is the case even when the problem itself is conceptually a prediction. In real life, even apparently simple prediction problems may need a neural network to get precise results or, as we hinted at in the preceding chapter, a combination of multiple models.

In this chapter, we'll explore further the capabilities of the ML.NET library and focus on the details of the more common tasks you can perform through the library. In doing so, we'll touch on scenarios like binary classification, clustering, and transfer learning.

The Overall ML.NET Architecture

As you saw in the preceding chapter, any programmatic interaction with the ML.NET application starts with getting a reference to the *MLContext* object. It represents the centralized context for all operations and the way to build and run the tasks in the machine learning pipeline, whether data preparation, feature engineering, training, prediction, or model evaluation.

Involved Types and Interfaces

Around the instance of the *MLContext* class, a full workflow develops for any possible learning operation conducted within the ML.NET library.

The Overall View

The interaction is facilitated by a number of interfaces that let involved parts communicate. Table 8-1 lists relevant types.

TABLE 8-1 Relevant Types Involved in the ML.NET Model Development Process

Type	Description
IDataView	This is the fundamental type for input and output in all data query operations. It wraps an enumerable collection (including schema information) and provides a cursor-based navigation system that proceeds row by row.
IDataLoader	This type is responsible for the actual loading of the data from some external data source and for returning a valid *IDataView* object.
ITransformer	This type represents the foundation of all components in the library that transform data. The trainer returns a transformer object for evaluation and for persistence of the model.
IEstimator	This type represents an algorithm yet to be trained on data. The term *estimator* comes from statistics jargon and is also used largely in the Spark literature.

In the big picture of ML.NET, the role of the *IDataView* type, which has a relevance comparable to that of *IEnumerable* in the whole .NET Framework, is remarkable. In the end, *IDataView* is an enumerable collection enriched with schema information.

Schema Information and Propagation

Note that both *IDataView* and *IEstimator* interfaces refer to a schema object. However, the *DataViewSchema* class is expressed as a collection of columns (features) and related types. In the context of an estimator, instead, the schema is an instance of the *SchemaShape* class and merely refers to a minimal set of schema requirements that incoming data must honor. The *IEstimator* interface, in fact, exposes the *Fit* method that trains the model on the provided data view and returns a transformer. The estimator uses *SchemaShape* to check that data has the structure necessary to be processed effectively. In addition, the *IEstimator* interface also exposes a *GetOutputSchema* method:

```
SchemaShape GetOutputSchema(SchemaShape inputSchema);
```

If the specified input schema matches the schema of the provided data view, the method runs and also returns the shape of the schema of the data after it is transformed by the algorithm. This feature is known as *schema propagation* for estimators.

The Graphical View

Figure 8-1 provides a graphical view illustrating how the constituent parts of the ML.NET pipeline interact and the involved interfacing types.

The raw data is loaded into the context object via *IDataLoader*, and it is persisted as a model at the end of training through the services of the *ITransformer* interface.

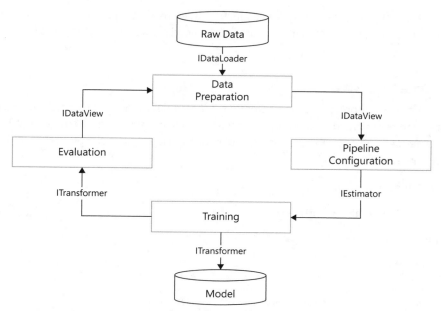

FIGURE 8-1 Connecting parts of the ML.NET pipeline

Data Representation

Let's take a deeper look at the *IDataView* interface and its usage within the pipeline. While most of the time you'll use predefined methods on the *Data* property of the *MLContext* class—the *DataOperationsCatalog* type—to point to a text file (e.g., a CSV file) and get an *IDataView* object back, it is interesting to explore the details of the interface and how to manually build data view objects.

The *IDataView* Interface

The following code snippet presents the definition of the *IDataView* interface as it appears in the source code of the ML.NET library:

```
public interface IDataView
{
    bool CanShuffle { get; }
    DataViewSchema Schema { get; }

    long? GetRowCount();
    DataViewRowCursor GetRowCursor(
        IEnumerable<DataViewSchema.Column> columnsNeeded,
        Random rand = null);
    DataViewRowCursor[] GetRowCursorSet(
        IEnumerable<DataViewSchema.Column> columnsNeeded,
        int n,
        Random rand = null);
}
```

The members of the interface provide two basic functionalities: navigating through the data and shuffling the data. However, the aspect that most justifies the need of an ad hoc data type is the support for schema.

Schema of a Data View

The schema of a data view is represented by the *DataViewSchema* class and is nothing more than a collection of columns and related reading methods. A column has a name, type, and annotations. When building the *DataViewSchema* class, you pass an array of columns. Here's some sample code to create a data view object from scratch:

```
public class SampleDataView : IDataView
{
    private readonly IEnumerable<SampleDataItem> _items;

    public SampleDataView(IEnumerable<SampleDataItem> data)
    {
        // Save raw data
        _items = data;

        // Build the data view on top of properties of SampleDataItem
        var builder = new DataViewSchema.Builder();
        builder.AddColumn("Property1", BooleanDataViewType.Instance);
        builder.AddColumn("Property2", TextDataViewType.Instance);

        // Set the schema
        Schema = builder.ToSchema();
    }

    // More code here for the other members of the interface
    ...
}
```

The data items to manipulate through the view are passed to the constructor of a sample class that implements *IDataView*. When this happens, data is stored in a read-only and private member, and a schema is built, adding one column for each property in the data item class (*SampleDataItem* in the snippet) you intend to support. Finally, the schema is saved.

In the sample code here, the schema is manually built, cherry-picking only some of the properties in the original array of data objects. In your tailor-made data view class, you have the full freedom of mapping properties to schema columns in the way that best suits your needs.

Navigating Rows in the View

The data view works like a plain enumerable object works in the .NET Framework and provides methods to count and visit all reachable elements in the collection.

As the name suggests, the *GetRowCount* method is designed to return null or a numeric value that denotes the number of data items in the view. It's interesting to note why a piece of information that is conceptually fixed is actually exposed through a method instead of a read-only property. The reason is that some implementations of the interface might have an intermediate cache that may return null or a partial value until it's fully populated. Most of the time, however, the *GetRowCount* method returns a fixed value.

Navigation is cursor-based and centered on the *GetRowCursor* method. The method just returns the cursor for the client application to use to move over the view in a forward-only mode. The method also allows you to access a subset of the columns available. Note that the *GetRowCursorSet* method returns an array of cursors to run in parallel to cover a larger section of the data view through multiple threads. If it is implemented, when calling this method, you can also set a limit on the number of cursors to be created and returned.

Shuffling Data in the View

In machine learning, shuffling the training data is generally a good practice to apply, especially during the initial preprocessing phase. In the preceding chapter, we briefly described how the Quicksort algorithm (for sorting data) may provide radically different performance depending on the order in which data is passed. Similarly, in machine learning, the original dataset can come presorted, and this may impact the split of the dataset in training and testing datasets. As a result, in fact, you could end up with two datasets that don't contain the same balance of relevant data items.

In the end, especially for classification tasks (but not just that), it may be generally useful to shuffle the original dataset before proceeding with training. Having said that, though, keep in mind that each situation is different and what works here may not work with the same effectiveness there.

In ML.NET, any object that implements the *IDataView* interface must declare whether or not it supports shuffling of data. This is done through the Boolean *CanShuffle* property exposed as a read-only member by the interface type. The data view object, however, is not expected to provide the ability to shuffle content. If supported by the data view, shuffling is performed by the *ShuffleRows* methods of the *DataOperationCatalog* object that the *MLContext* object exposes through the *Data* property.

Supported Catalogs

The whole set of capabilities of the ML.NET library is organized in catalogs. A catalog is a component that groups together trainers, transformers, and functions for loading and saving data and loading and saving models.

You can see an ML.NET catalog as the repository of a series of programming services dedicated to specific tasks. Catalogs are exposed through ad hoc properties from the programming interface of the *MLContext* object. We like to distinguish two families of catalogs: those that include trainers and tasks specific for a class of machine learning problems and those that collect cross-cutting operations.

Task-Specific Catalogs

Although named similarly, each catalog is different because each specializes in a specific area. All of them, however, are derived from a common base class. Task-specific catalogs refer to common machine learning classes of problems and related algorithms as shown in Table 8-2.

TABLE 8-2 Supported Task-Specific Catalogs in ML.NET

Catalog Property	Problem to Address	Sample Algorithms
AnomalyDetection	Detecting rare, and therefore possibly suspicious, data items that differ significantly from the rest of the dataset.	RandomizePca
BinaryClassification	Classifying all the items of a given dataset in one of two groups based on a set of classification rules.	SdcaLogisticRegression, LinearSvm, FieldAwareFactorizationMachine, and more
Clustering	Grouping items in such a way that items in the same group are more similar to each other than those in other groups.	KMeans
MulticlassClassification	Classifying all the items of a given dataset in one of multiple groups based on a set of classification rules.	NaiveBayes, SdcaNonCalibrated, OneVersusAll, SdcaMaximumEntropy
Ranking	Giving unknown data a score based on evidence.	LightGbm, FastTree
Recommendation	Producing a list of recommended products or services.	MatrixFactorization
Regression	Predicting numeric values.	OnlineGradientDescent, Sdca, LbfgsPoissonRegression

It is worth noting that the list of algorithms (trainers) supported by each catalog refers to those natively part of the ML.NET platform. More algorithms are (and will be) added through extension methods and additional Nuget packages.

Cross-Cutting Operation Catalogs

A number of other, more general-purpose catalogs exist in the ML.NET library. Those directly pointed to by the *MLContext* instance are listed in Table 8-3.

TABLE 8-3 Supported Cross-Cutting Operation Catalogs in ML.NET

Catalog Property	Description
Component	Methods in the catalog discover loadable components in specified assemblies and add them to the internal catalog of the library.
Data	Methods in the catalog allow operations on data, such as load, save, cache, filter, shuffle, and split data.
Model	Methods in the catalog allow you to load and save trained models from and to files.
Transforms	Methods in the catalog allow feature engineering operations such as data type conversions, categorical conversions, text processing, and feature selection. From this object, four additional catalogs are exposed: *Categorical*, *Conversion*, *FeatureSelection*, and *Text*.

It is worth noting that other catalogs are available in ML.NET for additional tasks such as dealing with forecasting, ranking, and time series and importing TensorFlow models. Later in the chapter, we'll talk more about the TensorFlow catalog.

In Chapter 6, "The .NET Way," as a way to get familiar with the ML.NET library, we discussed an example based on a linear regression task. In this chapter, instead, we'll look at some of the aforementioned catalog operations, trainers, and transformers in action in three macro areas: classification, clustering, and transfer learning.

Classification Tasks

As the name unequivocally suggests, classification is the problem of partitioning objects into homogeneous groups. The expected number of groups, whether exactly two or more than two, gives the problem significantly different connotations that lead not only to different names (binary and multiclass) but also to different families of algorithms and approaches to the solution.

Let's focus on binary classification first.

Binary Classification

A number of real-life examples easily fall under the umbrella of binary classification. A canonical example is the evaluation of patients' data to determine whether a given disease is present. Along the same lines, another example could be whether, given observed data, it might be safe for a financial institute to grant a mortgage. Whenever the answer can be expressed in either/or binary terms, then, from the machine learning perspective, you're facing a binary classification problem.

Simple Sentiment Analysis

Sentiment analysis is the process that attempts to extract the sentiment hidden in the folds of a text, whether a written comment or post or a sentence spoken over the phone. The intended output of the analysis is generally aimed at finding whether the mood is positive or negative. Hence, it seems a great example of binary classification. In this chapter, we'll see how to arrange the bare bones of a solution.

As a disclaimer, though, let us say up front that the approach presented, while working in some way, is not probably of the level of accuracy that most real-world systems require. In the next chapter, in fact, we'll build an end-to-end solution for applying sentiment analysis to a specific scenario. You will see, however, that although many more details will be taken into account, the core part of the work will be the same—providing a binary answer after processing a collection of sentences.

In the sample application, the dataset is made up of 4,000 sentences in some way correlated to opinions about a restaurant. The input text file has the following schema: a natural language sentence, a tab character, and then a 0/1 value to denote negative or positive feedback, as follows:

```
Not tasty and the texture was just nasty.    0
The selection on the menu was great and so were the prices.    1
```

The purpose of the training is returning the appropriate 0/1 value in front of any submitted sentence.

> **Important** As mentioned, the sample dataset contains sentences that rate a restaurant. Although the sentences can be associated with a number of like/dislike scenarios, the expected values are set to interpret the sentence as if it referred to a restaurant. In other words, the same sentence that is labeled positive when said about a restaurant might be labeled as negative if evaluated in another binary classification scenario.

Applying Necessary Data Transformations

When you load data in an *MLContext* instance from a text file, you need to instruct the system on the schema of the data. The generic version of the *LoadFromTextFile* method on the *Data* catalog does just that provided that the generic type has members decorated with the *LoadColumn* attribute. Here's a sample class you can use to build up the data view for the example:

```
public class SentimentData
{
    [LoadColumn(0)]
    public string SentimentText;

    [LoadColumn(1), ColumnName("Label")]
    public bool Sentiment;
}
```

The first column of data goes into the *SentimentText* property, and the second one (0/1) sets the *Sentiment* property. The property is also renamed *Label* for the purpose of the machine learning pipeline:

```
var filePath = ...;
var mlContext = new MLContext();
var dataView = mlContext.Data.LoadFromTextFile<SentimentData>(filePath);
```

For this example, only one dataset is available, so you'll face the problem of splitting it between a training and a testing dataset. In general, it is advisable to have different (and equally large) datasets, but sometimes it's impossible to have so much data during the development phase.

The split can be done manually, but it might be really problematic. You have to ensure, in fact, that the split returns two randomly distributed datasets. Machine learning libraries usually provide ad hoc tools, and ML.NET is no exception. The *Data* catalog just exposes the *TrainTestSplit* method, which takes an *IDataView* and a percentage and returns a *TrainTestData* object:

```
var splitDataView = mlContext.Data.TrainTestSplit(dataView, 0.2);
```

The percentage you provide (0.2 in the preceding line) indicates the share of the testing dataset. The net effect of this code is that the dataset undergoes an 80/20 split, where 80 percent of the data is retained for training and the remaining 20 percent is used for testing. The *TrainTestData* class is a mere container object made of two *IDataView* objects—*TrainSet* and *TestSet*.

> **Note** The model testing we're referring to here is comparable to unit tests in programming languages like Java and C#. The ultimate purpose of unit tests is not ensuring that the application satisfies all of the customers' requirements but, more simply, keeping the team confident about what they're doing and having a formidable tool to catch regression errors later in case of some deep refactoring. It's nearly the same here; the testing dataset gives only a necessary measure of quality but no guarantee that, when facing production data, the model will really perform that well.

Machine learning algorithms work on numbers. How can they deal with plain text? The answer is, they can't. To enable classification algorithms, you must take another preliminary step that is called *text featurization*. The ML.NET library provides the *FeaturizeText* method from the *Text* catalog, as follows:

```
var estimator = mlContext
    .Transforms
    .Text
    .FeaturizeText("Features", "SentimentText");
```

The method takes the *SentimentText* column and transforms it into a new column called *Features* made of an array of float values. Every value in the array represents the normalized count of discovered n-grams. An n-gram is a contiguous sequence of words discovered in a text. To grab a preview of the transformation being made by the *FeaturizedText* method, add a call to *Preview*, put a breakpoint in Visual Studio, and then explore the value of the *preview* variable:

```
var preview = mlContext
    .Transforms
    .Text
    .FeaturizeText("Features", "SentimentText")
    .Preview(splitDataView.TrainSet);
```

The *Preview* method applies the transformations to the provided data view and saves the snapshot to the local *preview* variable. Figure 8-2 shows a screenshot of the data view as being transformed.

The data view is now made of four columns—*SentimentText*, *Label* (originally *Sentiment*), plus two more. The third column, labeled *SamplingKeyColumn*, has been added for internal purposes during the training/testing split. The fourth column, *Features*, is a sparse vector of numeric values. Expanding the content of the column for the sample row, you can see a list of over a hundred float values, each representing the occurrence of n-grams as found in the content of the *SentimentText* column. Note also that values have been normalized in the 0–1 range.

FIGURE 8-2 The effect of text featurization on a sample dataset

Training the Model

The next step is appending a trainer to the machine learning pipeline, training the model, and evaluating the results:

```
// Appending the trainer (logistic regression algorithm)
var estimator = mlContext
          .Append(mlContext.BinaryClassification
          .Trainers
          .SdcaLogisticRegression("Label", "Features"));

// Fitting the model on the training dataset
var model = estimator.Fit(splitDataView.TrainSet);
```

The logistic regression algorithm is one of the trainers you can use from the *BinaryClassification* catalog, and it is considered the best-fit algorithm for the problem at hand (or at least the first option to try). Logistic regression works by modeling the probability of the default class in the dataset. In the example, the default class is the label value considered the default (or just more common) between positive or negative.

Another algorithm to try in the realm of binary classification is Support Vector Machine (SVM). This algorithm is offered by ML.NET through the *LinearSvm* method on the *BinaryClassification* catalog. Both algorithms provide nearly the same performance and the same accuracy on similar datasets, and neither one is affected by outliers. Furthermore, both algorithms are linear, so both can be trained well even on fairly large datasets.

The interesting thing is that the two algorithms come to their solution using radically different approaches. As mentioned, logistic regression uses a probabilistic approach and returns the likelihood that a data item falls into the default class. SVM, instead, tries to find the widest possible separating margin between data items that fall into each class.

Evaluating the Model

So how would you decide about the algorithm? Any machine learning library supplies easy ways to calculate metrics, and from statistics, you can borrow a number of techniques to evaluate the quality and the accuracy of an algorithm:

```
// Adjust testing data for testing the model
IDataView predictions = model.Transform(splitDataView.TestSet);

// Evaluating the model on testing data
var metrics = mlContext.BinaryClassification.Evaluate(predictions, "Label");
```

The returned object is a *CalibratedBinaryClassificationMetrics* object and groups together a number of relevant metrics for the problem. In particular, it tells you about the accuracy of the model—namely, the proportion of correct predictions in the test set (regardless of the value, either positive or negative). It also tells you about positive and negative recalls—namely, the proportion of positives (and negatives) detected as positives (and negatives). The harmonic mean of precision and recall is summarized in the F1-score (or F-score) metrics.

On the sample test dataset, the logistic regression algorithm—usually the first choice for binary classification problems—returns an accuracy of over 85 percent but a low F-score, around 30 percent, whereas the ideal value of F-score is 1. We'll return to metrics for evaluating algorithms in Chapter 10, "Metrics of Machine Learning," but for the time being, we'll add just the details to make another, more business-oriented point.

What should you do? Change the algorithm? Enlarge the dataset? Add new transformations? Well, the answer depends!

The actual business problem you're trying to address with binary classification will help you make a decision. Table 8-4 briefly defines the measures in which you might be interested.

TABLE 8-4 Common Measures for Binary Classification

Measure	Description
Accuracy	Indicates the percentage of items classified correctly in relationship to the entire test set. Needless to say, the ideal value is 100 percent.
Precision	Indicates the percentage of positives/negatives classified correctly in relationship to the number of predicted positives/negatives. In other words, it indicates how many of the positives/negatives detected were effectively so. The ideal value is 100 percent.
Recall	Indicates the percentage of items classified correctly in relationship to the items in the predicted class. In other words, it indicates the percentage of positives/negatives in the dataset correctly detected as positives/negatives. The ideal value is 100 percent.
F1-score	Indicates the harmonic mean of precision and recall. It can be calculated on each of the options. The ideal value is 100 percent.

The simplest measure to make sense of is accuracy, which, at the end of the day, just indicates how often the model makes good predictions, whether positive or negative. So, 85 percent can be considered quite good, although not certainly enthusiastic. In this example, the F1-score is fairly low, but on the other hand, it's a combined metric and doesn't represent a direct measure. Therefore, if accuracy (or precision or recall) is crucial in the scenario, you can blissfully ignore the F1-score.

The F1-score comes into play when the problem at hand doesn't give strict guidance on the ideal training approach and you want to compare multiple algorithms.

When a Combined Metric Helps

The role of the F1-score is crucial when your dataset is unbalanced in the sense that one of two scenarios occurs much more frequently than the other. In case of a balanced dataset, F1 can be ignored because, in the presence of good accuracy, the risk of erroneous classifications is really low. In case of unbalanced datasets, instead, it's all about the importance that each option has for the problem at hand.

If both scenarios should be taken into account carefully, the F1-score should be sufficiently high on both options to be safe about the quality of the model.

Sometimes, instead, one scenario is more important than the other for the business. A good example is fraud detection, where effectively labeling fraudulent transactions is much more important than dealing in any way with nonfraudulent transactions. In this case, you should look at the F1-score only for the option that is more important and pick the algorithm that maximizes the value.

Multiclass Classification

Conceptually, binary classification can be seen as a special case of multiclass classification when the number of classes to group on is limited to two. When it comes to the actual calculation, though, having exactly two classes or more than two makes a huge difference and leads to distinct families of algorithms.

Multiclass classification applies to any real-world scenarios in which a data item must be assigned to an existing category. To train an algorithm, you provide a sufficiently large set of classified elements and let the algorithm figure out where the new data item fits better. Unlike clustering (which we'll discuss next), multiclass classification is a form of supervised learning, meaning that the classes to choose from are known in advance.

The same problem of sentiment analysis that we approached as a binary classification can be rephrased as a multiclass classification problem by simply expanding the range of possible outcomes: positive, negative, neutral, and maybe more. This apparently trivial extension, though, has a dramatic impact on the various steps of the machine learning pipeline.

> **Note** Multiclass classification is different from multilabel classification where a single data item is assigned one or more categories. A good example of multilabel classification is music classification that attempts to assign multiple genres to each song. Multilabel is usually approached through multiclass or even binary classification on aptly transformed data and, more often, learning pipelines. For example, the solution can have a binary classification model for each of the possible categories.

Applying Necessary Data Transformations

The sample dataset to consider here comes from one of the samples available with ML.NET. It's a tab-separated file that contains a collection of over 10,000 Github issues. Each issue is characterized by a title, a description, and an area of interest. You want to train the model to guess the area of any new issue submitted just by looking at the title and description. Here's an example of the training dataset:

ID	AREA	TITLE	DESCRIPTION
24597	area-System.Net	HttpWebRequest Not Supported HTTP/1.0	...
24608	area-System.Data	sni.dll bug or problem using the same login	...

The *Title* and *Description* columns need to be featurized as done in binary classification. This is a necessary step to teach the algorithm how to grab the relevance of words:

```
_mlContext
    .Transforms
    .Text
    .FeaturizeText("Title", "TitleFeaturized");
_mlContext
    .Transforms
    .Text
    .FeaturizeText("Description", "DescriptionFeaturized");
```

In multiclass classification, another step is required: mapping the content of the column to predict numbers. The *Area* column in the dataset is textual, but you need to turn it into unique numbers in order to proceed with the training. You faced a similar problem in the preceding chapter while converting the text describing the payment mode of the taxi ride. In that case, though, you used the one-hot encoding technique.

The one-hot encoding technique works beautifully for categorical data—nearly the same as enumerated types in the .NET Framework. The one-hot encoding transformation creates additional 0/1 columns for each possible categorical value. It's acceptable as long as the options are limited to just a few.

The *Area* column is different. The distinct values in the column can be in the order of hundreds or even thousands in large datasets. This would make handling such a large number of features problematic. Therefore, you can opt for a different transformation: adding a new column that maps each distinct value in the *Area* column to a distinct numeric value, typically a progressive index.

```
// Map output column "Label" to input column "Area"
_mlContext.Transforms.Conversion.MapValueToKey("Label", "Area");
```

The *Label* column ends up holding values like 1, 2, 3 for each distinct string found in the *Area* column.

Training the Model

By design, the ML.NET library requires that all information to be learned from is concatenated in a single column named *Features*. In the previous example, the *Features* column was created as the result of the featurization of a single text column, the *SentimentText* column. In this case, you must create the Features column explicitly by concatenating previously featurized *Title* and *Description* columns:

```
_mlContext.Transforms.Concatenate("Features", "TitleFeaturized", "DescriptionFeaturized")
```

Depending on the algorithm selected, you might need to make multiple passes on the training dataset. To avoid reloading the same data over and over from the file on disk, you can force the algorithm within the pipeline to work on cached data. To do so, just add a call to the *AppendCacheCheckpoint* method. Note that the cache checkpoint must be added to the pipeline before the trainer is appended.

The resulting pipeline is obtained from the following sequence of operations:

```
var pipeline = _mlContext.Transforms.Conversion.MapValueToKey("Area", "Label")
    .Append(_mlContext.Transforms.Text.FeaturizeText("Title", "TitleFeaturized"))
    .Append(_mlContext.Transforms.Text.FeaturizeText("Description", "DescriptionFeaturized"))
    .Append(_mlContext.Transforms.Concatenate("Features",
                    "TitleFeaturized", "DescriptionFeaturized"))
    .AppendCacheCheckpoint(_mlContext);
```

Which algorithm should you use?

The *Trainers* collection on the *MulticlassClassification* catalog provide several options. Most of the algorithms, however, work by training one binary classifier for each class or combination of classes. It could be less than ideal performance-wise if the client application only needs a default/suggested value to categorize a new data item. This is the case for the *OneVersusAll* and *PairwiseCoupling* trainers. Another option is the *NaiveBayes* algorithm. Based on probabilistic theory, this trainer is recommended when the features are independent and the training dataset is small. Both options hardly apply here, where the dataset can be realistically made by millions of rows and features are correlated. What remains to consider are linear algorithms such as stochastic dual coordinate ascent (SDCA) trainers.

A linear algorithm generates a linear combination of the input data and a set of weights. The training effort is then aimed at finding the ideal weights to complete the linear formula. For a linear algorithm to work effectively, all features should be normalized to avoid one having more influence over the result than others.

> **Note** Featurization of textual columns is just aimed at turning text into numbers in full respect of normalization. Mapping keys to values doesn't alter calculation of algorithms as long as the mapped column is not included in the features (as in this example). If a text column must be considered for learning, instead you then should apply either one-hot encoding or featurization.

In general, linear algorithms are cheap to train and fast and cheap to predict. Given their inherent linearity, they also scale well with the number of features and the size of the training dataset. It is worth noting that linear algorithms need to make multiple passes over the dataset. Hence, if the size of the dataset allows, you might want to cache it in memory for a better training performance. Let's opt for the *SdcaMaximumEntropy* trainer for this example:

```
var trainer = _mlContext
    .MulticlassClassification
    .Trainers
    .SdcaMaximumEntropy("Label", "Features");
```

One more piece is needed in the pipeline before training: you need to convert the predicted value back to the expected text. For example, say that the area "System.Net" was mapped to 1. The trained model will then predict 1 for any new issue it determines falls in the System.Net class. The value 1, however, doesn't tell much to any client application. The pipeline, though, knows the mapping table, and a call to *MapKeyToValue* will do the reverse job:

```
// Add one more column (PredictedLabel) to contain the string of text actually predicted
pipeline.Append(trainer)
        .Append(_mlContext.Transforms.Conversion.MapKeyToValue("PredictedLabel"));
```

Note that the various linear algorithms for multiclassification vary for the technique each uses to select weights.

Evaluating the Model

The SDCA algorithms combine several of the best properties and capabilities of logistic regression and SVM algorithms and are a good fit for multiclass classification. How do you determine, however, if it is good enough for the problem at hand? Let's grab some metrics:

```
// Train the model
var model = pipeline.Fit(trainingDataSet);

// Grab some metrics
var testMetrics = _mlContext
    .MulticlassClassification
    .Evaluate(model.Transform(testDataSet));
```

The *Evaluate* method returns a *MulticlassClassificationMetrics* object. Table 8-5 lists some of the most-used metrics reported by the object.

TABLE 8-5 Some Metric Properties for Multiclass Classification

Property	Description
ConfusionMatrix	Returns the confusion matrix for the classifier. (See later description.)
LogLoss	Indicates the mean of the log loss values calculated for each class.
LogLossReduction	Indicates the percentage of the advantage that the classifier provides over a random prediction.
MacroAccuracy	Indicates the average of the F1-score calculated for each class.
MicroAccuracy	Indicates the F1-score for all predictions made by the model.
PerClassLogLoss	Gets the log-loss of the classifier for each class.

Both micro- and macro-accuracy refer to calculating F1-scores—namely, the harmonic mean of precision and recall. The difference is that micro-accuracy refers to the whole set of predictions, whereas macro-accuracy calculates F1-scores individually for each class and then returns the average.

In general, micro-accuracy is preferable if you have a large dataset with some relevant degree of class imbalance (that is, many more examples of one class than of other classes). Macro-accuracy, instead, counts more if you have an interest in evaluating the performance of the model on the various classes, including those with few occurrences in the training dataset.

The *LogLoss* metric measures the average level of uncertainty about the results of the classifier. The lowest is the best value. Ideally, the lowest possible value is 0. Figure 8-3 presents the list of *LogLoss* values reported for the more than 20 classes in the sample dataset. The resulting average is 0.91.

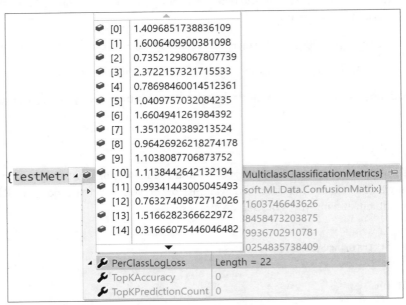

FIGURE 8-3 Values of the *LogLoss* metric for all the classes in the sample application

How would you combine accuracy and loss? A quick summary is that accuracy indicates the quantity of errors, whereas loss refers more to the quality of errors and how huge they were. Hence, low macro accuracy and high loss denote large errors on a lot of data—the worst-case scenario. On the contrary, low accuracy but low loss denote small errors but on a lot of data. In case of great accuracy, you have few errors but as large as the loss amount quantitatively says.

Looking at the Confusion Matrix

Yet another tool to evaluate the performance of a classifier is the *confusion matrix*. This matrix combines predictions and labels on the rows and columns of a square matrix, as you can see in Figure 8-4.

		Actual Class		
		Cat	Dog	Rabbit
Predicted Class	Cat	**5**	2	0
	Dog	3	**3**	2
	Rabbit	0	1	**11**

FIGURE 8-4 A sample confusion matrix for a multiclass classifier

The values in the columns (e.g., Dog) indicate how many times elements in the class have been predicted as any of the values in the rows. For example, the matrix in Figure 8-4 says that a dog was recognized twice as a cat, once as a rabbit, and three times as a dog. The *MulticlassClassificationMetrics* object exposes a property called *ConfusionMatrix* that gathers all values for such a matrix. In the sample application, the matrix is 22×22. The matrix is represented by a ML.NET class named *Confusion-Matrix* with predefined properties to calculate precision and recall on a per class basis. (See Table 8-6.)

TABLE 8-6 Properties of a Confusion Matrix

Property	Description
Counts	Returns an array of arrays, in which every element refers to a row and contains an array of values for each of the columns.
NumberOfClasses	Indicates the dimension of the matrix (number of rows/columns).
PerClassPrecision	Returns an array with the precision calculated for each class.
PerClassRecall	Returns an array with the recall calculated for each class.

As a reminder, the *precision* indicates the percentage of true class positives the model predicts with respect to the total number of actual positives in the dataset for the given class. The *recall*, instead, refers to the percentage of true class positives the model predicts with respect to the total number of positives detected for the given class.

Clustering Tasks

Clustering is the primary form of unsupervised machine learning. As discussed in Chapter 3, "Mapping Problems and Algorithms," a clustering algorithm processes a dataset and partitions it in an array of subsets. So far, it may look like multiclass classification, but there's a huge difference.

In multiclass classification, the training dataset provides the total number of output classes, and any of the data items will be placed in one of the provided classes—the one that fits better. In clustering, there's no known number of subsets, even though some of the algorithms may accept a maximum number of clusters to return.

Put another way, the clustering algorithm is left alone to figure out where and how data items naturally group together and return the number of clusters. Let's see how clustering can be implemented in ML.NET.

Preparing Data for Work

A canonical dataset for clustering exercises is the Iris dataset. It contains 150 lines of text, each describing a type of iris plant. The actual file, *iris.data*, can be downloaded from https://archive.ics.uci.edu/ml/datasets/Iris.

A Quick Look at the Data

The Iris database is fairly simple and small, but in the ML community it is considered a good starting point for clustering problems. The file contains lines of text as follows:

```
5.1, 3.5, 1.4, 0.2, Iris-setosa
4.9, 3.0, 1.4, 0.2, Iris-setosa
4.7, 3.2, 1.3, 0.2, Iris-setosa
```

The columns of data can be mapped to a C# class like the following:

```csharp
public class IrisData
{
    [LoadColumn(0)]
    public float SepalLength;

    [LoadColumn(1)]
    public float SepalWidth;

    [LoadColumn(2)]
    public float PetalLength;

    [LoadColumn(3)]
    public float PetalWidth;
}
```

The first two columns refer to the length and width of the sepal of the flower. (The sepal is a special kind of leaf that, along with petals, form the calyx of most flowers just beneath the corolla.) The next two columns refer to the length and width of the petal. The file also has a fifth column with the name of the iris flower.

Applying Transformations to Data

In this clustering scenario, all the data you need to process in the training phase is already numeric. So, you do not need to use one-hot encoding, featurization, or conversions. All you need to do is prepare the ML.NET pipeline for work by concatenating features to learn from into a single column:

```
var mlContext = new MLContext();
var dataView = mlContext.Data.LoadFromTextFile<IrisData>(irisDataFile);
var pipeline = mlContext
        .Transforms
        .Concatenate("Features", "SepalLength", "SepalWidth", "PetalLength", "PetalWidth")
```

At this point, the pipeline is configured to process the content of the Features column formed by the concatenated values of petal and sepal length and width expressed in centimeters.

> **Note** In ML.NET, column names if expressed with magic strings are case sensitive. To bypass the problem, however, you can use the C# newest *nameof* operator.

Training the Model

When it comes to clustering, the most popular algorithm is K-Means. It's not the only known clustering algorithm, as you saw already in Chapter 3, "Mapping Problems and Algorithms." However, it is an excellent compromise, and it is the only trainer that ML.NET supplies out of the box.

The K-Means Algorithm at Work

As mentioned, a cluster is a collection of data items that have been recognized to have similarities. The algorithm requires you to indicate a value K that is meant to be the number of clusters to split the dataset into. In other words, if you set $K=5$, the algorithm learns to return a value 1 through 5 for each input it receives.

The algorithm first selects a group of K points, referred to as *centroids*. Each centroid is assumed to be the center of a cluster. Next, it iteratively scans the dataset and tries to allocate each data item in the cluster that counts the minimum distance from the point. At the end of each iteration, the algorithm recalculates the centroid to be the point at the center of the group. The algorithm halts when centroids do not change anymore or when a given number of iterations has been performed.

Setting the Trainer

In ML.NET, you select the K-Means trainer using the following code. Note that you initially set the number of clusters to $K=5$:

```
// Set the trainer, number of expected clusters, and column(s) to work on
var trainer = mlContext.Clustering.Trainers.KMeans("Features", 5);

// Append the trainer to the pipeline
var pipeline = mlContext.Append(trainer);
// Fit the model
var model = pipeline.Fit(trainingDataSet);
```

Once in production, the clustering algorithm is expected to return two key pieces of information: the ID of the cluster that the data item is predicted to belong to and the distance between the data item and the center of the cluster. This distance should be minimal.

> **Note** A radically different clustering algorithm that doesn't require the number of expected clusters in input is Affinity Propagation. Presented in 2007, it works by measuring the affinity between data items. The function that measures affinity between data items is one of the hyperparameters of the algorithm. As an example, consider that K-Means was first proposed for application in the field of statistics back in 1955.

Evaluating the Model

Evaluating the performance of a clustering trainer may not be obvious. In most cases, data scientists resort to something called *external assessment*, which consists of using a well-known dataset (e.g., the Iris database) to see whether specific data items are placed in the right cluster. Let's set the groundwork to collect some metrics via ML.NET.

Collecting Metrics

You can slightly edit the code presented so far to split the dataset into train and test sets and call the *Evaluate* method on the trained model:

```
var split = mlContext.Data.TrainTestSplit(dataView, 0.2);

// Set the trainer and fit the model on 5 clusters
var trainer = mlContext.Clustering.Trainers.KMeans("Features", 5);
var pipeline = mlContext.Append(trainer);
var model = pipeline.Fit(split.TrainSet);

// Collect metrics about the model
var testingDataView = model.Transform(split.TestSet);
var metrics = mlContext.Clustering.Evaluate(testingDataView);
```

Here, the *Evaluate* method returns a *ClusteringMetrics* object with three properties, as in Table 8-7.

TABLE 8-7 Properties of the *ClusteringMetrics* Object

Property	Description
AverageDistance	Represents the measure of proximity of the data items to cluster centroids.
DaviesBouldinIndex	Returns the value of the Davies-Bouldin index, which measures how much scatter is in the cluster and the cluster separation.
NormalizedMutualInformation	Represents the measure of the mutual dependence of the variables.

The last two properties in the table refer to indexes for internal assessment of the performance of the algorithm. The first property—the *AverageDistance* property—is the most relevant here.

How to Define Quality of Clusters?

Overall, clustering is like pudding: you have to eat it to see if you like it. Any cluster analysis is done to make sense of largely unknown data. Therefore, clustering is good only when you can see a clear distinction between data items, which really helps draw reliable conclusions from the data.

The ultimate purpose of clustering is to provide a reliable tool to automate software decisions, whether plain categorization of data, fraud detection, medical diagnosis, or management decisions. Clustering comes into play when too much data is available that can't just be processed manually. Clustering helps when it comes to rationalizing the data available. The algorithm doesn't have to be fast and efficient; it does have to be reliable and provide insights and added value.

In the end, clustering shouldn't be used to find confirmation, but to learn new things.

External Assessment of the Sample Application

Let's see how external assessment really works. As mentioned, you have a known database—the Iris database—and the database is known to be made up of three classes of iris plants. The database is also known to be perfectly balanced: 50 data rows per class. Let's take three records out of the training dataset—one per known group—and train the algorithm on the remaining items. The required number of clusters is now set to three, as the number of clusters you know are in the actual dataset:

```
var trainer = mlContext.Clustering.Trainers.KMeans("Features", 3);
var pipeline = mlContext.Append(trainer);
var model = pipeline.Fit(trainingDataView);
```

Now you can load testing data and expose it as an *IEnumerable* type for looping over:

```
// Load testing data
var testingDataview = mlContext
    .Data
    .LoadFromTextFile<IrisData>(_testDataPath);

// Create the predictor
var predictor = mlContext
    .Model
    .CreatePredictionEngine<IrisData, ClusterPrediction>(model);

// Build an enumerable to loop over and make predictions
var listOfTests = mlContext
    .Data
    .CreateEnumerable<IrisData>(testingDataview, reuseRowObject: true);
foreach (var item in listOfTests)
{
    var prediction = predictor.Predict(item);
    Console.WriteLine($"Cluster: {prediction.PredictedClusterId}");
    Console.WriteLine($"Distances: {string.Join(" ", prediction.Distances)}");
}
```

The class used to receive the response of the model is *ClusterPrediction* and is defined as follows:

```
public class ClusterPrediction
{
```

```
        [ColumnName("PredictedLabel")]
        public uint PredictedClusterId;

        [ColumnName("Score")]
        public float[] Distances;
}
```

The class represents the response you'll get in production from the model. The *PredictedLabel* column contains the ID of the predicted cluster, and the *Score* column contains an array with squared Euclidean distances to the cluster centroids. The array length is equal to the number of clusters. Those columns are automatically bound to the properties of the C# class. Figure 8-5 shows the output as it goes in a console application where three tests are run.

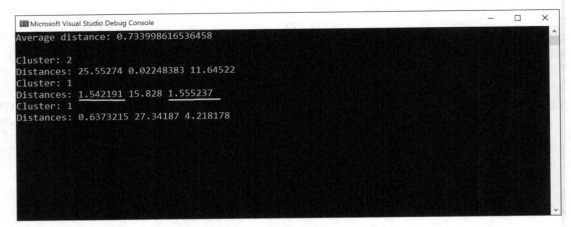

FIGURE 8-5 The prediction of the algorithm on a specific type of iris

The testing dataset contains three iris records, one per known cluster. Those records are not part of the training data. As you can see, the three records are reported to belong to only two distinct clusters. Note, though, that the distance between cluster #1 and cluster #3 in the second test case is minimal. This is acceptable for an external assessment scenario.

Transfer Learning

Most of the beauty of machine learning is crafting your own model to make it behave the way you want. In a way, this reminds us of the old days of software in which every single procedure had to be handcrafted and was hardly ever reused. Transfer learning is the same concept of software reuse (and modularity) applied to machine learning.

Transfer learning means that a model developed for a task (by someone else and possibly using a different platform) is reused as the starting point for a new model that accomplishes a different task. It's like using an existing, specialized library (or Nuget package) to build your own solution.

As the final example of the ML.NET capabilities, let's take an existing TensorFlow model and use it to build an image classifier.

Steps for Building an Image Classifier

Generally speaking, an image classifier is a module that takes an image and tells about its content, whether it contains a dog, a house, or a flower. To build such a module from scratch, you need to build and train a rather sophisticated neural network. You need millions of images and also deep learning skills. In addition, you also need relevant computing power.

With transfer learning, things can be much more simple.

Gaining Access to the Inception Model Library

The Inception Model (IM) is a general-purpose neural network written with TensorFlow and available for download from the TensorFlow website. You get the files for the model and can save them in one of the folders for your ML.NET project. The download URL for the latest version of the model is https://bit.ly/2ShnXSA.

When you unzip the file, you'll find the serialized model—a Protobuf .pb binary file—and a couple of text files. One is the license, and the other one is the list of 1,000 categories that the model can recognize in a submitted image.

Overall Purpose of the New Classifier

The purpose of this example is building a far simpler image classifier that can tag images with one of a few categories. In other words, what you're trying to do is create a plain multiclass classification, except that you want it done on top of images rather than text. Building your own neural network for processing images is out of the question, and no such support is built natively in any machine learning platform.

The idea, then, is to import the Inception Model and retrain it to match the simpler classification purposes. You need to instruct the neural network to map its native labels to the freshly provided labels. Transfer learning can be done in two main ways: you can retrain all layers of the network or just the penultimate layer. The purpose of this example is to override the output of the neural network and add an extra step. So, the approach is a kind of penultimate layer retraining.

In the next steps, you'll build your own pipeline as if it were a canonical multiclass classification and then just compose a slightly more sophisticated training infrastructure that includes the prebuilt TensorFlow model.

Applying Necessary Data Transformations

The training dataset is made up of two main pieces of information: the path to an image and the related label. You still need to train the final model on images because you want the model to classify the image and learn how to go from the native labels of Inception Model to the custom labels.

Defining the Image Dataset

The following C# class defines the typical data row in the training dataset. As mentioned, there are two string properties:

```
public class ImageData
{
    [LoadColumn(0)]
    public string ImagePath;

    [LoadColumn(1)]
    public string Label;
}
```

This time the dataset doesn't have to be that huge because you can rely on a fully trained model. Here's an example:

```
veggie.jpg      food
pizza.jpg       food
pizza2.jpg      food
teddy2.jpg      toy
teddy3.jpg      toy
teddy4.jpg      toy
toaster.jpg     appliance
toaster2.png    appliance
```

You load this file into the pipeline using the familiar *LoadFromTextFile* method on the *Data* catalog:

```
var mlContext = new MLContext();
var data = mlContext.Data.LoadFromTextFile<ImageData>(dataLocation);
```

As in the multiclass example shown earlier, you need to map class names to predict unique numbers. The dataset column to turn into numbers is *Label*, as in the *ImageData* class. The name for the new column is *LabelKey*:

```
// Add new column LabelKey with a numeric value for each distinct value in column Label
mlContext.Transforms.Conversion.MapValueToKey("LabelKey", "Label")
```

This is only the first step of the data transformation process. The most important part of this step is adding all necessary transformation that could enable the TensorFlow model to work properly.

Making Necessary Image Transformations

The image classifier you are building is not natively able to deal with images. It will rely on the Inception Model library for that. However, for this to happen, the training dataset must also include image information in a format that the underlying neural network can understand.

By referencing the *Microsoft.ML.ImageAnalytics* Nuget package, you have access to three estimators tailor-made for the Inception Model. The first transformation, carried out by the *LoadImages* method, adds a new feature named *input* to the dataset. The content of this column is then iteratively transformed by the chained action of the remaining estimators:

```
// Create dedicated estimators for the Inception Model
var loading = mlContext
    .Transforms
    .LoadImages("input", _trainImagesFolder, "ImagePath");
var resizing = mlContext
    .Transforms
    .ResizeImages("input", InceptionSettings.ImageWidth, InceptionSettings.ImageHeight,  "input");
var extracting = mlContext
    .Transforms
    .ExtractPixels("input", InceptionSettings.ChannelsLast, InceptionSettings.Mean);
pipeline.Append(loading).Append(resizing).Append(extracting);
```

The *LoadImages* estimator uses the content of the *ImagePath* column to locate the image and load its bitmap in the new Input feature. The *ResizeImages* estimator resizes the bitmap in the *Input* feature, and the *ExtractPixels* estimator extracts color information. At the end of the chain, the originally added *Input* feature contains pixel information about the image loaded from the path specified by the *Image-Path* column. The net effect is shown in Figure 8-6.

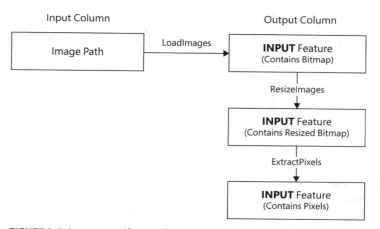

FIGURE 8-6 Image-specific transformations to invoke the Inception Model

Composing and Training the Model

Now that you've dealt with data transformations, it's time to compose the training infrastructure for the classifier. You first need to append the TensorFlow model to the ML.NET pipeline and then the specific trainer you want to use for multiclass classification.

Adding the TensorFlow Model to the Pipeline

The TensorFlow model to import is saved as a file somewhere in the project. To load it in the ML.NET pipeline, you need to know the path and call the *LoadTensorFlowModel* method from the *Model* catalog:

```
mlContext
    .Model
    .LoadTensorFlowModel(inputModelLocation)
    .ScoreTensorFlowModel(new[] { "softmax2_pre_activation" }, new[] { "input" });
```

The *ScoreTensorFlowModel* method invokes the previously loaded TensorFlow model by passing an array of output columns and a set of input columns. In the specific example, each array is made up of one column. The output column is *softmax2_pre_activation*. The input column is *input*. Those two columns form the output and input of the pretrained TensorFlow model. Via *input*, the model receives the image to process, and via *softmax2_pre_activation*, it returns the output of the neural network.

Retraining the TensorFlow Network

The final step to have a custom image classifier is to take the output of the Inception Model library and further use it for your own goals. To do so, you need to add the same operations you saw earlier for the multiclass classification example:

```
var trainer = mlContext
        .MulticlassClassification
        .Trainers
        .LbfgsMaximumEntropy("LabelKey", "softmax2_pre_activation");
var converter = mlContext
        .Transforms
        .Conversion
        .MapKeyToValue("PredictedLabelValue", "PredictedLabel"));

// Configure the pipeline
pipeline.Append(trainer).Append(converter).AppendCacheCheckpoint(mlContext);

// Train the model
var model = pipeline.Fit(dataView)
```

First, you set the multiclass trainer. In this case, you use the *LbfgsMaximumEntropy* algorithm. The algorithm takes the name of the column it will fill with the response. (It must be a key, numeric column.) It also takes the name of the feature it will use as its input. In this case, it gets the output of the TensorFlow model as the input. According to the documentation, the algorithm returns a response that is made by an index named *PredictedLabel* and an array of float values, each indicating the score for any of the possible classes. This property is named *Score*. The index of the class is not enough, though, so that's why you turn the index into a string value using the call to *MapKeyToValue*. As a result, the response of the model can be mapped to the following C# class:

```
public class ImagePrediction : ImageData
{
    public float[] Score;
    public string PredictedLabelValue;
}
```

When calling the composed model, you will pass an *ImageData* object and receive back an *ImagePrediction* object.

Testing the Model

The evaluation of the model follows the same rules you saw for multiclass classification. If the metrics of the model prove it can perform nicely, to see it in action, you can use the following code:

```
// The variable "model" refers to the model trained on top of the TF model
var predictor = mlContext.Model.CreatePredictionEngine<ImageData, ImagePrediction>(model);
var prediction = predictor.Predict(imageData);
```

The prediction contains the scored class and the percentage for each of the defined classes. (See Figure 8-7.)

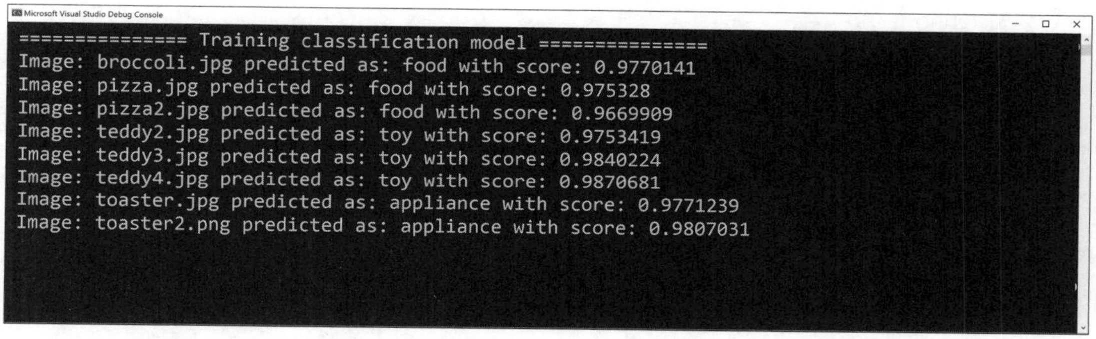

FIGURE 8-7 The image classifier in action

Margin Notes on Transfer Learning

Training a model from scratch is the most effective way to achieve what you intend to achieve. However, for complex scenarios such as those that require a neural network, training a model from scratch could be expensive and require exceptional skills. If the problem at hand allows some middle ground, transfer learning represents an interesting and powerful shortcut to success.

The example presented here showed that you can take an existing computer vision neural network and build a custom classifier on top of it. In a fraction of the time necessary to train a full network (and without dedicated hardware), you can build a model fairly quickly.

Last, but far from least, transfer learning works regardless of the technology used to build the underlying model. This means that your team can develop any complex model with, say, Python or TensorFlow, and you can blissfully import it in the ML.NET ecosystem or smoothly use it as is in a .NET application.

Summary

ML.NET enables you to add machine learning to any .NET applications. This means that you can create machine learning solutions right in .NET code and use the serialized model within another .NET application. However, it also means that you can take a model developed with, say, TensorFlow and seamlessly incorporate it in a .NET client application.

In this chapter, we reviewed a few examples of machine learning tasks, as supported by ML.NET. A task is the sequence of steps you need to code to arrange a learning pipeline for a specific problem such as regression, binary classification, anomaly detection, ranking, multiclass classification, and clustering.

The learning pipeline is not limited to preparing and training the model; it also includes metrics and evaluation. You've seen that when it comes to evaluating the quality and performance of a model, the real outcome depends on the nature of the real problem you're trying to solve. In the next chapter, we'll try to raise the level of samples—from basic exercises to a real-life problem.

## PART III

Fundamentals of Shallow Learning

## CHAPTER 9

Math Foundations of Machine Learning

If your experiment needs statistics, you ought to have done a better experiment.

—Ernest Rutherford

(Winner of Nobel Prize for Chemistry in 1908 and precursor of nuclear physics)

Too many people, regardless of a high or technical level of education, find it hard to figure out how machine learning works. Too often the algorithm is envisioned as a *deus ex machina* (a Latin phrase meaning "god from the machine") that suddenly appears on stage to abruptly resolve a seemingly unsolvable situation in the plot. In Greek tragedy, a mechanical device was used to bring actors on scene to let them play the role of some divinity, which is where the name "god from the machine" originated.

To many, machine learning algorithms just do magic. Whereas to others, machine learning algorithms can perform any imaginable wizardry, if only trained long enough. Machine learning algorithms are far from being magical or almighty, but they do have some kind of superpower that enables them to mine valuable gems of information apparently out of nowhere.

It's just the power of math and, in particular, statistics.

To fully comprehend the state of the art of machine learning and envision some of its possible future development, it is necessary to start from the foundation of statistics and spice it up with a bit of calculus, mathematical analysis, and probability.

Under the Umbrella of Statistics

Throughout the chapter, assume that you are working with datasets, namely structured collections of rows and columns. In this context, rows are often referred to as *observations*; columns, instead, are always referred to as *features*. Transforming raw data (say, emails) into a tabular dataset is a different problem that we'll address with concrete examples in a more hands-on chapter about sentiment analysis. (See Chapter 19, "Sentiment Analysis: An End-to-End Solution.")

Features have their own (rather high-level) type system, as summarized in Table 9-1.

TABLE 9-1 Type System of Features

Type	Description
Continuous	The feature can take any (numeric) value in a given range. For example, the rotation speed of a mechanical device is a continuous value.
Discrete	The feature can take only one of a few specific (numeric) values in a given range. For example, the marks at school are discrete values.
Categorical	The feature takes a discrete value from a nonnumeric set. In software terms, a categorical value is the same as an enumeration. Boolean values are typically represented via a pair of categorical values.
Text-based	The feature takes a descriptive value. In software terms, a text-based value is a string and, like a string, can represent any information that makes sense in the context (i.e., colors, states, emails, IP addresses).
Timestamp	The feature represents a specific time.

The table is purely indicative because sometimes you have to model information that logically sits across two types. For example, a feature that represents a temperature is borderline and can be continuous as well as discrete. The same can be said for colors whose exact representation depends on the problem and the role that colors play in that specific scenario.

In this chapter, we'll focus on datasets made of numeric values. It is a relatively fair operation that doesn't introduce a relevant loss of generality. Categorical data can always be expressed with numbers through a simple mapping table. Turning strings into numbers, instead, is a bit more complicated, and the actual solution typically varies with the specific scenario. In the simplest cases, it's a matter of finding an encoding; in other cases (i.e., sentiment analysis), it can be a count on the occurrences of specific words and substrings.

Now let's get back to main topic of the chapter. The beating heart of statistics is the *mean, mode,* and *median.*

The Mean in Statistics

The mean is one of the first things that every student learns in elementary school. It is a single numerical value that represents the average of a collection of numbers and attempts to synthetically describe the content of a dataset. There are three classical (also known as Pythagorean) types of mean. They are the arithmetic mean (AM), the geometric mean (GM), and the harmonic mean (HM).

The Arithmetic Mean

The arithmetic mean is by far the most popular type of mean. It is given by the sum of all values in the dataset divided by the total number of values:

$$M_a = \frac{1}{N}\sum_{i=1}^{N} x_i$$

The same formula can be rewritten to avoid the division and use a coefficient f for each value that indicates the frequency in which it appears in the dataset. The rewritten formula looks like the following:

$$M_a = \sum_{j=1}^{K} f_j x_j$$

It is interesting to note that the symbol K in the formula represents the number of distinct values found within a dataset of size N. The function f measures the frequency of each element and is expressed as the ratio between the number of appearances and the size of the dataset.

A bit more general is the concept of weighted mean, which is rendered in the following formula:

$$M_{aw} = \frac{\sum_{i=1}^{n} w_i x_i}{\sum_{i=1}^{n} w_i}$$

The weight is a value that measures the importance attributed to any value in the dataset. The weighted mean is the ratio between the sum of weighted values and the total of all weights. The whole point of a weighted mean is calculating an average value from a dataset, giving some selected values more emphasis and downgrading others.

The arithmetic mean works well with linear transformations. A linear transformation T of a value x is expressed as follows:

$$T(x) = ax + b$$

If you know (or calculate) the mean of a numeric column in a dataset, you can quickly obtain the mean of a linearly transformed version of the column by simply applying the same transformation to the mean value. In other words, you can substitute the column with its mean and apply equally effective transformations to the mean.

Note that the arithmetic mean is particularly sensitive to *outliers*, namely values that look anomalous in the dataset when compared to the majority of other values. Not surprisingly given the formula of the arithmetic mean, a large outlier raises the mean, whereas a small outlier brings it down.

The Geometric Mean

Opposed to the arithmetic mean, which is based on the sum of N numbers, the geometric mean attempts to discover the tendency of a dataset using the product. The geometric mean is defined as the nth root of the product of N numbers:

$$M_g = \sqrt[N]{\prod_{i=1}^{N} x_i}$$

The geometric mean has a couple of glitches.

First, if the dataset contains even a single value of 0, the entire mean is 0. Second, the geometric mean is computable only for positive numbers, and small numbers have a much larger impact on it than big numbers. For example, a small outlier can take the final average value down significantly.

In addition, the arithmetic mean is always greater or equal to the geometric mean, and the two coincide only if the collection of values taken into account is made by a single number repeated *N* times.

The Harmonic Mean

The harmonic mean is defined as the reciprocal of the arithmetic mean of the reciprocals of the single value. Sound complicated? Not much when you look at the actual formula:

$$M_h = \frac{n}{\sum_{i=1}^{n} \frac{1}{x_i}}$$

The harmonic mean looks a lot like the arithmetic mean, but it is much more influenced by small outliers than larger ones as is the case with the arithmetic mean.

Often, the harmonic mean is the least of the three Pythagorean means. To make it the least, in fact, it suffices that for all positive values in a dataset, there's just one pair of nonequal values. Given this, it turns out that typically the arithmetic mean is the highest, and the geometric mean is in between.

The Mode in Statistics

In statistics, the mode is the value (or the values) that appears more often in a dataset, and subsequently, it is the value with the highest frequency and the highest chance to be sampled. A dataset with two (or three) values that appear with the highest frequency is called *bimodal* (or *trimodal* or *multimodal*). Note, however, that multiple mode values might be the symptom of too sparse values and limited homogeneity.

Measure of Central Tendency

Like mean and median, the mode is a measure of central tendency, and as such, it can't be effectively represented by a value that sits at the beginning of a dataset. A measure of central tendency represents the typical value (or center point) of a dataset. For this reason, when the mode value coincides with the first (or the last) value in the dataset, it is commonly ignored.

It is thought that a measure of central tendency is significant only when placed in the middle of a distribution of values and gives an idea of their order of magnitude.

Graphical Representation of the Mode

As an example, let's consider the following dataset:

```
17, 12, 12, 21, 33, 21, 21, 12
```

The most frequent numbers in the dataset are 12 and 21 appearing three times. Hence, the dataset is a bimodal distribution of values, and the two modes are 12 and 21. For your information, the arithmetic mean of the dataset is 18.625.

Even with only eight numbers, it is quite problematic to spot the most frequent values. For this reason, alternative representations of the dataset have been introduced to quickly spot interesting densities. The most popular is the histogram, as in Figure 9-1.

12	21		
12	21		
17	12	21	33

FIGURE 9-1 The previous dataset represented as a very basic form of a histogram

A histogram is similar to a bar chart, but it differs for one key aspect. The bar chart is a way to show the relationship between two variables in a dataset. The histogram, instead, presents the data of a single feature. The source values are rendered on the X-axis, whereas the frequency of distinct values goes in the Y-axis. Figure 9-2 presents two sample histograms for modal and bimodal distributions.

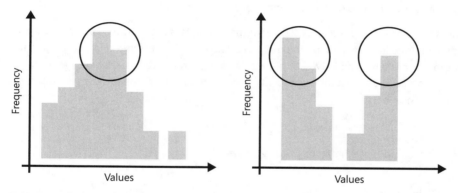

FIGURE 9-2 Two sample histograms for modal and bimodal distributions

The Median in Statistics

At first, the definition of median may seem quite an easy one. The median is just the value that separates a feature in two halves: values smaller than the median (*left tail*) and values greater than the median (*right tail*). So far so good, but the devil is in the details.

More precisely, the median is the number such that any other number in the feature is equally likely to be smaller or greater than it.

The Cumulative Distribution Function

To make sense of the median, we need to introduce the concept of the *cumulative distribution function* (CDF). The function *CDF(x)* expresses the probability (technically, the cumulative frequency) that the feature has a value comprised between the minimum and *x*. The CDF is used to discover the median, and the median is found when the returned value is 50. Figure 9-3 provides a graphical representation of the median in a feature column.

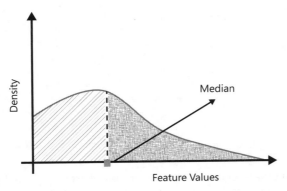

FIGURE 9-3 The areas left and right of the straight line with equation *X=median* are equal

The median is the center of the distribution—a concept that is probably easy to figure out for plain numbers but not for other types of data you may have in a feature.

What makes calculating the median easier for numeric values is that numbers can be easily sorted. In the case of a numeric feature, you get the median by sorting numbers and taking the value that cuts the sequence in two equally sized halves. If the size of the feature is even, you'll have two numbers right at the middle. In this case, you just take both and return their arithmetic mean. As an example, assume the following eight numbers:

12, 12, 12, **17**, **21**, 21, 21, 33

The median is the arithmetic mean of 17 and 21, namely 19.

Properties of Medians

The median is more robust than the mean because it is much less influenced by the presence of outliers. At the same time, though, the median is defined for only one feature at a time, whereas the mean (especially the geometric mean) can be defined for any number of features at a time.

When it comes to informational content and resilience to skewed data, mean, mode, and median show different properties.

- The mode delivers a low quantity of information because it doesn't result from any mathematical calculation. At the same time, though, it is insensitive to outliers, thus showing a significant robustness.

- The mean is not as robust as it is deeply affected by outliers, but it is full of information. Quite often, in fact, the mean is used to fill gaps in the dataset (especially, in time-series datasets).

- The median is right in the middle of mean and mode when it comes to information and robustness.

It is interesting to note that a particular data distribution exists where mean, mode, and median just coincide. This data distribution is known as the Gaussian distribution or just normal distribution. (See Figure 9-4.)

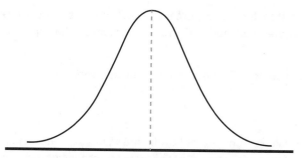

FIGURE 9-4 The representation of a Gaussian distribution

Quartiles

The median breaks up the feature in two parts. Another common way to break up the feature is through *quartiles*. Quartiles break up the feature in three segments of equal density. The median is ultimately the second quartile.

The first quartile is the value such that the likelihood for a number in the feature to fall left of it is up to 25 percent. The second quartile (or median) is the value such that the likelihood for a number in the dataset to fall left of it is 50 percent. Finally, the third quartile is the value such that the likelihood for a number in the dataset to fall right of it is again up to 25 percent. (See Figure 9-5.)

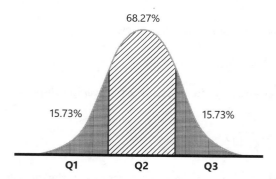

FIGURE 9-5 Three quartiles rendered around a distribution of data

Quartiles are useful to deliver information in a rather immediate way. The term *interquartile range* is often used to indicate the difference between the first and third quartile, which corresponds to the area of the central quartile or median.

Bias and Variance

The fundamental tools of statistics, such as mean, mode, and median, can certainly provide enough information about the order of magnitude of the values in the feature. None of these tools, however, can tell much about the distribution of the various values in the feature.

A common question to answer is: how distant are values from the mean? The question is relevant in machine learning modeling because it indicates the amount of error you may incur when approximating effective values with their mean.

The mathematical tool to deal with the distance of values from their mean is *variance*.

The Variance in Statistics

In strict statistics terms, the variance is the value that measures how far the values in a dataset fall from their average value. In the broader scope of machine learning, variance measures the distance between what the model can predict in production and what it has learned to predict based on training data. In other words, the variance is the primary tool to evaluate the goodness of a trained model.

Formalizing the Dispersion

The variance is the measure of an error. Specifically, the error indicates the distance between the values in the feature and their mean. Let's explore the different ways to measure the distance.

A first approach to measure the dispersion in a feature consists of calculating the difference between maximum and minimum values and dividing by two:

$$D = \frac{X_{max} - X_{min}}{2}$$

The simple difference between minimum and maximum value is also known as *range*:

$$R = X_{max} - X_{min}$$

Both forms of dispersion are not particularly precise. A better measure is the *average absolute deviation*:

$$\overline{|X - \tilde{X}|} = \frac{1}{N}\sum_{i=1}^{N}|X_i - \tilde{X}|$$

In the formula, $\tilde{X}$ represents the arithmetic mean of the feature X and X_i represents the ith element of the feature. Overall, the formula calculates the arithmetic mean of the absolute value of single errors. Again, in this context, the error is the distance between the actual value and the mean of the entire feature. Note that taking the absolute value is crucial to avoid errors with different signs balancing, thus producing false information.

Variance and Standard Deviation

The concept of *variance* goes only one step further. All you do is replace the absolute value of the error with the square value. Here's the formula for the variance of a feature X:

$$Var(X) = \frac{\sum_{i=1}^{N}(X_i - \tilde{X})^2}{N}$$

The variance of a feature X is also referred to as σ_X^2.

Using the square of the error provides a couple of benefits. First, you reduce the impact of small errors because the square of small numbers is even smaller. Second, you obtain an object that is easier to work with from a purely mathematical point of view. (The function "absolute value" is not differentiable in at least one point and differentiability is useful to minimize functions.)

In addition, by taking the square root of the variance, you obtain the *standard deviation*:

$$\sigma_X = \sqrt{\frac{\sum_{i=1}^{N}(X_i - \tilde{X})^2}{N}}$$

In summary, the variance is the estimation of how far a column of data spreads out from the average value. This basic definition is sufficient to assign variance a central role in data analysis, of which machine learning is the ultimate offspring.

A Slightly Different Formula

The majority of statistics books present a different formula for the standard deviation. The difference is the $N-1$ in the denominator:

$$\sigma_X = \sqrt{\frac{\sum_{i=1}^{N}(X_i - \tilde{X})^2}{N-1}}$$

There is one key reason for using $N-1$.

In statistics, you constantly work only with data samples (never with all possible data), and using a smaller denominator in the formula increases the standard deviation and subsequently the level of uncertainty. Why -1 and not, say, -2 then? The answer requires a deeper level of statistics. Technically, the short answer is that only with $N-1$ can you obtain an *unbiased estimator*.

In addition, it is interesting to note that in the edge case in which $N=1$—therefore, the feature is made by a single value—the standard deviation would be impossible to calculate. This makes perfect sense because you would be in a situation of full uncertainty due to a dramatic lack of data.

Anyway, in the case of very large datasets (as would be the case in machine learning), N or $N-1$ doesn't make any significant difference.

At this point, an interesting question is: why are we using the arithmetic mean to calculate the dispersion instead of, say, the median? The arithmetic mean has an interesting aspect summarized in the following formula:

$$\sum_{i=1}^{N}(X_i - M_a) = 0$$

The sum of all errors—namely, the difference between a feature value and the mean—equals 0. From here, you find that the following function is minimal for $c = M_a$:

$$\sum_{i=1}^{N}(X_i - c)^2$$

In other words, the arithmetic mean minimizes the sum of errors and then the standard deviation.

Expected Value

Another way to define the variance is through the concept of *expected value*. The expected value is nothing but the arithmetic mean. The expression $\mathbb{E}[X]$ indicates the expected value of a feature X. In light of this, the variance can be expressed as the expected value of the standard deviation:

$$\mathbb{E}[(X - \mathbb{E}[X])^2]$$

Here, you consider the mean of the square of difference between the values in the feature X and the mean. This is an equivalent formulation of variance with a key benefit: it makes it easier to calculate the variance. In fact, the formula can be rewritten as follows:

$$\sigma_x^2 = \mathbb{E}[X^2] - \mathbb{E}[X]^2$$

In this case, in fact, you can get the variance by simply calculating the mean of a feature and making a few square operations without calculating errors and taking square roots.

The Bias in Statistics

In general terms, the bias is any unjustified factor applied during an evaluation in favor, or against, the entity being evaluated. A biased judgment is, in fact, considered unfair because it is reckoned potentially erroneous. In statistics, it is nearly the same.

Estimator and Bias

The *estimator* $\hat{X}$ of a feature X is the function capable of predicting the value of a feature based on some observed data. The *bias* of an estimator is the error between the predicted value and the actual value:

$$Bias[\hat{X}] = \mathbb{E}[\hat{X} - X] = \mathbb{E}[\hat{X}] - X$$

The bias of an estimator is therefore the mean of the differences between the predicted value and the feature value. Technically, it is not impossible for this error to be zero; but it never happens realistically.

Mean Squared Error

Let's look at another concept—the *mean squared error* (MSE) of an estimator. MSE measures the mean of the (squared) difference between the mean of all the prediction and the mean of all feature values:

$$MSE[\hat{X}] = \mathbb{E}[(\hat{X} - X)^2] = \frac{\sum_{i=1}^{N}(\hat{X}_i - X_i)^2}{N}$$

Isn't it the same as variance? The variance of an estimator measures the distance between the prediction and the mean. The MSE, instead, measures the distance between the prediction and the real feature value (also referred to as the *true parameter*).

In the end, the MSE depends on both the variance and the bias. Not coincidentally, an alternative formula to calculate it is the following:

$$MSE[\hat{X}] = Var[\hat{X}] + Bias^2[\hat{X}]$$

Note that in those circumstances in which the estimator is unbiased, MSE and variance coincide.

Data Representation

The ultimate output of statistical analysis is the provision of a (significant) summary of observed data. There are a few common ways to represent data. They are

- Five-number summary
- Scatter plots
- Multidimensional analysis

Let's get into a bit more detail.

Five-number Summary

As the name suggests, the *five-number summary* is the collection of five relevant pieces of statistical information collected from a feature. They are

- Minimum value in the feature
- Value of the first quartile
- Median (value of the second quartile)
- Value of the third quartile
- Maximum value in the feature

These five numbers let analysts form an immediate idea about two datasets and compare two or more at just a glance. A five-number summary is often graphically rendered with a chart called a *box plot.*

A box plot is made by a box whose width represents the interquartile range (the median) connected at sides with segments ending with the minimum and maximum of the value. (See Figure 9-6.)

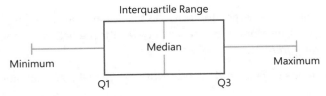

FIGURE 9-6 Schema of a box plot

With box plots, comparing the relevant facts of two features is immediate whether it is the values of two distinct features in the same dataset or the values of the same feature in different datasets taken from the same source in different moments. Figure 9-7 compares two box plots.

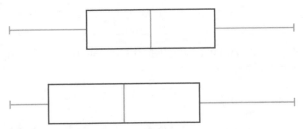

FIGURE 9-7 At-a-glance comparison of five-number summaries of two features

Histograms

A histogram is the representation of the distribution of numerical data and results from the union of bars of different heights. Each bar represents a range of values, and the height of the bar measures the density of values in that range.

A histogram is commonly used for univariate analysis performed on the values of a single feature. In this case, the X-axis shows the values of the feature and the Y-axis renders the frequency of each value. However, a histogram can also be used to render the relationship between two features in a dataset. In this case, the X-axis takes the value of one feature, and the Y-axis takes the values of the other feature. This is multivariate analysis. For example, in real estate you can have a histogram where the X-axis presents the square footage and the Y-axis has prices. (See Figure 9-8.)

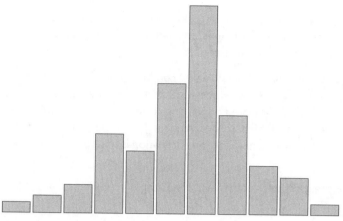

FIGURE 9-8 A sample histogram

If the represented variable takes continuous values, the histogram turns into a curve. If the values are categorical, the histogram turns into a bar chart.

The layout of the highest bars determines the symmetry of the histogram. The more the highest bars are in the middle of the histogram, the more the histogram is balanced and the mean is close to the median. Such a histogram is symmetric. Otherwise, the histogram has some distortion. (See Figure 9-9.)

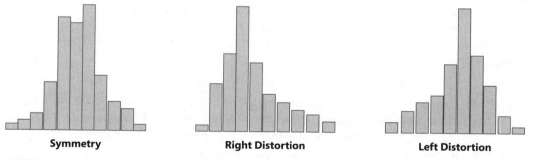

| Symmetry | Right Distortion | Left Distortion |

FIGURE 9-9 Symmetry and distortion in histograms

A histogram has a coefficient of symmetry that results from a well-known formula that would be uselessly complex to explain here. Anyway, what's interesting is the value the formula may return for a given histogram. If the value is between −0.5 and 0.5, the histogram (and subsequently the distribution of values in the feature it represents) is considered symmetric. If the coefficient is between −1 and −0.5, the distribution is moderately distorted on the right, and if it is between 0.5 and 1, the distribution is moderately distorted on the left. Outside −1 and 1, the distribution is considered significantly distorted.

Scatter Plots

Histograms are a valid option if the number of pairs in the Cartesian plane is not huge; otherwise, a different type of plot is preferable—for example, the scatter plot.

The scatter plot renders in a Cartesian plane all possible (x,y) combinations of the values that two observed variables (i.e., two features) take at the same time. Most of the time, the scatter plot is created to learn whether the rendered variables are correlated or not. The correlation may be positive—one grows when the other grows—or negative. In this case, one variable grows when the other decreases. The two variables can also be independent, meaning that no correlation is observed between their respective values.

The following formula defines the *covariance* of two features X and Y:

$$Cov(X,Y) := \sigma_{X,Y} = \frac{\sum_{i=1}^{N}(X_i - \tilde{X})^2(Y_i - \tilde{Y})^2}{N}$$

The covariance is the mean of the product of the squared errors of the features X and Y. This value gives an idea of how the two variables go together. The next formula instead defines the *correlation* between two features X and Y:

$$Corr(X,Y) := \rho_{X,Y} = \frac{Cov(X,Y)}{\sqrt{Var(X)Var(Y)}}$$

Correlation measures both the strength and direction of the (linear) relationship between values in two features. As you can see, correlation is a function of the covariance. It turns out that the covariance of a feature with itself is always 1, and two fully independent features have covariance equal to 0. Intuitively, the greater the covariance, the more the value of one feature helps predicting the value of the other.

> **Note** The concept of two fully independent variables is not completely accurate. It is more precise to say that the covariance is 0 in case of two *stochastically* independent variables. Stochastic is the attribute of a variable that has a probability distribution that can be analyzed through statistics but not predicted accurately.

Scatter Plot Matrices

Technically, a scatter plot is not limited to a single pair of variables. For example, using plots of different colors, you can render multiple variables in the same chart. However, what if you want to explore the correlation between three or more variables?

For three variables, you can try to render in a 3D space with the help of ad hoc software programs. For more than three variables, things are a bit more problematic. One workaround consists of rendering the first three variables in a regular 3D space. The value of the remaining variables is then turned into some sort of scalar transformation that results in a shade of the color. The color is treated like a fourth dimension whose value summarizes the values of all other variables.

Another workaround consists of using a scatter plot matrix.

With K variables to render, you build a K×K matrix and put on the nth row the values of the nth variable combined with all the others. The pairs on the diagonal are skipped as they plot the relationship of each variable with itself. (See Figure 9-10.)

Variables V1 - V1	Variables V1 - V2	Variables V1 - V3	Variables V1 - V4	Variables V1 - V5
Variables V2 - V1	Variables V2 - V2	Variables V2 - V3	Variables V2 - V4	Variables V2 - V5
Variables V3 - V1	Variables V3 - V2	Variables V3 - V3	Variables V3 - V4	Variables V3 - V5
Variables V4 - V1	Variables V4 - V2	Variables V4 - V3	Variables V4 - V4	Variables V4 - V5
Variables V5 - V1	Variables V5 - V2	Variables V5 - V3	Variables V5 - V4	Variables V5 - V5

FIGURE 9-10 A sample 5×5 scatter plot matrix

Plotting at the Appropriate Scale

All charts can help to spot symmetries, anomalies, and otherwise hidden dependencies visually. Needless to say, those aspects can also be noticed analytically, but as the common wisdom reminds, a picture is always worth a thousand words.

When you are plotting, the scale of values is critical. Suppose that the values in a column fall in a very large interval—10,000, 300,000, 1,000,000, or maybe hundreds of millions. The final chart won't likely fit in any monitor you may have, and even if it did fit, it would likely be nearly unintelligible.

The apt workaround for this problem is the use of a logarithmic, or semi-logarithmic, scale.

Usually, plotted charts follow a linear scale, meaning that dots on the X- or Y-axis are evenly distributed, and the distance between 1 and 10 is the same as between 100 and 110. In a logarithmic scale, instead, the dots follow the values of the logarithm function, most typically the log10 function. Concretely, a value of x is represented as if it were *log(x)*. Does this make a difference? You bet!

A value of 1 is represented as *log(1)*, which is 0. A value of 10 is represented as *log(10)*, which is 1. Even more interestingly, a value of 50 is rendered as *log(50)*, which is 1.69. (See Figure 9-11.)

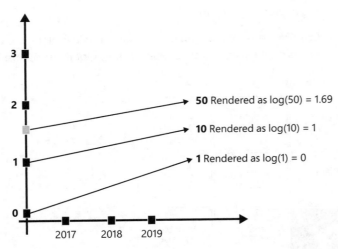

FIGURE 9-11 A sample logarithmic scale

In brief, a logarithmic scale reduces wide-ranging quantities to tiny scopes, thus making plotting far easier and sustainable.

Summary

Machine learning doesn't do any magic but simply leverages the hidden power of statistics. In this chapter, we just scratched the surface of the math (and the statistics) that provides the foundation for machine learning and data analysis.

We first reviewed some basic tools, such as the various means, the mode, and the median. Next, we covered variance and bias and ended with the tools for the visual representation of the content of a dataset: five-number summary, box plot, scatter plot, and scatter plot matrix.

In the next chapter, we'll touch on the metrics useful to evaluate machine learning models, such as data normalization, regularization, and confusion metrics.

## CHAPTER 10

Metrics of Machine Learning

Young man, in mathematics you don't understand things. You just get used to them.

—*John von Neumann*

At its core, machine learning is about devising, and then building, a software model that can predict a result given some input data. The key difference with any other kind of classic software is that the software behind a machine learning model doesn't walk its way through a set of predetermined logical routes. The software behind a machine learning model is opaque in the sense that it gives a result, but the steps taken to produce it are not visible and interpretable as the source code of a canonical routine.

You can see a machine learning model as a mathematical function that produces output as a prediction, and you want the distance between the produced output and the expected output to be minimal. Therefore, the major challenge of machine learning is finding a model (i.e., a mathematical function) that produces output with the smallest possible error.

In the preceding chapter, we presented a number of statistical tools and techniques that are relevant in machine learning. Most of the alleged "magic" performed by machine learning is based on statistics. But where's the boundary between statistics and machine learning? Are they the same thing? Does one include the other?

Let's find out more about the steps that lead from statistics to machine learning models and how to ultimately evaluate the goodness of a model.

Statistics vs. Machine Learning

First and foremost, statistics and machine learning are not the same thing although they are strictly related, in much the same way mathematics and physics are not the same thing but are tightly interconnected. For the most part, machine learning stems from statistics, but a further evolution of machine learning brings new energy to statistics in much the same way that in the past some observations from physics (specifically, the study of heat transfer) turned into a brand-new area of mathematical research (specifically, the Fourier analysis).

Statistics and machine learning, though, are profoundly different when it comes to their respective ultimate goals.

The Ultimate Goal of Machine Learning

The ultimate goal of statistics is learning about the properties of some input data. Statistical inference is, in fact, just the process of data analysis that aims at finding hidden relationships between existing segments of data. Understanding these relationships is the true objective of statistics. Predicting future occurrences of data is not a declared goal of statistics even though it is nearly a happy coincidence once the underlying model has been inferred.

Machine learning has a different ultimate goal.

Effective Predictions over Full Understanding of Data

The ultimate goal of machine learning is making predictions. Predictions must be as exact as possible and can be made only when starting with existing data. What is the difference with statistics then? In a way, it's the same difference between theory and practice.

Statistics is about finding the theoretical model that explains the existing data. Machine learning is about finding a practical model that allows you to make good-enough predictions. The model doesn't have to be the perfect theoretical model; it just needs to be good enough at making predictions.

In statistics, researchers work on a source dataset with a number of features. The whole dataset is dissected to find relationships between features. Only occasionally researchers test the model on data outside the source dataset. In machine learning, things go in a significantly different way.

In machine learning, the model is elaborated based on a subset of the source dataset, called the *training set*. The created model is trained to make predictions based on the relationships inferred from the training set. The remaining part of the source dataset (the *test set*) is used to verify the effectiveness of the model. The ultimate goal of machine learning, then, is making good predictions both on the training set (easy) and test set (not so easy).

Good-enough Predictions

The machine learning model is a black box that ingests data and returns predictions. It's not an open and transparent mathematical box as in statistics, but it's an opaque and complex (to some extent, even unintelligible) box that has learned to make good-enough predictions. Sometimes a machine learning model just works. When it doesn't work well enough, however, fixing it is mostly a matter of fine-tuning parameters, which means essentially taking a stab in the dark with no clear idea of why increasing (or decreasing) a given value delivers a given result.

The whole point of this chapter is to go through the consolidated practices of measuring the performance of a machine learning model. Put another way, in this chapter we'll go through the consolidated practices for deciding if the predictions you get from a model are good enough.

In general, we'll use the term *machine learning algorithm* to indicate the sequence of steps that produce a model for making predictions. In this regard, the model is the implementation of the *estimator* concept of a feature, as you saw it in the previous chapter. As a reminder, the estimator of a feature is the function capable of predicting the value of the feature based on some observed data.

> **Note** The reality of machine learning is that it just works, but it's not completely clear why it works. It's not pure magic though, and it doesn't strictly need a coherent and fully determined statistical model. Probably, the truly theoretical foundation of machine learning lies more in chaos theory than in statistics, but nobody has yet found concrete evidence for this speculation.

From Statistical Models to Machine Learning Models

A machine learning model is expressed by a mathematical function. This function takes input values from a training set and returns results that must be in line with expected values of the test set (in case of supervised learning) and coherent with the user expectations in case of unsupervised learning.

To find out more about the nature of this mathematical function, let's start from relationships between features in the training set. There are two classes of relationships: simple and not-so-simple.

Simple Relationships

In a perfect world, a relationship between two features X and Y is constant, free of uncontrollable elements, and not subject to error. Such a relationship is expressed with a function f such that

$$Y = f(X)$$

The function f is some mathematical transformation applied to X. In the real world, things are different, however. First and foremost, in the real world you hardly have a simple relationship of just two features. Most of the time, in fact, the number of features involved in an appropriate definition of the problem is much greater than two.

The right formula for f has to be guessed, so you use statistical methods to progressively approximate it. (This is what you do through algorithms like those discussed starting with the next chapter.) In addition, in the real world the equation for f has an additional term E for the error. The error is made of two parts: reducible and irreducible errors.

$$Y = f(X) + E$$

What machine learning provides, therefore, is not the ideal function f that fully describes the relationships between the features in the dataset, but an estimate of it. The reducible error is the error arising from the mismatch between the ideal function f and its estimate. The gap between the values returned by the ideal function and its approximation can be reduced by improving the composition of the estimator function.

The Irreducible Error

The origin of irreducible error is subtler. The irreducible error is due to the fact that X doesn't completely determine Y. In other words, the feature Y is mostly determined by X, but some other variables exist (outside X and independently from X) that still influence Y. The irreducible error is not reducible by successive approximation of the model, but only by identifying those influencers and making them part of the training set.

Let's work out a concrete scenario that shows the impact of the irreducible error.

Suppose you're developing a model to estimate the impact of different doses of some medicines on patients. The dataset will have columns with the different doses of the various medicines and expected features with the health parameters of the patients. Now, are the health indicators of a particular patient absolutely reliable? What if that patient had measured parameters altered by uncontrolled conditions such as allergies? Recorded health parameters are reliable, but they may not be completely determined by medications taken. As you can see, there's a lot of uncertainty hidden in a real-world relationship: measurement errors, dependency on multiple features, uncontrollable conditions.

An irreducible error can be removed only if its source is clearly identified and incorporated as a feature in the dataset. Aside from this, the best you can do is to focus on reducible errors.

Complex Relationships

As mentioned, you never have relationships of two features only. Most of the time, the relationship is expressed by the following formula:

$$Y \approx f(X1) + f(X2) + f(X3) + f(X4) + \ldots$$

Note the use of the symbol $\approx$ in the formula in lieu of the more familiar symbol of equality (=). By convention, the symbol $\approx$ is already the indicator of some nonzero error. In other words, Y is almost entirely determined by the function f applied to $X1$ and a number of other features:

$$Y \approx \alpha X1 + \beta X2 + \gamma X3 + \delta X4 + K$$

As you can see, in this case features $X1$ through $X4$ are multiplied by a coefficient expressed with a Greek letter. In addition, the formula also has a constant term, which could be zero but is not the error. For simplicity (and to have a nice graphical rendering), let's consider a linear relationship between two features. The formula is well represented by a straight line:

$$Y \approx \alpha X1 + K$$

Figure 10-1 shows a sample chart for the preceding function.

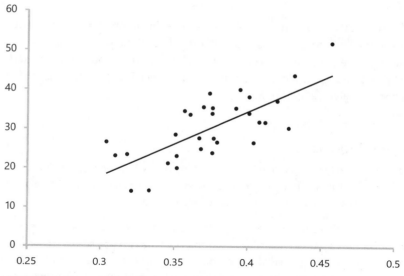

FIGURE 10-1 Linear relationship between two features

It's easy to spot errors because not all points resulting from the relationship between *X* and *Y* belong to the straight line. Yet, the straight line gives a quite clear idea of the ongoing trend of the relationship. Therefore, to reduce the error, you need to find a better-fitting line (in general, a different function) that collects the largest number of points. In doing so, you could even act on the constant elements of the formula (α and *K*) and modify the slope of the line.

However, not all relationships are linear like the preceding one.

In many real cases, in fact, you need to work with polynomial relationships or even exponential relationships. Exponential relationships, for example, express the dynamics of compound interests on loans. Other necessary relationships may be dependent on angles and then on trigonometric functions like sine and cosine.

Evaluation of a Machine Learning Model

What if the painstakingly devised machine learning model is not as precise as you wish? What does precision mean exactly? If you look at the chart in Figure 10-1, you can see that the natural definition of "precision" brings the line as close as possible to all plotted points. But can you bend the line into something like a curve that touches on all the plotted points?

From Dataset to Predictions

In general, the answer to the preceding question is yes, but it is not a good idea to warp and distort the model (the line in the example) to make it blindly fit a given training dataset (the set of points in the example).

> **Note** A straight line is just what its name says it is—a simple line connecting at least two points. Can you make the line more complex so that it touches all the points in a given set? You can use polynomial interpolation and generate a polynomial that touches on a fixed number of distinct points. For example, the Lagrange polynomial is the polynomial of lowest degree that does just that given a feature X.

Linear and Nonlinear Models

The ultimate purpose of machine learning is actively researching a way to predict the value of a feature looking at the value of other features. There's more to it though, as you also expect the final model to be able to effectively predict results from input features it has never seen before.

The linear model expressed with a straight line is a simple one and fit to only a small number of scenarios. The number of features at stake is usually greater than just the two you see related in a straight line or a polynomial. You can't realistically predict reliably how much rain will fall based only on irradiation or temperature. There are many more variables to consider for a model that can *reliably* predict the rain.

Many times, a linear model is just unfit because the problem to tackle is inherently complex, depending on multiple variables and multiple combinations of (linear and nonlinear) variables.

Dealing with Noise in the Dataset

To evaluate the performance of a machine learning model, you have to carefully consider the noise embedded in the data that you consider to train the model. Let's face it: all real-world data you can work on is dirty. In this context, "dirty" means that data contains irreducible errors coming from random sources, such as measurement inaccuracies and unavoidable impactful conditions.

Sometimes, improving a model to make it fit better to the available data only has the effect of making it fit better to the inherent noise embedded in the dataset. This is where you experience the true difference between statistics and machine learning. In machine learning, all you want is to be able to make reliable predictions. To achieve that, you need a model that, in some way, learns from the provided examples. In production, though, the model will likely never work on the same data it was trained on. Therefore, the more you make the model fit to the training set (inevitably padded with dirty data), the more you teach it about the noise in that specific dataset. In doing so, you teach the model things it will not be able to use in production because the noise will be different in any different dataset.

In other words, the noise in the data doesn't belong to the inherent relationships between the features you ideally want the model to capture.

> **Note** Keep in mind that machine learning models can only capture relationships that exist in the data. At the same time, a machine learning model can identify a relationship between data that doesn't exist but, in some way, returns reliable predictions.

Measuring the Precision of a Model

The precision of a machine learning model is expressed as the distance between the results produced by the model and the expected results. The dataset is split into two subsets. One segment of data is used to train the model while the remaining part is used to test the performance of the model. The precision of the models results from how the model works on the test set. The problem is that if you adapt the model too much on the training dataset, you run the risk that it won't be able to make reliable predictions on data it has not seen before.

To measure the distance between the predictions of the model and the expected results, you use the mean squared error (MSE). Hence, the lowest is the MSE; the most precise is the model. As discussed previously, MSE depends on both the variance and the bias.

Bias/Variance Trade-off

Bias is introduced whenever a model is used to approximate a true relationship. The bias of a model is the mean of the error between predictions and actual values found in the applied dataset. Variance of a model, instead, measures how far predictions fall from the average value in the applied dataset. To measure precision, you calculate the MSE of the model on the training set first. If it's small enough, you proceed to evaluate the model measuring its precision on the test dataset. You expect the MSE on the test dataset to be as similar as possible to the MSE of the training dataset and as close as possible to 0.

There's no guarantee at all that a model with a low MSE on training data will also have a low MSE on the test dataset. If too much of the training dataset (and its noise) was absorbed in the model, the model would likely be unable to generalize its behavior on a new dataset like the test data set. Figure 10-2 shows how bias and variance go as the complexity (or flexibility) of the model grows.

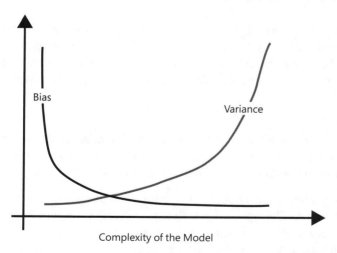

FIGURE 10-2 Curves describing bias and variance of a machine learning model

To reduce the bias, you can add complexity (or flexibility) to the model. Essentially, this means that you add details to the model that make it closer to the training set. In doing so, though, you tend to increase the variance of the model as the model absorbs too many details specific to the training dataset and will likely fail when making predictions on a different dataset, like the test dataset.

The chart shows that there's room to add flexibility without increasing variance. This is the true essence of training when you're making the model learn about the data. At some point, though, too much flexibility makes the variance grow and then explode. In the end, it's all about finding a trade-off between bias and variance. You use the MSE for this. (See Figure 10-3.)

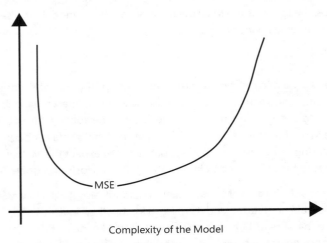

FIGURE 10-3 The MSE resulting from the previous bias and variance curves

As discussed previously, MSE can be calculated as the sum of variance and the square of bias. In light of this, Figure 10-3 shows the curve of the MSE. You are primarily interested in the MSE of the test dataset. You can assume, in fact, that the MSE of the training dataset is good enough; otherwise, you won't proceed to test the model. Finding the trade-off between bias and variance consists in minimizing the MSE function.

Underfitting and Overfitting

A model that returns a bias that is too high on the training dataset is simply a model that doesn't fit. Its predictions are wrong, meaning that the model is wrong—mostly, too simple. You need to change the features and/or change the algorithm. In the literature, this situation is known as *underfitting*.

A model with a good bias on the training dataset but a high variance is one that is not general enough and fits too much the training data. The algorithm is unfit too, as you fail to capture the inner relationships between data. In the literature, this situation is known as *overfitting*. Overfitting occurs when the model has a test MSE much higher than the training MSE.

In a nutshell, adding complexity is fine as long as you can keep variance under control. When variance explodes, the model is no longer reliable. Good bias/variance trade-off is the ideal good balance between underfitting and overfitting. (See Figure 10-4.)

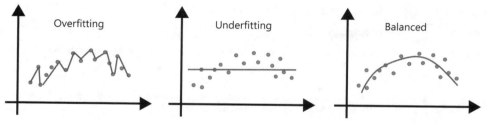

FIGURE 10-4 Comparing overfitting, underfitting, and good balance

Classification and Confusion Matrix

Considerations about bias and variance work well when the predictions you expect from the model are about a feature based on a continuous range of values. What if, instead, yours is a problem of classification and all you need is to determine the category a given record belongs to? In this case, you evaluate the precision of the model through a different tool—the *confusion matrix*.

Let's see how it works in a simple scenario like the binary classification. In this case, you expect the model to make a binary prediction: true or false. Overall, there are four possibilities:

- The model rightly classifies the feature as positive, and it's a true positive (TP) scenario.

- The model wrongly classifies the feature as positive, but it's a false positive (FP) scenario.

- The model wrongly classifies the feature as negative, but it's a false negative (FN) scenario.

- The model rightly classifies the feature as negative, and it's a true negative (TN) scenario.

You can represent the results as a 2×2 confusion matrix (see Figure 10-5). Starting from here, you generate indicators to estimate the precision of the model.

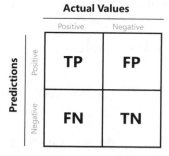

FIGURE 10-5 A sample confusion matrix

The rows of the matrix contain predictions, whereas the columns contain actual values. From here, you can generate three key performance indicators: *accuracy*, *recall*, and *precision*. (See Table 10-1.)

TABLE 10-1 Performance indicators extracted from a confusion matrix

Indicator	Formula	Description
Accuracy	$\dfrac{TP + TN}{Total}$	Indicates how often the model makes good predictions, including positives and negatives
Recall	$\dfrac{TP}{TP + FN}$	Indicates the percentage of true positives the model predicts with respect to the total number of actual positives in the dataset
Precision	$\dfrac{TP}{TP + FP}$	Indicates the percentage of true positives the model predicts with respect to the total number of positives detected

Accuracy is a subtle indicator and might not be truly useful if taken alone. Accuracy measures the percentage of good predictions—that is, when the feature was positive and was recognized as positive, and when it was negative and was recognized as negative. Imagine now you're classifying email messages to spot spam emails. Imagine also that the dataset contains 10 percent of messages that are truly spam. The model could deliver an accuracy of 90 percent without being able to recognize a single spam message as such!

That's why you need also to look at the recall indicator. The *recall* indicator measures how good the model is at identifying true positives (i.e., truly spam messages). Note that the denominator of the *recall* formula contains the sum of true positives and false negatives—namely, the total number of positives in the applied dataset.

Other indicators that can easily be extracted from the confusion matrix are those listed in Table 10-2.

TABLE 10-2 Positive and negative rates from the confusion matrix

Indicator	Formula	Description
True Positive Rate (TPR)	$\dfrac{TP}{TP + FN}$	Measures the proportion of actual positives that are correctly categorized as such. This is the same as *recall*.
True Negative Rate (TNR)	$\dfrac{TN}{TN + FP}$	Measures the proportion of actual negatives that are correctly categorized as such.
False Positive Rate (FPR)	$\dfrac{FP}{FP + TN}$	Measures the proportion of negative events that are wrongly categorized as positive.
False Negative Rate (FNR)	$\dfrac{FN}{FN + TP}$	Measures the proportion of positive events that are wrongly categorized as negative.

Not any indicator is relevant in the same way for just any problem. For a model designed to recognize spam messages, false positives (spam messages detected as regular messages) are largely preferable to false negatives (regular messages classified as spam). For a model designed to evaluate the credit rating instead, a false negative is preferable to a false positive. For a bank, in fact, it is preferable to deny credit to a reliable customer than to concede it to a potentially risky customer.

Cross Validation

The success of a machine learning model depends on its ability to make good predictions on data it has never seen before. To train the model, though, you have only one source dataset. How can you more effectively use the dataset to train the model?

Earlier in the chapter, we hinted at splitting the source dataset in two segments—one for training (approximately two-thirds of it) and one for test purposes. This corresponds to the basic cross-validation technique and is known as *holdout*. Limiting to *holdout* has two drawbacks. First, you use a subset of the available data to train the model. Second, you use a subset of data to test the model and, worse yet, a dataset that might not even be significant. A better approach is to apply the *holdout* technique multiple times. This is the essence of the *k-fold* technique.

In *k-fold*, the source dataset is partitioned into *k* subsets, and then *holdout* validation is repeated *k* times, each time using one of the *k* subsets as the test dataset. In each iteration, the remaining *k-1* subsets are grouped together to provide the training data. The final evaluation is made on the average MSE.

The *k-fold* technique is not subject to underfitting as long the algorithm is a good fit for the problem being tackled because the model is trained using all the available data. In addition, the variance of the model is minimized because the entire dataset is used to test the model. Note that when using *k-fold* with a dataset packed with a relevant percentage of outliers, the outliers are evenly split across all folds to evenly distribute the noise they produce in the data.

There are no strict rules for setting the value of *k*, but 5 and 10 are commonly used values. The *k-fold* technique is taken to its extreme with a variation known as *leave p out*. The *leave-p-out* technique sets a value for *p* and then proceeds to remove *p* elements from the source dataset. Those *p* elements form the test dataset. The value lies in the fact that all possible subsets of *p* elements from the source dataset are processed. As you can guess, with values of *p* larger than 1, the computational costs of the operation may be relevant. With *p*=1 instead, the technique has a lower cost (order of *N*) and is often implemented (the *leave-one-out* technique).

Regularization

Cross validation is not the only approach to avoid overfitting. Another commonly used approach is *regularization*. Regularization is about adding some penalty whenever a new feature is added to the model. Regularization intervenes in the training phase when results are not convincing and you are tempted to add more features to the model to achieve better results. In doing so, the risk is overfitting, namely a model too close to the source dataset.

To try to avoid that, regularization recommends to add a penalty to each new feature. Adding a penalty, however, automatically increases the error, so in the end, it becomes a matter of adding just the features that bring an inherent value and reduce the error. Regularization is a guard against making the model uselessly complex.

Preparing Data for Processing

The actual performance of algorithms also depends on the format of the data with which they work. Think, for example, of sorting algorithms. For some of them, the performance depends on the characteristics of the sequence of input data. The most illustrious example is the Quicksort algorithm, which performs worse if served already sorted data!

In machine learning, things are not much different. Some algorithms work well if trained on data where features have a given mean, few or many outliers, values in a given range, and so forth. Preparing data to obtain the best performance is therefore crucial. There are three main operations you can perform on data: scaling, standardization, and normalization.

Scaling

The purpose of scaling is to change the range of values of a feature without altering the distribution of values. For example, imagine a feature that takes values in the [0,100] range. In this case, a scaling operation can consist of dividing each value by 100, thus shifting the range of values in the 0–1 interval. Among other things, using a [0,1] interval also reduces the amount of memory necessary for the computation. There are two main algorithms for scaling data.

MinMax Scaler

The MinMax scaler is the core algorithm used to change the scale of values. For each value in the feature, the transformation goes through the following steps:

- The value is subtracted from the minimum value of the feature in the dataset.

- The resulting value is divided by the range—namely, the difference between the maximum and minimum value of the feature in the dataset.

The MinMax scaler doesn't alter the distribution of values and maintains the relative distance between values.

Robust Scaler

The robust scaler algorithm aims to reduce the importance of outliers. Each value in the feature is first subtracted from the median, and the result is then divided by the interquartile range (the difference between the third and first quartile). In this way, the distance between values in the scaled feature is reduced, and the relevance of outliers is reduced as their values are shifted closer to the median value.

In doing so, though, the distribution of values in the feature is altered, and the range of values for the feature is larger than what you can obtain with the MinMax scaler. It is worth noting that some algorithms prefer flattened outliers and others suffer with large ranges. For example, regression algorithms work better with smaller ranges. (We'll cover regression in the next chapter.)

Standardization

Standardization is another algorithm that is sometimes classified as a scaler. The standardization process aims at building a feature where the mean is equal to 0 and variance is equal to 1. Again, the reason for standardization is making the operation of some algorithms easier.

For each value in the feature, the standard scaler works by subtracting the mean of the feature and dividing the resulting value by the standard deviation. After this operation is completed, 68 percent of the values fall in the range [−1, 1]. The range of values is larger than the one obtained with the MinMax scaler.

Normalization

Scaling and standardization are algorithms that work on the values of a feature—namely, a column in the dataset. Normalization instead works on the rows of the dataset. There are two types of normalization: L2 and L1.

For each row in the dataset, the L2 normalization works as follows:

- Calculate the sum of squared feature values.

- Take the square root of the result.

The value obtained is known as *norm L2*. As the final step, each feature value in the row is divided by the norm. After all is done, in each row the sum of the square of the feature values equals 1.

The L1 normalization follows the same steps with one key difference: instead of summing the squared values of the features, you consider the absolute value.

A normalized row is useful in all those situations in which you're not much interested in the absolute count of occurrences but in the frequency. As an example, consider a dataset based on sentences in which each feature refers to a given word. The value of the feature is the number of occurrences of the word in the corresponding sentence. Are you interested in the absolute count of occurrences of the word or more in the relative frequency in which it appears? When you opt for the frequency, then you need to normalize the rows of the dataset.

Summary

In this chapter we discussed how to evaluate the performance of a machine learning model and how to modify the source dataset to maximize the performance of any chosen algorithms. A machine learning model is a function that makes predictions. All you want is to make sure to get reliable and precise predictions. The precision of the model is affected by bias and variance. The content of the chapter can be summarized by the following:

- If you face high variance, your model is probably facing overfitting; that is, the model is too close to the training dataset. To reduce variance, you can enlarge the training set, reduce the number of features involved in the calculation, and apply regularization. If you're already applying regularization, increase the penalty.

- If you face high bias, you can add more features in an attempt to add complexity (flexibility) with the declared goal of making the model more general. If it's not enough and you're applying regularization, you can reduce the penalty. If that approach still doesn't work, you might want to consider changing the actual algorithm.

In the following chapters, we'll start delving deep into classes of machine learning algorithms.

How to Make Simple Predictions: Linear Regression

Those who have knowledge, don't predict. Those who predict, don't have knowledge.

—Lao Tzu
(Chinese philosopher and founder of Taoism, sixth century BC)

In machine learning, regression leverages a technique borrowed from statistics to predict output values. Along with classification, regression is the typical choice for problems in which the solution consists of *predicting* output starting from some input. Classification and regression do the same job but with one important difference. The output of regression is numeric and in a continuous range, whereas the output of classification is categorical and based on values that fall in a discrete set.

In all the chapters in Part III, "Fundamentals of Shallow Learning," we will try to follow a fixed outline. First, we will describe the problem that the class of algorithms being presented addresses. Second, we will include some details about the steps of the algorithm.

Note that regression is not a single, well-defined algorithm, but it is more the moniker of a class of different algorithms. In this chapter, we'll cover linear, multilinear, and polynomial algorithms. In a way, the entire area of supervised learning falls under the umbrella of regression and classification as well. Nonlinear regression is, basically, everything else.

Let's start with linear regression.

The Problem

Anything related to predictions is a good fit for regression—for example, estimating real estate prices in a given area. In similar situations, a linear regression algorithm (or multilinear or polynomial) may be a good start for the job. It is hardly, however, the perfect fit.

Guessing Results Guided by Data

Regression is just about identifying some relationship existing between the provided records of data so that when passed other similar data, the algorithm can return reliable results. Don't be scared of hearing, or even using, words or phrases like *guess*, *intuition*, and even *taking a stab in the dark*. As discussed in the preceding chapter, statistics is about extracting a precise model from fixed data; machine learning is just about learning how to make reliable predictions by studying some data that you'll never deal with in production. There's a lot mathematics (mostly statistics) behind machine learning but also harder-to-formalize factors like intuition, experience, gut feeling and, yes, pure luck.

However, the solid foundation of regression (and machine learning algorithms in general) is the dataset. So, in our real estate example, the larger and more detailed the historical record of prices in the area you have, the better.

The Function Hidden in the Data

The ultimate goal of a linear regression algorithm is to identify a mathematical function whose curve closely approximates the (present and future) distribution of data in that specific business domain and bounded context. From this simple sentence, you should be able to see the inherent simplicity of a complex problem.

It's mostly about the data available, the underlying scientist's knowledge of the business domain, and how good you are at restricting it to reduce noise and go deeper. The present data you work on provides a snapshot of some past facts, but the algorithm is called to work on future data. The more bounded is the context, the more chances you have to come up with a reliable prediction mechanism. At the same time, the business that pays for the scientist's effort doesn't much like to be restricted to a relatively small subset of the domain.

The Size of the Context

To form a clear idea about the point we're trying to make here about the correlation between business domain and bounded context in regression, think of a very hot topic these days in the manufacturing industry: predictive analysis of mechanical and electronic parts of engines and industrial machines.

Is it enough to assume that, say, all wind turbines in a given area face physical wear in the same way? Is it enough to assume that wind force is exactly the same for each and every turbine in the area, and so is the same true for humidity, temperature, and air density?

Can you then find a model that predicts when any of the gearboxes of any turbines in the farm are about to fail? Or isn't it more realistic to expect to be able to guess when a component of a single turbine is going to fail? In the former case, you need to find a single regression for the entire wind farm. In the latter, instead, you are restricted to a bounded context of the problem and focus to find a regression function for each and every turbine in the farm—dozens or even hundreds.

Making Hypotheses About the Relationship

Because regression is expressed by a mathematical function, the key question to ask (and answer) is: what kind of function? Is it a straight line? Is it a polynomial? As foregone as the answer may sound, it's a plain and simple trial-and-error kind of thing. You take your first stab in the dark and proceed from what you get.

But there are a few high-level guidelines, however.

Linear and Multilinear Relationships

Past experience and statistical knowledge of the domain may tell you whether the model you're looking for can realistically be linear. Linear regression, in fact, is a possible scenario, but it's not the only one. A linear model is rendered through a straight line, meaning that all the data (present and future) will lay out around the plots of a straight line. If that assumption is correct, it's all about finding the formula of the line.

The concept of linear regression, however, is a bit more general than it may seem at first.

Most of the literature presents examples of linear regression in the bidimensional Cartesian plane. This is mostly a simplification done for the sake of learnability. Let's face it: linear regression in a bidimensional plane works only for toy applications because it would mean having only one feature direct the function of (only) another one. It's definitely possible, but not to tackle a real-world problem.

More in general, a linear relationship is a *multilinear* relationship of the following form:

$$f = c_1 \cdot X_1 + \ldots + c_n \cdot X_n + k$$

Each X_i in the formula is a feature, and each c_i is a coefficient. The preceding linear function therefore represents a straight line but in an *n*-dimensional space. Back to the prediction of real estate prices, multilinear regression would involve features like square footage, neighborhood, number of rooms, and possibly many others. Prediction of taxi fares is another intuitively linear problem in a number of features: predominantly the distance, but also time of the day, traffic conditions, area of the city, day of the week, and so forth.

Multilinear regression is a common scenario, but the vast majority of predictions need a nonlinear model. If you have a gut feeling that a linear model might be a good fit, it is probably worthwhile to investigate that option first.

> **Note** In the rest of the book we'll associate the adjective *linear* with terms like *relationship*, *regression,* and *model* to actually refer to a multilinear relationship, regression, or model.

Does the Linear Model Fit?

So, you assumed that the relationship is linear. What does that mean? It means that errors (or residuals) are nothing more than random fluctuations around the straight line. In other words, the variance remains substantially constant as the predictor processes values.

If the linear model makes sense, errors will have a nearly constant variance and a mean of zero, meaning that their values will be approximately normally distributed. By plotting the errors, you should get something like Figure 11-1 if the model fits.

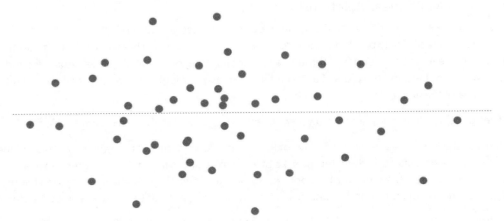

FIGURE 11-1 Errors randomly scattered around the line of zero

Each point plotted in the figure represents an error, and the vertical distance from the center line (where the error is zero) indicates the distance from the expected output. The more those points are normally distributed, the better the linear model fits. Let's look at Figure 11-2 now.

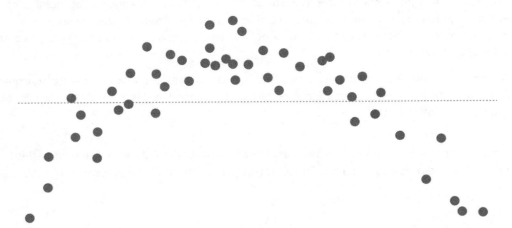

FIGURE 11-2 Plotted errors form a curvature due to systematic overpredictions and underpredictions.

The plotted points form a curve across the line where the error is zero. This indicates that the linear model systematically overpredicts some values and underpredicts some others. It's a sign that the linear model doesn't describe the problem well enough.

In yet another scenario, the distribution of errors forms a mass of points that fan out as the predictor proceeds with values. (This is referred to as *heteroscedasticity*.)

In general, therefore, anything different from a normal distribution of errors is an alarm ringing against the validity of the linear regression model.

Nonlinear Relationships

This point might be obvious, but it's definitely as simple as it sounds: if a relationship is not linear, then it is nonlinear. A nonlinear regression can therefore fit a broad range of curves, whether exponential in the feature or trigonometric or perhaps a sigmoid or a Weibull growth curve. (Polynomials, instead, fall in the linear case.)

Another interesting scenario is logistic regression. In this case, the function takes N input values but returns a dichotomic (e.g., true/false) answer, substantially classifying the input data into one of the predefined categories. A canonical example of logistic regression is determining whether an email message is spam or not. (We've seen logistic regression in action in Chapter 8, "ML.NET Tasks and Algorithms," to determine the sentiment of restaurant reviews.)

The Linear Algorithm

At its core, linear regression is all about finding the equation of the curve that best fits the data. To do that, however, you first need to identify a cost function and then the best way to minimize it. In the beginning, the cost function will have unexpressed coefficients. Finding the ideal values for those coefficients is the purpose of the minimization step.

The General Idea

To get a better visual idea of the next steps, let's start with a simple scenario: linear regression in a bidimensional space. In this case, there will be a single feature to determine the value to predict. It's clearly an unrealistic scenario as if, in predicting the price of a house, you would limit considerations only to, say, square footage, thus ignoring other aspects such as number of rooms and neighborhood. Figure 11-3 gives an idea of what linear regression algorithms do in a bidimensional space.

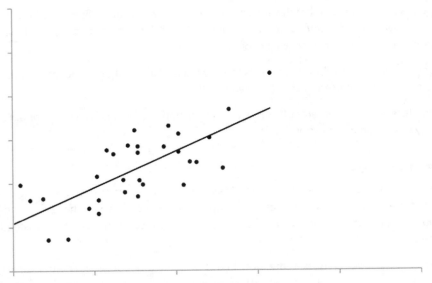

FIGURE 11-3 Truly linear regression in only two dimensions

Quite simply, the regression algorithm looks for the straight line that best fits the given data. A straight line has the following equation:

$$y = mx + b$$

The coefficient m indicates the slope of the line. The value b instead is referred to as the y-intercept and indicates the initial jump of the line in correspondence to the x=0 point.

> **Note** The regression line is unique in the simple bidimensional case but not necessarily in more complex scenarios such as multilinear and polynomial.

Identifying the Cost Function

To find the equation of the best-fit line, you first need to define a function that defines a cost to minimize algorithmically. The cost is the distance between the value the line calculates (predicts) and the expected values as set in the given data.

The Bidimensional Case

To formally express the cost, you use the squared errors to build this function and call it sum of squared error (SSE) or residual sum of squares (RSS). Here's how you define it. N is the number of records in the dataset:

$$SSE = \sum_{1}^{N} \left[y_i - \left(mx_i + b \right) \right]^2$$

Expanding the square of the binomial, you can rewrite the body of the sum as follows:

$$\sum_1^N y_i^2 - 2mx_iy_i - 2by_i + \left(mx_i + b\right)^2$$

And further, you can reformulate it like this:

$$\sum_1^N y_i^2 - 2mx_iy_i - 2by_i + m^2x_i^2 + b^2 + 2mbx_i$$

Note that SSE is equal to the mean square error (MSE) multiplied by the size N of the dataset. This is the same as

$$SSE = \left(y_1^2 + \ldots + y_N^2\right) - 2m\left(x_1y_1 + \ldots + x_Ny_N\right) - 2b\left(y_1 + \ldots + y_N\right) + m^2\left(x_1^2 + \ldots + x_N^2\right) + 2mb\left(x_1 + \ldots + x_N\right) + N \cdot b^2$$

The preceding formula expresses the function to minimize in a bidimensional case.

The Multilinear Case

In the more realistic scenario of multilinear regression, the formulation of SSE you have seen so far is a bit more general:

$$SSE = \sum_1^N \left[y_i - \left(\beta_1x_{1i} + \beta_2x_{2i} + \ldots + \beta_kx_{ki} + b\right)\right]^2$$

Instead of considering a single feature value, you now need to consider a vector of K feature. Put another way, you're shifting from a Cartesian plane (R^2) to an n-dimensional plane (R^k). The coefficients to discover in order to minimize the cost function are $\beta_1 \ldots \beta_k$ and b.

Whether you consider the linear or multilinear scenario, the next step consists of minimizing the cost function. After you identify the values of m (or $\beta_1 \ldots \beta_k$) and b, for which the expression reaches its minimum, you will find the straight line (in the considered space) that best fits the original dataset.

The Ordinary Least Square Algorithm

The first minimization algorithm to consider here is the ordinary least square (OLS) method that Carl Friedrich Gauss devised back in 1801 to calculate the orbit of asteroids.

Minimizing the Linear Cost Function

Let's bring back the definition of arithmetic mean as shown in Chapter 3, "Mapping Problems and Algorithms." $\tilde{Y}$ indicates the mean of the set of expected values Y:

$$\tilde{Y} = \frac{(y_1 + \ldots + y_N)}{N}$$

You can rewrite the equation as follows:

$$\left(y_1 + \ldots + y_N\right) = N \cdot \tilde{Y}$$

Further on, by multiplying every value in the feature X by values in Y, you obtain the mean of a new Z feature:

$$\left(x_1 y_1 + \ldots + x_N y_N\right) = N \cdot \tilde{Z} = N \cdot Mean()$$

The ultimate goal is still formulating the cost function in a way that makes it easier for you to find its minimum. Not coincidentally, the preceding equation matches one of the blocks in the previous cost function. The following equations will also help:

$$\left(y_1^2 + \cdots + y_N^2\right) = N \cdot \widetilde{Y^2}$$
$$\left(x_1^2 + \cdots + x_N^2\right) = N \cdot \widetilde{X^2}$$
$$\left(x_1 + \cdots + x_N\right) = N \cdot \tilde{X}$$

Armed with this information, you can now reformulate the cost function as follows:

$$SSE = N \cdot \widetilde{Y^2} - 2m \cdot N \cdot \tilde{Z} - 2b \cdot N \cdot \tilde{Y} + m^2 \cdot N \cdot \widetilde{X^2} + 2mb \cdot \tilde{X} + N \cdot b^2$$

This is the final function you will try to minimize.

It's now a function of only two variables, m and b. The mean of X, Y, Z, X^2, Y^2, in fact, will be calculated in the beginning and will be then treated as constant values. Most of the time, when rendered in a tridimensional space, the function is a paraboloid, like the sample in Figure 11-4.

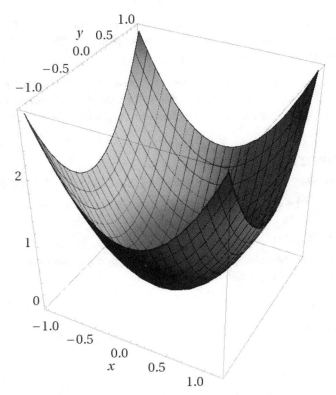

FIGURE 11-4 A paraboloid function like most of the cost functions

Your task is finding the lowest point of such a tridimensional surface. Some review of analysis may help here. In particular, Fermat's theorem ensures that the minimum (and maximum) point of a convex function like this is where the derivative is zero. Hence, let's calculate partial derivatives of *SSE* with respect to *m* and *b* and set them to zero. Here are the partial derivatives for *m*:

$$\frac{\partial SSE}{\partial m} = -2N \cdot \tilde{Z} + 2m \cdot N \cdot \widetilde{X^2} + 2b \cdot N \cdot \tilde{X}$$

And here's the derivative for *b*:

$$\frac{\partial SSE}{\partial b} = 2m \cdot N \cdot \tilde{X} - 2N \cdot \tilde{Y} + 2N \cdot b$$

Next, you can set them equal to zero and divide by 2*N*. You then get the following:

$$m \cdot \widetilde{X^2} = \tilde{Z} - b \cdot \tilde{X}$$

$$b = \tilde{Y} - m \cdot \tilde{X}$$

You know *b*, and if you replace the second expression in the first, you also get *m*:

$$m = \frac{\tilde{Z} - \tilde{X}\tilde{Y}}{\widetilde{X^2} - (\tilde{X})^2}$$

You're done! The actual algorithm will take the dataset, calculate all the necessary mean values, and then find slope (*m*) and y-intercept (*b*) for the minimal cost function. The minimal cost function is the line that best fits the training dataset.

Minimizing the Multilinear Cost Function

Let's look at how things change if we consider the more realistic scenario of a multilinear relationship between features and expected values. The cost function has the following form:

$$Y \approx \beta_1 X_1 + \beta_2 X_2 + \ldots + \beta_K X_K + \theta$$

In the formula, X_i are the feature values (*K* features in total), β_i represent the multidimensional counterpart of the slope, and θ is the counterpart of the y-intercept. In this multilinear case, taking the route of arithmetic mean values won't take you to an equally elegant formulation of the cost function. You can use vectors and matrices instead to represent the cost function.

$$Y \approx \begin{pmatrix} X_1 \\ \vdots \\ X_K \end{pmatrix} \cdot \begin{pmatrix} \beta_1 & \cdots & \beta_K \end{pmatrix} + \begin{pmatrix} \theta_1 \\ \vdots \\ \theta_K \end{pmatrix}$$

Assuming that you have a dataset with *N* rows and *K* features (namely, columns), you can define a matrix as follows, where $X_{i,j}$ indicates the value of the *i*th feature on the *j*th row:

$$A = \begin{pmatrix} X_{1,1} & \cdots & X_{1,K} \\ \vdots & \ddots & \vdots \\ X_{N,1} & \cdots & X_{N,K} \end{pmatrix}$$

As far as the β_i coefficients are concerned, you can group them in a β vector. You can also do the same for expected values grouped in a Y vector.

$$\beta = \begin{pmatrix} \beta_1 \\ \vdots \\ \beta_K \end{pmatrix} \qquad Y = \begin{pmatrix} y_1 \\ \vdots \\ y_N \end{pmatrix}$$

The overall cost function can be now expressed in terms of vectors and matrices like this:

$$A\beta \approx Y$$

To minimize the squared error with respect to β, you have the following:

$$r^2 = \left\| A\beta - Y \right\|^2$$

From here, using derivatives and linear algebra, you finally arrive at the β values that minimize the cost function:

$$\beta = \left(A^T A \right)^{-1} A^T \cdot Y$$

As you can see, β results from a few matrix operations such as multiplication, inverse (finding the matrix that multiplied returns the identity), and transpose (swapping rows and columns).

The Gradient Descent Algorithm

For multivariable mathematical functions, the *gradient* is a sort of a compass that shows the direction of the curve and can be seen as a further generalization of the concept of a derivative. The gradient of a function in three variables looks like the following:

$$Gradient\left(f\left(x, y, z \right) \right) = \frac{\partial f}{\partial x} \hat{x} + \frac{\partial f}{\partial y} \hat{y} + \frac{\partial f}{\partial z} \hat{z}$$

In the preceding definition, $\hat{x}$, $\hat{y}$, $\hat{z}$ represent Cartesian axes as vectors, and each axis plots values from one feature. In the same formula, $\frac{\partial f}{\partial x}$, $\frac{\partial f}{\partial y}$, and $\frac{\partial f}{\partial z}$ are the partial derivatives with respect to the features X, Y, and Z. The gradient is a vector and, subsequently, calculating the gradient is the same as finding a vector.

Note Partial derivatives are derivatives calculated with respect to a specific variable (i.e., a feature) and considering all other variables as constants.

An Example in Three Variables

The gradient is made of derivatives, and derivatives tell how much the function is growing with respect to a given variable. Because of this, the gradient will always move in the direction of the maximum growth of the function. In our scenario, though, we're not interested in maximizing the function, but we want to minimize it. Hence, we move in the exact opposite direction of the gradient.

The gradient descent is an algorithm to find the minimum of a function. It's an iterative algorithm that repeats calculations until the error reaches a fixed threshold, or when the gradient is sufficiently close to zero or when the error calculated at the current iteration is bigger than the last one detected. All these are equivalent conditions to stop the descent of the algorithm.

As an example, let's use two features (X_1 and X_2) to predict a third one indicated with Y. The multilinear model is the following:

$$f = m \cdot X_1 + n \cdot X_2 + b \approx Y$$

You want to use the gradient descent algorithm to find the ideal values of m, n, and b such that the mean squared error (MSE) is minimum. For that to happen, you must be able to calculate the partial derivatives of the MSE cost function with respect to m, n, and b. The MSE cost function is defined as follows:

$$MSE = \frac{1}{N} \sum_{i=1}^{N} \left(y_i - \left(m \cdot X_{1i} + n \cdot X_{2i} + b \right) \right)^2$$

Note that X_{1i} and X_{2i} indicate the ith element of the feature X_1 and X_2. The partial derivatives with respect to the variables you're interested in are

$$\frac{\partial MSE}{\partial m} = \frac{2}{N} \sum_{i=1}^{N} -X_{1i} \cdot \left(y_i - \left(m \cdot X_{1i} + n \cdot X_{2i} + b \right) \right)$$

$$\frac{\partial MSE}{\partial n} = \frac{2}{N} \sum_{i=1}^{N} -X_{2i} \cdot \left(y_i - \left(m \cdot X_{1i} + n \cdot X_{2i} + b \right) \right)$$

$$\frac{\partial MSE}{\partial b} = \frac{2}{N} \sum_{i=1}^{N} -\left(y_i - \left(m \cdot X_{1i} + n \cdot X_{2i} + b \right) \right)$$

The gradient descent algorithm starts assigning a given value to the three variables m, n, and b. It also needs to set a value called the *learning rate* that is indicated here with α. The learning rate indicates how much you move along the direction of the gradient at each iteration. Typically, the value of α is between 0 and 1 and tends to be quite small.

The Actual Algorithm Steps

At each iteration, you recalculate the partial derivative of the MSE function with respect to the variables m, n, and b and then determine the new values of m, n, and b, as follows:

$$m = m - \alpha \frac{\partial MSE}{\partial m}$$

$$n = n - \alpha \frac{\partial MSE}{\partial n}$$

$$b = b - \alpha \frac{\partial MSE}{\partial b}$$

Armed with the new values of *m*, *n*, and *b*, you recalculate the MSE and see if you like it. If not, you make another round. The gradient descent algorithm can be described by the following code:

```
var dataset = ...;
var next_m = 1;   // We start the search at a random point
var next_n = 2;   // We start the search at a random point
var next_b = 3;   // We start the search at a random point

var alpha = 0.01;              // Learning rate
var precision = 0.00001;       // Desired precision
var max_iterations = 10000;    // Maximum number of iterations

var cost = MSE(m, n, b);

for(var i=0; i<max_iterations; i++)
{
    // Set the current point
    var current_m = next_m;
    var current_n = next_n;
    var current_b = next_b;

    // MSE cost function in the current point
    var mse = cost(current_m, current_n, current_b);

    // Get the gradient and proceed in the direction to the next point
    next_m = current_m - alpha * partial_derivative_m(mse, dataset);
    next_n = current_n - alpha * partial_derivative_n(mse, dataset);
    next_b = current_b - alpha * partial_derivative_b(mse, dataset);

    // Calculate the distance between current and previous point
    var step_m = next_m - current_m;
    var step_n = next_n - current_n;
    var step_b = next_b - current_b;

    // Check precision
    if (stop_condition(precision, step_m, step_n, step_b))
        break;
}
```

Essentially, the algorithm proceeds, point after point, along the curve of the MSE function. After a point is reached, the gradient indicates the direction to go (opposite to growth), and the algorithm gets the next point in that direction. In doing so, it uses the value of the learning rate to determine how far it would go. The precision is evaluated, and if it's good enough, the algorithm ends.

The Learning Rate

The value of the coefficient α is crucial. If the learning rate is too small, the algorithm may be slow to reach the minimum and may not be able to get an acceptable value in the given number of iterations. On the other and, if the learning rate is too big, you take the risk of jumping over the value that minimizes the MSE function. This is an even worse problem because if you jump over the minimum, you will never get an acceptable level of precision, which would force you to repeat the algorithm with different parameters. (See Figure 11-5.)

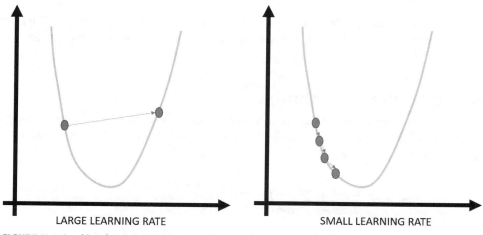

FIGURE 11-5 Looking for the right learning rate

Batch and Minibatch Gradients

As outlined in the script for the algorithm, each iteration of the gradient descent computes the partial derivative of the MSE function on the entire dataset. This is the scenario we have considered so far. A gradient descent algorithm that works over the entire dataset is referred to as *batch* gradient. If the size of the dataset is fairly large, there might be performance issues because computing the derivative for each variable on a large dataset is computationally heavy.

Another flavor of the gradient algorithm is the *stochastic* gradient, which works on a random element of the dataset at each iteration. With reference to the previous script, the following lines are affected:

```
next_m = current_m - alpha * partial_derivative_m(mse, dataset);
next_n = current_n - alpha * partial_derivative_m(mse, dataset);
next_b = current_b - alpha * partial_derivative_m(mse, dataset);
```

Instead of the whole dataset, a stochastic gradient descent would use a random dataset row. The MSE is also affected and would come without the sum and division by N.

Finally, there's also the *minibatch* gradient. In this case, you still don't use the whole dataset but instead use a smaller one made of K randomly selected rows at each iteration.

Important In practical machine learning solutions, you don't really write any algorithm most of the time. You just use existing libraries for the language of choice (mostly Python but lately also .NET) and instruct the library algorithm to behave in one way or the other through parameters. In the end, the whole linear regression approach is reduced to calling a single function from a linked library.

> **Note** Least square and gradient descent are not the only regression algorithms. Other popular algorithms are Stochastic Dual Coordinate Ascent (SDCA) and Poisson regression.

How Good Is the Algorithm?

To evaluate the goodness of a linear regression algorithm, you need an indicator that tells something about how you're capturing the variance of the feature to predict. A commonly used indicator is R-squared and is defined as follows:

$$R\text{ squared} = \frac{Explained\ variation}{Total\ variation\ in\ Y} = \frac{\sum_{i=1}^{N}\left(y_i - \left(m \cdot X_{1i} + n \cdot X_{2i} + b\right)\right)^2}{\sum_{i=1}^{N}\left(y_i - \bar{Y}\right)^2} = \frac{N \cdot MSE}{Var(Y)}$$

In the formula, the explained variation is the MSE of the model, and the total variation is the variance of the feature. The optimal value of R-squared is as close as possible to 1 in the presence of a low value of the MSE.

Improving the Solution

In the real world, linear regression can certainly address some problems, though likely in a multiple number of variables. However, the majority of problems that can be transformed in a prediction need more than a linear model to be effectively modeled. This where the polynomial route starts.

The Polynomial Route

Both the R-squared and the techniques unveiled in the preceding chapter (bias/variance trade-off, confusion matrix, and the like) are helpful to evaluate the model. If they are not good enough, however, one option to take into account is that the linear model is not appropriate for the problem. In Figure 11.6, you see a bunch of points that could be even approximate with a straight line, but probably the precision of the resulting model, though acceptable, would not be that great.

Given the distribution of data, it is hard to find a better line. In this case, you may look into polynomial regression. In polynomial regression, the function for the model is not simply linear, but some of the features are squared or more. The model in the figure is still linear in the coefficients m, n, and b, but not in the features. In the sample scenario in which you have a single feature X_1, the model has the following form:

$$Y \approx m \cdot X_1^2 + n \cdot X_1 + b$$

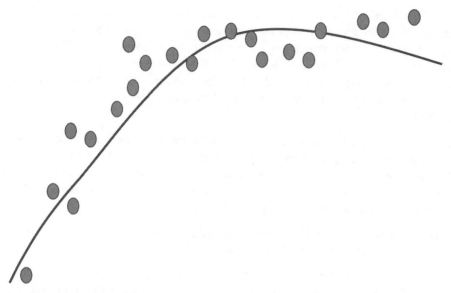

FIGURE 11-6 Polynomial regression

At the end of the day, it's as if you're adding a new feature to the source dataset that contains the values of the feature X_1 just squared. On this modified dataset, you can apply the same linear regression techniques to minimize the cost function. Adding a new feature means increasing the complexity of the model.

Regularization

As you might remember, in the preceding chapter we talked about regularization as the process of adding penalties to the model when a new feature is added, which increases the complexity. The goal, in fact, is having the minimum number of features that are necessary to produce good predictions. You can use regularization to reduce overfitting and minimize complexity.

Let's see what happens if we go with L2 regularization. When L2 is applied to a linear regression algorithm, you have something also called *ridge regression*. In L2, the penalty is given by an increase of the values returned by the error function you want to minimize. The squared error is usually given by the following:

$$ SSE = \sum_{i=1}^{N} \left(y_i - \left(\sum_{j=1}^{K} \beta_j x_{ij} + b \right) \right)^2 $$

In the formula, b is the y-intercept, and β_j values indicate the slope of the various K features. After applying L2 regularization, you end up minimizing the following error function instead:

$$ \sum_{i=1}^{N} \left(y_i - \left(\sum_{j=1}^{K} \beta_j x_{ij} + b \right) \right)^2 + \lambda \sum_{j=1}^{K} \beta_j^2 $$

The formula contains an additional term—the regularization term—that depends on λ. The regularization term sums over squared β values and multiplies the total by λ. With λ equal to zero, you're back to the previous, canonical situation. The net effect of λ is penalizing the SSE function when the model has high values of the coefficients β. The ultimate goal is having a model that is as simple as possible with as few features as possible. With regularization, you add the constraint to the error function that it must also minimize the β values. How this happens depends on the type of regularization chosen.

It is key to note that L2 regularization enforces the β coefficients to be lower, but it doesn't let them be zero. In this regard, it turns out that L2 regularization is good to avoid overfitting, but not to do feature selection. The technique, in fact, will not help identify irrelevant features (those with the β zeroed), but it simply minimizes their impact on the final model. You might end up with a few features of low relevance without tools to determine which one is truly relevant.

Note also that a value of λ that is too high may instead add too much relevance to the β coefficients, ultimately leading to underfitting and a poor model.

If you think you have too many features and want to try to remove some of them, you have to look into the L1 regularization, also known as lasso regression. With L1, the function to minimize takes the following form:

$$\sum_{i=1}^{N} \left(y_i - \left(\sum_{j=1}^{J} \beta_j x_{ij} + b \right) \right)^2 + \lambda \sum_{j=1}^{J} |\beta_j|$$

The interesting thing is that L1 uses absolute values in the regularization term. This difference has a huge impact on what you learn from the technique compared to L2. In particular, minimizing an error function with a term that is the sum of absolute values results in zeroing some of them. In this regard, L1 regularization not only punishes high values of the coefficients β but also sets them to zero when not relevant. Unlike L2, L1 regularization is then ideal to do feature selection in order to simplify a model.

Summary

In dictionaries, the term *shallow* is equated to *not deep* and sometimes to *superficial* or *not serious*, depending on the context. In the context described here, it just means not deep, as opposed to *deep learning*, which we'll cover in the next part focusing on neural networks.

In this chapter, we addressed the regression approach to prediction. Whenever your high-level problem can be reduced to a matter of guessing what could happen based on what has already happened, regression is generally a great fit. There are many faces to regression. In this chapter, we focused on linear, multilinear, and polynomial regression and ways to further optimize results via regularization.

The next chapter is about trees.

## CHAPTER 12

How to Make Complex Predictions and Decisions: Trees

The possible solutions to a given problem emerge as the leaves of a tree, each node representing a point of deliberation and decision.

—Niklaus Wirth
(Creator of the Pascal programming language and winner of the Turing Award in 1984)

In the preceding chapter, we discussed regression as a way to infer the hidden relationship between dependent features and use it to build an effective prediction engine. Regression uses tools from statistics to perform its magic. Well, it's not really magic—it's a pure math matter of minimizing the values of a function that measures the error—but it sometimes really looks like magic in the sense that you get good predictions out of the nowhere of pure mathematical theorems.

The preceding chapter focused on linear and multilinear relationships for continuous values. With a popular data structure like trees, you can go beyond that and cover classification problems and nonlinear relationships.

Conceptually, a tree-based algorithm is fairly simple to understand and doesn't (apparently) hide any complexity. It looks like a flowchart-based decision support tool in which you make a choice at each step and repeat it until you come to a conclusion. A tree-based algorithm is, in a way, fairly close to the perceived way of human reasoning.

In this chapter, we'll focus on two large classes of tree-based meta-algorithms (classification and regression trees) and explore a few specific algorithms.

The Problem

A classification problem is about building a decision tree—for example, estimating whether an individual is prone to a certain disease. In a typical classification problem, you have some input values (i.e., features) and a final decision to be made (i.e., output label). A decision tree works like a flowchart.

It starts from input features and then applies some business-specific logic to navigate in the tree until it reaches a leaf of the tree. The inherently perceived simplicity of the decision tree is based on the fact that any output stems from clear decisions made at each step.

A tree is also a good fit for nonlinear regression problems. The training of a tree-based algorithm iteratively partitions the space of the dataset in regions, ensuring that all elements in each region are as similar and homogeneous as possible. A tree-based algorithm easily and effectively captures nonlinear relationships between rows of data because it doesn't try to guess a function but simply aims at the maximum homogeneity possible in partitioned regions of the dataset. Homogeneity is implemented through an error function so that rows with similar values fall in the same region. In this way, any possible nonlinearity of the relationship is encapsulated in the grouping. You don't actually need to know the formulation of a regression function; you just have a tree-based path that helps make the prediction.

But what is a tree, exactly?

Note In machine learning, trees are also employed in multilevel decision algorithms as weak learners. Trees are easy to train and can capture nonlinear relationships. Their precision can be poor sometimes, but this is where composed models fit in. Random forests and gradient boosting algorithms, in fact, work by combining models created by weak learners like trees into strong learner models. (We'll cover strong learner algorithms in the next chapter.)

What's a Tree, Anyway?

In mathematics, and specifically in graph theory, a *graph* is a collection of nodes and (directed or undirected) links connecting them. Sometimes the term *edge* is used to refer to a pair of nodes connected together. Within a graph, a path indicates the route to go from one node to another.

A tree is a special graph with one root node. The root node is the only unparented node. All other nodes have one inbound and zero or more outbound paths. A node with no children is said to be a *leaf*. Also, links between the nodes of a tree never form a loop. The height of the tree is known as *depth* and is measured by counting the number of nodes laid out vertically. Figure 12-1 shows a sample binary tree. It is said to be binary because each node (except leaves) has exactly two children. The depth of the tree in the figure is three.

As you see in the figure, a tree starts with a single node—the root—and develops into multiple branches, each being the root of a subtree.

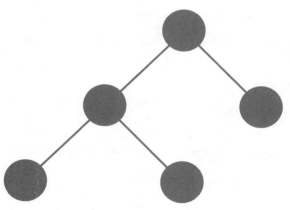

FIGURE 12-1 Sample binary tree

Trees in Machine Learning

In machine learning, a tree can be seen as a journey from one input feature to one of the many possible conclusions.

A tree-based algorithm is implemented as a visit that starts at the root and proceeds to a leaf crossing the depth of the tree. All intermediate nodes represent questions whose answers determine which child of the current node is the next to visit. The visit stops when a leaf is reached. Each node of the tree queries a feature against a particular value, and depending on the value of the input, one of the child nodes is picked up.

How, then, do you choose the feature to query at each step, and how do you pick up the value to split on? Here's an example of how a tree-based algorithm may work.

A Sample Tree-Based Algorithm

To solidify some exposed concepts, let's go through an example of a tree-based decisional process. Suppose you're going to go out, but the outside weather is not completely constant, so you need to make a decision about whether to bring a coat.

At a minimum, you need to answer a few questions. The list of questions is sort of arbitrary, but just asking the right questions can lead to a better model. Here's an example then:

- The first question could be something like "Is it raining?"

- If the answer is Yes, then you simply take a coat and go.

- If the answer is No, then you probably need more information to decide. Another question to answer could be "What's the outside temperature?"

- If the answer is less than 15°C (59°F), then you take a coat and go.

- If the answer, instead, is at least 15°C, you need more details. For example, you might want to ask if a temperature lower than 15°C is forecast in the next two hours.

- If the answer is Yes, you then take the coat.

- If the answer is No, you just go out with no coat.

This process is fairly simple, isn't it? More than anything else, it's close to the human way of reasoning about things. Such a decisional process can be rendered graphically (at least in such simple cases) as shown in Figure 12-2.

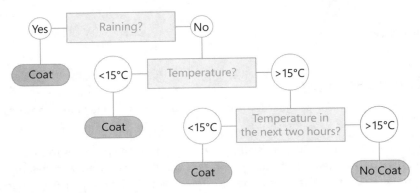

FIGURE 12-2 A tree-like decisional process

In a tree used in a machine learning scenario, each node is a feature, and each step of the visit (referred to as a *split*) is a business question to answer. Each branch from a node is an answer, and each leaf of the tree is a prediction. The prediction can be categorical (like coat/no coat) or continuous.

Each split partitions the dataset in distinct regions so that at each step a clear, univocal decision can be made. For example, <15°C or >=15°C cuts the dataset into two nonoverlapping areas. The reason why partitions (i.e., nonoverlapping areas) are important is that in this way each leaf has a different, unique set of conditions to be reached. Figure 12-3 provides a graphical explanation of this.

The idea that Figure 12-3 conveys is that all the rendered points are the rows in the source dataset, and the partitions are the leaves of the tree. In other words, each row is classified in one of the recognized partitions.

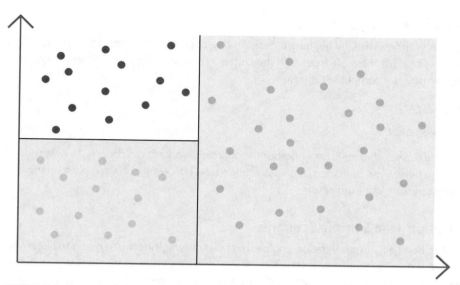

FIGURE 12-3 The area of the dataset partitioned to reflect all possible final decisions

Design Principles for Tree-Based Algorithms

A tree-based algorithm is essentially an algorithm that contains only conditional statements and can be really seen as a plain sequence of *IF* statements. In this, there's a clear resemblance with the way that the human brain works.

Another possible similarity you could get here is with expert systems—the first attempt to build intelligent software for making decisions considering a long (but fixed and hard-coded) list of parameters.

Decision Trees versus Expert Systems

A tree-based algorithm leading to a categorical decision is not the same as an expert system. The main difference is that expert systems are written by humans and are deterministic in what they can predict and how they predict it. In other words, the learning paths of an expert system are hard-coded.

In a tree-based algorithm, instead, the decision tree is built during the training phase. It's the algorithm that figures out how to implement splits and on which values. Back to the previous coat example, it's the algorithm that figures out the ideal temperature to branch on and how long to look ahead for weather forecasts. If you were to come up with an algorithm with those numbers hard-coded (as in the earlier illustrative example), you would have an expert system rather than a machine learning decision tree model.

Flavors of Tree Algorithms

All tree-based algorithms work by building a decision tree to process input data from root to leaves. Two main classes of algorithms use trees, and they differ in how some key parameters like *homogeneity* and *information gain* are computed. They are

■ Classification trees

■ Regression trees

In each of the classes, there will be a number of concrete algorithms to choose. To give some substance to the behavioral principles of a classification tree, let's work out a sample scenario and find out more about performance indicators.

A Classification Tree Sample Scenario

Say you want to build a recommendation engine that predicts whether you're going to like a new movie that comes out. The source dataset will contain a long list of movies you've watched in the past and will have tons of features, such as lead and supporting actors, genre, director, length, language, box office collection, awards won, and other similar things. The dataset also contains an output feature that indicates what you want to predict.

If the prediction can be expressed through a discrete, categorical range of values (e.g., 1 if you really disliked it through 5 if you really liked it), the classification tree is the ideal choice. If the prediction, instead, is a continuous value, a regression tree is the way to go.

With reference to the sample scenario, the (classification) algorithm will figure out how to route the information about a sample movie through consecutive decision points so that all movies with similar characteristics end up on a leaf with the same label (rating). During the training, the algorithm will therefore conceptually split the sample dataset in homogeneous groups. In other words, the vast majority of the movies rated 3 should then be classified in the same group.

To do so, the algorithm has to find out, in some way, why you may rate a movie with 1. It has to find out that you may not like movies directed by a certain name or movies with a certain combination of actors. A good algorithm must be able to figure out if you just can't stand any movies by, say, Woody Allen.

 Note If you build a decision system where you explicitly tell it to rate bad any movie directed by Woody Allen, well, that's not machine learning. That's just an expert system.

Homogeneity

Concepts like information gain and impurity are crucial to help the algorithm decide how to define split conditions and on which features. The goal of the algorithm is to ensure that the training dataset is split in homogeneous groups.

Homogeneity depends on the fact that all rows in the same group have the same level of information gain. Impurity is the measure used at the end of each iteration to determine if the groups obtained are sufficiently homogeneous.

Error Function

How do you measure impurity of grouping? Again, as in the preceding chapter, you need to bring to the table some formal definition of an error.

You can't use the squared error function here (as in the previous chapter) because, given the discrete nature of the output, you would end up with an error function that doesn't describe a continuous curve but rather proceeds by jumps. You need a different approach.

At the end of the algorithm, you want to obtain groups of movies (rows of the sample dataset) labeled 1 through 5, and you want those movies to be realistically labeled something very close to the assigned values 1 through 5. This final homogeneity descends from having homogeneity at each intermediate step when the algorithm does the split. Put another way, you want each split to partition the dataset in two and each group made by movies (rows) with the nearly the same value for the feature evaluated (e.g., the director). Impurity is the definition of the error you are looking for.

So, there are two classes of tree-based algorithms. Let's attack classification trees first.

Classification Trees

A classification tree is able to make predictions about discrete, categorical output (as opposed to continued output values). In a nutshell, a classification tree algorithm answers questions like "Given the present data, which of the following N (>0) facts would you predict?" To answer the question, the algorithm builds a decision tree with a well-identified root and well-known leaves. The power of the algorithm is how it fills the logical space between the root and the leaves—namely, how it operates to split the dataset in homogeneous groups.

The various classification algorithms primarily differ in the way they compute impurity and information gain. There are mainly two algorithms:

- CART (Classification and Regression Trees)

- ID3 (Iterative Dichotomiser 3)

Both algorithms follow the same script but different definitions of impurity.

How the CART Algorithm Works

It's not realistic to aim at perfectly homogeneous groups; therefore, the goal is reducing the impurity at each split as much as possible. The increase of homogeneity you get at each split is called *information gain*. Before we discuss the details of how algorithms calculate information gain and impurity, let's take a quick look at some script that describes the overall process behind a classification tree algorithm. The resulting classification is a binary tree.

Building the Tree Step by Step

When the algorithm starts, the tree is empty and will be built progressively, one split at a time. The actual algorithm for adding nodes to the tree is the same whether the node is the root, a leaf, or an internal node. Here's a high-level description of how it works:

```
var max_depth = 4;
var min_number_of_leaves = 5;
var max_number_of_leaves = 10;
var homegeneity_threshold = 0.97;

var tree = new Tree();
var canStop = false;
while(!canStop)
{
    var root_impurity = calculate_impurity(dataset);
    if (should_stop_based_on(
            tree,
            min_number_of_leaves,
            max_number_of_leaves,
            homegeneity_threshold))
    {
        break;
    }

    var feature_impurity_table = new Dictionary<object, object, object>();
    foreach(var feature in dataset)
    {
        var feasible_values = extract_distinct_values_for(feature);
        foreach(var value in feasible_values)
        {
            var value_impurity_table = new Dictionary<object, object, object>();

            var child_datasets = split_on(feature, value);
            var impurity_node1 = calculate_impurity(child_datasets[0]);
            var impurity_node2 = calculate_impurity(child_datasets[1]);
            var combined_impurity = combine_impurity(impurity_node1, impurity_node2);
            value_impurity_table.Add(feature, value, combined_impurity, child_datasets);
        }

        var best_feature_value_pair = value_impurity_table.Min();
        feature_impurity_table.Add(best_feature_value_pair);
    }

    // Here we have a dictionary with one entry for each feature
    // that relates to the best value for splitting
    var ideal_feature_value = feature_impurity_table.Min();
```

```
// Split on the feature/value pair with the best homogeneity
// and recursively repeat the procedure on the two split datasets
tree.AddNode(ideal_feature_value);
repeat_procedure(ideal_feature_value.child_datasets[0]);
repeat_procedure(ideal_feature_value.child_datasets[1]);
}
```

The algorithm to build the tree is inherently recursive and starts with an empty tree and the entire dataset. Note that the preceding sample script builds the tree in a depth-first, greedy way, but this is not necessarily the way to go because algorithms that use a breadth-first approach instead also exist.

> **Note** The main conceptual difference between depth-first and breadth-first algorithms is that the former type works on one (sub) dataset at a time and greedily tries to optimize it and starts adding leaves sooner. A breadth-first algorithm, instead, would work on two sub-datasets—the left and right node—at the same time.

The Actual Steps

The algorithm sets a few hyperparameters to better control the learning process and decide when to stop it. Typically, they are the minimum and maximum number of leaves, the maximum depth of the tree being built, and an acceptable level of homogeneity in the split datasets.

At each step, the algorithm has to decide which is the most relevant feature (and related value) to start from given the dataset section it is working on. In the beginning, it is the entire dataset. First, the algorithm computes the level of homogeneity of the rows in the dataset. The lower the impurity, the higher the homogeneity. Next, for each feature, it takes all known values the feature assumes in the dataset and tries to split. In other words, the algorithm tries to separate the dataset rows where the feature takes a value less than or equal to the value considered from those where the value is higher. Note that if the feature takes values in a continuous range (and not in a categorical range), instead of looping over all possible values of the feature, the algorithm uses the mean value.

Further on, the algorithm measures the impurity of both child datasets and picks up the feature (and value) that maximizes the information gain. The information gain is a weighted value that results from both the child datasets. The dataset is then split on that pair feature/value, and the two datasets are recursively processed.

At the beginning of the loop, there's some check to stop the algorithm in case the depth of the tree is too high, which would make you at risk of overfitting, or the maximum number of leaves has been reached or a sufficiently good level of homogeneity has been reached. In general, with a too-deep tree, the algorithm would inevitably adapt too much to the training data. At the same time, depth depends on how precise you expect the prediction to be. The deeper the tree, the more precise the prediction can be. It's a trade-off between overfitting and precision.

Important The problem of constructing the optimal decision tree is a known NP-complete problem, based on the work of Ronald Rivest and Laurent Hyafil (1976). A problem belongs to the class of NP problems if it can't be solved in a polynomial time. An NP problem is also said to be NP-complete if (and only if) every other NP problem can be polynomially reduced to it. This said, however, a number of (greedy) optimizations exist to make the building of an acceptably good decision tree feasible in a relatively quick (polynomial) time.

Information Gain and Impurity

Classification trees measure the inequality of the data distribution (impurity) in a dataset through an index called the Gini index, from the name of the Italian statistician Corrado Gini. The Gini index for a (sub) dataset S is given by the following formula:

$$Gini(S) = 1 - \sum_{i=1}^{K} P_i^2$$

In the formula, K is the number of the possible categories, and P_i is the frequency of elements in the dataset with the given value. In the movie example, K equals 5, the number of allowed rates. As an example, if the dataset has 20 movies, 8 of which rated 1, 3 rated 2, and 9 rated 4, the Gini index is the following:

$$Gini(S) = 1 - \left(\frac{8}{20}\right)^2 - \left(\frac{3}{20}\right)^2 - \left(\frac{9}{20}\right)^2 = 1 - 0.385 = 0.615$$

Let's try to figure out the whys and wherefores of the formula using a simpler scenario of binary classification. Predictions can have only two values, 0 or 1. In a complete partition, the sum of all frequencies is just 1 because the completeness of the partition covers all possible cases. For a binary classification, you then have the following:

$$(False\ Positive) + (False\ Negative) + (True\ Positive) + (True\ Negative) = 1$$

The same concept can be equivalently expressed as follows:

$$P(Actual = 0) \cdot P(Predicted = 1) +$$
$$P(Actual = 1) \cdot P(Predicted = 0) +$$
$$P(Actual = 1) \cdot P(Predicted = 1) +$$
$$P(Actual = 0) \cdot P(Predicted = 0) = 1$$

In the formula, P indicates the probability of the specified condition. Moving elements around, it becomes

$$P(Actual = 0) \cdot P(Predicted = 1) + P(Actual = 1) \cdot P(Predicted = 0) =$$
$$1 - P(Actual = 1) \cdot P(Predicted = 1) + P(Actual = 0) \cdot P(Predicted = 0)$$

In a binary classification scenario, the member on the right of the equation can be further transformed. If you name P_0 and P_1 the probability that the element takes the value of 0 and 1, you obtain

$$P(Actual = 0) \cdot P(Predicted = 1) + P(Actual = 1) \cdot P(Predicted = 0) = 1 - \left(P_0^2 + P_1^2\right)$$

In the current form, the member on the right looks exactly like the Gini index. The part on the left, however, is now self-describing. The Gini index measures the frequency of erroneous predictions—namely, the elements of the dataset classified in an erroneous way (the *actual* value is different from the *predicted* value). Therefore, the result is that the Gini index is an indicator of homogeneity.

The following formula calculates the Gini Gain (GG)—namely, the information gain due to a split on a feature A in a dataset S:

$$GG(S, A) = Gini(S) - \sum_{i=1}^{T_A} P_i \cdot Gini(i)$$

In the formula, T_A refers to all the possible values that the feature A takes in the dataset. In the same formula, P_i is the frequency of the ith value for the feature in the dataset. Finally, $Gini(i)$ is the Gini index computed on the subset of the dataset made by all the elements, where the feature A takes the value i. Most of the time, the split is binary, so 2 is the typical value of T_A.

The whole formula for the information also can be seen as a weighted mean of the Gini index on the groups created by the split. The weight is given by the frequency of the value i in the feature A. The information gain therefore measures the decrease of the impurity before and after the split.

How the ID3 Algorithm Works

Iterative Dichotomiser (ID3) is another algorithm used to build classification trees that makes use of a different measure of homogeneity called *entropy*. Because of the definition of entropy, ID3 is more susceptible than CART to outliers. (We will discuss this issue in more detail later.)

In the original formulation, the ID3 algorithm was not designed to handle missing values and numeric (noncategorical) values. However, a more recent version of it, known as C45, fixed the shortcomings so that now the only key difference between CART and ID3/C45 is the definition of homogeneity (entropy versus Gini index). In particular, missing values are filled with mean values. Another aspect of ID3 fixed by the newer-version C45 is the reduction of the risk of overfitting, thus adding a further step of manipulation called *pruning*. We'll describe pruning in a moment when we introduce regression trees.

How the Algorithm Works

ID3 builds a classification tree in the same top-down fashion as CART does. It starts with an empty tree and the full dataset, and for each step, it loops over the list of features (those that have not been selected in previous steps) and their feasible values.

It picks the pair feature/value for which the entropy is minimal. It then adds a new node to the tree and splits the dataset into two regions: the rows where the value is less than or equal to the selected feature value and the rows where it is higher. Finally, the algorithm is recursively repeated on the two generated (sub) datasets.

Important A good question to ask is, What are the differences between CART and ID3/C45? A noticeable one is that the ID3/C45 family of algorithms is greedier and stops using a feature after a split on it has been made. On the other hand, CART can reuse the same feature over multiple splits. This difference results in CART typically producing larger trees but also with more chances to contain better splits. Aside from the size (and subsequently performance of CART), another drawback of CART is the lack of support for pruning—namely, rule sets defined as hyperparameters to make decisions at each split iteration.

Information Gain and Entropy

As mentioned, ID3 uses a different measurement than CART for impurity based on the concept of entropy. Entropy of a dataset S is defined as follows:

$$H(S) = \sum_{i=1}^{K} -P_i \cdot \log_2 (P_i)$$

In the formula, K is the number of categories to predict (i.e., the possible rates for a movie), and P_i is the frequency of elements in the dataset S with a category value of i (i.e., the number of movies rated in a given way in the training dataset). Note that a frequency value is never greater than 1; therefore, the logarithm (base 2) is negative. Subsequently, the value you sum is always positive.

In ID3, the goal is getting a very low entropy, falling close to 0. Such a low entropy would mean highly homogeneous splits. As an example, if the dataset has 20 movies, 8 of which rated 1, 3 rated 2, and 9 rated 4, the total entropy is the following:

$$H(S) = -0.4 \cdot \log_2 (0.4) + (-0.15 \cdot \log_2 (0.15) + (-0.45 \cdot \log_2 (0.45))$$

The information gain (IG) produced by a split on the feature A in a dataset S is defined as follows:

$$IG(S, A) = H(S) - \sum_{i=1}^{T_A} P_i \cdot H(i)$$

In the formula, $H(i)$ indicates the entropy of the subset of the dataset made by all the elements where the feature A takes the value i.

Impact of Outliers

One of the most relevant differences between CART and ID3/C4.5 is the impact of outliers, which is much higher in ID3/C4.5 than in CART. The reason for this lies in the mathematical definition of the Gini index and entropy. In particular, the Gini index is obtained as the sum of squared frequency of feature values, whereas the entropy results from the sum of the frequency multiplied by the logarithm of the feature value.

Figure 12-4 presents in the same graph the curves generated by the logarithm (multiplied by –1 as in the entropy formula) and square (x^2) functions. The X-axis shows the frequency of feature values. As you know, frequency values are in the [0, 1] interval. Keep in mind, however, a frequency of 0 is impossible because the logarithm is defined for 0.

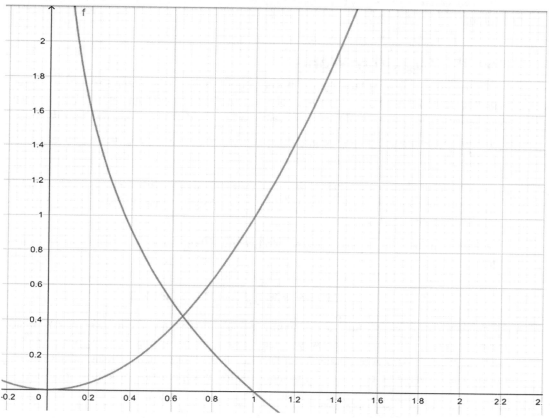

FIGURE 12-4 Comparing the growth of the (negative) logarithm and square functions

An outlier value has a frequency value very close to 0.

From the figure, you see that the entropy takes very high values (vertical asymptote) the more the input value approaches 0. In comparison, the square function shows a more linear growth, even a sublinear growth. Therefore, the impact of outliers is much higher (infinite versus 0) when entropy is used instead of the Gini index.

Regression Trees

A regression tree is designed to predict a continuous value rather than a discrete value, as in classification. Actual regression tree algorithms build the tree through the same binary recursive partitioning we discussed for CART and ID3/C45. Compared to classification trees, though, regression trees use yet another indicator to decide about the split.

A regression tree is typically built using a specific algorithm known as the Regression Tree Algorithm.

How the Algorithm Works

The high-level description of the algorithm is analogous to that of CART and ID3 and is centered on the (repeated) split of the dataset on the value of a feature. Each split cuts the dataset into two parts and recursively proceeds on each of them. Compared to CART and ID3, there are two key differences:

- With continuous values to predict, neither impurity nor entropy works well, so you need to get back to the concept of squared error.

- The value of the feature to split on is not a specific value the feature takes, but having to predict a continuous value, it is the mean of the values the feature takes in the region of the dataset being considered.

At each split step, the dataset is divided into two distinct regions R_1 and R_2 and the SSE is calculated as follows:

$$SSE(S, R_1, R_2) = \sum_{i=1}^{K1}\left(y_i - \tilde{Y}_{R1}\right)^2 + \sum_{i=1}^{K2}\left(y_i - \tilde{Y}_{R2}\right)^2$$

In the formula, K_1 and K_2 indicate the number of elements in the split regions. $\tilde{Y}_{R1}$ and $\tilde{Y}_{R2}$ indicate the mean of the feature Y in the region. All you need to do at each step is find the regions R_1 and R_2 that minimize the error. However, because R_1 and R_2 result from a split, what you really need to identify is a feature A and a value to split on. Here's pseudocode for the repeatable part of the algorithm:

```
var sse = calculate_sse_for(dataset);
foreach(feature in features)
{
    // Calculate the mean for the current feature
    var mean = calculate_mean(feature);

    // Obtain regions R1 and R2 for the feature
    var regions = split_on(feature, mean);

    // Calculate SSE for split regions R1 and R2
    var sse_r1 = calculate_sse_for(regions[0]);
    var sse_r2 = calculate_sse_for(regions[1]);
    features_sse_list.Add(combine_sse(sse_r1, sse_r2));
}
```

```
// Best SSE of all features
var best_sse = features_sse_list.Min();

if (best_sse >= sse)
{
    // Best result reached
    break;
}
```

The procedure in the pseudocode will be recursively repeated for each dataset. The exit points from the function can be reaching the limit of the SSE, the depth of the tree, or the number of leaves, much the same as what we saw for CART and ID3.

Tree Pruning

With regression trees, the risk of overfitting is inherently higher than with classification trees. Again, there's a mathematical foundation for this. Continuous values to predict (as opposed to categorical values) make for much more room for calculations. There's always a value that can be made smaller with one more iteration. If not properly managed, the situation can easily degenerate into overfitting.

One way to reduce the risk of overfitting is to introduce a threshold so that the algorithm will continue only if the split improves the SSE at least for the given threshold. This method works, but it's rather rudimentary though. A better way consists of adopting a technique similar to the ridge regularization described in the preceding chapter so that the growth of leaves is penalized. This process is known as *pruning*. The idea is letting the tree grow until a minimum number of leaves is reached, usually no fewer than five. Next, pruning is applied. Pruning consists of removing a number of leaves from the calculated decision tree T. You don't want to alter the binary structure of the tree, so you would always remove an even number of leaves anywhere. Let's call this number $2p$. After pruning, you obtain a new tree called $(T - 2p)$.

Overall, the goal is shrinking the tree without also shrinking the accuracy of the predictions the tree can make. For this reason, pruning also comes with a cost-complexity function defined as follows:

$$R_\alpha(T - 2p) = \sum_{i=1}^{\#T} SSE(T - 2p) + \alpha \cdot \#(T - 2p)$$

In the formula, $\#T$ refers to the number of leaves in the tree T. From a mathematical perspective, pruning consists of minimizing the function $R_\alpha(T - 2p)$. The parameter to act on is the number $2p$ of leaves to remove. Along with the $2p$ parameter, there's the learning coefficient α to define and vary for better results. The more you increase α, the more the pruned tree shrinks, and the more you risk losing in terms of accuracy. To evaluate the performance of the coefficient α, you use a k-fold cross validation where typical values of k are 5 or 10.

Summary

Machine learning tree algorithms do a good job when it comes to classification and decision-making problems and also provide a nonlinear way to regression, expanding on what you saw in the preceding chapter about linear and multilinear regression.

Tree-based algorithms are divided into two families: classification and regression. All algorithms in both families, however, work inspired by the same principle and around the same logic. In particular, two major algorithms such as CART and ID3/C45 fall under the umbrella of classification. All tree algorithms work nearly the same way, essentially by looping on the set of features and their values, trying to find the optimal feature/value combination that can split the dataset in two homogeneous regions. In the end, a decision tree is built during the training phase that is more or less able to classify and predict test data in production. The way in which the optimal split is determined sets the difference between the various tree algorithms.

It is worth noting that this chapter doesn't cover all that's relevant to know about trees in machine learning. In the next chapter, we will expand to other classes of algorithms based on trees like random forests and gradient boosts.

## CHAPTER 13

How to Make Better Decisions: Ensemble Methods

We need to solve the unsupervised learning problem before we can even think of getting to true AI.

—*Yann LeCun*
(VP and Chief AI Scientist at Facebook)

At the end of the day, the problem of machine learning is always the same: building more and more accurate predictive models. The basic tools available for building solutions are the tools of mathematics we touched on in previous chapters, and the tools to evaluate the quality of the model are bias, variance, and errors. Tree-based algorithms are good for classification problems—which, of a few known labels, is the best to describe the observed data item—but the algorithms presented in the preceding chapter are simple overall and, in some ways, *weak learners*.

The ensemble methods discussed in this chapter refer to a few classes of algorithms that generate a predictive model from the combination of multiple learning techniques. Essentially, they group weak learners together to form one stronger learner.

Two main classes of ensemble methods specialize in different directions. They are *bagging* methods to decrease variance and *boosting* methods to reduce bias.

The Problem

The preceding chapter described how to build decision trees for classification and regression scenarios. It didn't look like a super complex thing to do and, in a way, as humans, we could even follow the reasoning of the algorithm and interpret its steps. This is a sign that the model is not necessarily powerful in its overall simplicity. This awareness raised the notion of weak learners.

A weak learner is an algorithm that always learns something from the training data and will then always perform better than just guessing. In other words, when it comes to assigning a label (therefore, classifying) an observed data item, any of the decision trees shown in the preceding chapter have good but not great chances to be as accurate as expected in the detection of the relationships between input and target.

This problem has been seriously addressed in the literature since the mid-1990s and led to the development of ensemble methods in just a few years.

The core idea of ensemble methods is putting together simpler models, letting each work, and then evaluating the response to orchestrate the final response from the unified model. In other words, having a single tree is good, but it might not work at its best (not enough wood, not enough shade, not enough fruits); having a forest of trees is much better. This is the metaphor that led to ensemble methods.

As mentioned, there are two main classes of ensemble algorithms. One is called bootstrap aggregating, but the name is often shortened to *bagging*. The other is known as boosting.

- **Bagging.** In this technique, weak learning models are independent and weighted the same way. The learning models combined can be of the same type or even heterogeneous. Concrete bagging algorithms let weak learners go and then return a weighted average of their results as the final score. Bagging increases the stability of the model and reduces the variance, making the model much less sensitive to the training data.

- **Boosting.** In this technique, weak learning models are applied sequentially rather than in parallel (as with bagging). At each iteration of the boosting algorithm, a new model is created to predict the error of the applied learner. Consequently, in the successive step, the applied learner incorporates the errors captured in the previous iteration. Boosting reduces bias, but at the same time, it is more inclined to overfitting.

Let's look in more detail at these two classes of algorithms.

The Bagging Technique

There's a quick and direct way to start with bagging: choosing a classifier algorithm and running it on a couple of small subsets of the dataset. When both are done, you take the average and compare what you get with the results of the same algorithm on the entire dataset. If this method works, great! Otherwise, you should probably consider larger subsets.

Note, though, that larger subsets of data don't guarantee better results.

In the case of a small training dataset, you generate additional datasets for training from the original dataset by using combinations with repetitions. In this way, you amplify the size of the original dataset and get a better score by aggregating the scores of multiple subsets. If the results obtained from a traditional classifier are good enough, you can't just expect to improve indefinitely.

Random Forest Algorithms

You might have figured out already from what you've read in this book that in machine learning more than the name or the implementation of a specific algorithm, it's the class or the general approach to a solution that counts and that is referred to in the literature. So, today the term *random forest* or *random decision forest* doesn't refer to a specific algorithm, but rather it is the general name of an ensemble learning method suited for decision-making tasks that revolve around the classification of data items or the prediction of a particular label.

What Are They For?

Before we get into more details about the random forest algorithms, it's crucial to mention what they are (mostly) for. Consider that the class of random forest algorithms is extremely popular, and with reason, because it enables you to make more insightful decisions in an acceptable time. As the name may suggest, a random forest is made of trees (though, in general, other types of basic models can be used as well), and its output is an aggregation of the results obtained by the constituent models. In particular, random trees are more accurate than regression trees whenever there's a nonlinear relationship in the data to model.

A first great concrete example of a nonlinear relationship is the recommendation engine of an e-commerce online shop. In general, everything that falls under the umbrella of suggestions is a good fit for random forests, including, for example, medical analysis, skimming of financial transactions for fraud detection, and financial assessment for loans or investment tips.

The Overall Idea

Unlike a single (classification or regression) tree, at training time, a random decision forest is made up of a multitude of individual decision trees, and the final score is given by the mode of the classes detected by individual trees. This happens in case of classification. In the case of regression, instead, the final score is the mean of the values predicted by the individual trees. Historically, the first algorithm for random decision forests was created by Tin Kam Ho in 1995.

Figure 13-1 provides a graphical representation of the overall idea behind a random forest.

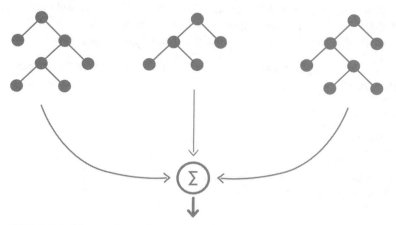

FIGURE 13-1 Schema of a random forest algorithm

The random forest algorithm mostly uses decision trees (classification or regression, based on the actual problem) as weak learners and runs them in parallel. However, because they are built out of the same dataset and the same set of (fixed) hyperparameters (i.e., for deciding when to stop), it is reasonable to expect that each of the learners will produce nearly the same output.

So, what's the point of building a forest? This is just where the *random* in the name of the ensemble algorithm kicks in.

Randomness Is King

In a random forest, each learning tree is built on randomly selected features. Unlike a canonical decision tree, in which each split step results from a careful picking of the feature (and value) that maximizes the information gain, in a random forest scenario, each learner operates on a random subset of features.

In addition, individual learners are trained on segments of the original datasets obtained with the *bootstrap* method. In statistics, the bootstrap is a technique for estimating quantities by averaging estimates from multiple small data samples (and duplicating rows in case of small datasets). In the end, a random forest gets a number of bootstrapped datasets from the original dataset and trains each on a randomly selected number of features. Put yet another way, the canonical decision tree operates on a random selection of rows and columns of the original training dataset.

Each learner adopts different stop parameters that are part of the overall configuration of the random forest algorithm. A few guidelines exist for those values, but in the beginning, they might just as well be random.

Steps of the Algorithms

Random forests, as well as all the algorithms discussed in previous chapters (and those that will be discussed in the upcoming chapters), find one or more effective implementations in a number of Python and .NET libraries (e.g., Scikit-learn, ML.NET). Developers and data scientists are not likely to write algorithms from scratch; more often than not, they limit use to call library functions.

Yet, it is interesting to at least know the steps to achieve the solution of a problem. Here's how a random forest algorithm works:

```
var forest = CreateRandomTrees(100);
var m = NumberOfFeaturesToConsider;
var results = new List<TreeResult>();
foreach(var tree in forest)
{
    // Select the given number of (random) features to use
    var features = select_features_randomly(m, dataset)

    // Extract a subsample of the dataset
    var bootstrap = select_bootstrap(dataset);
```

```
    // Train the model
    results.Add(tree.Fit(bootstrap, features, /* other hyperparameters */));
}

// Jump to conclusions
var score = pick_best(results);
```

The end of the loop gives the number of trees (100 in the example) trained and ready to make predictions. The final result comes from a voting mechanism that picks up the best prediction from the set of all predictions made by the various trees. If the algorithm is used for a classification problem, the voting mechanism will select the most predicted label (the mode). In the case of regression, it will pick up the mean of all predictions.

Number of Trees in the Forest

When the random forest came out, there was no specific indication about the optimal number of trees to grow in the forest. The claim was that because the algorithm would never run in to overfitting, one could use any (large) number of trees to reach the desired level of precision and computational capabilities.

Later on, the landscape changed a bit. In an article in 2004, researcher Mark Segal demonstrated that in case of poor-quality datasets (packed with incomplete, inconsistent, or even meaningless data), the random forest algorithm tends to overfit. Therefore, the number of trees has become a key hyperparameter of the algorithm. Today, a widely accepted idea sets the optimal number of trees somewhere in between 64 and 128. Any number in this range ensures a good trade-off between accuracy, processing time, and resource consumption.

Going beyond the threshold of 128 trees reduces the gain in accuracy proportionally unless a strong and serious computational environment is available. Keep in mind, however, that a random forest is fairly fast to train, but if a large number of trees is used, it may become slow at making predictions at runtime.

Other Hyperparameters

In addition to the number of trees (sometimes also referred to as estimators, mostly in statistical literature), the behavior of the random forest algorithm is influenced by other parameters, such as the maximum number of features to select in the various bootstraps.

Another important hyperparameter is the number of features to consider when looking for the best split. A commonly used value (for example, the one used by the Scikit-learn implementation) is the square root of the total number of features in the dataset.

Yet another parameter that mostly impacts on the speed of the algorithm (both training and runtime) is the maximum depth of the tree. If this parameter is not set, the algorithm proceeds until no further split is possible. Some implementations of the algorithm also stop processing if a given maximum number of leaves is reached.

While we're speaking of the algorithm, we also need to mention the subsets of data used to train the various random trees. The number should be significantly smaller than the size of the dataset, and there should not be partitions involved, meaning that two subsets may contain the same data rows. An acceptable value is the square root of the size of the dataset.

Pros and Cons

Random forests were introduced to make it simpler to make even better decisions than with classic decision trees. As with anything else, there are pros and cons to using them. These are the major pros:

- **Model nonlinear relationships.** Although the bagging technique can be used to combine heterogenous learners, random forests are about combining trees. As such, a random forest algorithm preserves the major value of trees—the ability to manage nonlinear relationships. Also, random forests are less sensitive to overfitting.

- **Support feature selection.** In complex problems, when large datasets must be prepared and shaped, a common problem is the actual relevance of features. A random forest is therefore good at telling which features in a dataset are the most relevant. A fine-tuned algorithm may perform bagging and explore which features are most classified out of random selection. This information can be used to fine-tune datasets even for problems not directly solvable with a random forest.

- **Mitigate dataset imbalance.** The random nature of the algorithm tends to mitigate the possible imbalance of the training dataset. In supervised learning, a training dataset is defined as imbalanced when it doesn't contain a relatively equal set of data points per class. It doesn't strictly have to be an even split, but when the distance between extremes is too wide (i.e., 90/10), some manipulation is in order. However, data manipulation is not strictly necessary with an imbalanced dataset if a random forest is used. The reason is that data is sampled in bootstraps, and this tends to absorb and mitigate imbalance.

Because a random forest is definitely a forest, the size does matter! The more learners you involve, the more the final unified model is slow to train and, worse yet, slow at work in production. Overall, a random forest is an excellent compromise between the time it takes and the accuracy it provides. If the results a given model delivers aren't sufficient for the problem at hand, other techniques can be employed, such as neural networks. (We'll get to neural networks in a few chapters.)

One final point to consider is that a random forest model is hardly interpretable. In machine learning, interpretability of the model refers to the end-user perception of the correctness of the received answer. No matter the ultimate point of making accurate classifications and predictions, end users will need to make decisions out of predictions, and they tend to always prefer suggestions that are intelligible and understandable. In a classic decision tree, the process is simpler overall, and to some extent, the end user (expert of the domain) can have a better time trying to mentally validate the response.

A random forest model is not very interpretable because it results from the combined predictions of a high number of randomly built and distinct decision trees. On the other hand, experience proves that random forests are pretty successful.

> **Note** The limited interpretability of the model is not necessarily a negative point. In fact, you can even read it as a sign of deeper analysis taking place beyond the level of human perception. Hence, a model that is hard for humans to interpret may even be more insightful and truly more useful in practice.

The Boosting Technique

The meaning of the word *boost* contains elements that overall indicate piecemeal progress, step-by-step increments, and a slow-but-steady march toward better results. This is just what we try to achieve in machine learning with the boosting technique for classification and regression problems.

The Power of Boosting

Unlike bagging (of which random forests are the quintessential example), boosting proceeds sequentially and comes to an end after a number of iterations. To compare the two techniques, you can informally think of a common procedure to select a restaurant to try.

With bagging, you ask a subset of your friends the same question and then make a final decision based on the suggestion receiving the most votes. With boosting, instead, you talk to one friend at a time and adjust the question you would ask the next friend based on the feedback from the previous one. Then you stop asking any questions when you feel confident enough with the answers you've got.

Ideal for Imbalanced Data

Like random forests, boosting is about classification and regression. However, the internals of the boosting algorithms make them particularly suited for anomaly detection and for building ranking models within information retrieval systems. Anomaly detection is a hot area because it concretely touches on domains such as fraudulent financial transactions or even tracked activity that is suspicious in light of cybersecurity.

The key fact is that boosting algorithms work well on imbalanced data. If you're looking for outliers (as in an anomaly detection scenario), the algorithm also performs well on highly imbalanced data. In general, it works acceptably well on heterogeneous data where linear approaches (i.e., multilinear regression) fail. If you're engaged in a classification problem with too much heterogeneous data, looking at a neural network is probably a better option.

Quick Classification of Boosting Algorithms

Overall, we can identify two main classes of boosting algorithms: adaptive boosting and gradient boosting. The former class descends from the first boosting algorithm ever proposed—the AdaBoost (Adaptive Boost) algorithm. Created by Yoav Freund and Robert Schapire in 1997, the algorithm has been a milestone in its area of application and brought its authors the Gödel Prize in 2003.

> **Note** The Gödel Prize awards the most outstanding papers in theoretical computer science annually. It is jointly assigned by the European Association for Theoretical Computer Science and the special focus group on computational theory within the Association for Computing Machinery. Interestingly, the 2019 prize was awarded to Irit Dinur for her new demonstration of the probabilistically checkable proof (PCP) theorem. The PCP theorem states that any decision problem in the class NP of hard problems has a polynomial proof that can be checked by a randomized algorithm of logarithmic complexity. The PCP theorem is considered the most relevant advance in theoretical computer science since the early 1970s when, thanks to Cook's theorem, the definition of NP completeness was set.

Later on, Leo Breiman from the University of California, Berkeley reformulated the boosting problem as an optimization problem using the gradient descent tool—an optimization algorithm largely used in functional analysis for finding the minimum of a function. The work of Breiman gave the spark to further research and optimization, which led to today's algorithms (e.g., XGBoost) that are hard-coded in many machine learning development kits.

Aside from the different formulation of the problem, AdaBoost and Gradient Boost follow the same conceptual steps. Let's take a quick look at adaptive boosting.

The Original Adaptive Boosting Algorithm

As a first step, the adaptive boosting algorithm builds and trains a tree in which each data row in the dataset (observation) is given the same relevance. After the first tree is ready, an evaluation phase determines which rows in the dataset have been correctly classified. A second tree is then created and trained on a dataset in which the rows that were determined to be incorrect at the previous step are now given a higher relevance. The predictions of the model that results from the concatenation of the previous two are evaluated and contribute to creating a third tree trained on the dataset with updated weights on the rows.

The process continues iteratively until the nth weak learner has reached an acceptable level of error. At that point, the final prediction of the overall (stronger) model is given by the combination of the results produced by the various weak learners. Let's look at a graphical representation. Figure 13-2 represents the sample dataset originally used for training.

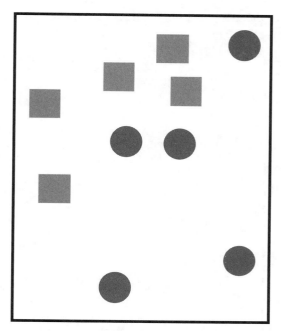

FIGURE 13-2 A graphical representation of a bidimensional dataset

The first run of the boosting algorithm will build a weak decision tree that only recognizes, say, the squared boxes near the left edge. In the second run, unrecognized squared boxes will be given a higher weight, and the second learner trained on these altered values will split the dataset in two halves, the largest of which may include all squared boxes and some circles. A third step will raise relevance of the circles, and a third decision tree will draw a horizontal line to include most of them, as in Figure 13-3.

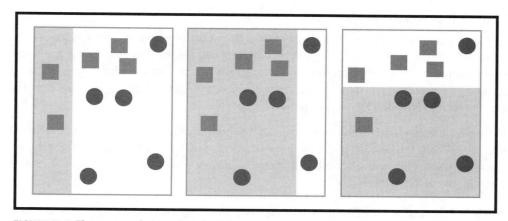

FIGURE 13-3 Three steps of a boosting algorithm

From the figure, the concept of weak learners is pretty clear. The model counts three decision trees, each of which is not really working great. However, their combined effect teaches the resulting strong learner how to recognize nearly all cases correctly. (See Figure 13-4.) There's still some error left, but that depends on the hyperparameters set on the algorithm.

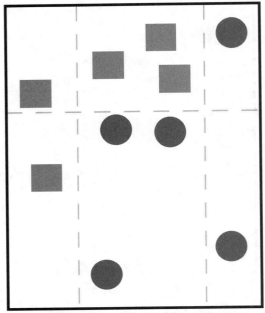

FIGURE 13-4 The original dataset as classified by the strong learner built using the boosting algorithm

The areas delimited by the dashed lines in Figure 13-4 represent the actual leaves of the tree resulting from the combination of all (weak) decision trees built along the way.

Gradient Boosting

As mentioned, gradient boosting looks at trained models as the sequence of steps toward the finding of an optimal result. Instead of improving results obtained at each step through the application of different weights on data points, gradient boosting adds a new feature at each iteration that represents the error on the prediction. In the end, the final prediction is the sum of the originally predicted value plus all the corrections added at each subsequent step.

In gradient boosting, each iteration determines new coefficients for a loss function, called a training loss function. This is the function that is ultimately minimized using the gradient descent technique. The gradient of the training loss function after each iteration is used to adjust the coefficients of the function for the successive tree.

High-level Steps of the Gradient Boosting Algorithm

Let's try to express the steps of the gradient boosting algorithm in a slightly more formal way. In a gradient boosting algorithm, the weak learners can be of any type (e.g., linear regression algorithms, Bayesian trees). However, most of the time they are just decision trees because they're simple and fast to train and can capture nonlinear relationships. Overall, the final model has the following form:

$$F(X) = f_0(X) + f_1(X) + \ldots + f_m(X)$$

In the formula, any of the $f_i(X)$ members represent weak learners. The X is the dataset, and m is the number of trees. Here's the sequence of steps:

- You create and train a decision tree without much care and attention. A model that just fits the dataset is acceptable at this stage. Let's call this model $f_0(X)$.

- You calculate residual errors of the model and train another decision tree $f_1(X)$ to predict those errors. You then have a new model as $F(X) = f_0(X) + f_1(X)$.

- Repeat the process of calculating the residual error of the current model $F(X)$ and training a new weak learner to add to the list, thus coming to a new enlarged definition of $F(X) = f_0(X) + \ldots + f_m(X)$.

- You stop when you reach a level of error sufficiently low or anyway acceptable for the problem at hand.

Essentially, at each step the algorithm allows you to add a new black box determined by the hyper-parameters that have been set (e.g., the loss function). To some extent, you can instruct the algorithm on how to build the black box, but when you get it, you can only use it as is. In this regard, it is correct to say that the way additional weak learners work is not completely under your control. Figure 13-5 provides a graphical representation of the gradient boosting algorithm.

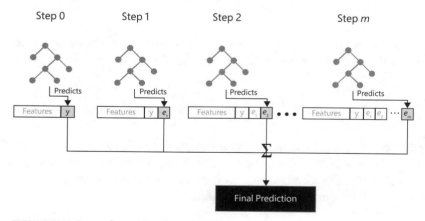

FIGURE 13-5 Steps of a gradient boosting algorithm

Inside the Gradient Black Box

The key thing going on in Figure 13-5 is that, at the end of each step, a new column is added to the dataset, and a new weak learner is trained to predict just the values of the newly added column. The newly added column measures the error between the prediction made and the expected values.

In the first step of the algorithm, an initial weak learner is defined; it returns a constant value regardless of the input values. In other words, if you stopped here, a fixed and a constant value would be returned by the model for whatever is the submitted set of input values. The constant value is defined as the value α such that the sum of errors calculated by the function L on the expected value y_i and α is minimal. The function L is one of the hyperparameters of the algorithm. In symbols, it is like that shown here. The notation arg_α min indicates the value α that minimizes the summation. A commonly used L function is the mean squared error (MSE) function:

$$F_0(X) = arg_\alpha \min \sum_{i=1}^{N}(y_i, \alpha)$$

Note that in the formula, X denotes the training dataset, N is the number of rows in the dataset, and y_i is the expected value for the ith row. The algorithm runs for a fixed number M of iterations. For any of the subsequent iterations, the following steps are accomplished. Let's say you're in the middle of the mth iteration.

For each row x_i in the dataset, the algorithm calculates the partial derivatives of the function L with respect to the function parameter $F(x_i)$:

$$g_{i,m} = -\frac{\partial L(y_i, F(x_i))}{\partial F(x_i)}$$

Note that the function F indicates the final result of the application of all previously calculated weak learners. At the mth step, the function F is like the following, where f_i is the ith weak learner in the chain:

$$F(X) = \sum_{i=0}^{m-1} f_i(X)$$

The calculated values $g_{i,m}$ are the values that form the new column to add to the dataset in use. On this extended dataset, a new weak learner f_m is trained. Finally, the algorithm calculates the step size to advance the gradient. The step size is not a fixed value but changes for each iteration. This is the formula that calculates the α for the mth step of the algorithm:

$$\alpha_m = arg_\alpha \min \sum_{i=1}^{N} L(y_i, F_{m-1}(x_i) + \alpha f_m(x_i))$$

It is the value that minimizes the sum of the errors between expected values and values calculated by the existing total function plus the newly trained weak learner. The calculated α value ends up being the coefficient that weighs the new learner in the chain of strong learners. The output of the mth iteration is a new model as follows:

$$F_m(X) = F_{m-1}(X) + \alpha_m f_m(X)$$

This is the substance of the mathematics behind the gradient boosting algorithm. Some further techniques are employed, however, to reduce the overfitting of the solution. One of these is called shrinkage, and it alters the preceding formula as follows:

$$F_m(X) = F_{m-1}(X) + \gamma \; \alpha_m f_m(X)$$

A coefficient γ greater than 0 and less than or equal to 1 is used to multiply the α_i weight. This is done to slow down the descent and allow more time to understand data. Heuristics show that small shrinkage values (< 0.1) produce significantly more general models at the cost of raising both the training time and the time it takes to query the deployed model.

Common Hyperparameters

Gradient boosting algorithms support a number of tuning parameters that may be slightly different in different implementations. However, the most common parameters are the *learning rate*, which, much like the gradient descent we've met in linear regression, helps to determine the variation of the coefficients of the loss function for the next round, and the maximum depth that each decision tree is allowed to reach.

Other parameters can be the percentage of the dataset to be actually used by each tree to train and the percentage of features. Note that taking a small percentage of the dataset may lead to underfitting, but choosing a high number of features may determine overfitting. Even for boosting algorithms, the number of trees is crucial, but a value of 100 is commonly accepted.

Finally, most actual algorithms allow you to choose the loss function to be used depending on the problem at hand, whether regression, classification, or classification problems with probability.

Popular Actual Algorithms

The two most popular implementations of the gradient boost technique are XGBoost and LightGBM. Both use decision trees as weak learners and introduced variations essentially for performance reasons. Both algorithms have been created in the past few years.

The XGBoost algorithm improves the way that splits are calculated after the first step. In particular, more data is added to help subsequent models make better decisions. Furthermore, the algorithm is able to skip rows that are missing an entry for the feature being processed. In this way, on sparse datasets, the algorithm produces a nearly linear performance on the feature without missing values.

LightGBM is an algorithm developed at Microsoft in 2017 and fully supported by the ML.NET framework. It uses XGBoost as the starting point and proceeds with further sophisticated optimizations, so that in the end, it outperforms XGBoost as far as the speed of training is concerned and also can handle larger datasets. The accuracy of both algorithms instead is nearly identical.

Pros and Cons

Gradient boosting algorithms are inevitably more prone to overfitting than random forests. Furthermore, they are more problematic to configure. In addition to the learning rate that determines how close you get each time to an acceptable error level, there's the maximum number of weak learners to create and all the sets of parameters for them.

Gradient boosting is inherently slower than random forests because it works sequentially even though XGBoost and LightGBM are great just at finding shortcuts to provide an excellent average performance.

On the contrary, gradient boosting algorithms are more accurate than random forests and can work on any loss function with enough mathematical characteristics to produce a gradient (the loss function must be differentiable). This makes the algorithm the only way to go for problems, such as ranking of information and expected counts of events (Poisson regression).

Summary

Ensemble methods refer to a class of algorithms that collectively attempt to solve the problem of not just making decisions, but making decisions better and faster and in a more accurate way. Sounds like magic?

Well, not exactly! It sounds more like mathematics.

Ensemble methods combine machine learning models (mostly, but not necessarily, decision trees) to form a single predictive model that can offer better performance in terms of accuracy. The trick is connecting multiple weak learners and letting them emerge as just one.

Ensemble methods take two main forms: random forests and gradient boosting algorithms.

Random forests are fast to train and so simple that it is hard to build a bad random forest! The reason is that it works in parallel, it is also fast to run and, on top of that, it returns a pretty good indication of the relevance that each feature in the dataset can have.

Gradient boosting algorithms are more flexible in how they can be programmed to search for the best results, and this makes them the perfect (fast) fit for some particular classes of problems that are hard to tackle with other algorithms. The most prominent of all is anomaly detection.

In the next chapter, we'll continue our journey through the major algorithms for shallow learning and talk about the Naïve Bayes and Bayesian classifiers. They can be extremely fast compared to other classification algorithms and work on the foundation of the Bayes theorem of probability to predict the class of unknown data points.

## CHAPTER 14

Probabilistic Methods: Naïve Bayes

*A mathematical theory is not to be considered complete until you have made it so
clear that you can explain it to the first man whom you meet on the street.*

—David Hilbert, father of metamathematics

A trained model can give only a peremptory and assertive answer, but no probability about it. Is this a problem? As usual, the answer depends on the nature of the problem you're trying to address with machine learning. To come to a conclusion, the question to the answer is: Would you accept a prediction that the same algorithm may score as quite unlikely?

At some point in history, the scientific community felt the need to add a probabilistic dimension to classification (and regression) problems. Hence, in this chapter, we'll enter the world of Bayesian statistics and focus on a new type of classifiers, known as naïve Bayes classifiers.

Quick Introduction to Bayesian Statistics

In the late 1960s, a new approach to statistics flourished, adding an innovative and probabilistic dimension to classic problems of classification (and also regression). As a result, new types of classifiers appeared specifically designed to do text analysis and catalogue documents using the frequency of words as a measure. Those classifiers were baptized *Bayesian classifiers* because of their working principle deeply rooted in Bayesian statistics.

Today, Bayesian classifiers are widely used in medical diagnosis, weather forecasts, sentiment analysis, and for quick classification of documents (e.g., spam/nonspam). For a better understanding of Bayesian classifiers, a quick tour of Bayesian statistics is in order.

Note Weather forecast algorithms employ numerical models that, fed daily with information, predict the value of several variables such as temperature, humidity, wind, and pressure. Altogether these variables correspond to define the atmospheric pattern for a given period. The problem is the granularity at which such a pattern applies, which is typically for squares several kilometers large. Finer-grained forecasts are then obtained combining observations with historical data. Recent developments in weather forecasting have used Bayesian statistics to identify the segment of historical data with the highest likelihood to be relevant for predictions.

Introducing Bayesian Probability

The name *Bayesian* refers to the work attributed to Thomas Bayes, an English statistician and philosopher who lived in the first half of the eighteenth century. Even though the name Thomas Bayes appears everywhere in the literature, it seems that others did a significant part of the work we today label as "Bayesian."

It seems certain that Thomas Bayes condensed his work in a manuscript that he never managed to publish. After his death in 1761, his fellow mathematician Richard Price got the manuscript and published it with some significant revisions but still under the name Bayes. So, apparently Richard Price took no credit for the work he undoubtedly did.

Furthermore, a decade later French scientist Pierre-Simon Laplace presented an analogous theory he developed in full autonomy and unaware of the Bayes and Price work. Laplace, however, went well beyond the point of formulating the theory, and today he is unanimously considered the developer of the (Bayesian) *interpretation of probability*.

According to this vision, the probability of an event is defined as the result of a state of knowledge rather than the result of the frequency of an event. Hence, probability is the degree to which it is believed that an event will occur. This is the key fact about Bayesian statistics that Bayesian classifiers (and regressors) leverage.

Important It is key to notice up front that, although Bayesian statistics can be applied to both classification and regression problems, from a purely computational point of view, a probabilistic approach to regression is highly expensive. We'll return to this point later in the chapter.

Some Preliminary Notation

Before we get our hands on the theorem, let's start clarifying some of the necessary notation around the Bayes formula. The first concept on the table is *conditional probability*.

Conditional Probability

Conditional probability is defined as the probability that an event *A* will occur given that an event *B* has already occurred. The function *P* refers to the probability function. The notation used for conditional probability is $P(A|B)$ and is read as "the probability of *A* given *B*."

$$P(A|B) = \frac{P(A \cap B)}{P(B)}$$

In plain terms, the conditional probability of *A* is the ratio between the probability that both *A* and *B* will occur and the probability that B will occur. Needless to say, the formula of conditional probability is valid only when $P(B)$ is greater than 0.

Intersection of Two Events

In the formula of conditional probability, the notation $P(A \cap B)$ indicates the probability that both events *A* and *B* will occur. This is also referred to as the *intersection of events*. The intersection of events can be also expressed as follows:

$$P(A \cap B) = P(A) \cdot P(B|A)$$

The probability that two events will occur results from the probability that the former event occurs multiplied by the probability that the latter event will occur given the former. The preceding formula assumes that events *A* and *B* are interrelated and one influences the other. As we'll see in a moment, there's also the scenario in which two events are independent, meaning that one doesn't influence the other. In this latter case, the formula $P(A \cap B)$ assumes a simpler form.

Intersection of Multiple Events

The formula that expresses the intersection of events can be easily generalized to any number of events using the so-called *chain rule*. For example, if you consider three events *A*, *B*, and *C*, you obtain

$$P(A \cap B \cap C) = P(A) \cdot P(B|A) \cdot P(C|A \cap B)$$

For any number *N* of events $A_1 \ldots A_n$, it becomes

$$P(A_1 \cap \ldots \cap A_n) = \prod_{i=1}^{n} P(A_i | \bigcap_{j=1}^{i-1} A_j)$$

As mentioned, all events are assumed to be interrelated. Now, another key concept to introduce is the concept of independent events.

Independent Events

Two events *A* and *B* are said to be *independent* if the occurrence of one doesn't influence the occurrence of the other. In the case of independent events, the intersection of two events *A* and *B* takes a simpler form:

$$P(A \cap B) = P(A) \cdot P(B)$$

The intersection of two independent events is simply the product of the respective probabilities. Also, the formula of conditional probability gets simplified if you consider independent events:

$$P(A \mid B) = \frac{P(A \cap B)}{P(B)} = \frac{P(A) \cdot P(B)}{P(B)} = P(A)$$

It is read like this: "the probability that an event A will occur given the occurrence of an event B is the same that the event A will occur."

Partitions of Events

Event partitioning is the final stop on the way to formulation of Bayes' theorem. In general, the partition of a set is a collection of subsets such that every element of the original set belongs to exactly one of the subsets. Let's apply the concept of partitioning to the probability space.

The set you want to partition is the space of all possible outcomes of some random experiment. The partition of this set is a collection of events $A_1, \ldots A_n$ that fully describe what can happen. Each event A_i has a probability greater than 0 and the sum of the probabilities of all events is 1:

$$\sum_{i=1}^{n} P(A_i) = 1$$

Knowing that only a number of events $A_1, \ldots, A_n$ may occur, what is the probability that a given event B will occur? You can split the calculation of $P(B)$ over the various partitions of the probability space and take the sum of them all:

$$P(B) = \sum_{i=1}^{n} P(B \cap A_i) = \sum_{i=1}^{n} P(A_i) \cdot P(B \mid A_i)$$

The probability of B is the summation of the probability of B and all of the $A_1, \ldots, A_n$ events. This is intuitive because the probability of the intersection of a specific event B with the space of all possible events is just B. This formula for getting the probability of an event B given a number of other events will be useful in a moment.

Bayes' Theorem

Bayes' theorem provides a formula to calculate the probability of an event given the occurrence of some other (related) events. The key fact about the theorem is that it focuses on the causes of events going beyond the plain frequency of observed events. Causes of events express prior knowledge of occurred conditions. Just this latter point makes it interesting for machine learning scenarios. Prior knowledge of occurred events is just what you get from the training dataset.

Here's the canonical formulation of the theorem:

$$P(A \mid B) = \frac{P(B \mid A) \cdot P(A)}{P(B)}$$

The formulation reads like this: "the probability that an event *A* will occur once another event *B* has occurred is given by the known probability that in the past *B* occurred given *A* multiplied by the overall probability that *A* will occur. The obtained value is then divided by the overall probability that *B* will occur."

In plain English terms, the theorem can also be summarized as follows:

$$P(Cause \mid Effect) = \frac{P(Effect \mid Cause) \cdot P(Cause)}{P(Effect)}$$

In many real-world scenarios, in fact, you know the probability of the effect and the probability of the cause. From historical data, you could also get to know a good probability estimate of the effect given the cause. Bayes' theorem allows you to get the fourth element of the picture: the probability of the cause given the effect!

Yet another plain English formulation can be the following:

$$Posterior = \frac{Prior\ Knowledge \cdot Likelihood}{Normalization}$$

Sounds too abstract and lightyears away from the real world? Let's look at an example then!

A Practical Code Review Example

Suppose that a team of four developers check in code to a project. Out of the statistics from the source code management tool in use, the project manager receives the data in Table 14-1.

TABLE 14-1 Sample Historical Data Available to a Project Manager

Developer	Percentage of Code Contributed	Percentage of Bugs	
DEV1	30	4	
DEV2	23	1	
DEV3	27	3	
DEV4	20	2	

The project manager decides to run a code review session and randomly selects a sample of the code in the repository. Given that the selected code sample is found to have a bug, what's the probability that it was contributed by Dev2?

Table 14-1 tells a great deal but not everything, so both event partitioning and Bayes' theorem will help you find an answer. Let's call D_i the event that the *i*th developer contributed the code to the repository and *B* the event that a randomly selected piece of code contains bugs. Table 14-2 presents the same information as Table 14-1 in the form of probabilities.

TABLE 14-2 Probability of Contributing Code and Bugs per Developer

Probability of Code per Developer		Probability of Bugs per Developer	
$P(D_1)$	0.3	$P(B\mid D_1)$	0.04
$P(D_2)$	0.23	$P(B\mid D_2)$	0.01
$P(D_3)$	0.27	$P(B\mid D_3)$	0.03
$P(D_4)$	0.2	$P(B\mid D_4)$	0.02

Recall the question to answer: given that the selected code sample is found to have a bug, what's the probability that it was contributed by Dev2? In light of the earlier notation, the answer can be expressed as follows:

$$P(D_2\mid B)$$

The event partitioning formula tells you the following:

$$P(B) = \sum_{i=1}^{4} P(D_i) \cdot P(B\mid D_i)$$

The numbers in Table 14-2 allow you to calculate the probability $P(B)$ that the selected code contains at least one bug.

$$
\begin{aligned}
0.30 \times 0.04\ + \\
0.23 \times 0.01\ + \\
0.27 \times 0.03\ + \\
0.20 \times 0.03 = 0.0284
\end{aligned}
$$

It means that 2.84 percent of the total code contains at least one bug. This is only an intermediate step; to get the final answer, you need to apply Bayes' theorem:

$$P(D_2\mid B) = \frac{P(B\mid D_2)\cdot P(D_2)}{P(B)}$$

You hold the values needed for the final calculation:

$$P(D_2\mid B) = \frac{0.01\cdot 0.23}{0.0284} = 0.08$$

Now you have the number: when the project manager gets to review some bugged code, the likelihood that it was contributed by Dev2 is 8 percent.

Applying Bayesian Statistics to Classification

The missing link before we can embark on a discussion about Bayesian classifiers and related algorithms is the probabilistic formulation of the problem of classification.

Initial Formulation of the Problem

Given a set of features $X_1, ..., X_n$, you want to calculate the (posterior) probability for each of the possible known outcomes (i.e., classes) $C_1, ..., C_k$.

In other words, you not only want to know in which of the predefined classes a given data item will be catalogued (as in a canonical classification algorithm), but you also want to know the probability that the data item will fit into any of the predefined classes. The set of classes forms a partition of the probability space, and the total of all probabilities will still sum up to 1.

Bayes' theorem gives you a nice equation to calculate the probability that the data item X (set of features) belongs to the C_j class:

$$P(C_j \mid X_1, ..., X_n) = \frac{P(X_1, ..., X_n \mid C_j) \cdot P(C_j)}{P(X_1, ..., X_n)}$$

Let's put aside the denominator for a moment and focus on the numerator. The reason is that the denominator doesn't depend on $C_1, ..., C_k$ and the values of X_i (the features) are given. Hence, the denominator is constant.

The numerator expression $P(X_1, ..., X_n \mid C_j)$ is only a simplified notation for the chain rule discussed earlier and indicates the joint probability that all X_i values (the features) belong to the C_j class. According to the chain rule, the probability of the intersection of $X_1, ..., X_n$ is as follows:

$$\prod_{i=1}^{n} P\left(X_i \mid \bigcap_{j=1}^{i-1} X_j\right)$$

The resulting formula is quite expensive to compute because it requires multiple applications of the conditional probability formula. Is there any way to simplify it?

No, unless you release some of the constraints and opt for a sort of naïve approach.

A Simplified (Yet Effective) Formulation

The assumption made to simplify calculation is that all X_i features are mutually independent. Under this assumption and using the formula of independent events, you can wildly simplify Bayes' theorem as shown here. The final result is often referred to as the *posterior* probability.

$$P(C_j \mid X_1, ..., X_n) = P(C_j) \cdot \prod_{i=1}^{n} P(X_i \mid C_j) \cdot \frac{1}{P(X_1, ..., X_n)}$$

In this formulation, each conditional probability has to be calculated separately for each feature, regardless of the others. This reduces the complexity from that of a multidimensional problem to that of a one-dimensional problem just solved repeatedly.

The (naïve) assumption of mutually independent features makes applying Bayes' theorem to classification a fairly quick thing. Subsequently, in this simplified form, Bayesian classifiers have become the algorithm of choice for a number of applications required to give a response in nearly real time.

> **Note** In most formulations of the naïve Bayes formula, the denominator is omitted, and proportionality is introduced. As a result, the sign of equality (=) disappears from the formula replaced with the sign of proportionality (α).

Where's Naivety?

In the literature, Bayesian classifiers are referred to as *naïve classifiers*. The reason lies in the assumption that all the features are treated as independent from one another. From a purely statistical point of view, in fact, the assumption is quite strong and just doesn't model the real world well.

Such classifiers are defined *naïve* because, although it is known that features are almost never truly independent, they still make the assumption and go ahead. But, wait! Doesn't such naivety in the algorithm affect the outcomes?

That's the interesting part of the story: in spite of an objectively naïve assumption, the algorithm works surprisingly well for most classification tasks even if when the involved features are not truly independent.

Why Do Naïve Classifiers Work Anyway?

Classification is a problem that we find in the field of statistics as well as in machine learning. There's a core difference, though, between statistics and machine learning. Statistics performs a post-mortem analysis of data aimed at dissecting it and building a model for accurate estimations. Machine learning, instead, uses the data to become good at making predictions and classifying.

A machine learning algorithm doesn't have to be accurate in its estimations as long as it's good at making predictions and giving responses. This is just what happens with naïve classifiers. They are just good (and extremely fast) at predicting the class the data item belongs to.

How is that possible? Using Bayes' theorem, a classifier gets the likelihood that a data item belongs to any of the given classes. With all the probabilities collected, the response that the classifier returns is subject to a decision rule that each specific algorithm may implement differently. In the end, though, each classifier selects the class that gets the highest score—whatever that means, most likely the highest probability.

So, what happens is that naïve classifiers calculate the probability badly but still classify fairly well. On the other hand, correct estimations (like in statistics) imply accurate predictions, but accurate predictions (like in machine learning) don't strictly require correct estimations. More pragmatically, what happens is that the errors in probability hardly change the name of the highest ranked class.

Practical Aspects of Bayesian Classifiers

The sole application of Bayes' theorem is not sufficient to have a (naïve) classifier. A Bayesian classification algorithm is characterized by three components:

- A decision rule engine
- A module to calculate any prior probability $P(C_j)$
- A module to calculate conditional probabilities $P(X_i | C_j)$

A decision rule serves the purpose of deciding which class should be used for classifying the data item with the provided features. A frequently used rule consists of picking the class with the highest probability. This is known as the *Maximum a Posteriori* (MAP) rule.

To compute the prior probability $P(C_j)$, classifiers follow two common strategies. One considers all classes equally probable and sets the prior probability to $1/n$, the reciprocal of the number of classes. The other strategy considers the distribution of each class in the training dataset. The probability is then given by the number of items in the dataset that belongs to the class on the total number of items in the dataset.

Finally, to calculate conditional probabilities, a few distinct approaches lead straight to different implementations of the naïve classifier algorithm: multinomial and Bernoulli.

Naïve Bayes Classifiers

A naïve Bayes classifier is a probabilistic machine learning algorithm that's mostly used for classification tasks. The foundation of the classifier is Bayes' theorem and the assumption that features are mutually independent. A model based on a naïve Bayes classifier is easy to build and fairly quick in production. Hence, it is particularly useful when employed to scan and classify large volumes of data. In spite of their declared algorithmic naivety, naïve Bayes classifiers are often known to outperform other more sophisticated classification models.

Naïve classifiers come in two main flavors: those able to work with discrete features and those designed for continuous features. In the first group are two main families of algorithms: multinomial and Bernoulli classifiers. To work with continuous features, instead, you have to look into the Gaussian classifier.

> **Note** As a reminder, a discrete feature is one that only assumes well-defined values in a finite or infinite enumerable interval of any type (numbers, strings, dates). A continuous feature is one that can assume any value in a given interval. For example, features representing measures (such as height, width, temperature, pressure) are likely to be continuous features.

The General Algorithm

Both the Multinomial Naïve Bayes (MNB) classifier and the Bernoulli Naïve Bayes (BNB) classifiers share the same core algorithm. The steps are outlined here in C# pseudocode:

```
string NaiveBayes(string[] classes, object[] features)
{
    // Holder of the probability for each class
    Dictionary<string, float> probability = new Dictionary<string, float>();

    // Holder of posterior (final) probability for each class
    Dictionary<string, float> posterior = new Dictionary<string, float>();
```

```
    // Calculate the probability for all classes
    probability = CalculateProbabilitiesForAllClasses(classes);
    // Loop over classes
    foreach(var class in classes)
    {
        // Gets the prior conditional probability
        var prior = CalculatePriorProbabilityForClass(features, class);

        // Get the posterior probability based on conditional probability
        posterior[class] = CalculaterPosterior(probability[class], prior);
    }

    // Make the final decision
    return BestOf(posterior);
}
```

Essentially, the algorithm follows the steps of Bayes' theorem. It gets the list of classes and features and, first thing, calculates the prior probabilities $P(C_j)$ for all classes. Next, for each class, it gets the product of all conditional probabilities of the individual features given the class. The formula is $\prod_{i=1}^{n} P(X_i | C_j)$. Note that the denominator can be omitted because it is constant. The algorithm then obtains the posterior probability as the product of the previous values: $P(C_j)$ multiplied by the products of conditional probabilities. Finally, the algorithm applies the decision rule and picks up the value to return from the list of computed posterior probabilities.

As mentioned earlier, under the hypothesis of discrete feature values, you can distinguish two main families of naïve classifiers: multinomial and Bernoulli. They differ in the way in which the conditional probability is calculated.

> **Important** Both multinomial and Bernoulli classifiers do the same job of classifying data items, but each uses a different way to calculate the prior (conditional) probability. In fact, the concept of "prior" probability (and subsequently, the probability distribution employed) reflects the knowledge of the business domain. For this reason, multinomial and binomial apply to different business scenarios.

Multinomial Naïve Bayes

Multinomial Naïve Bayes (MNB) is largely used for text analysis and subsequently document classification. It is ultimately used, for example, to tag an article as news, sports, the economy, or maybe politics and comes to this conclusion after analyzing the words in the text. The algorithm works particularly well when the features it receives in input represent the words found in the text, and the actual value is the frequency of that word in the text.

The Multinomial Distribution

In statistics, multinomial distribution is used to determine probabilities in experiments where more than two outcomes are possible, trials are independent (the outcome of one trial doesn't affect the outcome of successive trials), and each outcome has a constant probability on each trial.

The canonical example provided to explain multinomial distribution is the rolling of a k-sided die: each roll is independent, and each of the k sides has its own distinct and constant probability to be rolled.

The MNB classifier assumes a *multinomial* distribution of the features. What does this mean concretely?

Distribution of Words

Mapped to the text analysis scenario, a multinomial distribution of the features simply means that each word found in the text (hence, a feature) has its own distinct and constant probability of appearing in a document of a given class (e.g., news, sports, politics).

To apply the naïve Bayes' theorem, you need to be able to calculate the probability that a word X_i appears in the text, given that the text belongs to some class C_j. This is nothing more than the formula you've seen many times already: $P(X_i | C_j)$. How do you do it?

In MNB, such a probability is expressed as the ratio between the number of times the word X_i appears in documents of class C_j and the total number of documents of class C_j:

$$P(X_i | C_j) = \frac{Number\ of\ documents\ of\ class\ C_j\ that\ contain\ the\ word\ X_i}{Number\ of\ documents\ of\ class\ C_j}$$

With a training dataset available, finding those probabilities is obviously no big deal.

The Zero Probability Problem

Applying the preceding formula, as is, at some point poses a terrible problem. Let's assume you train the naïve classifier and put it in production ready to analyze incoming articles and make a prediction about the class it belongs to.

What if the article contains a word never found in the training dataset related to a given class? In this case, the probability calculated for the word in relationship to a given class would be 0. And this raises a serious concern. In fact, having a zero probability in a product of probabilities would take everything down to 0. As a result, the probability that the article is tagged with the given class would be 0.

Having zero probability ultimately affects the accuracy of the overall response. It could mean that the use of an "unusual but still legitimate" word in the jargon of, say, sports could qualify the whole article as non-sports-related! More precisely, without countermeasures, even when all words have a 99 percent probability to refer to sports, a single word with a probability of 0 would take the estimation down to 0.

To avoid that, you add a small and nonzero coefficient α to the numerator and denominator in the previous $P(X_i|C_j)$ formula. The fix is known as *Laplace smoothing*:

$$P(X_i|C_j) = \frac{\textit{Number of documents of class } C_j \textit{ that contain the word } X_i + \alpha}{\textit{Number of documents of class } C_j + (\alpha \cdot n)}$$

The *n* in the formula is the number of features being considered.

If α is zero, no smoothing is applied. Usually, the smoothing factor is a small number in the order of 0.001. In some cases, though, it can be close to 1, especially in the case of very large datasets.

The Final Expression

The MNB variation of the algorithm sets a formula for calculating the conditional probability of a feature given a class that is like the following:

$$P(C_j) \cdot \prod_{i=1}^{N} P(X_i|C_j)^{f_i}$$

In the formula, $P(C_j)$ is the prior probability of the class and f_i is the frequency with which the word X_i appears in the text. N is the number of words to take into account.

> **Note** Sometimes the value resulting from the preceding formula is too small. This phenomenon is known as *underflow*. To overcome the issue and work with numbers of a manageable size, you can shift to a logarithm scale and just return the logarithm of the found number.

To successfully apply MNB to real-life applications, some good feature engineering is often required. In particular, you might want to preprocess the features to remove *stop-words*. In natural language processing, a stop-word is any word removed from text for clarity and to avoid misleading interpretations. A stop-word is any word considered essentially devoid of significance for the purpose of classification. No universal list of stop-words exists, so any application may define its own. In general, however, conjunctions, articles, and verbal forms are great candidates to be treated as stop-words. For example, the text "The game is over" can be treated like "Game over" removing "the" and "is" without altering the originally intended meaning.

Other forms of feature engineering that could make the MNB classifier more effective are lemmatization (grouping together different variations of the word such as singular, plural, past participle) and *n-grams*. An n-gram consists of grouping sequences of words instead of single words.

> **Note** The MNB is ideal for analyzing long texts because it works on the frequency of values. Would it work also for nontext classification? Yes, of course. Would it be effective in the same way for nontext data? Well, the answer depends. The algorithm always uses the frequency of data, and if using the frequency of nontext data is still relevant for the problem at hand, then, yes, the MNB algorithm would also still be effective for nontext data.

Bernoulli Naïve Bayes

The Bernoulli Naïve Bayes (BNB) classifier can be considered as a simplified version of the multinomial Bayes classifier that just assumes a different distribution of probabilities. BNB can be used in the same business scenarios as MNB, except with differently shaped features.

The Binomial Distribution

In statistics, the binomial distribution (or Bernoulli distribution) is used to determine probabilities in experiments where only two outcomes are possible, trials are independent, and each outcome has a constant probability on each trial. In other words, binomial is the simplified version of multinomial in which the space of outcomes counts only two options.

The canonical example provided to explain binomial distribution is the toss of a coin. The coin is two-sided, each toss is independent, and each face of the coin has its own distinct and constant probability to be tossed.

The BNB classifier assumes a *binomial* distribution of the features. Ultimately, it works in nearly the same way as MNB, except that the features it deals with are assumed to be Boolean values.

Distribution of Words

Mapped to the text analysis scenario, a binomial distribution of the features means that each word found in the text (hence, a feature) still has its own distinct and constant probability of appearing in a document of a given class (e.g., news, sports, politics). This probability is 50 percent: either the word exists in the document of a given class, or the word doesn't exist. In the training dataset, there are columns for words, and the value is no longer the frequency of that word in the text but a simpler Boolean: found/not found.

To apply the naïve Bayes' theorem, you need to be able to calculate the probability: $P(X_i | C_j)$. How do you do it? In BNB, you model a Bernoulli distribution for the various classes and the set of features:

$$P(X_i | C_j) = \theta^{x_i} (1-\theta)^{1-x_i}$$

Note that X_i can take only 0 or 1 as its value. The θ indicates the probability that in the C_j class you'll find occurrences of the word X_i. In the literature, the θ is sometimes labeled with a subscript θ_{ij} just to indicate that it refers to the probability of the ith feature being found in the jth class.

The Final Expression

The BNB variation of the algorithm then sets a formula for calculating the conditional probability of a feature given a class that is like the following:

$$P(C_j) \cdot \prod_{i=1}^{N} \theta^{x_i} (1-\theta)^{1-x_i}$$

In the formula, $P(C_j)$ is the prior probability of the class. As mentioned, given the Bernoulli distribution, X_i can be only 0 or 1. This means that two possible values for the probability to multiply are θ (when $X_i = 1$) and $1-\theta$ (when $X_i = 0$).

The BNB classifier is therefore particularly suited to analyze short articles in which the absence (or presence) of a word represents a strong signal of belonging to a given class.

> **Note** A naïve Bayes classifier with a Bernoulli event model is quite different from a multinomial classifier in which the frequency is set to 1. The difference is that a Bernoulli classifier uses a different distribution of probability to address, in a more specific way, different business problems. The BNB is particularly suitable for analyzing short texts.

Gaussian Naïve Bayes

The Gaussian Naïve Bayes classifier gets into play when all features take continuous values and follow a normal (Gaussian) distribution. The hypothesis about the normal distribution is not restrictive at all and fairly common in statistics because of the mathematical foundation represented by the Central Limit Theorem.

The Gaussian Distribution

Also known as the bell curve, the Gaussian distribution is a continuous function that provides the probabilities of occurrence of the continuous values of a random variable (e.g., a feature). The values end up distributing along a curve with some crucial properties:

- The shape of the curve is symmetric.

- The curve has a bump in the middle.

- Mean and median are the same and are placed right in the middle of the distribution.

The typical bell curve is shown in Figure 14-1.

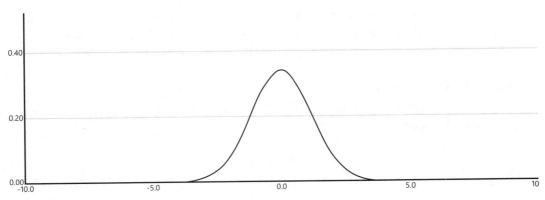

FIGURE 14-1 The typical bell curve representing the Gaussian distribution

When you look at the curve, the probability of values (in a continuous interval) tends to concentrate around the mean.

> **Note** The Gaussian distribution of probability is only one of the most commonly used ones, and it works well with most continuous features met in the context of most problems. However, for certain problems, a different distribution may be more useful, such as the Poisson distribution. In particular, the Poisson distribution is a discrete (not continuous) distribution and expresses well the probability of a given number of events that occur in a fixed interval of time.

Probability Density versus Probability

Intuitively, the probability is the ratio between positive cases and the total number of cases. When continuous values are involved, though, the preceding concept of probability becomes pointless. In a continuous scenario, a feature can take an infinite number of values, and subsequently, the probability that it will take a specific value is always 0. The reason is that the denominator—the number of possible values—tends to be infinite, and consequently, the numerator is a finite value. The result is 0.

In a continuous scenario, you need to assume a distribution of probability. Any distribution has its own density function. In light of this, the probability of a feature is calculated within a range of values as the area under the density function, above the horizontal axis, and comprised between the lowest and greatest values of the range. (See Figure 14-2.)

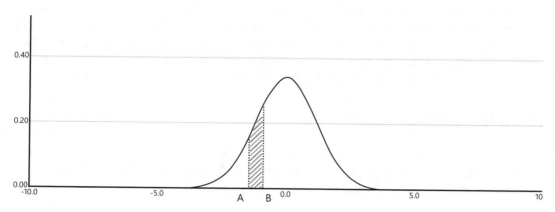

FIGURE 14-2 The dashed area indicates the probability that the feature falls in the [A, B] interval.

It is worth noting that the density function is always nonnegative, and the entire area delimited by the density function and the part of the X-axis that includes the domain of the feature is equal to 1.

> **Note** The probability of a continuous variable assuming values in a given range is the integral of the density function in the same range. By the same mathematical token, the density function is a derivative of the probability function.

The Gaussian Naïve Classifier

The Gaussian distribution has the following density function:

$$p(X_i \mid C_j) = \frac{1}{\sqrt{2\pi\sigma_j^2}} e^{-\frac{(i-\mu_j)^2}{2\sigma_j^2}}$$

In the formula, σ_j is the variance of the feature X_i with respect to the class C_j. At the same time, μ_j is the mean of the feature X_i with respect to the class C_j. To calculate this value, you go over the dataset, take the rows labeled as C_j, and calculate mean and variance of the various features.

The whole Naïve Classifier algorithm remains the same with some small adaptations. As the starting point, you calculate the probability of all classes. Next, for each known class, you first compute mean and variance for the features at hand and next compute the conditional probability using the preceding exponential function. Finally, you compute the product of all conditional probabilities for the various classes and return the class with the highest score.

The Gaussian Naïve classifier is frequently used in nontext classification problems when continuous values are available. This is certainly the case with medical diagnostics. The Gaussian classifier works only with continuous features. So, what if only a few of the features are continuous? In this case, a bit of feature engineering is necessary to turn continuous values into discrete values using quartile values to break continuity. The opposite, namely turning discrete values into continuous values, while technically possible, is pointless because it would make "continuous" calculations on data with clear gaps.

Naïve Bayes Regression

In this chapter, we focused on Bayesian classifiers and only briefly hinted at the existence of Bayesian regressors. Applying the naïve Bayes' theorem to regression is definitely possible, although at the cost of some additional computational effort.

Foundation of Bayesian Linear Regression

Compared to traditional linear regression (also sometimes referred to as frequentist regression), a Bayesian regressor has two major benefits:

- Any uncertainty about predictions is explicit.

- There is a possibility of incorporating prior knowledge in the model.

In particular, the second point deserves some further thinking.

Benefits of Aprioristic Knowledge

As you saw earlier, the Bayesian model builds a posterior probability proportional to the inherent likelihood of data multiplied by the aprioristic probability of parameters. The more aprioristic knowledge you can add to the model, the more information you can hard-code in it. This brings two more advantages.

First, it allows you to fight overfitting effectively, even with a limited dataset available. Second, it keeps the computational effort of the algorithm, when used in production, to a minimum because some numbers that would be costly to calculate can be taken for granted as aprioristic assumptions.

Incremental Learning

The mechanics of Bayesian learning, so solidly founded on prior knowledge of fact and the ability to incorporate it in the formula, also allows for incremental building of trained models.

The more sophisticated the problem, the larger the dataset and the more expensive the training phase in terms of computational resources. Bayesian learning, instead, allows you to change the prior knowledge when new observations are available and incorporate as "known" facts the results of previous trainings done on a smaller dataset.

As a result, training can be done incrementally with one smaller dataset at a time, just changing the formulas for likelihood and prior probability based on what appears to be acknowledged facts.

Revisiting Linear Regression

Let's try to understand how linear regression, which we discussed in Chapter 11, "How to Make Simple Predictions: Linear Regression," can be revisited and reformulated in a Bayesian scenario. Here's the classic, frequentist expression:

$$y_i = \alpha + \beta x_i + \varepsilon$$

Once revisited in probabilistic terms, it becomes a normal distribution of the following form:

$$y_i \approx N(\mu_i, \sigma^2)$$

In the formula, N indicates the normal distribution, $\mu_i = \alpha + \beta x_i$ is the value of the feature, and σ^2 is the variance and incorporates the error. The fundamental difference with classic regression is that the training is not aimed at guessing the single optimal values of α and β, but will try to guess a distribution so that the values of α and β result from prior knowledge and evidence (likelihood).

> **Note** The interesting thing to notice is that the more you know about the observations (i.e., the dataset), the less relevant the selection of the distribution becomes. In case of a very large dataset (potentially infinite), in fact, values tend to be the same you would get through a frequentist approach.

Applications of Bayesian Linear Regression

What's the field of application for Bayesian linear regression? First, the Bayesian approach works in regression problems for which there's only a limited amount of data likely insufficient to produce a good response with the classic approach. Second, it works when some prior domain knowledge is available, and it is desirable to incorporate it in the model.

The use of a Bayesian model gives an explicit measure of the uncertainty: you get not only a prediction but also the likelihood of it as estimated by the model. Bayesian regression therefore works when too little data is available or is too large to process in a single shot. In both cases, the approach allows you to build an initial estimate and improve it later as more data is acquired or just made available.

While the Bayesian approach also works for regression, it remains an approach mostly used for classification. As a forward reference, consider that in practice a neural network is often preferable to a Bayesian regressor.

Summary

In some real-life types of predictions and classifications, knowing the likelihood of the response would help make better and more insightful decisions. There are problems in which classic regression and classification algorithms work beautifully and problems in which a probabilistic dimension would be valuable when not strictly required.

Bayesian algorithms are largely used in sentiment analysis and recommendation systems and whenever quick and relatively effective screening of data is vital.

All real-life applications of Bayesian statistics have a key point in common: not only does the predicted value matter, but also the likelihood of the prediction is crucial. Think, for example, of the diagnosis of an important disease: you want to know whether the patient has (or can develop) a given disease, but also with which probability. Put another way, you want to know how *sure* the algorithm is about its response. Over two centuries later, Bayes' theorem is still the foundation of an entire sector of statistics and the basis for a number of machine learning techniques.

In this chapter, we provided an overview of some key concepts from probability theory and then moved on to discuss the impact of Bayes' theorem on classification. We discussed various meta-algorithms such as multinomial, Bernoulli, and Gaussian classifiers and briefly hinted at Bayesian regression.

In the next chapter, we'll tackle clustering and data grouping. The next chapter completes our overview of shallow learning algorithms.

## CHAPTER 15

How to Group Data: Classification and Clustering

If a machine is expected to be infallible, it cannot also be intelligent.
—Alan Turing, from "Computing Machinery and Intelligence", 1950

In the previous chapters, you encountered the term *classification* many times. Classification is one of the most common problems in machine learning, and it can be tackled in various ways, including decision trees, Bayesian classifiers, and even logistic regression.

In this chapter, we'll present two more sophisticated algorithms for classification, and then we'll move on to address a subtly similar problem—*clustering*. According to most dictionaries, classification is the act of arranging a group of things in homogeneous classes based on their characteristics. Clustering, instead, is defined as the act of putting together a number of things of the same kind. The border between classification and clustering is very thin. Curiously, if you look for synonyms, you can hardly find *cluster* and *classify* set as synonyms, but both are usually presented as synonyms of the term *group*.

In machine learning, classification is a form of supervised learning and refers to the process of classifying labeled data. Clustering is a form of unsupervised learning and refers to the process of classifying unlabeled data. In classification, all training data items have a feature indicating the name of the category. In clustering, there's no such explicit labeling feature in the training dataset. In classification, a new data item is then predicted (or classified) into one of the known categories, based on the information the model has learned during training. (The capability to make predictions on the basis of learned information is what turns plain learning into supervised learning.)

In clustering, there's no distinction between preliminary training and production. All you do is run an algorithm on a dataset to obtain a partition in which items in the same cluster are determined to have something in common. Next, to make sense of the output, data scientists and domain experts have to look into the content of each cluster.

Let's look at more sophisticated algorithms for classification.

Note Although machine learning algorithms are commonly split into supervised and unsupervised, an unsupervised algorithm alone can hardly be the solution of a real-world problem. More often, it is the first step run to clean data (e.g., multidimensionality reduction) before further acting on it with a combination of other (mostly) supervised techniques.

A Basic Approach to Supervised Classification

As mentioned, classification is about predicting the (known) category in which a new data item would fit. In this chapter, we'll examine approaches to classification that are more flexible and sophisticated than decision trees, regression, or Bayes classifiers. The first algorithm we present—the K-Nearest Neighbors algorithm—is straightforward to grab, is easy to implement, and works very well in some specific scenarios such as recommendation systems.

The K-Nearest Neighbors Algorithm

The K-Nearest Neighbors (KNN) algorithm classifies data items using an intuitively simple approach summarized by the proverb "Birds of a feather flock together." The algorithm, in fact, assumes that similar data items (the birds of a feather) lie sufficiently close to each other in the dataset (flock together).

All the algorithm does is measure the distance between the data item to classify and all items in the dataset, take the K nearest neighbors, and put the data item in the class that is most common in the group of neighbors. To work, KNN needs two core parameters. One is the size of the group of neighbors, which is just what the K in the name symbolizes. The other is the function that measures the distance between two data items.

Number of Neighbors

Honestly, determining the most appropriate value of K is far from easy. The quick rule that always works is "pick the value of K that gives you the best results on the actual dataset." There are a couple of general considerations to make.

First, the value of K indicates the level of farsightedness you want. The smallest possible value of K is 1, but it essentially means running the algorithm with blinders on. A value of 1 prevents the algorithm from gaining any broad understanding of the data and just makes no sense—neither computational (it won't make it faster) nor business. A value of 1 doesn't give you any reliability on the result because the variance is incredibly high. It is not really much better than making a random choice.

Second, a very high value of K (close to the size of the dataset) stabilizes the variance but at the cost of missing possibly important details, and it essentially means running the algorithm with some binoculars. Here the metaphor of farsightedness is truly appropriate: with blinders on, you can't see beyond your nose; with binoculars on, you can't see much up close.

At any rate, a starting point is necessary. A pragmatic rule suggests initially setting K to the square root of N, where N is the size of the dataset, and adjusting as appropriate. Another pragmatic rule suggests always picking an odd number if the number of classes is two and you're essentially doing binary classification.

Calculating the Distance Between Data Items

Neighbors are defined as the K items in the dataset nearest the data item to classify. The most common function used to calculate the distance is the Euclidean distance, defined as follows:

$$D(X_1, X_2) = \sqrt{\sum_{i=1}^{M}(X_{2,i} - X_{1,i})^2}$$

Given two data items X_1 and X_2, you calculate the difference between the values of the ith feature $X_{2,i} - X_{1,i}$. In the formula, M is the number of features considered; therefore, the number of features you're interested in considering to calculate the proximity of two data items. The squares of all differences are then summed up, and the Euclidean distance between two data items is finally defined as the square root of the summation.

Another slightly different function for the distance is the so-called taxi distance or Manhattan distance:

$$D(X_1, X_2) = \sum_{i=1}^{M}|X_{2,i} - X_{1,i}|$$

In this case, the distance is the summation of the modules of differences, feature by feature. The name *Manhattan* refers to the highly geometric layout of the streets in the city. In fact, the algorithm measures the distance as if it were traveling using parallel and perpendicular lines. The Euclidean distance, instead, connects two points, building a triangle in which the direct line is the hypotenuse. (See Figure 15-1.)

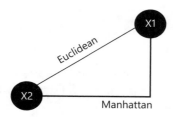

FIGURE 15-1 Comparing the Euclidean and Manhattan distance

It is key to notice that Euclidean and Manhattan distances work well for numerical values of the features. In this context, values can be continuous or discrete without affecting the calculation of the distance.

When strings are involved, you might want to use the Hamming distance or the Levenshtein distance. Both work calculating the minimum number of edits necessary to turn one string into the other. Hamming assumes strings of the same length, whereas Levenshtein works on any two sequences of characters.

> **Note** The Euclidean and Manhattan distance are two particular instances of the more general Minkowski distance. The Minkowski distance with a parameter of 1 is Manhattan and with a parameter of 2 is Euclidean. You will find out that the Minkowski distance is the default distance parameter in the KNN implementation of the popular Python library *scikit-learn*.

Dealing with Categorical Data

What if you mixed numerical and categorical fields in your dataset? In this context, good examples of categorical values are payment types, colors, vendor name, gender—all stuff that, as a developer, you want to treat through an enum type.

In case of categorical data, you might want to apply the one-hot encoding technique (see Chapter 4, "General Steps for a Machine Learning Solution") and turn each categorical feature into a collection of Boolean features.

> **Important** The selection of the ideal distance is not an obvious step. As foregone as it may sound, you need to find a distance function that works for your data. There's an entire field of research about it, and it is called Neighborhood Components Analysis. Euclidean and Manhattan are two examples, but many more distances exist. The good news is that most common distances are provided out of the box by libraries; the bad news is that if none of them work the way you need, you have to run your own KNN algorithm. But, fortunately, the implementation isn't that hard!

Steps of the Algorithm

Once the number of K and the distance metric have been identified—at least, for a good start—coding the algorithm is a relatively easy task. As you'll see in a moment, in fact, the sequence of steps and the underlying logic of the algorithm are fairly straightforward to capture.

The ultimate goal of the algorithm is to predict the category (label) that a given data item belongs to, given the dataset as currently classified.

Brute-Force KNN Implementation

In its simplest and probably most naïve form, the KNN algorithm takes a brute-force approach and computes the distance between the data item to classify and all the items in the dataset. This results in a computational complexity of $O(DN^2)$, where D is the number of features. Here's some C# pseudocode:

```
var itemToClassify = ...;
var K = ...;
var sortedList = new SortedList();

// Build the table of distances
foreach(var item in dataset)
{
    var distance = CalculateDistance(itemToClassify, item);
    sortedList.Add(item, distance);
}

// Pick the neighbors
var neighbors = sortedList.Top(K);

// Get the labels to predict from the neighbors
var labels = ExtractLabelsToPredict(neighbors);

// Take the mode (the most used value)
return ExtractMostFrequentlyUsedLabel(labels)
```

As you can see, the algorithm first makes a pass over the entire dataset and builds the table of distances between the item to classify and all items in the dataset. Next, it extracts the nearest K element from a sorted list of distances. The next step is predicting the category the item is determined to belong to. The category is selected by looking at the categories of selected neighbors and picking the one used most often. (This is nothing more than the old familiar concept of mode.)

 Note In case the KNN algorithm is used for a regression task, everything works the same except that the mean of the feature to predict is returned rather than the mode.

More Efficient KNN Implementations

For large datasets, calculating distances with all the data items soon becomes impractical. The brute-force implementation can be made more efficient by reducing the number of necessary distance calculations.

One approach uses a data structure called *K-D tree* to store the list of distances. A K-D tree is a binary tree in which the leaves are the data items, and all nonleaf nodes split the space in two halves based on the value of one particular feature. A K-D tree is typically a balanced tree, meaning that each leaf node is approximately the same distance from the root. Building a K-D tree takes $O(D \cdot N log N)$, where D is the number of features. The core of building a K-D tree is having all data sorted in all dimensions—hence, D multiplied by the typical cost of sorting.

The *D* in the complexity makes a KNN founded on a K-D tree at the risk of performance when *D* grows indefinitely. Be aware that, beyond the cost of building the tree, you also have to consider the cost of finding the neighbors. For large values of *D*, the usual logarithmic cost of visiting a balanced tree query grows significantly to the point of pragmatically resulting in nearly a linear cost plus the overhead of using a tree structure. The bottom line is that a KNN based on a K-D tree works beautifully for relatively small values of *D*, typically up to 20 or even 30. For higher values, another data structure is used, which leads to another variation of the KNN algorithm.

The Ball Tree is a binary tree in which every node defines a D-dimensional hypersphere (also known as the ball) containing a subset of the data items to be searched. The complexity loses the *D* factor and is only $O(NlogN)$.

Also, heuristics say that a KNN grows based on both the Ball Tree and K-D tree as the size of neighbors. When the size of *K*—the neighbors—grows large compared to *N*, a brute-force implementation might be the optimal choice.

Training of the KNN Algorithm

In the landscape of machine learning algorithms, KNN is an exception because its learning pipeline is unusual; the algorithm, in fact, needs no canonical training and validation phases. The algorithm just matches the live data to the dataset you specify. In other words, the training dataset is used for queries as is and as if it were the result of some preliminary training.

So, no model is built, but how would you assess the quality of the response? You can use cross-validation, typically on 5 or 10 folds, and see the metrics. This works much better than splitting the dataset between training and test data.

The larger the dataset, the more accurate the result can be; but the larger the dataset, the more it takes to get a prediction. Nothing is easy!

Business Scenarios

The most common scenario for KNN is recommendation systems where all you want to do is recommend similar items to customers who have showed interest in a given data item. For example, you can compare a set of customers who like each data item. When you find that two similar sets of customers like two different data items, you can conclude that the data items themselves are likely similar and can be recommended to both sets of customers.

Although KNN is not as sexy as a neural network or the Support Vector Machine (more on this in a moment), it works nicely for recommending products to buy, media content to consume, or suggestions to share with users of a software network. Another area of application for KNN is concept searching—finding documents (e.g., emails, contracts) relevant to a project.

 Note KNN is probably slower than a neural network or Support Vector Machine, but it's quick and easy to set up (not having a training phase does help) and highly readable by humans.

Support Vector Machine

Admittedly, the name of the algorithm—Support Vector Machine (SVM)—is quite intimidating, and so is some of the mathematics behind it. Overall, SVM is a supervised algorithm that can be effectively employed to address both classification and regression problems. It is frequently used for text classification, spam detection, and sentiment analysis. It also performs well when used on images to recognize patterns, whether handwritten notes or digits and objects or faces.

It delivers quite accurate responses even when trained on relatively small datasets, as long as the data in them is clean and with limited overlapping. With larger datasets, it tends to be less effective because of the much longer time it takes to train. In fact, the mathematics it relies on is fairly sophisticated—intuitive to grab but hard to digest and apply.

Let's keep this description to the absolute minimum that's legally possible!

Overview of the Algorithm

Technically, the SVM algorithm is a binary classification algorithm. It splits the n-dimensional space of data into two halves and fits any given data item in one of two. Don't be fooled by the fact that it's a binary classification algorithm. In the end, this is only a technical detail. Sophisticated compositions of the core algorithm exist to make it suitable for any classification tasks.

How does SVM cut an n-dimensional space in two? From a purely mathematical perspective, well, that's not trivial at all. However, sometimes a picture is worth a thousand words. (See Figure 15-2.)

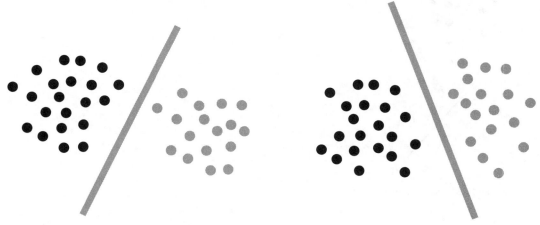

FIGURE 15-2 Two examples of splitting a dataset in two halves

The Concept of a Hyperplane

The message to get from Figure 15-2 is that SVM manages to find a line that cuts the space of data into two distinct parts. The figure doesn't lie, but it makes the concept too simple. In machine learning, the space of data—the dataset—is made up of a collection of data rows each with n features. In geometric terms, the dataset is therefore an R^n space, where n is the number of features. Figure 15-2 just illustrates the behavior of SVM in a simple and unrealistic R^2 space—as if the dataset counted only two features. To understand the behavior of SVM in an n-dimensional space, you first need to understand the concept of a *hyperplane*.

A hyperplane is a subspace whose dimension is one less than the dimension of the parent space. In R^n, a hyperplane is then a subspace of the $n-1$ dimension. Subsequently, a hyperplane is a straight line in R^2 (as in Figure 15-2) and a plane in R^3.

As mentioned, the SVM algorithm operates in the R^n space, where n is the number of features, and all it does is look for a hyperplane to split the dataset in two. In general, there might be infinite hyperplanes that could cut the space in two. SVM looks for the hyperplane that maximizes the minimal distance between the two resulting subsets. In other words, SVM picks the hyperplane such that the distance between the hyperplane and the nearest points in both subspaces is maximum. The distance to maximize is called the margin. (See Figure 15-3.)

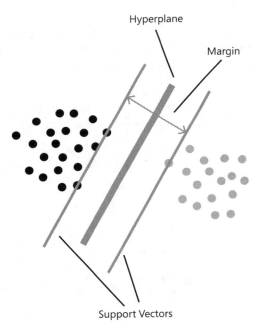

FIGURE 15-3 Hyperplane and support vectors

The Concept of a Support Vector

The name of the algorithm—Support Vector Machine—comes from yet another concept well illustrated in Figure 15-3. The points of each subspace nearest the hyperplane are called *support vectors*, just because they sustain and support the separation space.

A support vector is the last point of each subset before running across the hyperplane. SVM selects the hyperplane whose support vectors are at the greatest distance. Most of the complexity of SVM is finding those vectors.

Nonlinearly Separable Datasets

Admittedly, the SVM scenario depicted so far is still simplistic because it assumes one key fact: a linear separation exists between the points in the dataset. This is not always true and depends on the actual content of the dataset. For a two-dimensional example, look at Figure 15-4. Given the represented distribution of data points, how can you find a straight line to separate the space? Well, you can't.

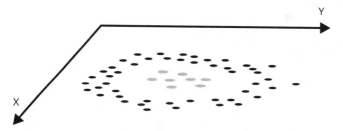

FIGURE 15-4 A bidimensional example of a nonlinearly separable dataset

Again, an intuitive solution exists, but putting it into practice may be challenging. In plain terms, to split a nonlinearly separable dataset, you project it in a larger dimensional space where a hyperplane exists. For example, you can project the R^2 plane of Figure 15-4 in an R^3 space, and this would give you one additional dimension along which the data points can be distributed. How would you do this? As an example, you can take each data point x_1, x_2 in R^2 and project it to R^3 by adding a third coordinate z, as shown here. (The sum of the squares is just an illustrative example.)

$$z = x_1^2 + x_2^2$$

In the new R^3 space, a separating hyperplane exists for some $z = k$, as shown in Figure 15-5.

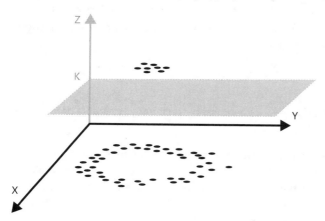

FIGURE 15-5 Graphical representation of the separating hyperplane

In the example, the equation of the hyperplane is $x_1^2 + x_2^2 = k$ and turns out to represent a circumference. (See Figure 15-6.)

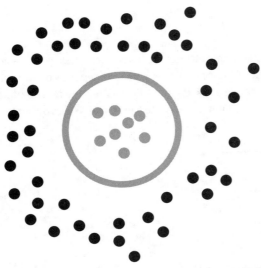

FIGURE 15-6 A nonlinear hyperplane splits the dataset into two halves.

In general, the hardest part of nonlinear scenarios is identifying the actual function that would optimally project data points in the larger space. It's not a trivial point and requires deep analysis of the data and advanced mathematical skills, specifically in the area of functional analysis (e.g., Mercer's theorem).

> **Note** The projection work is performed through something called a *kernel function*. A kernel function takes in input vectors in the original space and returns the scalar product (dot product) of the vectors in the target space. A kernel function K is expressed as $K(x, z) = \gamma(\varphi(x) \cdot \varphi(z))$, where φ is the mapping function and can take various forms: polynomial, exponential, and sigmoidal. The coefficient γ controls the margin between support vectors and the hyperplane. The higher the coefficient, the more precise the algorithm, although the risk of overfitting is always around the corner.

Linear or Nonlinear

We have two variations of the SVM algorithm—for linearly and nonlinearly separable data. How do you know which one to use?

To cut a long story short, linearly separable datasets are much more the exception than the norm. Using the projection trick (also referred to as the kernel trick) is usually fast enough after you have identified the best set of parameters—the type of kernel and the γ coefficient. So, it's recommended that you go directly with a nonlinear SVM. If the results of a nonlinear algorithm are accurate enough, you can infer that the dataset is nonlinearly separable!

Beyond that, truly linearly separable datasets are rare and easily recognizable, just plotting some data even in a small number of dimensions. In addition, with linearly separable datasets, you probably can obtain good results even without resorting to SVM but stopping at simpler algorithms such as logistic regression.

> **Note** Even though the action of the kernel function can be described as projecting the dataset in a larger space, that never happens in practice, and you'll never duplicate the dataset in the target space. This is the reason that ultimately makes the projection trick quite effective from a computational perspective. For the kernel function to work, in fact, it suffices that the scalar product of each data point in the source and target space (with the additional coordinate added) is calculated.

A Quick Mathematical Refresher

We've already mentioned the scalar product of two vectors, and in the rest of the SVM section, we will mention fundamental operations between vectors. Let's briefly recap some key facts. (Feel free to skip this section if you're familiar with the topic.)

Basic Operations on Vectors

Like numbers, vectors can be summed and subtracted from one another. If you represent vectors using the $(x_1, x_2, \ldots, x_n)$ numeric notation, the sum of two vectors X and Y merely consists of the sum of the elements in the same position:

$$z_i = x_i + y_i$$

Similarly, the difference of two vectors results in a new vector of the same dimension in which the value of corresponding elements has been subtracted:

$$z_i = x_i - y_i$$

Likewise, you can multiply a vector by a scalar value (i.e., a number). That results in a new vector of the same dimension in which each constituent element has been multiplied by the scalar:

$$z_i = scalar * x_i$$

Scalar Product of Vectors

The scalar product of two vectors is not a new vector but a scalar number. The resulting value is calculated as follows:

$$X \cdot Y = \sum_{i=1}^{n} X_i * Y_i$$

Related to the scalar product of two vectors is the concept of *norm*. Technically, the norm of a vector is defined as follows:

$$|X| = \sqrt{X_1^2 + \ldots + X_n^2}$$

The net effect of the norm is that dividing the scalar product of two vectors X and Y by the norm of any vector just simplifies the expression as if vectors were plain numbers:

$$\frac{X \cdot Y}{|X|} = Y$$

Lagrange Multipliers

Employing Lagrange multipliers is a strategy used in mathematical optimization to find the local maximum and minimum of a function when other conditions should be satisfied by the chosen values.

The idea is to convert the function f into a new function L, as follows:

$$L(x, \lambda) = f(x) - \sum_{i=1}^{m} \lambda_i * g_i(x)$$

The added member refers to the known constraints so that the function to optimize is a plain unconstrained function to minimize.

Steps of the Algorithm

In spite of the rather sophisticated logic of hyperplanes, support vectors, and kernel functions, getting a prediction from a trained SVM model is a simple question of calculating a scalar product and checking the value against a threshold. Let's examine the mechanics of the prediction first and then move on to see what really happens during the training phase.

Mechanics of the Prediction

At the end of the day, to predict a data point P in one of the two subsets (left or right) in which the hyperplane splits the dataset, the algorithm uses the following formula to get a value:

$$value = W \cdot P$$

The W in the formula is a vector perpendicular to the identified hyperplane, and it is determined during the training phase. The calculated value in the formula is the scalar product of W and P. If the value is greater than or equal to $1 + b$, the data point is predicted in the right half. If the value is less than or equal to $-1 + b$ the data point is predicted in the left half. The coefficient b is also determined during the training phase.

Note What if the point to predict falls outside the interval $(-1+b, 1+b)$? Technically, it would mean that the algorithm doesn't know very well what to say. Some implementations smooth the preceding constraint and opt for one of the halves, depending on how the value compares to the sole $1+b$ threshold. However, maintaining a larger interval is the sign that you might want to retrain the model. In fact, a data point that falls in the comfort zone around the separating hyperplane would be a great candidate to become a new support vector. Finally, note that most implementations of SVM also let you set a worker variable (known as *slack variable*) to restrict the interval if necessary.

Figure 15-7 provides a visual explanation of the prediction mechanism in a bidimensional space.

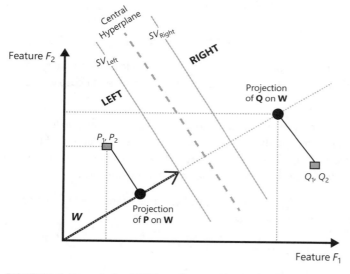

FIGURE 15-7 How a trained SVM predicts two data points P and Q

The plane in the figure has dataset features on the X- and Y-axes. From the origin of the plane, a vector W departs and proceeds perpendicularly to the separating hyperplanes. It's three hyperplanes: the central hyperplane and the hyperplanes passing for the left and right support vector points. A given point P with feature values P_1, P_2 is predicted in the left or right half, depending on where its orthogonal projection lies on W. In the figure, the projection of P on W determines a point in the left half. The projection of the data point Q, instead, falls in the right half.

Important When you look at Figure 15-7, it might seem blatantly obvious that P belongs to the left half and Q to the right half. It isn't obvious at all, however, in a more realistic R^n space when many more features are involved. In addition, consider that hyperplanes and support vectors are just numbers and have no visual representation in the algorithm! Figure 15-7 just shows, graphically, how the prediction mechanism of SVM works.

Mechanics of the Training

As visually explained in Figure 15-7, you need the vector W, perpendicular to the hyperplanes, to make the prediction. The vector results from the conditions in Table 15-1.

TABLE 15-1 Conditions for the Vector W

$W \cdot P + b \geq 1$	Data point P is in the right half. If a slack variable is defined, it is summed here to 1.
$W \cdot P + b \leq -1$	Data point P is in the left half. If a slack variable is defined, it is summed here to -1.

In particular, for the special points SV_{left} and SV_{right} selected as the support vectors, the following equations hold:

$$W \cdot SV_{left} + b = -1$$

$$W \cdot SV_{right} + b = -1$$

Note that the use of the factor 1 here is arbitrary but doesn't cause any loss of generality. In fact, if you use any value δ, you could always normalize dividing by the same factor, ending up with a value of 1.

SVM is a supervised algorithm, so you can assume a binary classification scenario. In light of this, you know which feature you intend to predict and the (binary) value it has for each element of the dataset. Hence, you add a new feature column Y that maps labels to predict 1 and -1. Let's say that the feature Y gets -1 if the feature has the value you expect for the left half and 1 for the right half.

Let's now define the distance $SV_{right} - SV_{left}$ between the two hyperplanes that pass for the support vectors. Using the preceding equations, you can write

$$W \cdot SV_{right} - W \cdot SV_{left} = 1 - b + 1 - b = 2$$

If you divide both members of the equations by the norm of the vector W (indicated as $|W|$), you obtain the following:

$$SV_{right} - SV_{left} = \frac{2}{|W|}$$

This distance indicates the margin around the central hyperplane and determines the decision boundary of the algorithm. This is the value you want to maximize during training. For the ease of mathematical computation, though, instead of maximizing the distance, SVM chooses to minimize the reciprocal of the distance in which the norm is replaced with its square:

$$\frac{1}{2}|W|^2$$

Note that neither the presence of the multiplier nor the square in this context introduces a significant deviation. At the same time, though, the resulting function is convex, which makes it noticeably easier to get its derivative.

Discovering the Coefficients for Prediction

The actual problem that the SVM training needs to solve—minimizing the reciprocal of the distance function—is one of *constrained optimization*. In mathematics, constrained optimization is the process of optimizing a function with respect to some variables with respect to constraints set on the variables. In this case, the constraint to match is $Y * (W \cdot P) \geq 1$, where Y is the additional feature added to the dataset (set to 1 or –1 and mapped to the label to predict) and P is an element of the dataset.

A constrained optimization problem is commonly solved using a technique known as Lagrange multipliers. The technique transforms the original function into a new function that embeds the constraints and assigns each a coefficient α_i—the multiplier. The new function is as follows:

$$\frac{1}{2}|W|^2 - \sum_{i=1}^{n} \alpha_i [Y_p (P \cdot W + b) - 1]$$

The index i refers to the rows of the dataset, and P is any of the elements in the dataset. The Y_p member refers to the value of the Y feature in the P element of the dataset. By incorporating constraints in the new Lagrange function, you reduce the constraint optimization problem to a classic optimization problem.

To find the minimum, SVM calculates partial derivatives with respect to W and b and sets them to zero while ensuring that α_i multipliers are greater than or equal to 0. Here are the results of partial derivatives:

$$W = \sum_{i=1}^{n} \alpha_i Y_{p_i} * P_i$$

$$\sum_{i=1}^{n} \alpha_i Y_{p_i} = 0$$

When you replace the new expression of W in the Lagrange function (after some further steps omitted for brevity), you obtain a function where the only unknown members are the coefficients α_i. These coefficients are then discovered using a classic minimization technique, such as any of those encountered in the preceding chapter, most commonly online gradient descent and variations such as Stochastic Dual Coordinate Ascent (SDCA).

Note In Chapter 8, "ML.NET Tasks and Algorithms," the implementation of the example about multiclass classification used a weird trainer called *SdcaMaximumEntropy*. It was one of the trainers natively provided by the ML.NET library for multiclass classification. What kind of algorithm is it? *SdcaMaximumEntropy* is a special flavor of SVM that uses SDCA to find the actual α_i coefficients.

Inside the Trained Model

Now that you know in some detail what happens during the training of the SVM, let's look back at the mechanics of the prediction to gain a formal—rather than visual—perspective of it. At the end of the day, the output of the SVM training is the following function. For a data point P, the prediction is a function f such that

$$f(P) = \sum_{j \in SV} \alpha_j Y_j * (X_j \cdot P) + b$$

The index j ranges over the two support vectors—selected elements of the dataset. Y_j refers to the value of the column Y for the support vectors, and X_j are the two support vectors. The training phase then is aimed at selecting the support vectors, the α_j coefficients, and b.

Important We discussed the mathematics of SVM and its training phase in the context of linearly separable data. As mentioned, however, linear SVM is not very common, and nonlinearly separable data is more frequent. How does the algorithm deal with the nonlinearity of the dataset? Is anything slated to take its place in some radically different way? The interesting thing is that all we said holds true also for nonlinear scenarios, with a minimal and reasonable change. Because prediction is only a matter of calculating the scalar product of support vectors and data points, all you need to do is use the kernel function of choice that gives you the scalar products in the transformed space.

From Binary to Multiclass Classification

In this chapter, we presented SVM, for the purpose of using it for binary classification. The binary nature, however, applies only to the core algorithm and its underlying mathematics. In the real world, there are some versions of SVM that support multiclass classification. These versions of SVM use an approach called *One vs One*.

Quite simply, One vs One reduces SVM multiclass classification to multiple instances of SVM binary classification. The data point is predicted against all possible pairs of classes, and the most voted class is finally predicted.

SVM is one of the most commonly used algorithms for any form of classification, one of the most mathematically elegant, and because of that, one of the most flexible. Figure 15-8 makes a quick visual comparison between SVM and decision trees. Decision trees can only classify using squares, meaning rigid rules based on feature values. SVM, instead, especially in its nonlinear form, can shape nearly any area of data distribution.

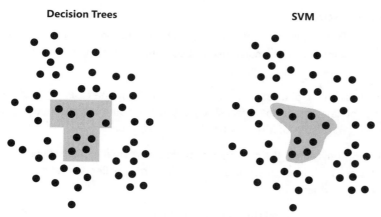

FIGURE 15-8 Visual comparison of decision trees and SVM

Unsupervised Clustering

KNN and SVM are two supervised algorithms that excel at grouping data. A common and key factor in these two algorithms is that both extensively rely on any pre-existing knowledge in the training dataset for predicting the class.

In some circumstances, however, there's no pre-existing classification to learn from for building a classifier. Yet, for some business reasons, you might need to group data as homogeneously as possible. This makes the case for using algorithms of unsupervised learning.

A Business Case: Reducing the Dataset

Before we dig out some unsupervised learning algorithms, let's go through the steps of a realistic and nontrivial business scenario in which you may need unsupervised learning.

As an example, imagine you have a very large dataset and plan to run some canonical forms of supervised learning on it. The humongous size of the dataset, however, is a big obstacle. You may not have sufficient computer power or just the time it may take to train such a huge block of data.

Reducing the Number of Features

In similar situations, a common workaround is managing to reduce the size of the dataset. How would you do that? You can proceed horizontally on columns or vertically on rows.

A first option is trying to reduce the number of features (columns). To do that, you can use Principal Component Analysis (PCA) as discussed in Chapter 4. PCA estimates the variance of features and can select only those that are more relevant to explain the nature of the dataset.

A second option is using unsupervised learning.

Using Clusters to Reduce Rows

You want to cut rows from the dataset, but you want to do that to further process it with supervised algorithms. In other words, you want to drop as many rows as possible but without altering the knowledge in the dataset.

The idea is to make a first pass on the dataset to create clusters of rows. In this case, you don't pay any attention to the features you later intend to predict. The goal (and the ultimate goal of unsupervised learning) is returning a list of clusters of (presumably) homogeneous data.

After the unsupervised algorithm returns the clusters, you build a new, smaller dataset, just picking a few rows from each cluster. This approach ensures that you obtain a smaller dataset but with the same level of homogeneity as the original one.

Let's now look into a couple of unsupervised clustering algorithms.

The K-Means Algorithm

At the highest level of abstraction, the K-Means algorithm splits the dataset into K partitions. Unlike other unsupervised clustering algorithms, K-Means requires that you pass the number K of clusters to return. In addition, it is crucial to note that returned clusters form a partition, meaning that the entire dataset is covered and each element belongs to exactly one cluster.

The algorithm extensively uses the concept of mean, and for this reason, it can work only on numeric features.

Steps of the Algorithm

The goal of the algorithm is building K clusters in which the variance is as low as possible—namely, clustered data points are then determined to be similar. In each cluster, data points place themselves around a central element known as a *centroid*. The centroid is the mean point of the cluster.

To start, the K-Means algorithm selects K data rows in a random way. (Alternatively, you can provide ad hoc centroids.) These data rows are set to be the initial centroids. From a mathematical viewpoint, a centroid data row is a vector of M elements, where M is the number of features in the dataset. In the beginning, in the selected centroid, the values of the features are random in the range of feasible values for the feature.

The second step of the algorithm assigns each row in the dataset to its nearest centroid. The distance used to measure proximity is the square of the Euclidean distance. The square is added for computational reasons to ensure a quicker convergence of the minimization function. The distance between two points P and Q is as follows:

$$Dist(P,Q)^2 = \sum_{i=1}^{n} P_i - Q_i$$

The algorithm looks for the centroid C_i among the K available that have the minimum distance from a given point in the dataset. At this stage, you have K clusters and a first raw partition of the dataset.

Next, the algorithm enters in a loop and runs until a stop condition is met. For each iteration, the centroid is recalculated, and rows are redistributed among the list of new centroids.

The centroid is defined as the mean point of the cluster. This means that after a few data rows have been added to any cluster because of the calculated proximity, you need to check if the current centroid is still the mean point. The algorithm calculates the mean of each feature for all elements in the cluster and sets the centroid accordingly. After that, it calculates a new partition of the dataset in light of the new centroids. In this phase, some elements may be moved from one cluster to another.

The loop ends after a fixed number of iterations or when no row is moved from the currently assigned cluster. Stop conditions are usually configurable as hyperparameters.

Devising the Ideal Number of Clusters

It goes without saying that the effectiveness of the K-Means algorithm depends on the choice of K. At the same time, picking the right value of K is a bit like taking a stab in the dark. In fact, it is not always possible to guess for it in a reliable way. That depends on your knowledge of the data, but at the same time, often you use unsupervised learning just when you don't know much about the data!

So, what's the best practice?

As weird as it may sound, using a random value for K is a common start—preferably a small number like 3 that will grow after a few attempts. However, there are some methods with a more solid mathematical foundation to evaluate the feasibility of the number of clusters after a partition has been obtained.

The *elbow* method works by computing the sum of the distances between the points in each cluster and the centroid. The more you grow K, the more the distances shrink because, by adding a new cluster, you group together closer elements. However, at some point, the marginal gain that the new cluster produces drops, meaning that the elbow is reached and you're really near the optimal value of K for the dataset.

Another approach is the *silhouette* method that measures the quality of clustering. Essentially, the method calculates a metric and determines how well each object lies with its peers within the cluster. A value close to 1 means the dataset row likely fits in the right cluster; a value close to –1 indicates that the row is probably placed in the wrong cluster. Based on the number of misplaced data rows, you can decide whether or not to increase the value of K.

The K-Modes Algorithm

The K-Means algorithm is an extremely popular and effective algorithm, but as mentioned, it works only for numeric features. A variation of it—the K-Modes algorithm—can be used when a lot of categorical values or numeric but largely discrete values exist in the dataset.

The main difference between K-Means and K-Modes is that the latter uses the mode rather than the mean. In addition, another aspect that differentiates the two algorithms is the definition of the distance.

The Dissimilarity Measure

K-Modes measures the distance between centroids and data points using a variation of the Hamming distance known as *dissimilarity*. In the context of the algorithm, here's the definition of the dissimilarity measure for two data points X and Y:

$$D(X,Y) = \sum_{i=1}^{n} \delta(X_j, Y_j)$$

In the formula, n indicates the number of features and δ is defined as follows:

$$\delta(X_j, Y_j) = \begin{cases} 0 \ if \ X_j = Y_j \\ 1 \ if \ X_j \neq Y_j \end{cases}$$

In the end, the distance is the number of the features in the two data points that have matching values.

> **Note** The dissimilarity measure is a generalized form of the aforementioned Hamming distance that, in information theory, expresses the distance between two strings of equal length as the number of positions at which the corresponding symbols are different.

Steps of the Algorithm

Aside from the definition of the distance function, the K-Modes algorithm is nearly the same as K-Means. Moreover, it was expressly defined to extend K-Means to the case of non-numerical features.

The value of K is selected according to the same heuristics discussed for K-Means, and a number of K centroids are randomly selected from the dataset to define the initial set of clusters. All the data rows in the dataset are then assigned to the cluster where the distance between the data row and the centroid is at a minimum according to the dissimilarity measure.

Then the algorithm enters a loop, and for each iteration, it recalculates the centroid of each cluster as the element in which every feature assumes as its value the mode of the feature (i.e., the most frequently used value) calculated on all elements in the cluster. After the algorithm updates the centroid, the dataset is rescanned and data rows are assigned to the cluster to minimize the distance (dissimilarity) with the centroid.

The DBSCAN Algorithm

The two clustering algorithms considered so far require that the number K of clusters is specified as a hyperparameter. This is often a problem, especially when you have no idea of the number of clusters that may be (reasonably) hidden in the dataset and have no easy way to plot it (e.g., too many features) to let clusters emerge visually to some extent.

Another family of algorithms exist that perform clustering without requiring that a fixed number of clusters is set in advance. They are known as *density* algorithms, and DBSCAN is the most illustrious representative.

Density-Based Clustering

DBSCAN, short for density-based spatial clustering of applications with noise, is a relatively recent algorithm, at least compared to K-Means. It was proposed in the late 1990s, some 15 years after the paper that officially presented K-Means to the world. (Seeds of the K-Means algorithm, however, date back to the 1960s.) In other words, DBSCAN, and the field of density-based clustering, originated from the desire to find a different approach for clustering that could find out the (ideal) number of clusters algorithmically.

The core idea of density-based clustering is grouping together data points that lie in a neighborhood defined by a distance (usually Euclidean distance). Also rooted in the idea is that each group should contain a minimum number of points and that data points in low-density regions are subsequently marked as outliers. Any such algorithm depends on three parameters:

Distance Function. This measurement is used to determine how close two data points are. As mentioned, the Euclidean distance is a common choice.

Density. This is the minimum number of points that form a dense region. Under this threshold, points are considered outliers. As you can understand, it's an extremely critical parameter to set.

Proximity. This is the maximum distance allowed between two data points to consider them as neighbors and therefore part of the same cluster. Note that in the literature this value is often referred to as *eps* or *ε*.

Let's see how the algorithm works internally.

Steps of the Algorithm

In a nutshell, DBSCAN is implemented as a full dataset scan; for each unvisited (not assigned to any cluster) point along the way, it attempts to build a new cluster and, if successful, then iteratively tries to expand it, including the neighborhood of each point captured in the cluster. Here's some C# pseudo-code for DBSCAN:

```
function(dataset, distanceFunction, proximity, density)
{
    var clusterIndex = 0;
    foreach(var point in dataset)
    {
        if (AlreadyAssignedToCluster(point))
            continue;

        // Find the neighborhood of the point given distance and proximity
        var neighbors = SearchNearbyPoints(point, dataset, distanceFunction, proximity);
        if (neighbors.Count() < density)
        {
```

```
        // Assign the point to some Outliers cluster (mark as a noisy point)
        AssignToCluster(point, "Outliers");
        continue;
    }

    // Assign the point to a newly defined cluster
    clusterIndex ++;
    AssignToCluster(point, clusterIndex);

    // Try to expand the cluster: add neighbors of each point in the neighborhood
    foreach(var p in neighbors)
    {
        if (AlreadyAssignedToCluster(p))
            continue;

        // Assign the neighbor to the new cluster and get the related neighborhood
        AssignToCluster(p, clusterIndex);
        var relatedNeighbors = SearchNearbyPoints(p, dataset, distanceFunction, proximity);

        // Add more neighbors to further investigate
        if (relatedNeighbors.Count) >= density)
            neighbors.AddRange(relatedNeighbors);
    }
  }
}
```

DBSCAN is generally good at detecting outliers, and the *noise* in the name just refers to this inherent ability. The typical stop condition occurs when there are no more unassigned points. However, in some implementations, the stop can be determined even when the number of unassigned points is so small that it is acceptable to ignore them.

Comparing K-Means and DBSCAN

There are two main differences between K-Means and DBSCAN. First, K-Means is much faster, although the actual performance of DBSCAN is really poor mostly on large datasets. Second, DBSCAN doesn't require that you know the number of clusters in advance.

DBSCAN is fairly intuitive in its behavior and fails when set to work on a dataset with large differences in densities. The reason is that proximity and density parameters can only be set for the entire dataset, and then in case of relevant differences, the value may not be appropriate for certain areas of the dataset. The alternative is using a non-density-based approach—therefore K-Means!

On the other hand, DBSCAN can find arbitrarily shaped clusters and even clusters surrounded by different clusters if the gap is greater than the defined proximity. In DBSCAN, the choice of hyperparameters is crucial. As mentioned, the most commonly used distance function is Euclidean, but this distance becomes expensive to calculate as the number of features grows—the nefarious *curse of dimensionality* problem. As far as the cluster density is concerned, a broadly accepted rule is to never pick up a value smaller than 3 and usually a value greater than the number of features in the dataset. However, the larger the dataset is, the larger the density should be.

Even more delicate is the choice of proximity. The general rule is to pick a small value because a large value would generate too few clusters. At the same time, a too small value would result in a huge number of outliers. The value to start with is usually identified by rendering a *K-Nearest Neighbor graph* (K-NNG). Such a graph connects together each point to its K nearest points. (See Figure 15-9.) An acceptable value of K to find the ideal proximity is density − 1.

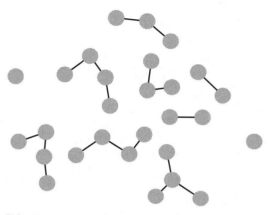

FIGURE 15-9 A sample K-Nearest Neighbor graph

Finally, DBSCAN is mostly insensitive to the order of points in the dataset. However, points located on the edge of two different clusters might result in different clusters if the algorithm is run using a different order of the dataset.

Summary

Grouping data is necessary for statistics as well as machine learning, and there are only two ways to approach the problem: you know how to group them, or you don't know how to group them. You know how to group data if you know the data, and more importantly, you know the classes you want to obtain. If you are in such a situation, you have a classification problem.

A classification problem can be solved in many ways—decision trees, logistic regression, naïve Bayes classifiers. In this chapter, we presented two approaches: K-Nearest Neighbors and, more relevantly, Support Vector Machine.

On the other hand, if you don't know what data you have, you can't even guess how many and which classes you want to obtain. In this case, you have a clustering problem. For quite some time since the 1960s, clustering has been addressed by the K-Means algorithm and its variations. More recently, the DBSCAN algorithm has been introduced, tackling the problem from a different perspective.

Classification is a form of supervised learning, whereas clustering is a form of unsupervised learning. However, most of the time, unsupervised learning is only the first preliminary step to clean and prepare data for some form of supervised learning.

This chapter concludes our exploration of shallow machine learning techniques. The next part of the book is about neural networks and deep learning.

Fundamentals of Deep Learning

## CHAPTER 16

Feed-Forward Neural Networks

Despite all the hype and excitement about AI, it's still extremely limited today relative to what human intelligence is.

—Andrew Ng
Former director of Google Brain and former chief scientist at Baidu

In the course of this book, you've encountered and examined a number of algorithms, some more complex than others, some more suitable than others for classification tasks, some tailor-made for regression problems. What if, however, at the end of the training pipeline, you find out that no algorithms work as the customer demanded? What if the input is not numbers but images, videos, or sound? And what if it is made by time-series but the succession of events is crucial to extract valuable information?

Beyond a certain level of inherent complexity, in the problem and/or in the data source, you need to go beyond shallow learning and move toward a deeper form of learning. Curiously, it's a deeper form of learning but also, quite counterintuitively, way older than many recent algorithms.

Welcome to the dazzling world of neural networks!

A Brief History of Neural Networks

The history of neural networks is longer than many think and even longer than the history of computers. Embryos of the modern computer, in fact, appeared in the 1950s, devised around the model of the von Neumann machine—a combination of central processing unit, memory, storage, and I/O devices.

Well, believe it or not, an embryo of a neural network appeared even earlier than that.

The McCulloch-Pitt Neuron

Back in 1943, at the peak of the Second World War, as Alan Turing and team were fighting hard at Bletchley Park to mechanize attacks against the Nazis' Enigma code, in the United States Warren McCulloch (neuroscientist) and Walter Pitts (mathematician) devised a mathematical model to describe the processing that takes place in the brain when the brain deals with the recognition of highly complex patterns. The model was designed by connecting many basic cells together in the same topological way that neurons are connected in the physical brain. Not coincidentally, those processing units are just called artificial neurons or MCP (McCulloch-Pitts) neurons.

In the paper "A Logical Calculus of the Ideas Immanent in Nervous Activity," published in the *Bulletin of Mathematical Biophysics*, McCulloch and Pitts also gave an elementary but functional model of an artificial neuron. Theirs was only a mathematical model, though, with no concrete mapping to anything physical such as valves, diodes, and resistors.

After that, the next major development in neural networks was the concept of a *perceptron* that Frank Rosenblatt introduced 15 years later, in 1958. Essentially, the perceptron is an evolution of the MCP neuron with an additional preprocessing layer responsible for the detection of patterns. Today, the perceptron is considered the simplest form of artificial neuron and is replaced by more sophisticated forms, such as sigmoid neurons, in real-world applications.

Artificial neurons are the constituent blocks of neural networks.

Feed-Forward Networks

In this chapter, we'll focus on *feed-forward networks*—the most common type of neural network—in which the information flows forward only from the input layer to the output. In Chapter 18, "Other Types of Neural Networks," however, we'll explore other, and more sophisticated, types of neural networks.

In a nutshell, a neural network is a web of computing units (artificial neurons) whose overall behavior is meant to loosely resemble the behavior of the human brain. Artificial neurons are organized in homogeneous layers, and each layer is connected to the next so that information flows from the previous to the next layer, always in the form of real numbers. Each connection between layers mimics the behavior of synapses in the human brain. (See Chapter 1, "How Humans Learn.")

Today, neural networks are commonly used for some specific problems such as cognitive functions (vision, speech recognition and analysis, medical diagnosis, gaming, sophisticated sentiment analysis) and for all those apparently simpler problems (mostly prediction and classification) for which shallow learning algorithms are not found to work appropriately.

More Sophisticated Networks

Not all neural networks are the same, and not all of them can achieve the same results on the same problems. A feed-forward neural network has some limitations, the most relevant of which is that it is essentially stateless and keeps no memory of whatever happens. Every prediction is independent from any previous and subsequent prediction.

In addition, a feed-forward neural network can't handle images or audio files and is not designed to generate new content. To overcome these limitations, other types of neural networks have been arranged, such as recurrent neural networks (for stateful networks), convolutional neural networks (for computer vision), and generative adversarial neural networks (for content creation *à la* FaceApp).

In spite of the more or less sophisticated architecture they may have, at the end of the day, neural networks are made of artificial neurons and associations between layers. Let's find out more then!

Types of Artificial Neurons

To capture the essence of neural networks, let's look into feed-forward neural networks and the first-ever type of artificial neuron—the perceptron.

The Perceptron Neuron

Abstractly speaking, you can think of an artificial neuron as a function that takes a few values in input and returns a single binary value. (See Figure 16-1.) Originally, input values also were devised to be binary values. Today, instead, they're just real numbers.

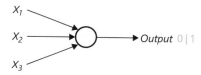

FIGURE 16-1 Overall schema of a perceptron

Introduced with the perceptron but today common to any type of an artificial neuron is the concept of an *activation function*.

The Activation Function

In a nutshell, the perceptron does two key things:

1. It multiplies each value it receives in input for a corresponding coefficient called *weight* and calculates the sum of all products. You can think of this operation as a scalar product of two vectors—input data and weights.

2. It returns 1 if the calculated value equals or exceeds a given threshold and 0 otherwise.

Expressed through a formula, it turns out to be the following:

$$Output = \begin{cases} 1 \ if \ \sum_{i=1}^{n} X_i * W_i \geq threshold \\ 0 \ otherwise \end{cases}$$

You can make the function a bit more general by adding an arbitrary term—the *bias*—independent from input and weights. The preceding formula then becomes the form shown next. Note that the following formula uses a more compact notation for the scalar product of the input vector X and vector of weights W:

$$Output = \begin{cases} 1 \ \ if \ \ X \cdot W + b \geq 0 \\ 0 \ if \ \ X \cdot W + b < 0 \end{cases}$$

Such a function is called an activation function. The threshold reminds us of the electrical threshold necessary to activate a synapse in the human brain. Figure 16-2 offers a graphical view of the activation function that Rosenblatt defined for the perceptron.

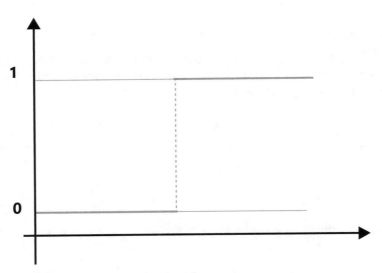

FIGURE 16-2 The activation function of a perceptron

The perceptron weighs any received input and makes a decision (that is, it returns 1) only if the actual value is beyond a given level of confidence. The perceptron is a very simple neuron; it is merely a binary and linear classifier, and all it does is draw a hyperplane. In its simplicity, though, the perceptron has a very interesting property: it can be used to simulate a *NAND* gate.

NAND and Functional Completeness

In electronics, a NAND gate is a logic gate that returns false if all of its inputs are true and true otherwise. Its output is complementary to that of an AND gate, and in fact, the NAND gate is the combination of an AND gate and a NOT gate.

NAND gates are functionally complete, meaning that all other logic gates (AND, NOT, OR) can be implemented through a combination of NAND gates. For example, the AND gate can be obtained as a concatenation of two NAND gates. In other words, when you have NAND gates, you can implement any logical expressions. The interesting fact is that by choosing the proper combination of weights and bias, a perceptron can be used to simulate a NAND gate.

The perceptron in Figure 16-3 has a bias of 3, and –2 is the weight for X_1, X_2 input parameters. Supposing a binary input of 00 (all false), you can see that in the former case the total calculated is 3, which equals the threshold and makes for a response of 1. Conversely, assuming an input of 11 (all true), you obtain –1, which is not equal to or greater than the threshold, resulting in a response of 0. The same happens for any other variation of 0 and 1 in the input. Hence, the perceptron works as a NAND gate.

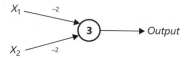

FIGURE 16-3 Using the perceptron to simulate the NAND gate

Where do you go from here?

The NAND equivalence gives perceptrons full expressivity, and by fine-tuning weights and bias, you can calibrate the neuron to make it calculate certain things. In other words, you can build a training process on top of perceptrons to discover the ideal values of weights and bias that more accurately compute what you want or expect.

Feed-Forward Layers

More in general, the power of perceptrons lies in the chance it gives you to approach the flow of any function by simply adding more layers, more inputs, and more connections. The idea is to forward the output of a neuron and make it be the input of another neuron in a subsequent layer of perceptrons. In this way, the information travels forward only until it reaches the end of the chain.

This is, in essence, a feed-forward neural network. The first layer of neurons is the input of the network, and the last node is the output. All intermediate layers—those whose neurons are neither input nor output of the network as a whole—are known as hidden layers. (See Figure 16-4.)

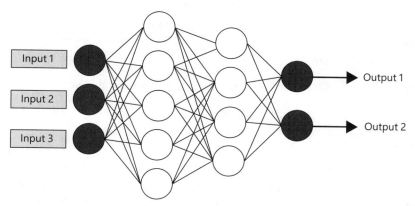

FIGURE 16-4 A sample feed-forward neural network

All neurons belonging to a successive layer receive as input the output calculated by connected neurons of the previous layer. The output of a neuron is obtained through the activation function. Each layer of neurons has its own activation function.

A feed-forward neural network is much more scalable in terms of functionality compared to the basic linear classifier of a simple perceptron. Each layer, in fact, adds both complexity and abstraction because you don't work with the raw input data anymore but only with some of its transformations. Here's where the popular term *deep learning* comes from—the depth of the neural network (or the number of layers in the network). We can also define deep learning as made of neural networks with hidden layers between the input and the output layers.

Finally, note that in Figure 16-4 the output layer presents more than just one value. This is absolutely viable: both input and output of a neural network are vectors.

> **Note** We already mentioned this earlier, but it helps to reinforce the point here. Feed-forward neural networks in which the information travels forward only and never backward are just a particular type of a neural network. In Chapter 18, we'll explore types of neural networks where the information travels back and forth.

Enabling the Network to Learn

So, you now have a neural network that can perform a large set of calculations. The accuracy of those calculations, though, depends on weights and bias. Although you can set these values beforehand, it would be great if the network could learn those values by itself. In real-life scenarios, in fact, setting weights and bias manually might be highly impractical given the huge number of connections and weights to deal with.

To set up an effective learning mechanism, though, you need more control over the output. In other words, if you slightly change one of the weights or biases, you also want the output to change slightly and continuously. In this way, through successive refinements, you could manage to obtain just the value you were looking for by simply acting on a specific input without drastically altering all the others and their connections to the output layer.

To enable learning across a neural network, you need another, and more sophisticated, activation function.

The Logistic Neuron

The perceptron neutron considered so far employs a *step function* as its activation function, as shown in Figure 16-2. In mathematics, a step function is a piecewise constant function whose entire output is determined by applying constant subfunctions to specific segments of the input. A step function is neither continuous nor differentiable.

To enable learning, instead, you intuitively need more (mathematical) continuity. Mathematical continuity is the key factor to prevent a minor change in the input from inducing a large change in the output. To enable learning, a binary 0/1 choice is no longer enough; you need to attack the entire space of real numbers between 0 and 1.

The Sigmoid Activation Function

Here's a new type of neuron that replaces the perceptron. The new neuron to consider is called *logistic* (or sigmoid) and has an activation function that is mathematically continuous:

$$\sigma = Output(Z) = \frac{1}{1 + e^{-Z}}$$

In the formula, Z is given by $X \cdot W + b$, where b is the bias, X is the input vector, and W is the vector of weights. The preceding function is a sigmoid, and its curve is plotted in Figure 16-5.

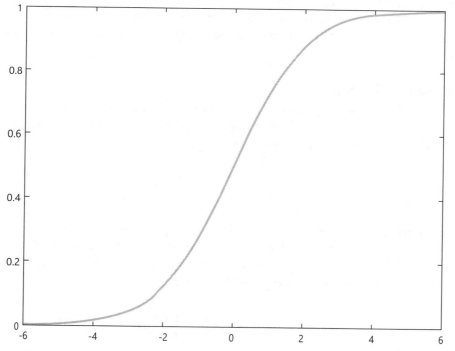

FIGURE 16-5 The sigmoid function

In mathematics, a sigmoid function is a bounded and differentiable function defined for all real input values. Its output varies between 0 and 1 with continuity (neither 0 nor 1 is ever reached).

From Step Functions to Sigmoids

By using a sigmoid, you're not changing the structure of the feed-forward neural network (e.g., the number of layers and connections) but just the value that each neuron forwards to its connected peers on the next layer. The value is no longer a binary value but a continuous value in the 0–1 range.

As you can see in Figure 16-5, for large values, the sigmoid activation function approaches 1, and for very small values, it stays close to 0. At the extremes, therefore, the behavior of the function is the same as the step function in perceptrons.

We started our analysis of feed-forward neural networks from perceptrons because of their inherent learning value. However, nobody uses perceptrons anymore in real life. The mathematical worth of working with continuous values is invaluable and will come in handy when dealing with the actual training of a neural network.

Compared to perceptrons, by using a logistic neuron, you introduce a sort of probability on the output that is not simply 0 or 1 but can be any value in between. What if, instead, you're still interested only in a binary outcome? How can you get that from a logistic neuron? In this case, you just add some software wrapper around the call to the network and map the outcome to 0 or 1, depending on how the outcome falls with respect to 0.5.

The Derivative of a Sigmoid

The sigmoid function σ has a non-negative derivative for each point. In addition, the derivative is bounded and also relatively easy to compute. This is another aspect of sigmoid that you will find enjoyable later when looking at the training of a neural network. Here's the derivative:

$$\sigma'(Z) = \frac{e^{-Z}}{(1+e^{-Z})^2} = \sigma(Z) * (1 - \sigma(Z))$$

A differentiable activation function guarantees that small changes in the input determine small changes in the output. This stems from the definition of differentiability: in a small neighborhood of a point, the values of the function change in such a way that the variation can be expressed with a linear transformation. You can even attempt to make an estimation of it:

$$\Delta Output = \frac{\partial Output}{\partial b} \Delta b + \sum_{i=1}^{J} \frac{\partial Output}{\partial W_i} \Delta W_i$$

In the formula, Δ indicates the variation. Partial derivatives of the activation function, calculated with respect to bias and weights, are multiplied for the corresponding small variation of bias and weights. In the formula, J is the number of weights.

Training a Neural Network

Except for some exceptions that we'll discuss in Chapter 18, neural networks are only for supervised learning, and the training is not different from the training of any other machine learning supervised artifacts. The key step still consists of identifying the function that represents the best measure of the distance between the predictions of the network and expected values.

The Overall Learning Strategy

Once you have a distance function—the major cost of the network—the ultimate goal of training is finding the coefficients that minimize it. For a neural network, the coefficients to find are bias and weights.

If the chosen distance function is convex and differentiable, it would then be possible to use the gradient descent to explore its minima. Under this condition, the training phase is all about making the gradient of the cost function, calculated with respect to all weights and all biases, descend toward the minimum.

Formalizing the Gradient Descent Step

The following two formulas indicate how the gradient descent proceeds and how weights and bias change, iteration after iteration:

$$W_{j,i} \rightarrow W_{j,i} - \frac{\alpha}{N} \sum_{k=1}^{N} \frac{\partial E(X_k)}{\partial W_{j,i}}$$

With $W_{j,i}$ you indicate the ith weight of the jth neuron, whereas B_j indicates the bias associated with the jth neuron. The new value of $W_{j,i}$ is then given by the sum of the partial derivative of the cost function E with respect to the $W_{j,i}$ variable. In the formula, the cost function E is calculated on the kth element of the dataset.

Analogously, you express the variation of the jth bias iteration after iteration:

$$B_j \rightarrow B_j - \frac{\alpha}{N} \sum_{k=1}^{N} \frac{\partial E(X_k)}{\partial B_j}$$

In the formula, α indicates the learning rate, and N is the size of the dataset. Speaking of gradient descent, the learning rate indicates how much you move along the direction of the gradient at each iteration. Typically, the value of α is between 0 and 1 but tends to be quite small. (We discussed the learning rate role in Chapter 11, "How to Make Simple Predictions: Linear Regression.") Finally, note that the partial derivatives are calculated across the entire dataset, and the arithmetic mean of the results is taken.

Minibatch

In real-life, for performance reasons, the gradient is not computed on the entire dataset but only on a restricted group of rows, and the mean is calculated on the size of the group rather than the size of the dataset. This approach is known as *minibatch*. Common sizes for a minibatch are 32, 64, and 128 elements. For example, when you train a TensorFlow model with ML.NET, the *BatchSize* parameter to be provided just refers to the minibatch concept.

You choose a size for the minibatch and randomly select the first chunk of elements to proceed. You update the weights and bias for the selected batch of rows and then repeat with another batch of elements until you complete the dataset (or some other stop condition is met). This is referred to as completing an *epoch*. At the end of an epoch, either you run another epoch or the training is over.

Finding the right size for the minibatch is sort of an art because a too-small size puts the model at serious risk of overfitting, whereas a too-large size may dramatically reduce accuracy. This is precisely one of the scenarios where an AutoML framework proves useful. A recent research paper also proposes to increase the batch size as training goes on instead of decaying the learning rate. (The paper is available at https://arxiv.org/pdf/1711.00489.pdf.)

> **Note** A trained neural network is a sort of black box. The number of weights, biases, and neurons may be so high that it is nearly impossible to figure out the whys and wherefores of any decision. A neural network is the apotheosis of flexibility and lack of interpretability. When it comes to classification, the best shallow learning algorithm—the Support Vector Machine algorithm—can reach a very high level of accuracy if all of its parameters are set appropriately—a sort of best-case scenario. On the other hand, a neural network can reach at least the same precision just out of training. But, again, a neural network is often a black box.

> **Note** Keep in mind that the previous statement "A trained neural network is a sort of black box" is challenged by new research and approaches. The interpretability of a neural network is being increased by techniques such as the saliency method and feature attribution. (See https://towardsdatascience.com/interpretability-of-deep-learning-models-9f52e54d72ab.) The interpretability of a neural network is a crucial problem in business areas subject to strict regulations such as finance. In these cases, in fact, authorities want to know exactly what happens, and a black box is not particularly easy to see through!

The Backpropagation Algorithm

So far, we have only scratched the surface of how the training of a neural network actually takes place. We haven't defined a real cost function and subsequently have never concretely worked out the calculation of the gradient. In other words, we haven't yet outlined any training algorithm.

You need a training algorithm that could work with a general, multilayer neural network. The most common algorithm to train a multilayer feed-forward network leverages the backward propagation of errors—a technique known as *backpropagation*.

The General Idea of the Backpropagation Algorithm

The backpropagation algorithm was first devised in the late 1960s, but it was never seriously applied to machine learning until the mid-1980s. Today, no better algorithm is known, and nobody is rushing to create a new one.

The backpropagation algorithm is an implementation of the gradient descent. It is therefore a tool to find the minimum of a function by exploring values in the direction of the steepest descent. Within the backpropagation algorithm, the calculation of the gradient proceeds backward through the network, from the last to the first layer of neurons. The gradient is first calculated on the weights on the final layer, and the error information is pushed backward on the previous layer where the calculation is repeated on the local weights. The process goes on and on until it reaches the initial layer. (See Figure 16-6.)

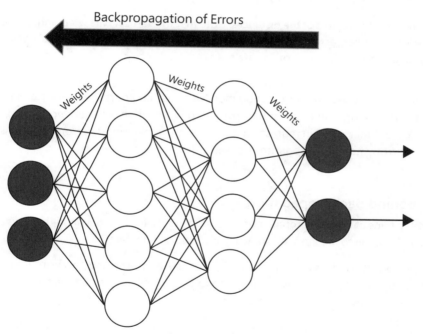

FIGURE 16-6 Error information flows backward from the final layer to the first layer.

In backpropagation, the rule to change the values of the various weights is recursive and proceeds backward from the output layer toward the input layer.

Note Backpropagation is the generalization of another, simpler algorithm—the *delta rule*—that works only for single-layer neural networks. The delta rule makes use of the gradient descent to find a minimum and set the optimal values for the weights. The new value of any given weight is set to the old value plus a delta that results from a number of parameters, including the error, learning rate, weights, input values, and output of the activation function of the neuron. Backpropagation extends the delta rule by adding some recursively defined expressions involving neurons of different layers.

As an example, consider the following cost function for the backpropagation algorithm:

$$C = \frac{1}{2N} \sum_{i=1}^{N} |Y(X_i) - O(X_i)|^2$$

Here N is the size of the dataset, and $Y(X_i)$ is the expected output of the given row of the dataset. At the same time, $O(X_i)$ is the final output returned by the network for the X_i row.

The cost function sums the squares of the distances. Note that the vertical bars wrapping the distance between prediction and expected value indicate the absolute value in case the neural network has a single output value and the vector norm in case the output is a vector.

Note We assumed the preceding cost function mostly for learning purposes because of its immediacy. In the real world, variations of the cross-entropy function are used most often, such as categorical or binary, and in regression scenarios, the mean square error function is used. The cross-entropy function is logarithm-based.

The Rationale Behind Backpropagation

Before we get into the folds of the backpropagation algorithm, it's useful to understand the whys of it. So, let's look at a cost function to minimize via some form of gradient descent.

In a multilayer network, this means calculating (partial) derivatives proceeding backward from the output layer to the input layer. It's ultimately a matter of applying the *chain rule* formula for computing the derivative D of the composition of two or more functions:

$$D(f(g(x))) = f'(g(x)) * g'(x)$$

The first (and rather rudimentary) idea that may spring to mind is using a sort of brute-force approach: manual estimation of the derivative of the cost function. The following formula estimates the value of the (partial) derivative of the cost function with respect to i weight associated with the j neuron in level l:

$$\frac{\partial C}{\partial W_{j,i}^{l}} \approx \frac{C(W + \Delta W_{j,i}^{l}) - C(W)}{|\Delta W_{j,i}^{l}|}$$

The formula attempts to estimate the difference quotient of the cost function for a very small variation $\Delta W_{j,i}^{l}$ of the i weight associated with the j neuron in level l. Conceptually, the numerator calculates the cost with respect to two different matrices of weights. The denominator, instead, presents the norm of the variation. Because the derivative is defined as the limit of the expression for the variation that approaches 0, by taking a very small value for the variation, you can get an estimate of the derivative.

What if the neural network has tens of thousands of connections? A brute-force, manual approach requires thousands of calculations for each step of the descent, which is definitely unmanageable for any realistic scenarios. Backpropagation is a (much) more efficient approach that ends up calculating all the necessary derivatives in a single step as the product of the output of level $l-1$ and the error of level l. In other words, the computational cost of backpropagation is nearly the same as calculating the output: training and computation are then symmetric.

Steps of the Algorithm

The backpropagation algorithm is articulated in four key steps nested in three different loops. The outermost loop is on the epoch. As mentioned, an epoch is a training session that touches on the entire dataset. For each epoch, you divide the training dataset in minibatches of a given m size and the attack with the second loop on every minibatch of rows. Finally, the innermost loop goes over the data rows in the current minibatch. Here's some pseudocode:

```
foreach(var epoch in epochs)
{
    var batches = SplitDatasetInMiniBatches(sizeOfBatches);
    foreach(var batch in batches)
    {
        foreach(var row in batch)
        {
            // Step 1: Calculate the output for the given row
            // Step 2: Calculate the final vector of errors
            // Step 3: Calculate the error vector for all intermediate layers
            // Step 4: Apply updated weights proceeding backwards
        }
    }
}
```

The first step is the classic feed-forward calculation visible in Figure 16-4. The neural network receives the features of a given data row and returns an output vector (or, in simpler cases, just a scalar value).

The heart of backpropagation is in step 2 and step 3. The error vector is first calculated for the final layer of the network, and then, proceeding backward, it is calculated for all intermediate layers.

The reason is that getting errors is easy once the computation has reached the final stage. However, you need to update the weights along the entire set of layers and can do that only by proceeding backward, from final layer to the input.

When all errors at all stages are known, the algorithm proceeds with the gradient descent calculation and finds the weights that minimize the cost function. Even this step is accomplished recursively from the final layer of neurons to the first. (See Figure 16-7.)

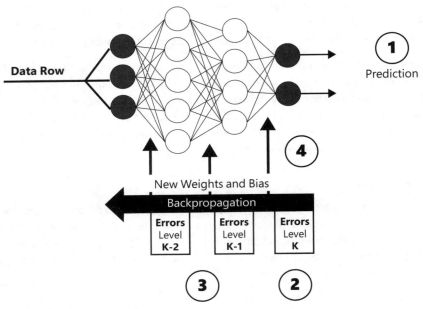

FIGURE 16-7 Schema of the backpropagation algorithm

Let's learn more about each step.

Calculating the Output of the Network

In this classic feed-forward step, the features of the processed data row become input of the neural network. Input values are combined with assigned weights and bias and move to the next layer after being further transformed by an activation function defined for the layer. Keep in mind that all neurons in the same layer are homogeneous and share the same activation function.

At the end of the step, the algorithm knows the predicted value(s) for the given input and is able to compare with the expected value(s). Given the definition of the cost function, the distance between points constitutes the error.

The rest of chapter is about the math that expresses the vector of errors. If you don't feel comfortable with that, just jump straight to the conclusions!

Getting the Vector of Final Errors

In the quite unrealistic case of a single-layer network, getting the error (or the vector of errors) is a simple operation. Trying to fix the weights and bias is simpler and can be tackled with the aforementioned delta rule approach. This approach doesn't work with a generic, multilayer neural network.

You need a formula that expresses the vector of errors. A formula possibly enables you to recursively connect errors at level L with errors at level $L-1$. From the earlier definition of the cost function and some sophisticated mathematics, you capture the vector of final errors (namely, those captured at final level L) by using the following equation:

$$\delta^L(x) = \nabla_a C_x \circ \sigma'(Z^{x, L})$$

The notation $\delta^L(x)$ refers to the vector of errors at level L captured starting from the x data row. The expression $\nabla_a C_x$ indicates a vector whose elements are the partial derivatives of the function cost with respect to the output of the activation function of the level for the same x data row.

The notation $\sigma'(Z^{x, L})$ refers to the first derivative of the activation function σ calculated on the weighed input of level L.

What about the weird symbol $\circ$ in the middle of the equation? It refers to the elementwise product of two matrices. Known as the Hadamard product, the operation applies to two matrices of the same size and returns a new matrix of the same size in which each element results from the product of corresponding elements in the matrices.

With the quadratic cost function assumed earlier, the member $\nabla_a C_x$ of the equation takes the familiar form of a vector whose elements are the difference between one output of the network and the corresponding expected value.

Obtaining Error Vectors for All Layers

When you have the final vector of errors, you need to figure out how much things went wrong (or how much they could be improved) at intermediate levels. The following formula links together the error vector of some level l and the error vector of level $l+1$:

$$\delta^l(x) = ((W^{l+1})^T \delta^{l+1}(x)) \circ \sigma'(Z^{x, l})$$

The vector of errors at level l results from the elementwise product of the activation function output at the level and the vector resulting from the following expression:

$$(W^{l+1})^T \delta^{l+1}(x)$$

The expression refers to a matrix by vector product and gives you an estimation of the error you have when leaving level l. $(W^{l+1})^T$ is the transpose of the matrix that contains all the weights applied at level $l+1$. The transpose of a matrix is an operation that returns a new matrix with rows and columns swapped. Once they are transposed, the matrix of weights has as many rows as neurons in level l and as many columns as neurons in level $l+1$. The number of columns matches the size of the vector with errors calculated at level $l+1$. Hence, the result is a vector with as many elements as neurons in level l.

Getting Updated Weights and Bias

At this stage, you have a complete list of vectors with errors as computed at each level of the neural network. What remains to be done is some optimization and, for that, you use the gradient descent approach.

Starting from the end, for each layer of the neural network, the algorithm recalculates the weights and bias for the neurons to use next. For a given level l, the new weight changes for a small delta, and its new value results from the following formula:

$$W^l - \frac{\alpha}{m} \sum_{i=1}^{m} \delta^l(x)(O(x)^{l-1})^T$$

The variable m indicates the size of the minibatch. The expression $\delta^l(x)$ refers to the error calculated at the current layer, and it is multiplied by the transpose of the vector of output values of the previous layer.

Likewise, the bias of a neuron changes for a delta. The new bias results from this formula:

$$b^l - \frac{\alpha}{m} \sum_{i=1}^{m} \delta^l(x)$$

In the formula, b^l refers to the bias at layer l, and all other elements that appear are the same as for weights.

Note As a final note on the training story of feed-forward neural networks, consider that normalizing input data is not strictly necessary because the neural network should be able to make sense of the input anyway. However, starting with normalized data may speed up the training process.

Summary

Over the centuries, scientists and polymaths often tried to develop models of the human brain, and many times their efforts were jeopardized by their lack of knowledge about the internals. In the 1940s, McCulloch and Pitts devised a mathematical model to explain the behavior of the brain. Nothing was built in hardware from it—probably because there was not much to build—but only 15 years later it represented the starting point for some research in the new field of artificial intelligence.

Neural networks are not a recent discovery in computer science, but for business and computing reasons, they have received a boost in the past decade. New types of neural networks have flourished, expanding the capabilities of the first canonical type of network created—the feed-forward neural network. In a feed-forward neural network, information flows in only one direction—from the input nodes to the output nodes, traversing any layer of intermediate nodes that may be defined.

In this chapter, we reviewed the structure of a feed-forward neural network, the types of neurons you can have, and how the training of a neural network takes place through a backpropagation technique. In the next chapter, we'll add some considerations about the design of a neural network. Bear in mind, though, that in the real world, very few people will really create deep learning architectures from scratch, so the relevance of these chapters is purely educational, probably analogous to explaining the mechanics of a car engine when all you will likely be doing is driving. Keeping to this analogy, driving here is training the existing model to do things like transfer learning.

## CHAPTER 17

Design of a Neural Network

The human brain has 100 billion neurons, each neuron connected to 10 thousand other neurons. Sitting on your shoulders is the most complicated object in the known universe.

—Michio Kaku, professor of theoretical physics and science communicator

Generally speaking, neural network architecture is always coupled with the problem that it is expected to solve, the training data available, the expected input, and the desired output. However, the number of people who have successfully built a neural network is not that large, and chances are good that not one of them is within your reach.

The purpose of this chapter is to provide some advice that could point you in the right direction and enable you to find an appropriate answer to questions like "Which activation function should I use?" and "How many layers and neurons should I employ?"

We'll also try to address a deeply rooted point—when you should use a neural network instead of a plain shallow learning algorithm—and provide an example of a simple neural network written in Python.

Aspects of a Neural Network

There is no magic rule or secret recipe for finding the most appropriate neural network architecture. For the most part, it's a trial-and-error experience. However, you have to start somewhere and somehow.

In general, *architecture by example* is a nefarious antipattern that happens when you design your software system around the pillars that others have employed for similar (or only apparently similar) problems. *Neural network by example*, instead, is much better given the nature of the neural network. Consequently, if you don't know where to start, look at what others have done for similar problems. Consider that similarity of problems is a relative topic, and similarity in neural networks is much closer to an effective affinity than similarity in user requirements and business use cases of a generic software project.

The best places to look for inspiration are the websites of popular neural network frameworks such as Keras, TensorFlow, or PyTorch. If problems match to some extent, that's the best way to learn because those architectures were likely selected after several trials and several mistakes and represent a contribution to posterity!

To give you more background, let's delve deeper into some aspects of neural networks that we only touched on in the preceding chapter.

Activation Functions

An extremely important part of a neural network is the activation function or transfer function. In the preceding chapter, you saw two types of neurons—the basic perceptron and the more realistic logistic neuron. There are many other types of neurons, and they differ in the capabilities and features of the activation function.

As a refresher, an activation function has to be bounded, differentiable, and preferably also monotonic (increasing or decreasing). Each layer of a neural network can have its own activation function.

Linear Functions

Be advised that this section is only for completeness. You'll never realistically use a linear function in a neural network. Yet linear functions meet the requirements of a typical activation function. The most basic example of a linear function is the identity function:

$$\sigma(Z) = Z$$

The identity function is differentiable and continuous and very easy to work with. However, it just doesn't help at all with the complexity that typically surrounds a neural network. On the other hand, you typically end up trying to use a neural network when no simpler approach works. Hence, you need more sophisticated mathematical tools than the identity function and any other linear function. At the end of the day, an activation function can realistically be only a nonlinear function in hidden layers. It can sometimes be a linear function in the output layer.

The Sigmoid Function

We covered the sigmoid function in the preceding chapter but are adding some more thoughts here. The sigmoid is extremely popular in neural networks and always returns a value between 0 and 1. In addition, its first derivative is very handy to work with. Here's its formulation.

$$\sigma(Z) = \frac{1}{1 + e^{-z}}$$

The Z refers to the vector of weighted input data that the activation function works on. In the preceding chapter, however, we didn't mention a drawback of using the sigmoid. In particular, the first derivative of the sigmoid is a function bounded in the $(0, 1/4)$ interval. (The peak comes for $x = 0$.)

$$\sigma'(Z) = \frac{e^{-z}}{(1 + e^{-z})^2} = \sigma(Z) * (1 - \sigma(Z))$$

Boundaries on the derivative lead to a problem known as the *vanishing gradient*. In other words, during backpropagation, small numbers proliferate, causing very tiny variations of weights and bias. Quite paradoxically, it happens that the greater the input, the smaller the gradient.

As a result, the sigmoid is not ideal for use in a neural network with many layers (deep learning). You therefore must apply some normalization strategy on the input to learn successfully.

The Softmax Function

The softmax function is a generalization of the sigmoid and is helpful in the output layer of a neural network for multiclass classification problems. The relationship with the sigmoid is that the sigmoid is a softmax function that can handle only two classes. If you set the number of components to consider to K, the softmax function will return one vector in which the jth element is as follows:

$$\sigma(Z)_j = \frac{e^{Z_j}}{\sum_{i=1}^{K} e^{Z_i}}$$

The function arranges a distribution of probability for the K elements, and the sum of values for all the K elements constantly equals 1. Softmax gives more relevance to bigger numbers and reduces the importance of small numbers.

The TanH Function

TanH, or the hyperbolic tangent, is another S-shaped curve similar to a sigmoid but with a key difference: its range of output values goes from –1 to 1 instead of being between 0 and 1. (See Figure 17-1.)

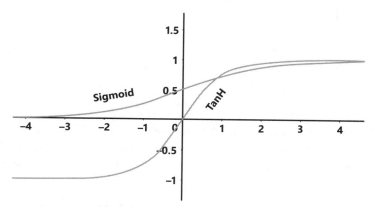

FIGURE 17-1 Sigmoid and TanH functions plotted side by side

The analytic form of TanH is as follows:

$$\sigma(Z) = \frac{1 - e^{-2Z}}{1 + e^{-2Z}}$$

The advantage that TanH provides over the sigmoid is that negative input values remain negative in the output and positive input values remain positive in the output. In addition, input values near zero remain near zero in the output too. Like the sigmoid, the TanH function also is subject to the vanishing gradient problem.

The ReLu Function

The ReLu function, short for Rectified Linear Unit, is probably the most used activation function. Its analytical form is fairly simple and intuitive:

$$\sigma(Z) = \max(0, Z)$$

The function is monotonic (also the first derivative of the function is monotonic), and its output ranges from 0 to infinite. The function returns 0 before x = 0. After the origin, it works as a linear function. (See Figure 17-2.)

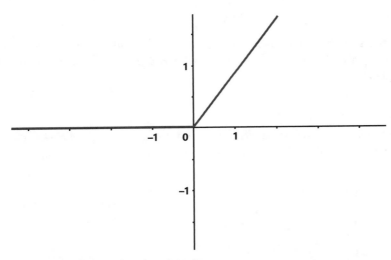

FIGURE 17-2 The ReLu function plotted

The function is beneficial because it is easy to compute, at least compared to other activation functions. Neural networks based on ReLu functions converge faster because weights stabilize quickly. Furthermore, the ReLu function is not subject to a vanishing gradient and not even to an exploding gradient. The first derivative, in fact, is 0 for negative input and 1 for positive input.

On the downside, the function can explode as the input grows, and negative values are mapped to 0 regardless, which may not be ideal in some situations. To improve on this aspect, a slightly modified version of the function has been introduced. The modified ReLu is as follows:

$$\sigma(Z) = \max(aZ, Z) \quad when \ a \ll 1$$

Usually, the value of *a* is very small and in the order of 0.01. Figure 17-3 compares the ReLu and modified ReLu functions.

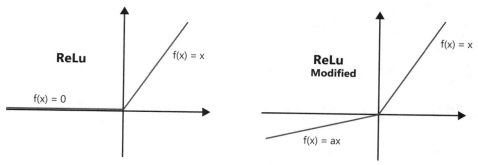

FIGURE 17-3 Comparing ReLu and modified ReLu functions

Now that we've discussed the activation functions, let's switch to hidden layers and figure out their number and other characteristics.

Hidden Layers

The beating heart of a neural network is the collection of intermediate hidden layers. Those layers are the actual repository of the logic, whether classification or regression logic. Any nontrivial neural network therefore will have a few hidden layers. Two points here deserve attention:

- How many layers?

- How many neurons in each layer?

The number of neurons may be different in the various layers, and also the type of neuron may be different in different layers (e.g., different activation function). The only constraint is that all neurons in a hidden layer must be homogeneous.

Visualizing the Role of Neurons

In a discussion of machine learning solutions, as a first step, it is common to try to visualize the interacting parts in bidimensional space. The 2D rendering doesn't help much in solving the real-world problem but helps a lot in grasping a sense of what happens under the hood in the very intricate space of *N* dimensions.

To visualize the actual work done by neurons and the role played by hidden layers of neurons, imagine a dataset sprinkled across the 2D plane and suppose you want to train a neural network to classify data points. Figure 17-4 presents the starting point of this exercise.

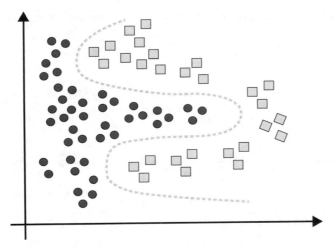

FIGURE 17-4 Classifying the items in a sample dataset

In the figure, circles and squares denote data points known to belong to different classes. All you want is to find a curve that could effectively separate circles from squares. Armed with a neural network, you can think of a neuron as a linear classifier for each feature. (More precisely, the actual linearity of the neuron depends on the actual linearity of its activation function.)

The dashed curve in Figure 17-4 will be approximated with a sequence of intersecting lines intuitively working as classifiers. Each line denotes a neuron in a first hidden layer. As you can see in Figure 17-5, three intersections exist between lines. The presence of intersections denotes the need for some additional layers. So, visually, the two leftmost intersections (those outlined in the figure) connect two neurons from the previous layer.

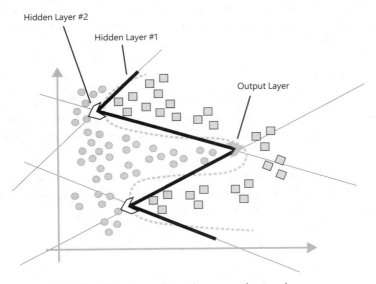

FIGURE 17-5 Classifying data points using a neural network

Finally, the two connected levels are further connected in the final output level, as in Figure 17-6.

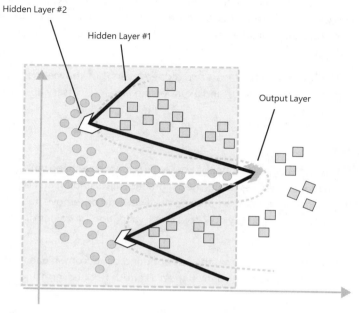

FIGURE 17-6 Connecting layers into the output layer

Figure 17-5 and Figure 17-6 identify the need for a neural network with three layers, and Figure 17-7 presents its schema. Four neurons appear in the first hidden layer (one per segment) and two neurons in the second hidden layer (one per outlined intersection), and a third layer—the output layer—connects the neurons of the previous layer to produce the final result.

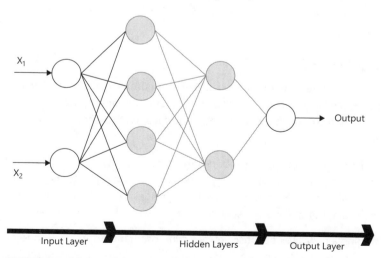

FIGURE 17-7 Schema of the neural network excerpted from Figure 17-6

Remember that this is only a nice learning exercise. This sketching technique can't be used in practice because if you were able to do it, there would be no need for a neural network to classify things. The general rule is that there's no general rule to estimate the ideal number of hidden layers beforehand. Usually, you start from some heuristics, build a network, test it via cross-validation, and then make changes.

One rule of thumb suggests that you start with at least two hidden layers, but knowledge of the problem, any past experience available as a reference, and a gut feeling about necessary abstraction required may suggest different options.

Ideal Number of Neurons

No certain rules exist in this field, even though a number of academic papers have been written on the subject. Indeed, it is a fascinating area of research. The pragmatic rule is finding an acceptable initial number, training the network, and seeing what happens if you add or remove neurons. Repeated tests are the only way. To test, you typically do k-fold cross-validation for values of k, typically 5 or 10.

Having said that, a documented formula exists to set the upper bound of neurons in each hidden layer—the number you should never exceed to save yourself from a serious risk of overfitting.

$$Upper\ bound = \frac{\#rows\ in\ dataset}{\gamma * (\#Input\ neurons + \#output\ neurons)}$$

As you can see, the scaling factor γ in the formula is broadly accepted to be in the 2–10 range, with some experts also suggesting that you restrict the range to 5–10.

Another tip is to make sure that, at least initially, the number of intermediate neurons in each hidden layer is between the size of the input and the output. Some also suggest you choose twice the size of the input layer as the initial value.

Adding Neurons or Adding Layers?

To make the neural network more expressive, should you add more neurons to a layer or add an entirely new layer? Having multiple layers makes the network deeper and more capable of recognizing and processing specific aspects of the data. In a way, an additional layer further specializes the network, adding some missing capabilities.

From a more mathematical perspective, a new layer brings more nonlinearity to the calculation by the means of some (nonlinear) activation function that allows you to pass from one layer to the next. If you stay in the same layer, you can only receive linearly combined input values. So, adding more neurons to a layer allows for more local accuracy, but the overall capabilities of the network remain unchanged.

There's more power in adding a new layer because you are composing more functions together. On the other hand, if the problem is linearly separable, you probably just need more accuracy in each of the existing layers, so adding a neuron is a better choice.

The Output Layer

The output layer of a neural network is not necessarily made of a single neuron, although this is a rather common scenario. As expected, the nature of the problem at hand gives you the best suggestions. For example, for a multiclass classification problem, it makes sense to have an output neuron for each possible category.

In a classification scenario, manipulating the response in such a way that the sum of all outputs is 1 greatly simplifies the training of the network. Each output value, in fact, indicates the probability that a given element belongs to category that the neuron represents. (See Figure 17-8.)

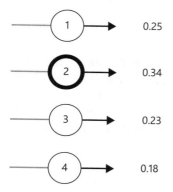

FIGURE 17-8 Multiple output neurons whose total response adds up to 1

Training the network becomes a simpler task than if you had a single output. With multiple outputs, all you need to do is have the network predict a value that is the highest of all responses for the neuron corresponding to the expected class. With a single output, instead, you need to fine-tune the network to produce exactly the value that identifies the category index. In other words, the error function always returns 0 or 1 (right or wrong), whereas with multiple outputs, you have continuous values and more controllable errors.

As mentioned, though, the approach you choose depends on the problem. Having multiple outputs works beautifully for a classification problem but not for, say, a regression problem. Think of the taxi ride cost prediction demo described in Chapter 7, "Implementing the ML.NET Pipeline." You solved that problem by using two linear regression models—one for predicting the time of the ride and the other to predict the fare also based on the time. Had you approached the problem with a neural network, you would have needed one output neuron—the fare to pay—and a hidden layer to calculate the time for the ride as a necessary input for the output layer.

But then again, the fact that regression works with a single output neuron is no general rule either. In other regression scenarios, multiple outputs may be more than welcome. For example, say you want to get a price and ideal date to buy some stocks.

Building a Neural Network

Admittedly, you won't get any further without at least a cursory understanding of the mechanics of shallow learning algorithms or neural networks. At the same time, unless you are an expert data scientist (or an academic researcher or mathematician), you will hardly be devising and implementing a neural network entirely from scratch. (In any such cases, you wouldn't likely be reading this book!)

So, in the end, in everyday life—whether you're a machine learning developer or data scientist—you just make calls to some machine learning or deep learning frameworks. There are quite a few frameworks for neural networks.

Available Frameworks

In an effort to show that there's life beyond Python in machine learning, in Chapter 6, "The .NET Way," we briefly described some popular frameworks for deep learning. Let's recap the highlights of the top deep learning frameworks here. If you look around, many blogs or individual articles attempt to rank deep learning frameworks. Each ranking may be biased and (more or less strongly) opinionated. However, we believe that the frameworks in Table 17-1 are certainly among the most popular...and with good reason.

TABLE 17-1 Popular Deep Learning Frameworks

Framework	URL
TensorFlow	www.tensorflow.org
Keras	https://keras.io
PyTorch	https://pytorch.org
Caffe	https://caffe.berkeleyvision.org

The order in this table is neither alphabetical nor random but attempts to reflect the perception of power and popularity.

TensorFlow

TensorFlow is by far the most complete and powerful platform today for writing neural networks. It may not have the most comfortable learning curve, but it is reliable, battlefield-tested, and widely adopted by large corporations. If you look at metrics of usage and adoption, TensorFlow has three times the largest Github activity than the second framework in line, at least twice as many books on the subject, and three times more job offerings. The only metric in which it doesn't excel—with reason—is the number of articles.

TensorFlow provides native bindings for Python, C++, and R and can be easily used from Java and Go. TensorFlow is associated with Google and still relies on the original core of the Google documentation. However, it relies on a very active community of developers and passionate people who constantly supply support and updates.

Note You can train a TensorFlow model using C# through the help of TensorFlow.NET (https://github.com/SciSharp/TensorFlow.NET). Interestingly, with ML.NET, you can load and retrain models (as we demonstrated in Chapter 8, "ML.NET Tasks and Algorithms"), but starting with version 1.4, you can also train a TensorFlow model directly from ML.NET.

Keras

Admittedly, discussing Keras at this level may be inadequate. Keras is more a high-level API on top of TensorFlow, and in this regard, it is not comparable to TensorFlow, PyTorch, or Caffe. With regard to TensorFlow training, Keras and ML.NET 1.4 are at the same level.

However, written to smooth the intricacy and low abstraction of the TensorFlow API to the extent that is possible, Keras is gaining a lot of popularity primarily because of its quick-prototyping nature and friendliness to beginners.

Keras is the natural choice for any beginners who prefer to use Python and is the environment of choice for any prototyping or relatively quick development. Keras runs on Python and—not a secondary point—can be used for building feed-forward neural networks and also recurrent and convolutional networks. As mentioned, Keras runs on top of TensorFlow.

If you look at usage and adoption metrics, Keras is second to TensorFlow for job offerings, books, and Github activity. Plus, it overtakes TensorFlow for the number of articles, which is not surprising if you consider that most articles you run into if searching for "neural networks" are beginner-level articles claiming to explain how to go from Zero to Hero in half an hour.

Note For .NET developers, it'll be a lot easier to use ML.NET as soon as the capabilities of the library are expanded to cover all scenarios. If you are a .NET developer, you can use TensorFlow.NET as the low-level API bindings for TensorFlow.

PyTorch

Built by Facebook on top of an existing library called Torch, PyTorch is rapidly gaining popularity for a couple of key reasons. First, it's a solid deep learning framework and more modern in many aspects than TensorFlow and Caffe. Second, it is a lot easier to use, and it was specifically devised to iron out some of the wrinkles discovered in TensorFlow over the years.

In raw terms of popularity, though, at the moment PyTorch is one step behind the raw use of Tensor-Flow and the use of a TensorFlow facilitator like Keras.

Caffe

Caffe is a highly specialized framework for image recognition, and in this area, it really provides amazing performance without requiring powerful and expensive hardware. Caffe works with C, C++, Python, and MATLAB. It also provides a command-line interface. Coming from Berkeley, it has the pragmatic cut of the academic perspective of things, and it is expressive, not hard to code, and highly and simply extensible to encourage testing and experimentation.

The Caffe framework also counts on some pretrained networks to address tasks beyond image recognition, including regression, large-scale visual classification, and speech. It doesn't seem to be good outside those areas, and it doesn't represent, for example, a choice for building recurrent networks.

> **Note** Another framework worth a mention is MXNet from Apache, which is used at Amazon, and the Microsoft Cognitive toolkit, which is an open-source comprehensive framework that supports both convolutional and recurrent neural networks and provides respectable performance. Last but not least is Theano. Theano was one of the first frameworks to appear somehow related to deep learning. It is strong at performing numerical computation, particularly those calculations typical of the training of a neural network. However, to build a neural network, you don't want to use Theano directly but pass through one of the Python libraries that hide most of its nitty-gritty details. One of these libraries is Lasagne; another one is Keras.

Your First Neural Network in Keras

This book is not designed to be a how-to book in which every statement is supported by a reproducible sequence of actions in some programming environment. Yet, at some point, we have to show and discuss some code. Let's look at what it takes to build a neural network in Python, using the Keras library. The sample neural network will have four neurons in input and four in output and will count on an intermediate hidden layer of eight neurons (twice the size of the input).

Preparing the Environment

For this basic example, we used JetBrains PyCharm Community Edition as our favorite editor. As long as you have Python support installed in Visual Studio 2019, you can even go for that.

After you create a new *neural.py* file in the project directory, the first concrete step to do in the code is to import all the necessary packages. In particular, import *NumPy* for text manipulation and the segments of Keras that have to do with layers, feed-forward networks, and metrics:

```
# Import external packages
from numpy import loadtxt
from keras.models import Sequential
from keras.layers import Dense
from keras import metrics
```

The next step is loading data from some CSV file somewhere on disk. The *loadtxt* method from *NumPy* will just return an in-memory copy of the data. Note that you need to instruct *NumPy* to use the comma as the delimiter for the lines in the selected text file:

```
# Load the dataset
dataset = loadtxt('some_dataset.csv', delimiter=',')
```

The dataset must be sliced vertically in two parts to separate the columns of data to use as the input (call it *X*) and the column(s) of data to use as the output (call it *Y*). As mentioned earlier in the chapter, this is a supervised learning context; therefore, *Y* refers to score feature(s) and *X* to the training dataset.

```
# Separate feature columns (X) to be treated as input and
# score column(s) to be treated as output (Y)
X = dataset[:, 0:4]
Y = dataset[:, 4:1]
```

The colon (:) refers to the slice operator of *NumPy*. The net effect of the first line is to assign the *X* variable the vertical slice of the dataset, which includes four columns starting from the first. As a result, the *Y* variable gets the vertical slice of the dataset, which includes only the fifth column. (Note that the :1 has been included for clarity and can be omitted.)

Modeling the Neural Network

In Keras, you can create the model of a neural network in two ways: using the sequential or functional API. The sequential API is the choice for feed-forward networks because it allows you to add layers one after the next in a forward-only way without any chance to connect layers differently. Conversely, the functional API gives you more freedom as far as connections between layers are concerned, thus enabling you to create more than just feed-forward neural networks:

```
# Create the model of our feed-forward neural network
model = Sequential()
```

At this point, you haven't specified anything significant. The subsequent step consists of adding the first hidden layer and connecting it back to the input. A layer is defined through an instance of the *Dense* class. The first argument to pass to the constructor of the class is the number of neurons in the layer. Two more parameters are crucial to pass. One is the activation function. In this example, you use the *ReLu* function.

When adding the first layer to the model, you also need to specify the size of the input layer. This can be done by using a scalar or using a *shape*. A shape is a more general way to express the size because it can express the size of a multidimensional object. In this case, you only need to tell the model that the input layer has four neurons. Hence, the following two expressions are equivalent:

```
sizeOfInput = 4
shapeOfInput = (4,)   # Note that the comma is necessary when it's only one dimension
```

To indicate the size of the input as a scalar, you use the *input_dim* parameter; otherwise, you use the *input_shape* parameter. The code to add to the Python file is as follows:

```
# Add the first hidden layer to the model:
# The hidden layer has 8 neurons, ReLu activation and is connected to 4-neuron input layer
layer = Dense(8, input_shape=(4,), activation='relu')
model.add(layer)
```

To add a further layer, you just create a new *Dense* object and add it to the model. Note, though, that *Dense* objects added after the first don't have to specify the size of the input. In other words, the definition of the input layer is implicit in the addition of the first layer. As a result, after the first call to the *add* method, the model has two layers, the first of which is the input layer. The second layer will be considered the output layer if you don't add more layers; otherwise, it will be considered the first hidden layer of the network.

Because the initial idea was creating a neural network with one hidden layer, you need to add yet another layer to serve as the output layer:

```
# Adding the output layer and making it use a sigmoid as the activation function
model.add(Dense(4, activation='sigmoid'))
```

The output layer has four neurons and uses the sigmoid function as the activation mechanism. You're almost done! The next step is training the network.

Training the Network

To train the network, you need to complete the configuration indicating the function cost to minimize, the minimization algorithm (a concrete implementation of what we generically referred to as *gradient descent* earlier), and the metrics to show. You set all such parameters via a call to the *compile* method:

```
# Final configuration of the model
model.compile(loss='mean_squared_error',
              optimizer='sgd',
              metrics=[metrics.categorical_accuracy])
```

In this example, the mean squared error (MSE) function is selected as the cost and the Stochastic Gradient Descent (SGD) as the optimization algorithm. Finally, you indicate a single metric to return—the accuracy. Now the model is ready for training:

```
# Train the model, evaluate the result and show accuracy metrics
model.fit(X, Y, epochs=150, batch_size=10)
accuracy = model.evaluate(X, Y)
print('Accuracy: %.2f' % (accuracy*100))
```

The *fit* method starts the training process and fires the backpropagation algorithm you saw in the preceding chapter. The *fit* method receives the input columns and the score columns, the number of epochs to go through, and the size of the batches. The evaluation process is triggered by a call to *evaluate*.

Note It is interesting to consider what happens when the input to a neural network is an image. The input data is the matrix of pixels and related colors. So, assuming the image to process is 300 × 300 and uses RGB colors, the input layer of the neural network would be a shape (300, 300, 3).

Note The example here uses the SGD gradient algorithm. Recently, another gradient algorithm has been gaining traction and being used more and more often—ADAM. Short for Adaptive Moment estimation, ADAM estimates the first and second moment of the gradient to find out the ideal learning rate for each weight of the neural network. The nth moment of a random variable is the expected value of that variable to the power of n.

Neural Networks versus Other Algorithms

Neural networks can approximate any linear and nonlinear function to an arbitrary level of precision. All you do is add and configure neurons and layers. The magic, or the trick (any magic has tricks behind it), is made possible by weights and bias. Furthermore, the output of a neural network can be a step function, and with the aid of a step function, you can approximate virtually every function.

Binary Classification Comparison

To find some visual evidence of how neural networks and shallow learning algorithms work on the dataset, you should spend some time looking at Figure 17-9. This figure presents the work done by various algorithms in the case of a nonlinear binary classification problem. In particular, areas with different shades of gray represent the decision boundary used by the algorithm, which can be read as the level of confidence in the output. Solid colors represent a strong certainty for either class. The numbers you see measure the accuracy.

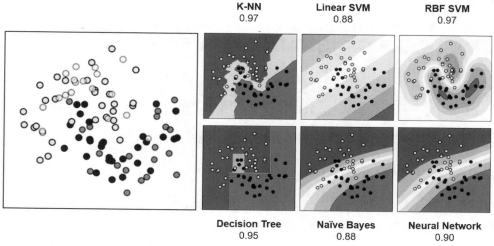

FIGURE 17-9 How different binary classification algorithms split the data space

Methodology and Considerations

Table 17-2 summarizes some points based on the charts in the figure. The table doesn't include the chart attributed to a neural network; that deserves a bit more space and focus.

TABLE 17-2 Notes About the Behavior of Algorithms in Figure 17-9

Algorithm	Notes
K-NN	The clustering algorithm reaches a noticeable accuracy and seems to fit nicely on a provided dataset. The decision boundary is due to the distance you set.
Linear SVM	This algorithm does not provide great accuracy, and the decision boundaries (lines) show it. It is just unfit for such a dataset. Using this algorithm on this dataset is only a bit better than a random guess, which would have at worst 0.50 accuracy!
Radial (RBF) SVM	This algorithm is a nonlinear version of SVM and uses a radial basis kernel (RBF) function. It has smooth and precise decision boundaries and high accuracy.
Decision Tree	The chart is almost full of solid colors, meaning that the algorithm is kind of binary in its decisions. Decision boundaries are fairly clean, which is in the either/or nature of the algorithm. It provides very good accuracy indeed.
Naïve Bayes	This algorithm shows smooth decision boundaries, but it's quite simplistic for the dataset at hand. It seems confident, though, in its results. The score is poor.

The charts in Figure 17-9 were obtained using the Python code provided through the classifier comparison page of the *scikit-learn* library. You can download the code at *https://scikit-learn.org/stable/auto_examples/classification/plot_classifier_comparison.html*.

All charts were therefore produced using one of the *scikit-learn* algorithms, as in Table 17-3. All algorithms worked on an autogenerated dataset created using the following code snippet:

```
make_moons(noise=0.3, random_state=0)
```

In the *scikit-learn* library, the *make_moons* function is specifically designed for binary classification and generates data points using a swirl pattern, similar to nesting two moon-like shapes.

TABLE 17-3 *Scikit-learn* Code Snippets Used to Implement Binary Classification Algorithms

Algorithm	Scikit-learn specific code
K-NN	KNeighborsClassifier(3)
Linear SVM	SVC(kernel="linear", C=0.025),
RBF SVM	SVC(gamma=2, C=1)
Decision Tree	DecisionTreeClassifier(max_depth=5)
Naïve Bayes	GaussianNB()
Neural Network	MLPClassifier(alpha=1, max_iter=1000)

In particular, the neural network chart was obtained running an instance of the *MLPClassifier*. In *Scikit-learn*, the class implements a multilayer perceptron (MLP) network with default configuration for activation function (ReLu) and hidden layers. This is to say, the not-exactly-exciting score of the neural network is due to the fact that we used a built-in neural network. This leads to a more general consideration.

Shallow Learning over Deep Learning

For simple problems in two dimensions, traditional machine learning, simpler than a neural network, usually works better. The same can happen for many tabular data-based use cases. It's still a general consideration and not a strict rule, but experience teaches that in these cases a shallow algorithm not only works better but also takes fewer resources when training in terms of time and computing power. Consider that, to train a large neural network, you probably need cloud resources, and that can add up to a huge bill.

On the other hand, note that for many other scenarios, specifically image and sound analysis, speech analysis, and video processing, a neural network not only works better but also is often the only viable way in terms of results.

Summary

In the preceding chapter, we presented the anatomy of a feed-forward neural network, roles and capabilities of neurons, and the (backpropagation) training algorithm. A number of things, however, didn't get their due diligence and coverage. In this chapter, we focused on the tasks related to the actual design and the building of a feed-forward neural network.

First, we completed the annotated overview of the aspects to consider in a neural network, such as the activation function and hidden layers. We discussed a number of different activation functions and common rules to help in deciding how to initially design the network. At the end of the day, no fixed rules exist to dictate the ideal number of hidden layers or the preferable number of neurons that each layer needs to have. More than ever, neural networks are in the wild territory of trial and error in which there's no other law than "try this and make it fit."

In the second part of the chapter, we used Keras—an extremely popular Python framework—to build a hello-world style demo of a neural network. The point of the demo was not to build some concrete functionality but rather to show how to use concretely the theoretical concepts we presented in the previous two chapters.

The big picture about the most common type of neural network—feed-forward neural networks—is now complete. These days, in the real world, neural networks are called to make truly amazing things, thus really marking a neat boundary between classic shallow learning and deep learning. In the next chapter, we'll look into other, more connected, and intricate types of neural networks, such as convolutional and recurrent neural networks.

## CHAPTER 18

Other Types of Neural Networks

Either mathematics is too big for the human mind or the human mind is more than a machine.

—Kurt Godel, author of the Incompleteness Theorem

In the preceding two chapters, we presented neural networks as an extremely sophisticated and accurate tool to use for classification and regression tasks when everything else fails. Unfortunately, there are some problems that the same neural networks can't solve well with the required level of precision. Under which conditions can a feed-forward neural network underperform? And where else can you turn when a canonical feed-forward neural network doesn't work as expected?

These are the questions that we'll try to answer in this chapter, looking at newer and even more sophisticated types of neural networks, such as recurrent neural networks (RNN), convolutional neural networks (CNN), and generative adversarial neural networks (GAN).

To start out, let's briefly recap a few concrete scenarios where feed-forward neural networks are not the most appropriate solution.

Common Issues of Feed-Forward Neural Networks

As the name itself suggests, feed-forward neural networks can perform their calculations in a forward-only way—that is, proceeding end to end from the input to the output layer. This marks the first big drawback of such a neural network.

A feed-forward neural network doesn't implement the concept of state or memory. In this regard, a feed-forward neural network works in much the same way as an HTTP server. Two consecutive requests are treated as fully independent requests over HTTP, and two consecutive predictions are treated as fully independent predictions by a trained network. The concept of state applies to both training and production.

The point is that in some real-life scenarios there are predictions that can't be made without carefully considering what has happened before. If you try to reliably predict the price of a given stock, the sole history of the stock may not be sufficient, so you need to take a look at the most recent quotes of the stock—which is data not necessarily incorporated in the trained model. Another example involves time-series data. If you want to predict or classify, say, the fault of some hardware device, the sole snapshot of signals observed at a given time is not sufficient, so you need to correlate those to the signals detected in a previous time frame. Essentially, a feed-forward neural network just can't do anything like that. To approach these problems, therefore, you need a type of neural network that supports the concept of state and keeps track of whatever prediction the network has made since training. This particular drawback is mitigated with the introduction of recurrent neural networks.

Classifying data is one thing, but classifying images or audio files is quite another. If you want to automatically tag zillions of images using a number of predefined tags related to the actual content, well, that's another complicated task for which a feed-forward neural network is not much help again. Convolutional neural networks, instead, are pretty good at that.

A feed-forward neural network is likewise unfit to generate new content (e.g., text or images) based on acquired patterns. This is the job of yet another new type of neural network: generative adversarial.

Recurrent Neural Networks

As humans, we continually make predictions ourselves. When we listen to someone speaking, sometimes we can rightly guess that person's next few words. When we make decisions, we don't simply evaluate the pros and cons as they appear from the available input data, but we integrate that data with experience and past memories of similar or related facts.

The purpose of recurrent neural networks is integrating the concept of state in neural networks and making them able to predict based on past predictions and related input.

Note A rudimentary approach to the problem may consist of increasing the size of the input. For example, while predicting a stock quote, you could add new features to the input to incorporate opening and closing prices in the past five days. Clearly, adding features is not a scalable approach. The moment you realize that five days earlier is not enough, you need to train the network again on a modified input. A feed-forward neural network has input and output layers of a fixed size.

Anatomy of a Stateful Neural Network

To make a neural network stateful, you have to build the notion of state right inside the network itself. A recurrent neural network is then a neural network in which the information flows forward from the input layer to the output, but every prediction leaves a track. In other words, every prediction is made based on the input that results from the combination of the direct input and the state that previous predictions may have determined.

A new logical component of the neural network must then be introduced—the memory layer A—that manages the (hidden) state vector H.

Architecture of the Memory Context

Figure 18-1 presents a high-level view of the component that serves as the memory context. As mentioned, it is a logical component of the architecture and not necessarily a distinct piece of software. In some RNN implementations, in fact, it is treated just as an additional hidden layer of a feed-forward neural network placed right after the input layer.

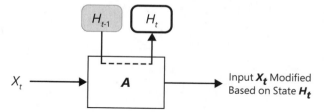

FIGURE 18-1 Schema of a memory context in a recurrent neural network

At the time t of the ongoing prediction, the component receives a vector of values X from the client application. The input X, combined with the current state H_{t-1} determined at the time $t-1$ of the last prediction, produces an update of the current state to H_t. The output of the component is a modified version of the original input transformed in some way based on the state. (We'll see details of this in a moment.)

The output of the component is typically used as input of a regular feed-forward neural network.

Architecture of a Recurrent Network

Figure 18-2 presents the most common (and basic) component architecture of a recurrent neural network. As you can see, at least in its simplest form, a recurrent neural network is the concatenation of a memory context and a classic feed-forward neural network.

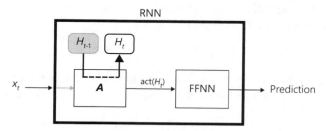

FIGURE 18-2 Component architecture of RNN

The bottom line is that a recurrent neural network is a feed-forward neural network plus an additional component that deals with the state of the network. The schema in the figure can be made as complex as needed, and multiple memory contexts can be concatenated. The same FFNN can be split into smaller pieces, and memory contexts can be added in between.

The state is a property of the memory context and is sometimes referred to as a *hidden state vector* just because of this attribute. The cumulative nature of the memory context is the key to guarantee the scalability of the approach, at least compared to the rudimentary approach of just increasing the feature list of a canonical feed-forward neural network to incorporate known facts.

Figure 18-3 shows the effect of state on a sequence of predictions done by a recurrent neural network on a timeline.

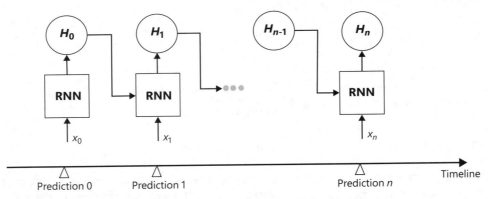

FIGURE 18-3 Impact of state management on the sequence of predictions made by RNN

Mechanics of State Management

Let's now review the steps that an input vector goes through when processed by a recurrent network. You can assume that the input comes in at some time *t*. This means that the memory context component has information up to time $t - 1$ in store.

The memory context component receives the input that the client application has provided. This is unfiltered, direct input data to be used for making a prediction.

First, the memory context *A* updates its own state vector *H*, which is the repository of historical information. Changes to *H* result from the application of some function *f*, typically *tanH* (hyperbolic tangent). Here's the formula that updates the state from time $t - 1$ to *t*:

$$H \rightarrow f(W_{hh} * H + W_{xh} * X_t)$$

In the formula, $W_{hh} * H$ indicates the product between the matrix of historical weights and the state vector *H* as of time $t - 1$. Instead, $W_{xh} * X_t$ is the product between the matrix of weights to apply to any input data and the same vector of input data.

The output generated by the memory context O_A consists of the value calculated by some activation function *g* specified as a hyperparameter of the network—mostly commonly, ReLu:

$$O_A = g(W_A * H)$$

In the preceding formula, W_A is the matrix of weights, as you saw in the previous two chapters for feed-forward networks. As in Figure 18-2, this output is then injected into a classic feed-forward neural network or anyway used in the context of the network.

The training phase of a recurrent neural network produces three weight matrices instead of one as for plain feed-forward networks. As mentioned, one is W_A and represents the classic matrix of weights of all neural networks. Another is W_{hh}, which indicates the relevance of the current state for the prediction. The third one is W_{xh}, which indicates the relevance of the current input for the prediction.

From RNN to Deep RNN

The diagram in Figure 18-2 presents the simplest form a recurrent neural network can take. You can extend the schema in various ways as it most suits your needs. For example, you can add one or more hidden layers in between the input and the memory context. Or you can have multiple memory contexts, differently configured. (See Figure 18-4.) A real-life scenario in which a more complex RNN architecture is necessary is speech recognition. In this case, in fact, it could make sense for the network to try to predict the next word based on what has been pronounced to date.

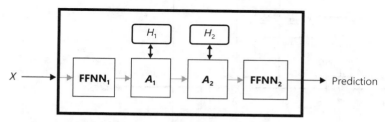

FIGURE 18-4 Possible schema of a "deep" RNN

From an algorithmic point of view, training an RNN is pretty much the same as training a classic feed-forward neural network, and backpropagation is still the key approach. In particular, unrolled over time as in Figure 18-3, the RNN can be assimilated to a chain of feed-forward neural networks that develop the internal state (possibly, multiple hidden states) over the course of the dataset. The variation of the backpropagation algorithm used here is called "backpropagation over time."

> **Important** For a recurrent neural network, even more than for a feed-forward neural network, working on normalized input data is crucial. You not only observe a faster convergence of the training process, but you also reduce dramatically the insurgence of the vanishing gradient phenomenon that in a simple RNN is amplified by cyclic access to memory states. (The vanishing gradient doesn't happen in the LSTM recurrent networks we'll introduce next.)

LSTM Neural Networks

The RNN architecture discussed so far presents a noticeable drawback: inputs that come sufficiently spaced out may not influence each other as you wish. In other words, the hidden state held by the memory context component has a too-short lifetime. This has brought about a new branch of research that has culminated in the definition of a Long Short-Term Memory (LSTM) neural network.

Overall, an LSTM neural network differs from a plain RNN in that it implements a more sophisticated version of the memory context.

Anatomy of an LSTM Memory Context

To prolong the lifetime of the hidden state, the neural network architecture adds a second level of memory. This longer-term memory is referred to as *cell state*. This state at time t is commonly indicated as C_t. The cell state works side by side with the shorter-term hidden state H_t, analogous to the memory of a plain RNN.

The big picture of an LSTM memory context is shown in Figure 18-5.

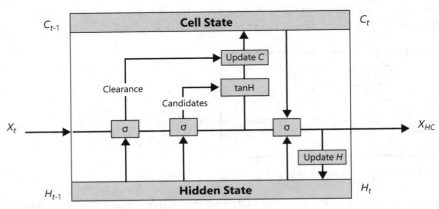

FIGURE 18-5 Schema of an LSTM memory context

The input X_t goes through several steps within the memory context. The context sends out a filtered version of the original input X_{HC} modified to take into account the short- and long-term memory. When the memory component sends its output, both types of state are updated to current time t.

Next, let's dig out the details of the various steps that transform the input based on the current states C_{t-1} and H_{t-1}.

Internal Mechanics of an LSTM Memory Context

The first step consists of clearing the current state of the longer-term memory. Through the application of the sigmoid function, some elements of the current state C_{t-1} are marked for later removal. The so-called forget gate layer f of the memory context is responsible for this:

$$f_t = \sigma(W_f * [H_{t-1}, X_t] + b_f)$$

The W_f in the formula is a matrix of weights specifically calculated during training to decide whether a piece of information is still relevant to stay in memory. Note that the sigmoid (logistic function) σ has an output in between 0 and 1, so each output value tells how relevant every element of the longer-term state is. The b_f is a bias coefficient also determined at training time. The interesting thing to notice is that the forget gate layer works on incoming data and data in the short-term memory to determine whether some of the information in the longer memory can now be considered outdated and removable. As an example, consider a text analysis scenario. In longer-term memory, you may have information about the current subject of the sentence. However, the combination of newer information may change that; hence, the element in longer-term memory is marked for deletion.

The second step identifies existing information in the cell state that needs be updated. The input gate layer i is responsible for the second step, and the formula to use is the same one shown above except for a different matrix of weights and bias:

$$i_t = \sigma(W_i *[H_{t-1}, X_t]+b_i)$$

The third step consists of identifying new value candidates to be stored in the longer-term memory as of time t:

$$a_t = tanh(W_c *[H_{t-1}, X_t]+b_c)$$

The W_a in the formula is yet another matrix of weights specifically calculated during training to identify data candidates to be placed in the cell state.

At this point, you have the entire list of changes for the cell state: items to remove, items to update, and new values to store. In the fourth step, the context physically updates the state, making it evolve from C_{t-1} to C_t. Here's the operation:

$$C_t = f_t *C_{t-1} + i_t *a_t$$

The term $f_t *C_{t-1}$ refers to the information you intend to remove from the cell state, and the term $i_t *a_t$ identifies the information to add or update. Because you've addressed the cell state, you can now take care of the shorter-term hidden state. This new hidden state H_t will remain in the memory context as short-term storage. Interestingly, the new H_t coincides with the externally available output of the component that in Figure 18-5 was referred to as X_{HC}. In the calculation, you first filter the original input through the shorter-term memory:

$$O_t = \sigma(W_o *[h_{t-1}, X_t]+b_o)$$

Again, bias and matrix of weights are calculated at training time. The O_t value is then combined with the freshly updated cell state:

$$H_t = O_t *tanh(C_t)$$

From LSTM to Deep LSTM

The preceding description of the LSTM doesn't represent the only possible implementation, but in a sufficiently general way it still wraps up the mechanics of past data in the context of a prediction. Text analysis and speech recognition are excellent examples of RNN with an LSTM memory context.

Figure 18-4 can then be updated to the case of LSTM memory and show that the actual topology of the neural network is up to you (and the problem at hand), so you have to decide if you need memory and what kind of memory and where in the flow. (See Figure 18-6.)

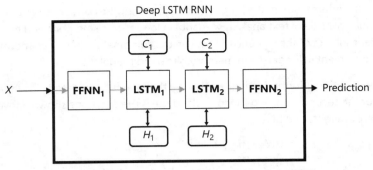

FIGURE 18-6 Possible schema of a "deep" RNN with LSTM memory

Convolutional Neural Networks

Feed-forward neural networks were the first type of neural network introduced to solve relatively simple regression and classification problems. As you saw at the end of Chapter 17, "Design of a Neural Network," a neural network may be overkill for simple data in just a few dimensions, but such networks become more and more precise as the complexity and dimensionality of data grow. And they usually grow with the complexity and intricacy of the problem.

Then you saw that a memory-based neural network is necessary for tasks such as those falling under the umbrella of natural language processing (NLP). If you need to deal with images instead, yet another approach is recommended because it works better than other known approaches may do.

Image Classification and Recognition

An image is nothing more than a matrix of pixels; therefore, you could think of breaking it up into small vectors (say, 10×10) and processing it through a deep neural network. Can you successfully predict what the image contains? It can realistically happen for basic, artificially built images such as simple diagrams but certainly not for real-world pictures. Using the classic (recurrent) feed-forward approach on a large image would lead to losing information about the disposition of pixels and, with it, the chance to teach the network what the image really contains.

A new approach is required. Enter convolutional neural networks. A convolutional neural network (CNN) is the primary tool used for image classification and recognition, and its use is extended to video and audio processing and, by further extension, to natural language as well. The training of a CNN goes outside the scope of the book, so we won't be covering it. However, suffice it to say that a CNN is trained along the same general ideas as backpropagation and gradient descent.

The Convolutional Layer

Much like an RNN, a CNN results from a combination of a plain feed-forward neural network with multiple, dedicated components. A convolutional neural network incorporates a special layer called the convolutional layer. Its purpose is reducing the usually large images to a more manageable form without losing relevant information that might be critical for making a good prediction.

The problem with images is that they are cumbersome objects to deal with. As an example, think of a 4K image such as those taken by a modern high-end smartphone. It's 16M pixels, and each pixel takes at least 3 bytes for the RGB channel—another 16M points. There should be a way to reduce such a huge amount of data. Mathematics comes to the rescue through the *convolution* operation.

The Convolution Operation

In mathematics, convolution is an operation between two functions and produces a third function that overall indicates how the shape of one is modified by the other. In real life, convolution is applied to figure out the correlation between two signals, to perform pattern matching or, as in the case here, to apply filters to incoming data. In this context, a filter is a process that removes some unwanted information from incoming data.

For continuous functions, the convolution is calculated as the integral of the product of the two functions after one is rotated by 180 degrees. If the functions involved are not continuous, instead, pieces of their product are simply summed. This is what happens when images are involved.

If this process sounds overly complex, well, it isn't, and moving on to consider images may prove it.

Convolution of Images

Let's say you have a matrix *I* that represents an image. For the moment, let's assume it is a grayscale image with a color depth of one. (Each value of the matrix indicates the level of gray of the corresponding pixel.)

Let's take another (arbitrarily smaller) matrix *K* called the kernel. In this case, the convolution consists of moving the kernel matrix over the entire surface of the original image, starting from position 0,0. The kernel will move one cell at a time along the width first and move one cell down after it has reached the right edge. The operation is summarized in Figure 18-7.

At each step, the kernel matrix is multiplied element by element (Hadamard product) to the corresponding section of the original image. Note that the color depth of the kernel has to be the same as the color depth of the original image. The resulting intermediate matrix has the same size as the kernel. All the elements of the resulting matrix are then summed up, and the value is written to a new matrix—the convolution matrix.

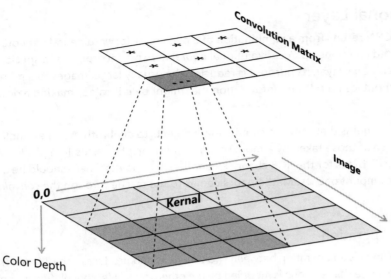

FIGURE 18-7 The convolution operation on one level of depth

The size of the convolved matrix depends on both the size of the image and the kernel. The formula is

$$(W_{Image} - W_{Kernel} + 1) \;*\; (H_{Image} - H_{Kernel} + 1)$$

The dimension of the kernel is a hyperparameter of the CNN, whereas its values are figured out during the training.

In case of multiple levels of colors such as RGB or CMYK, the convolution repeats for each of the color components, and multiple intermediate matrices are generated and then summed up together in a single value. The resulting convolved matrix always has the preceding dimension regardless of the color depth. (See Figure 18-8.)

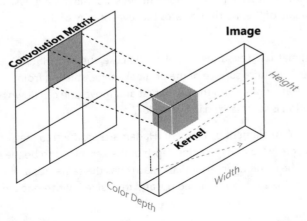

FIGURE 18-8 The convolution operation with a realistic color depth

At the end of the day, the convolution matrix compresses the information of the full image to a fraction of its size while hopefully preserving the same informational content.

Aspects of the Convolutional Layer

A CNN is not necessarily made up of a single convolutional layer. More often than not, there's a first convolutional layer that captures the low-level features of the image (corners, colors, curves, background) and then one or more additional layers responsible for identifying higher-level elements such as objects, faces, people, trees, and the like. Additional layers are ultimately responsible for abstracting pixels to real objects.

There are two main types of convolution. One is *valid padding* and is aimed at reducing the dimension of the image. The other is called *same padding* (SP). The effect of SP is ensuring that the convolved matrix has the same size as the image being convoluted. In fact, if the dimensions of the image and the kernel do not match properly, the convolved matrix may be smaller than the original image. To avoid that, the original image is padded with zeros before convolution takes place. As a result, the kernel may slip outside the original input map and will find neutral zeros all around. Zeros are added symmetrically all around the borders, as in Figure 18-9.

0	0	0	0	0	0
0	12	20	30	0	0
0	8	12	2	0	0
0	34	70	37	4	0
0	112	100	25	12	0
0	0	0	0	0	0

FIGURE 18-9 Zero padding turning a 4×4 image into a 5×5 image

Note It is interesting to note that some of the commonly used filters in image processing tools (e.g., the Gaussian blur) are obtained as a plain convolution between a fixed matrix and the original image.

The Pooling Layer

The convolution layer is only the first step that a CNN performs. The second step is pooling. The purpose of pooling is reducing the size of the convolved matrix even more to get rid of all noise and keep only the relevant and dominant features.

Max and Average Pooling

Pooling consists of moving another smaller matrix over the surface of the convolved matrix. In this case, we won't call it a kernel matrix because all that matters is the size and not the content. The moving matrix is a sort of window that shows what's underneath, applying one of two simple mathematical filters.

One is max pooling, which returns the maximum value found in the section of convolved matrix. The other is average pooling, which returns the arithmetic mean of the values observed. Figure 18-10 shows how to extract a pooling matrix from a 4×4 convolved matrix using a window size of 2×2.

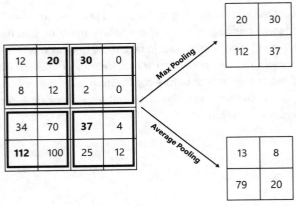

FIGURE 18-10 Max pooling versus average pooling

Even though convolutional and pooling layers are conceptually distinct, often they are combined in a single comprehensive layer. As mentioned, in a single CNN, there might be multiple convolutional and pooling layers. The more layers, the more powerful the network is, and conversely, the more computing power it requires.

The ReLu Activation Function

A CNN layer is usually characterized by a ReLu activation function. As you may recall from Chapter 17, ReLu (Rectified Linear Unit) is a function that returns the maximum between 0 and the value. The ultimate purpose of a ReLu layer is removing all negative values from the convolved matrix. (Negative values in the convolved matrix are possible if the kernel has negative values in it.)

Making a pass with a nonlinear function like ReLu increases the nonlinearity of the stream of values. The effect on the convoluted image is that the resulting image has fewer colors with more abrupt changes between nearby pixels.

The ReLu function is preferable over, say, the sigmoid because ReLu is easier to compute and also alleviates the vanishing gradient problem, as discussed in Chapter 17.

Note Increasing the nonlinearity of the data that flows through the neural network is crucial because, at the end of the day, the image classification function the network is trying to learn is nonlinear. Hence, without strengthening, the nonlinearity of transformations would lead to building a large and complex linear classifier, entirely missing the point of doing image classification on real-world images or text prediction on spoken human communication.

The Fully Connected Layer

Much like the recurrent neural network we discussed earlier, a real-world CNN has a complex structure and ultimately results from the composition of multiple convolutional and pooling layers. The union of these layers is responsible for feature mapping, namely a learning step aimed at extracting relevant information about the content of the image. Each CNN layer is specialized in some kind of feature detection.

The result obtained from CNN layers is passed to the fully connected (FC) layer that finalizes the process. (See Figure 18-11.)

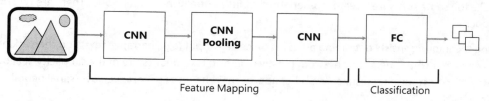

FIGURE 18-11 Schema of a deep CNN

The FC layer receives the output from the various CNN layers and processes them to create a sort of a model. It's called "fully connected" because it consists of multiple layers (as it appears necessary) that connect all inbound feature maps to build a classification model. (See Figure 18-12.)

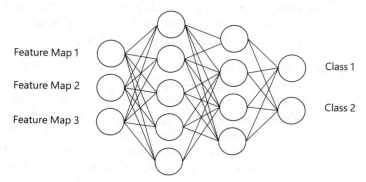

FIGURE 18-12 Schema of a fully connected layer

The purpose of the FC layer is putting together the discovered features to relate them in order to classify the image. The FC layer has ReLu as the activation function and includes a final multiclass classification layer commonly with a softmax activation.

Note that the fully connected layer can, in theory, be connected to other neural networks, thus configuring deep convolutional neural networks.

Further Neural Network Developments

Neural networks have been studied for decades, but only in recent years have we seen noticeable development, essentially because the greatly increased computing power has made it possible to tackle problems that were too hard to address otherwise.

In this context, one of the most interesting areas is generative neural networks, which are able to generate creative content.

Generative Adversarial Neural Networks

It is one thing to make a smart piece of software extract information from numbers; it is quite another to make the same software "create" something that fits naturally in the real world. There are two main approaches.

One technique consists of training an LSTM on certain input (e.g., narrative text) and then asking it to predict what comes next. This network mostly works on text, but in spite of the simplicity, it allows you to achieve astonishing results. The other approach is known as generative adversarial neural network (GAN).

The Overall Idea

GAN is based on a simple and brilliant idea. Two neural networks are trained to work together: one serves as the generator and one as the discriminator.

The discriminator is trained to understand whether or not a given input is realistic. In other words, the purpose of the discriminator is to measure the truthfulness of the submitted text or image. The concept of "truthfulness" is part of the definition of the discriminator and the training.

The generator, instead, is responsible for creating the content that the discriminator will judge. The generator submits its work to the discriminator and uses the feedback to make changes. To start the ball rolling, the generator initially submits random generated content. The discriminator evaluates the probability that the submitted creation comes from the training dataset. When the discriminator can't distinguish between the item in the dataset and the re-created content, the training ends. The moment the discriminator accepts the input, the created content is determined to be realistic. After the training, when a GAN model is released and runs in production, it just takes input and creates content based on that.

Now let's look at a couple of interesting applications of generative adversarial networks.

Applications of GANs

In 2017, a group of academic researchers created PassGAN, a password-guessing tool based on a GAN. They took a published database of tens of millions of passwords leaked from a gaming site and trained the adversarial network to generate new passwords. When done, they asked the model to generate several million new passwords.

Checked against a known database of real-world passwords leaked from LinkedIn, it turned out that 27 percent of PassGAN-generated passwords were used by some real LinkedIn users! For more information on PassGAN, refer to https://arxiv.org/abs/1709.00440. Amazing, but scary!

Another great example of real-life use of GANs is FaceApp, the popular mobile photo editor app (https://www.faceapp.com). Apparently, FaceApp does nothing particularly fancy that hundreds of other similar apps and online sites aren't already doing. It applies multiple graphical filters to a picture that contains a human face. Conceptually, it does nothing really different from sharpening the contours of a photo, blurring, or smoothing the image.

The interesting thing is that under the hood FaceApp applies filters as they were generated by a trained GAN. Reasonably, the training of the FaceApp GAN used tons of images of any specific type, such as beard, mustache, male, female, old, young, different hairstyles, and the like. Hence, the GAN learned how to transform an input photo in a way that the discriminator (during training) determined to be acceptable.

Auto-Encoders

Yet another interesting idea that brings neural networks into the territory of unsupervised learning is auto-encoders. An auto-encoder is a system made up of two connected neural networks in which the output of the first becomes the input of the second.

Anatomy of an Auto-Encoder

You can think of an auto-encoder as a two interacting networks—an encoder and a decoder. An auto-encoder network is depicted in Figure 18-13.

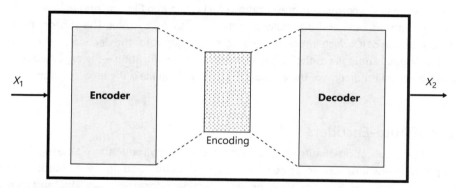

FIGURE 18-13 Schema of an auto-encoder neural network

The overall auto-encoder receives an input X_1 and passes it to the first layer (the encoder). The encoder encodes the input, creating a more compact representation known as *encoding*. Typically, the encoding creates single-dimensional data compared to n-dimensional data being the input. The encoding is then passed to the second layer (the decoder), which tries to re-create the original input as X_2. If X_1 and X_2 are close enough, the intermediate representation (the encoding) is a more compact representation of the original input.

Notice that Figure 18-13 illustrates the schema of the network as it is trained. Once the network is trained and deployed to production, it gets the input X_1 and outputs its compact representation (the encoding). Therefore, the point of the auto-encoder is to reduce the feature dimensions.

> **Note** The encoder element of an auto-encoder network is a special layer that is also referred to as an *embedding layer* if used in the context of any other neural network and not specifically an auto-encoder. An embedding layer takes an input vector and returns a denser and more compact version. When used in the context of a problem-specific neural network, the training of the layer depends on the training of the whole surrounding network.

Training of an Auto-Encoder

From a theoretical point of view, an interesting aspect of auto-encoders is that they ultimately address unsupervised learning scenarios but transform each into a supervised scenario. We said that an auto-encoder is made up of two neural networks, so the first idea might be training each network separately. If you do so, however, you run into an unsolvable issue: how do you choose the label for the encoder and training dataset for the decoder?

This means that the encoder and decoder are two dedicated macro layers that internally can expand in convolutional layers or feed-forward layers as appropriate for the problem at hand. These two macro layers, though, should be handled as a single one from the perspective of training. If you do so, then the input data is both the input for the encoder and the target label for the decoder. This, in fact, reduces the learning to a supervised learning.

Let's say you want to find a compact representation of a large audio file. The original file is the input to the overall auto-encoder and, internally, also the input to the encoder. The encoder produces a compact representation of it, which immediately becomes the input for the decoder. The decoder, however, uses the original audio file as the target to match in its classification—the expected result. The distance between the prediction of the encoder and the original file is the error function to minimize.

Applications of Auto-Encoders

The primary business application of auto-encoders is dimensionality reduction—a classic unsupervised problem—where you aim to condense larger data into perhaps fewer features without a loss of information. Other applications are anomaly detection, information retrieval, and image processing.

Training an auto-encoder for anomaly detection requires using only canonical data points so that the performance is optimal on standard elements and poor on unseen and anomalous data. Hence, the auto-encoder for anomaly detection will return a Boolean answer based on the distance between the original input value and the value reconstructed from the encoding.

Information retrieval, especially when large objects are involved (e.g., images), is simplified by checking the encoding rather than the whole object. This leads to a third application: image processing and, in particular, image compression. Other scenarios are image denoising and increasing resolution. Image compression is ultimately a form of dimensionality reduction, and interestingly, experiments with auto-encoders have been run to compress images that are competitive with the JPEG standard.

> **Note** If you review the entire workflow of JPEG compression—devised back in the early 1990s—it looks like the layers of a neural network. A first step performs a sort of a convolution, taking mini blocks of pixels over the surface of the image and applying the discrete cosine transformation function. Next, the output undergoes a quantization process in which elements near zero are converted to zero (similar to ReLu). Finally, data is encoded.

Summary

As fascinating as it may sound, a human neuron is an incredibly complex machine, only a small part of which we fully understand today. Conversely, a software neuron in a neural network is overall a simple mathematical function able to emulate a small fraction of the complexity of a human neuron. The funny thing is that while the industry and academic world strive to deliver complex structures of neural networks (recurrent, LSTM, convolutional, adversarial), we're still at a long distance from our brain.

In this chapter, we presented an overview of the most advanced types of current neural networks, such as those able to connect past experiences with current input (memory-based recurrent networks), those able to emulate vision and extract content and context from images, and those able to create new content.

This chapter completes our overview of deep learning. In the next chapter, we'll try to wrap up everything by presenting a neural network for sentiment analysis. In doing so, we'll go through the various steps of the learning pipeline again, from data loading to preparation and from training to production.

## CHAPTER 19

Sentiment Analysis: An End-to-End Solution

No problem can be solved from the same level of consciousness that created it.
—*Albert Einstein, Nobel Prize 1921*

Sentiment analysis aims at the systematic extraction and quantification of the polarity of a given text, whatever the original form is—spoken language, document, plain article. It's about understanding the combination of words and sentences that make up the natural language—spoken or written. In a growingly digitalized world, sentiment analysis is a formidable tool to measure the reaction of people to events, most commonly through public reviews, survey responses, and social media activity.

Marketing, customer service, e-commerce, and health care are business fields in which sentiment analysis is crucial and widely applied. Being able to automatically classify any form of feedback, and directly from its natural form of expression, delivers an incredible power but, even more, adds one more level of intelligence to software.

Determining the polarity of a text—whether the expressed mood is positive, negative, or neutral—is not an easy task. The natural language has so many nuances and variations, including humor and sarcasm, that it doesn't always match one-to-one with the known mood that a dictionary may statically assign to words and sentences. The same sentence, given the perceived context, may transmit a radically different meaning.

Grabbing the hidden meaning of text and its components—and in a reliable way—is the ultimate purpose of sentiment analysis. Sentiment analysis is clearly a matter of learning. You start with a long list of sentences with a known polarity and find the most effective way to teach the software to classify any new sentence it may face in production.

In this chapter, we'll process a public database of movie reviews and build a neural network to figure out the sentiment.

> **Note** Sentiment analysis is a good example of the delicate art that machine learning some-times turns out to be. The accuracy of the prediction depends on the quality and quantity of the input data but also on the expected results. If you're simply looking for a yes/no kind of answer, you can reasonably go with a binary classification algorithm as demonstrated by the ML.NET example in Chapter 8, "ML.NET Tasks and Algorithms." If you're aiming at more detailed output (e.g., good, not-so-bad, neutral, not-so-good, bad), you might need a neural network to obtain a more precise analysis.

Preparing Data for Training

Machine learning—and more in general, the whole field of artificial intelligence—is the software way to solve a well-formalized real-life problem. Machine learning, in fact, adds a new dimension to the space of problems that software can address: intelligence. Intelligence is also, in some way, the lever that brings solutions from the real world to real life. In the real-world space, problems need be solved to run business effectively. In the real-life space, there are more human-friendly solutions to business problems—in one word, intelligence.

At the root of everything, there should be a problem. So, before we get into the building of a classic machine learning pipeline—data preparation, training, evaluation, client application—let's spend some time neatly formalizing the terms of the sample problem for which we came to the conclusion that a machine learning solution is worth the cost.

Formalizing the Problem

A popular website whose business is built on the reliability of reviews and general feedback publicly shared by users hired Acme Corp to carefully review the whole repository of comments and propose a way to quickly and automatically rank the reviews. Users of the popular website are encouraged to leave a review and express a vote from 1 to 10, with 1 meaning profound dislike and 10 indicating a wonderful experience.

At a random check, owners of the website noted some occasional discrepancies between the (human) perceived sense of words and the given vote. Sometimes, the vote was too high for the perceived sense of words; sometimes it was too low for the enthusiastic words in the comments. Hence, they asked Acme Corp to build, as a proof of concept, a parallel and completely independent evaluation engine that could be run against the original database of reviews to compare evaluations and possibly lead to different business strategies.

Experts at Acme Corp suggested building a sentiment analysis system as a classifier and decided to skip over any simpler classifier algorithms to go directly with a bidirectional Long Short-Term Memory (LSTM) neural network. The point they made was that with 10 options to choose from and the subsequent need to capture any nuance and subtlety in the text, chances were good that a plain classification algorithm would be too big for the high expectations set.

Getting the Data

The success of a machine learning project is heavily influenced by the maturity of data within the organization. A data-mature organization is well aware of the data it owns, knows the meaning of the data, and ensures that any data is accessible to whoever needs it.

All three points are crucial to save time and budget on a machine learning project. Even in a small sample project like the one presented here, retrieving and shaping data in a suitable format took the lion's share of time and effort, well beyond 70 percent. For an organization willing to squeeze the most out of machine learning, knowing what you have in store and storing it in a way that allows you to reshape it into any requested form are vital. A data lake is a powerful tool for collecting data as it comes, but a tidy and clean structuring is necessary—whether in the form of a data warehouse, relational database, or similar.

Any machine learning projects are built on data, and the success depends on the ability to procure, clean, curate, and analyze. In the scenario set up for this chapter, we needed a dataset for sentiment classification and selected the dataset at http://ai.stanford.edu/~amaas/data/sentiment. It contains a set of 50,000 movie reviews, half for training and half for testing.

The dataset comes as a collection of distinct text files—one per review—and the title indicates the sentiment, ranging from 1 to 10.

> **Note** The dataset comes from the proceedings of the 49th Annual Meeting of the Association for Computational Linguistics: Human Language Technologies. It was written in June 2011 by Andrew Maas, Raymond Daly, Peter Pham, Dan Huang, Andrew Ng, and Christopher Potts. The full paper "Learning Word Vectors for Sentiment Analysis" is available at www.aclweb.org/anthology/P11-1015.

Manipulating the Data

Fifty thousand raw small text files are definitely not easy to work with. In a way, this project represents the metaphor of taking usable data out of an unstructured data lake. As a first step, the sample project groups the content of the dataset into a single location that is easier to work with. Note that the new form that the content assumes may likely be application specific and not reusable in other projects. This is an intermediate format because it only serves the ultimate purpose of making data usable for training the chosen algorithm.

An intermediate format can be a relational database, and a relational database can be a good source for a machine learning project run through ML.NET, but not necessarily for a Python training algorithm. In summary, there's a general pattern for data manipulation: going from an unstructured repository to a structured repository and from there up to a format readymade for the machine learning work. Figure 19-1 shows the general process and the instance of it in the sample project.

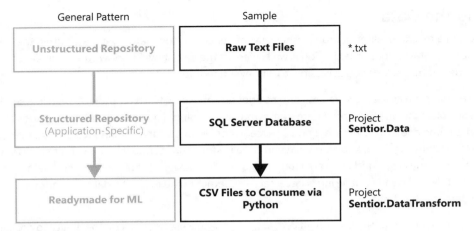

FIGURE 19-1 Reasonable pattern for transforming data for training

The implementation of the general pattern of data transformation collects raw text files from the downloaded dataset and creates a SQL Server database with two tables. One table contains the reviews. The project responsible for creating the table just loops through the text files, reads the content, and adds a record. The Boolean column *Test* indicates whether the review is for training (false) or testing (true).

```
public class Review
{
    [Key, DatabaseGenerated(DatabaseGeneratedOption.Identity)]
    public int Id { get; set; }
    public string RawText { get; set; }
    public bool Test { get; set; }
}
```

The second table contains the sentiment associated with the review. The following class shows the schema. The ID of the review is mapped to a value (1 to 10) that indicates the reported (or expected) sentiment. As mentioned, the sentiment is embedded in the filename. All raw input files are named *[number]_[sentiment].txt,* where *number* is a progressive index.

```
public class Label
{
    public int ReviewId { get; set; }
    public int Sentiment { get; set; }
}
```

The project *Sentior.Data* does all of this work. The project is a .NET Core console application. Internally, it may or may not use ML.NET for data manipulation. At this stage, in fact, there's nothing strictly related to machine learning, so the full power of the .NET Core framework can be leveraged. To sum up, this step is pure file and database work and can be accomplished with any appropriate tools.

Note The use of the *Test* column to split between train and test data is debatable. If you don't have a relational background, or if you find working with a relational DBMS to be expensive, well, don't do it. Both Python libraries and ML.NET offer effective in-memory methods to split between training and testing data. Moreover, those methods are guaranteed to return balanced datasets, which is not necessarily guaranteed if you pick up test rows manually.

Considerations on the Intermediate Format

So far, we have managed to have the content of the downloaded dataset locked down in a relational database. The decision to use (or not use) a database depends on the skills available to further manipulate data.

The format of the database mostly reflects the original structure of the data, but no feature engineering has been made yet, whether through Python, ML.NET, or SQL tools. Moreover, during the training phase, it may be necessary to get back and add or drop columns or compact columns in some way.

In a nutshell, it's highly recommended that you create an intermediate and flexible data structure. Given their skills, experts at Acme Corp opted for a relational database.

The intermediate format can be the format you directly use for training, or it can be the source for generating text files. Your choice depends on the technology you employ for training. When using Python, you probably do most of the data preparation without a relational database. At the same time, holding data in a relational database, as an intermediate format, can be helpful to quickly generate different text files. On the other hand, if data preparation is done through a relational database, you can train directly from it using the database services of ML.NET.

Having said that, holding data in a relational database can simplify a number of data cleanup scenarios, such as removing anomalous, null, or patently inconsistent rows; normalizing values; or generating new columns.

You can effectively do data preparation using text files in both Python and ML.NET, and you can do data preparation using a relational database—whatever you feel more comfortable with. When it comes to training, by using ML.NET, you can even train directly from a database. This is a usual case in enterprise scenarios.

Training the Model

The next decision to be made is about the training ecosystem and the algorithm. Both decisions can have an impact on the format of the data, so some further manipulation may be necessary, beyond further feature engineering.

Choosing the Ecosystem

Even though Python is by far the most commonly used ecosystem for machine learning projects, recall that it is mostly for convenience and an innate attitude to repeat successful practices. As we discussed in Chapter 6, "The .NET Way," the Python machine learning ecosystem rocks, but it doesn't mean at all that you are unable to use other languages and platforms. It's all about having (and using) the right tools for the job that *you feel comfortable with*. Yes, not just the right tools, but the right tools you know how to use. Table 19-1 shows that life exists beyond Python as far as machine learning is concerned.

TABLE 19-1 Major Machine Learning Libraries for Major Languages

Language	Library
Java, Scala, Kotlin, Clojure	DeepLearning4j
C++	MLPack
Go	GoML
C#, F#, Visual Basic	ML.NET

A major parameter to help you choose the target ecosystem is the actual form of learning you intend to use. If you believe that your project needs deep learning, TensorFlow is probably your best option, and that, for example, cuts off the newest ML.NET platform, which allows you to wrap some existing TensorFlow libraries but not to create a neural network. Another C# library (Accord.NET) does provide the ability to create simple neural networks, but it is now dismissed.

If you want to try using a neural network, your best option for training is the Python ecosystem, whether using TensorFlow directly or via Keras. Experts at Acme Corp opted for Keras.

Using a Python-based infrastructure forces you to have training and test data loaded into Python-compatible data structures. This also suggests that you extract data from the relational database and save it in the form of CSV files. The project *Sentior.DataTransform* just queries data from the previously created database and creates two files: *training.csv* and *test.csv*. Those two files will be the input to the Python-based training project.

> **Note** As emphatic as it may sound, saying that machine learning can only be done in Python is like saying that database access can only be done in .NET (or Java or Visual Basic or whatever other language).

Building a Dictionary of Words

The problem we're trying to solve involves analyzing text, but text is made of words. The source files, as copied in the database, are still in the form of sentences. One further step to take is breaking sentences into a dictionary of words and creating output CSV files.

To build the dictionary, all sentences in the review table are concatenated together and then punctuation is stripped off and the text is converted to lowercase. A further step tokenizes into words and builds a collection of unique elements. Each word has a unique ID that refers to its position in the dictionary.

Hence, the CSV training and test files have one entry for each sentence, but the sentence is represented by the concatenated sequence of indexes identifying constituent words in the dictionary. Here's an example:

```
68|4|3|135|37|46|7091|1351|15|3|5386|512|45|16|3|602|131|11|6|3|1306|467|4|1854|217|3|0|6386|308
|6|659|82|34|1941|1109|2810|33|1|946|0|4|29|5473|477|9|2766|1854|1|212|60|16|56|809|1339|828|251
|9|40|100|125|1491|55|143|36|1|1070|140|26|659|125|1|0|405|58|94|2184|299|768|5|3|881|0|20|3|180
4|690|29|124|71|22|226|103|16|47|50|625|33|739|81|0
```

The algorithm will be called to predict one out of 10 classes—the values in the range 1 through 10. Subsequently, the score class takes the form of an array of integers with values 0/1. For example, the output for a sentiment 4 is

```
0,0,0,1,0,0,0,0,0,0
```

A dictionary of words is needed because machine learning algorithms can only crunch numbers. A dictionary helps you turn sentences into an array of integers. In particular, the sample code builds a dictionary with the 10,000 most-used words.

Choosing the Trainer

A classification problem can be solved in many different ways, but a difference of learning power exists between shallow and deep algorithms. A neural network has the potential to learn to predict a more accurate response than other algorithms, and sentiment analysis is a delicate matter in which a too-sharp response may be even pointless sometimes.

> **Important** In general, any decision you make about algorithms should be supported by strong evidence rather than by speculation, but it's also true that you need to start in some way and from some firm point. No matter the intentions and commitment, sometimes you proceed led only by the wind of speculation and known examples and then change routes on the fly. Automated machine learning (AutoML) is crucial to mitigate this problem but can hardly solve it.

The Role of AutoML

In general, AutoML is a tool that enables developers with limited machine learning expertise to train high-quality models specific to their business needs. Any AutoML tool relies on some underlying learning framework and suggests the ideal algorithm (and configuration thereof) for a specific dataset and problem.

The AutoML framework of choice should be able to specifically understand the business domain and bridge over shallow and deep learning scenarios. The Google Cloud AutoML platform has a specific service for natural language processing that can be used for sentiment analysis. It gets you a trained model obtained via transfer learning from one of the (internal) pretrained models, likely based on both shallow and deep learning algorithms. The Microsoft AutoML.NET is driven by the set of the ML tasks supported in ML.NET and is limited to shallow algorithms.

Bidirectional LSTM

Acme Corp experts opted for a rather sophisticated neural network to build with Keras. The most relevant layer of the resulting network is a bidirectional LSTM. The complete schema of the network is shown in Figure 19-2.

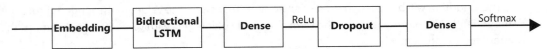

FIGURE 19-2 Constituent layers of the neural network in the example

In Chapter 18, "Other Types of Neural Networks," we learned that an LSTM network has a double layer of memory (hidden and cell state), but the flow of information within the network is forward only. This means that the state information that helps generate the output is based only on previous inputs. A bidirectional LSTM, instead, receives the input once from the beginning to the end and once from the end to the beginning in reverse order. Both passes of data processing have the effect of updating the memory context. The general schema of a bidirectional LSTM is shown in Figure 19-3.

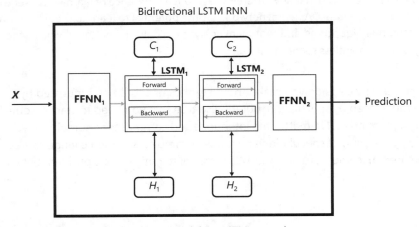

FIGURE 19-3 Schema of a bidirectional deep LSTM network

The double pass allows these networks to learn faster and grab a more accurate sense of the context because the state information includes two views of the same data. In text processing, this means that the network has a chance to look first at the flow of words from start to finish and then from finish to start, making it easier to figure out connections between words.

The Neural Network in Keras

Here's the Keras code in Python used to create the network. The routine takes three parameters: the size of the dictionary, the maximum number of words in a sentence, and the size of the word embedding layer.

```
def create_model_rnn(dictionary_size, max_words, EMBEDDING_DIM):

    # Create the neural network model
    model = Sequential()
    model.add(Embedding(dictionary_size, EMBEDDING_DIM, input_length=max_words))
    model.add(Bidirectional(LSTM(128, dropout=0.2, recurrent_dropout=0.2)))
    model.add(Dense(512, activation='relu'))
    model.add(Dropout(0.50))
    model.add(Dense(10, activation='softmax'))  # output layer
    model.compile(loss='categorical_crossentropy',optimizer='adam', metrics=['accuracy'])
    return model
```

As in Figure 19-2, the first layer is an embedding layer that serves the purpose of turning any input vector of integers into a more compact (denser) representation made of real numbers. The goal of this layer is reducing the size of the input for further flow within the network. Then there is the bidirectional LSTM with 128 neurons, followed by a plain hidden layer with a *ReLu* activation function and fairly large layer with its 512 neurons. Then, a dropout layer and another smaller hidden layer being the output with the expected 10 neurons. Reasonably, the activation function is *softmax*.

The network uses *Adam* (an adaptive learning rate method) as the gradient descent algorithm and *categorical_crossentropy* as the error function instead of the popular mean squared error. Note that *categorical_crossentropy* is ideal in classification problems where only one result can be correct but requires that the activation function of the output node is *softmax*.

Preparing the Neural Network for Training

As mentioned previously, the training project is a Python project (Acme Corp used Visual Studio 2019 Python extension for that) in which training and test data, as transformed from the database, are first loaded from CSV files and then mixed up to produce new random training and test sets. Here's the Python code to prepare data for training the preceding model:

```
def load_data(path):
    # Import data from CSV files

    train_data = pd.read_csv(path + '/training.csv', sep='|')
    test_data = pd.read_csv(path + '/test.csv', sep='|')

    # Load labels as vectors
    train_labels = pd.read_csv(path + '/training_labels.csv', sep=',')
    test_labels = pd.read_csv(path + '/test_labels.csv', sep=',')

    # Concatenate training and test data
    features = pd.DataFrame(np.concatenate((train_data.values, test_data.values)))

    # Concatenate training and test output labels
    labels = pd.DataFrame(np.concatenate((train_labels.values, test_labels.values)))
```

```
# 80/20 split of features and labels to get training and remaining dataset
# Note that [:index] means up to index and [index:] means from index
numberOfTrainingFeatures = int(0.8*len(features))
train_x = features[:numberOfTrainingFeatures]
train_y = labels[:numberOfTrainingFeatures]
remaining_x = features[numberOfTrainingFeatures:]
remaining_y = labels[numberOfTrainingFeatures:]

# 50/50 split of remaining features and labels between validation and test datasets
val_x = remaining_x[:int(len(remaining_x)*0.5)]
val_y = remaining_y[:int(len(remaining_y)*0.5)]
test_x = remaining_x[int(len(remaining_x)*0.5):]
test_y = remaining_y[int(len(remaining_y)*0.5):]
```

```
# Return training features/labels, test features/labels and validation features/labels
return train_x, train_y, test_x, test_y, val_x, val_y
```

To have a solid model, you might want to randomly split the dataset into three datasets: training, validation, and test. In the preceding code, the full data, which includes training and test datasets as downloaded and stored in the database, is split 80/20, so 80 percent goes for training and the remaining 20 percent is split 50/50 between testing and validation sets. The validation set is passed to the training method and is used to calculate the specified metrics. Based on the metrics, you fine-tune the model, and when ready, you get the final evaluation by running the model on the test dataset:

```
# Fit the model over 200 epochs (using validation data)
model.fit(train_x, train_y, batch_size=200, epochs=20, validation_data=(val_x, val_y))

# Final evaluation of the model (using test data)
score, accuracy = model.evaluate(test_x, test_y, batch_size=batch_size)
```

Note that in the preceding code, an epoch refers to one training pass made over the entire dataset. Batch size, instead, refers to the number of data points to consider in advance to cover the entire dataset during an epoch. (We'll discuss this issue more in a moment.)

Best practice ensures you can get an unbiased model that learns from training data and is able to later deal with totally unseen data.

Saving the Model

Once trained, the model must be persisted to be hosted and proxied in some way. If you don't have the model on disk, it would be problematic to reuse it in a real-life application. If not saved, it remains an in-memory resource.

```
# Train the model
model = train_model(model,train_x, train_y, test_x, test_y, val_x, val_y, batch_size, path)

# Serialize the model
model.save (path + "/model.pb")
```

The *.pb* file is then shared even across platforms and, for example, can be loaded as an external file in an ML.NET-based C# project.

Other Aspects of the Network

A few aspects of the sample neural network that we briefly touched on in past chapters are worth a second look in light of a concrete example.

The Embedding Layer

The first aspect we focus on is the presence of an embedding layer. We introduced embedding layers in Chapter 18 in the context of auto-encoding neural networks. Conceptually, an embedding layer plays the role of the encoder in an auto-encoding neural network: it condenses the input vector of numeric values into a more compact representation made of real numbers. An embedding layer can be used as a standalone component in any flavor of a neural network.

Keras provides a dedicated component for adding an embedding layer. Adding an embedding layer is recommended whenever you want to embed high-dimensional data into a lower-dimensional space. Concretely, the Keras embedding layer turns positive integers (commonly, indexes of words in a dictionary) into dense vectors of some fixed size:

```
model.add(Embedding(10001, 50, 100))
```

The first argument here is the size of the input—namely, in this case, the size of the dictionary plus one (10001). The second argument is the dimension of the dense embedding that each input integer will be subjected to (50). The third argument (100) is the maximum length of input sequences (i.e., words in the dataset).

Note that an embedding layer can be only the first layer of a neural network.

The Dropout Parameter and Dropout Layers

Dropout is a characteristic of a neural network layer that consists of ignoring—at training time—a certain number of randomly selected inputs, whether variables from the input data point or activations from a previous layer. The size of dropout is expressed as a percentage. For example, a dropout rate of 0.2 will actually ignore 20 percent of inputs.

Why do you need to silence input of a neural network? Dropout is a technique that greatly helps prevent overfitting. In a fully connected scenario—each neuron connected to any other neuron in the subsequent layer—some sort of interdependent learning between neurons is established during training. Dropout is then a form of regularization that penalizes the automatic building of such interdependencies.

By silencing a share of random neurons during training, dropout forces the neural network to learn more foundational and robust connections that happily survive the occasional shutdown of neurons. The facts that remain verified across many different random subsets of the other neurons are the facts that are worth learning.

In Keras, you can add dropout regularization as a separate layer—the Dropout layer—or as a parameter within an LSTM layer. A dropout layer usually sits between two dense layers and restricts the given percentage of the output of the previous layer from being the input of the next layer. In the following example, only 50 percent of the output of the ReLu layer makes its way into the output layer:

```
model.add(Dense(512, activation='relu'))
model.add(Dropout(0.50))
model.add(Dense(10, activation='softmax'))  # output layer
```

An LSTM neural network can also have a dropout mask applied internally to its input and its recurrent input (hidden state):

```
model.add(Bidirectional(LSTM(128, dropout=0.2, recurrent_dropout=0.2)))
```

In Keras, you control those aspects via the *dropout* and *recurrent_dropout* parameters of the LSTM method.

Epochs of Training

In deep learning, an epoch is one training pass made over the entire dataset. Epochs split training in distinct steps, like in a loop, thus giving a chance to provide feedback about the progress and evaluation. If you also have specified a batch size—a number of data points considered together—the ratio between the size of the dataset and the batch size will determine how often the model is updated during an epoch.

The number of epochs necessary for training a model is traditionally large, often on the order of hundreds or more. More epochs allow the learning algorithm to progressively minimize errors, run after run.

Because epochs are iterations of the learning process, plotting time and error level on a 2D chart helps diagnose the learning curve of the model. They can also give visual evidence of the fitting level of the model over the training dataset. (See Figure 19-4.)

```
embedding_1 (Embedding)      (None, 200, 100)       1000100
bidirectional_1 (Bidirection (None, 256)            234496
dense_1 (Dense)              (None, 512)            131584
dropout_1 (Dropout)          (None, 512)            0
dense_2 (Dense)              (None, 10)             5130
==================================================================
Total params: 1,371,310
Trainable params: 1,371,310
Non-trainable params: 0
None
W0810 20:49:44.873805 10764 deprecation.py:323] From C:\Program Files (x86)\Microsoft Visual Studio\Shared\Python36_64\lib\site-packages\tensorflow\python\ops\math_grad.py:1250: add_dispatch_support.<locals>.wra
pper (from tensorflow.python.ops.array_ops) is deprecated and will be removed in a future version.
Instructions for updating:
Use tf.where in 2.0, which has the same broadcast rule as np.where
Train on 39123 samples, validate on 4890 samples
Epoch 1/20
2019-08-10 20:49:48.123513: I tensorflow/core/platform/cpu_feature_guard.cc:142] Your CPU supports instructions that this TensorFlow binary was not compiled to use: AVX2
39123/39123 [==============================] - 913s 23ms/step - loss: 1.9214 - acc: 0.2751 - val_loss: 1.7642 - val_acc: 0.3548

Epoch 00001: val_acc improved from -inf to 0.35481, saving model to C:/Data/Projects/Youbiquitous/Book/Sentior/Sentior.Builder/Output/model.hdf5
Epoch 2/20
9750/39123 [======>.....................] - ETA: 12:37 - loss: 1.6812 - acc: 0.3666
```

FIGURE 19-4 The training process of the sample model

The sample neural network counts over a million trainable parameters (e.g., weight coefficients) and has been trained over 39,000 records and validated on 5,000. For 20 epochs, it took an average of two hours of training.

The Client Application

For the convenience of Acme Corp, the entire solution lives within Visual Studio 2019, but more importantly, the solution is made up of four distinct projects, as shown in Table 19-2. (Admittedly, if you want to write Python code, Jupyter or Azure Notebooks also are valid and popular options.)

TABLE 19-2 Projects in the Sample Solution

Project	Platform	Description
Sentior	.NET Core	Console application; it is the client code that consumes the trained model via ML.NET.
Sentior.Data	.NET Core	Utility to process raw files from the downloaded dataset and import into a relational database. It uses Entity Framework Core to deal with the database. It also uses ML.NET for some data transformation. However, using ML.NET at this stage is not a strict necessity.
Sentior.DataTransform	.NET Core	Console application; it reads from the database and creates CSV training and testing files. It uses ML.NET, but, then again, its use is not strictly necessary.
Sentior.Builder	Python/Keras	Python application; it uses Keras to build and train a neural network. The neural network is then saved as a ProtoBuf (*.pb) file to be imported via ML.NET in the client application.

It is key to note that any real-life machine learning solution is a mix of different projects, some of which result in console, command-line applications. At the very minimum, you need a project for training the model and a distinct one for the client application. The schema that too many articles and posts offer—a single procedure to load/clean data, train/test, and consume the model—is good for demos and conference talks but not for the real world.

Loading data into a manageable repository—whatever manageable means to you—is the first step. You may consider this repository as a sort of permanent cache to quickly create new views of the data for different attempts of training. The second step is training and testing, and you can choose the platform that most suits you—Python, .NET, Java, or even others. In between caching and training, there might be other helper utilities such as the CSV creator used in this example.

Finally, let's look at the client application.

Getting Input for the Model

The client application uses the trained model as if it were an external library or a microservice. The trained model has its protocol for calls, and the implementation of this protocol may be smoothed by the use of wrapper libraries. If you have a .NET application, ML.NET wraps most of the effort and exposes a developer-friendly API. Other options exist, but consuming a model essentially means calling into a host—often via a REST interface or a proxy.

In the sample, the client application is a plain console that captures a string of text and further processes it via the model:

```
var textToAnalyze = Console.ReadLine();
```

Unfortunately, the user information that a realistic client application can collect—plain text—is not good for a neural network that can only process real numbers. It is then necessary to turn the text into numbers before the model can start working. The client application or an embedded application service takes care of the extra work:

```
public IDataView TransformInputData(MLContext context,
            IDictionary dictionary,
            int maxLengthOfWords,
            string textToAnalyze)
{
    // Removes punctuation, blanks and lower text
    var data = new[] { new TextToPredict() {
                    Text = Regex.Replace(toAnalyze, @"[^\w\s]", string.Empty)
                            .ToLower()
                            .Trim()
            }
        };

    // Map the provided string to the provided dictionary
    var dataView = context.Data.LoadFromEnumerable(data);
    return MapToDictionary(dataView, dictionary, maxLengthOfWords);
}
```

The *DataView* object returned from this helper method will be used later before invoking the model for a prediction.

Getting the Prediction from the Model

You load the TensorFlow model created via Keras and saved as a *.pb* file into a newly created ML.NET context and then fit the model on the data view for word-index mapping:

```
var dataView = TransformInputData(mlContext, dictionary, 100, textToAnalyze);
var model = mlContext.Model.LoadTensorFlowModel(modelLocation);
model.Fit(dataView);
```

Next, you create a prediction engine to work with the model. The *CreatePredictionEngine* method takes the type through which the model receives the input (*TextToPredict*) and the type through which it will return a response (*SentimentPrediction*).

```
var engine = mlContext.Model.CreatePredictionEngine<TextToPredict, SentimentPrediction>(model);
```

Helper classes for consuming the model are listed here:

```
public class TextToPredict
{
    public string Text { get; set; }
}

public class SentimentPrediction
{
    // 10-elements array of 0/1 integers
    public int[] Sentiment { get; set; }
}
```

The following code invokes the engine for making a prediction:

```
var response = engine.Predict(new TextToPredict { Text = textToAnalyze });
```

The raw response is an array of integers that is not exactly nice for the end user.

Turning the Response into Usable Information

The final step of the client application is making the input understandable for the end user. More in general, the client application is responsible for two data transformations—from high-level user input to raw model input and from raw model output to high-level user output.

How the output is turned into usable information depends on the application, the expected users, and the data. In this case, you receive an array of 10 integers and all you do is pick the maximum value and classify it in some way against an application-specific scale. The simplest is positive feedback for values greater than 0.5 and negative feedback for values less than 0.5.

The ONNX Format

In the end, any machine learning model contains the analytical definition of a computation graph to be executed in the host environment when the model is invoked in production. The syntax used to express the graph varies with the software framework used to train the model. So TensorFlow, PyTorch, *scikit-learn*, and ML.NET have their own formats.

ONNX (https://onnx.ai) defines a common and extensible computation graph model, built-in operators, and standard data types aimed at making various models interoperable. The initiative started in 2017, driven by the efforts of Facebook and Microsoft, but other big companies active in the machine learning domain announced their intention to join the initiative: Amazon, IBM, Huawei, and Intel, among others.

ML.NET fully supports importing and exporting through the ONNX format.

Summary

Sentiment analysis is one of those problems that are most talked about these days when there is growing interest about machine learning. It's perceived as important because it promises to turn natural language into formal code that a machine can easily interpret. This is exactly the turning point of artificial intelligence—the point that increases the perception of software as intelligent software.

Beyond this, sentiment analysis is a canonical classification problem with some additional issues. One is that any client application can provide text, and any machine learning artifact must be crunching numbers. Word index mapping is, therefore, the first extra problem to face. Related to it is the problem of collecting data and shaping it in a truly usable way. The issue here is that, despite its same nature, data is not structured and must be organized into clean structures with proper sentiment formalization and then turned into plain, unintelligible numbers.

Classification is a tricky problem for which SVM and other shallow learning algorithms can be applied, but a neural network is an option with the potential to be more accurate, even though only evidence can show that. And accuracy is vital in sentiment analysis. Which neural network then? A plain feed-forward neural network or something more sophisticated and deeper in its ability to learn?

In this chapter, we first used a couple of .NET Core consoles to copy the downloaded dataset into a sort of permanent cache represented by a relational database and then to create CSV files for a Python script to consume. We used Keras to build a bidirectional LSTM neural network with a dropout layer and an embedding layer at the gate. Finally, we used ML.NET to import the serialized model into a .NET Core application.

This chapter ends our excursion into the world of deep learning and in general in the space of pragmatic machine learning. The final part of the book is about general consideration of how the industry is tackling artificial intelligence and cloud services.

Final Thoughts

## CHAPTER 20

AI Cloud Services for the Real World

Part of the inhumanity of the computer is that, once it is competently programmed and working smoothly, it is completely honest.

—Isaac Asimov, I, Robot, 1950

Today cloud platforms offer a number of stunning AI-oriented services for rather advanced scenarios such as computer vision and speech analysis. These services, however, taken singularly, are only (rather sophisticated) tools for building end-to-end solutions. The cost of the end-to-end solution is on top of the services, although the services can unleash the building of rather futuristic and imaginative scenarios.

Machine learning enables two main families of end-to-end solutions. One consists of developing a machine learning solution from scratch. The other is about using prepackaged machine learning services like those exposed by most cloud platforms. Collecting data is necessary in both cases, but all other steps of the learning pipeline (data processing, feature engineering, training, evaluation) happen in a slightly different way if prepackaged services are used.

Prepackaged machine learning services are essentially software as a service (SaaS) products to be integrated into an end-to-end solution. They provide building blocks already trained and tested on hidden (but reliable) data. As a developer, you just consume these services as an API, and all you need to do is adjust some settings (also referred to as *hyperparameters*) to obtain exactly what you want. A great example of prepackaged services is Azure Cognitive Services, which provides out-of-the-box advanced services such as image and speech recognition, natural language processing, and semantic searching.

In this chapter, we'll explore the machine learning services and products available on the Microsoft Azure platform.

Azure Cognitive Services

Azure Cognitive Services is a collection of prepackaged services that developers can incorporate into desktop, web, mobile, and bot applications via an API. Cognitive Services do use machine learning internally but do that using hidden models pretrained on Microsoft-provided data. You don't need to know anything about the internals of these services; you only learn how to consume them and how to integrate them into your applications.

The services in Azure Cognitive Services empower applications to interact with end users through natural methods of communication, including speech, common language, and visuals. Table 20-1 provides a list of available services.

TABLE 20-1 Directory of Azure Cognitive Services

Category	Service	Actual Capabilities
Vision	Image classification	Recognizes scenes, activities, celebrities, and landmarks in images with OCR capabilities. Also supports customizable image recognition.
	Face recognition	Detects faces and emotions in images, with the ability to identify individuals and recognize groups and similar faces.
	Video indexer	Recognizes faces, scenes, objects, and activities in videos. Also able to extract metadata and audio and to perform keyframe analysis.
	Content analyzer	Detects explicit or offensive content in images and videos. Also able to block or filter content with external human moderation.
Speech	Transcript and pronunciation	Performs speech-to-text and text-to-speech with customizable models to deal with accents or ad hoc vocabularies.
	Speaker recognition	Recognizes a given speaker from samples.
	Translation	Provides real-time, automated, and largely customizable translation services.
Language	Contextual understanding	Understands the meaning of unstructured text and recognizes the intent behind pronounced words.
	Text analytics	Extracts key phrases and named entities and performs sentiment analysis.
	Spell-checking	Performs multilingual, Bing-based spell checking of terms.
Knowledge	Q&A	Semantically extracts Q&A from unstructured text.
	Search	Searches on the web for text, news, images, and videos and autocomplete phrases.

These services are not free of charge and must be used while connected. On average, the cost per batch of 1,000 transactions is about $4. Face detection, for example, is around $1, and Bing search and speech recognition are around $7. Full details about the costs can be found at https://azure.microsoft.com/en-us/pricing/details/cognitive-services.

Note that charges apply per transaction and not per API call. The definition of a transaction changes per category of service. For example, a transaction is a POST request (not all the API calls it may generate under the hood) for computer vision, or it is an utterance of 15 seconds for speech recognition.

Important These services are also available as Docker containers to be installed in your own environment. Docker must be configured to allow the containers to connect with and send billing data to Azure. Text and images are processed within the local container and never sent to the cloud. A connection to Azure is only required for billing.

The Azure Custom Vision cognitive service is a bit different because it lets you build and deploy your own image classifier. Put another way, it allows you to train the model over Azure using your own labels. As a developer, you submit groups of images and label them as you think appropriate. Then the algorithm trains itself to this data the best it can. The interesting thing is that after the algorithm is trained, tested, and accepted, you can also export the model itself for offline use. In other words, you pay for training but not for use of the trained model. Various export formats are supported, such as ONNX but also TensorFlow for Android devices and CoreML for iOS.

Azure Machine Learning Studio

Azure Machine Learning Studio (ML Studio) is an interactive and visual workspace to build and evaluate models for predictive analysis. It doesn't strictly require programming skills and can be powerful for data scientists to use. It drives users through the steps in the classic learning pipeline as reproduced in Figure 20-1.

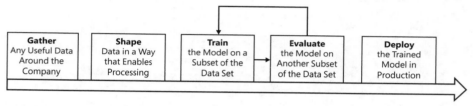

FIGURE 20-1 The learning pipeline

ML Studio essentially lets users compose an experiment by connecting datasets and *analysis modules* to select a specific subset of columns and perform some common cleaning tasks, such as removing rows that have any missing values. You can do all of this visually, by dragging and dropping and editing property panes. (See Figure 20-2.)

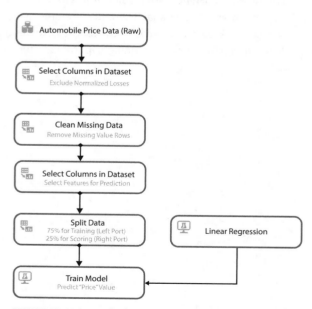

FIGURE 20-2 A sample data science experiment in Azure Machine Learning Studio

In Figure 20-2, one sample dataset full of automobile price data is connected to a list of data analysis modules for selecting a subset of columns, removing rows with missing values, selecting output columns (features), and splitting the data (75/25) between training and testing data. Finally, a linear regression algorithm component is added to the artifact before the model is trained. Figure 20-3 shows what happens after the training phase.

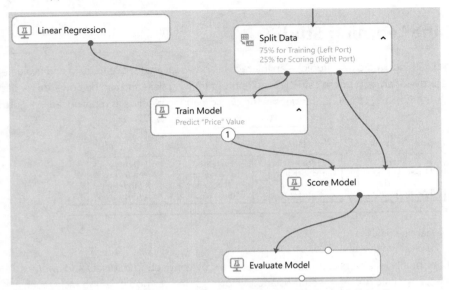

FIGURE 20-3 A sample data science experiment in Azure Machine Learning Studio

The live environment allows you to select a number of machine learning algorithms for anomaly detection, classification, clustering, various forms of regression, text analytics, and computer vision. You can use built-in blocks and import Python-based or R-based modules. In the end, it's like designing a workflow and running and evaluating it live with the freedom of changing hyperparameters from one of the web page sidebars. (See Figure 20-4.)

Properties   Project

◢ **Linear Regression**

Solution Method

| Ordinary Least Squares ⌄ |

L2 Regularization Weight

| 0.001 |

☑ Include Intercept Term

Random Number Seed

| |

☑ Allow Unknown Categ...

FIGURE 20-4 The property pane to configure the parameters for the linear regression block

When you're ready, you can convert the training experiment into a predictive model and publish it as a web service. Having the one-click capability to publish the model as a web service is immensely helpful and powerful because it makes the model accessible to other applications, including business intelligence and office applications.

Finally, note that ML Studio requires no coding and allows you to visually build and expose models. Compared to using Python or ML.NET, there are some cons, too. One is that you need an Azure subscription and then pay per model execution. In addition, the model is deployed as an HTTP service in Azure and can work only while you're connected (and you pay per use as well). Because it doesn't let you export the model offline (at least not yet), you can't build on top of it using transfer learning as ML.NET allows you to do.

Furthermore, the size of the dataset you can train on is limited, and you still need to upload the datasets to the cloud. Depending on the customer, uploading datasets might be challenging due to company policies or due to the large size of datasets.

Azure Machine Learning Service

Azure Machine Learning Service (ML Service) is the underlying machinery that backs up Azure Machine Learning Studio. Therefore, it is a cloud-based set of services that can be used to prepare, train, and deploy machine learning models. It also works as a repository of projects so that anything you do can be further managed and automated as appropriate.

When you create an experiment in ML Studio, you're actually telling ML Service to work out an internal script that goes after the steps of the experiment. With reference to Figure 20-4, it does the following:

- Loads data from an external file
- Filters columns and normalizes data
- Defines features to return
- Applies a linear regression algorithm
- Trains the model

Multiple algorithms can be concatenated and interspersed with further data manipulation blocks and externally loaded Python or R scripts. In turn, Python scripts may be import libraries such as TensorFlow.

If you opt to use ML Service directly, the workflow follows this sequence:

- Develop machine learning training scripts using Python and any of the popular packages such as TensorFlow, PyTorch, *scikit-learn*, Keras, and the like.
- Create and configure a compute target such as your local computer, the same ML Service, a Linux virtual machine in Azure, or perhaps Azure Databricks.
- Train the script.
- Submit the script to the compute target to run.

During training, the script can read from or write to a configured back-end storage, commonly an Azure blob container. Records of activity also are saved to keep track of all the steps of the experiment. If the run doesn't produce a satisfactory outcome, you make changes to the script and reiterate the loop.

If the trained model works as expected, ML Service requires that you load it into the model registry and develop a scoring script. A scoring script is simply the code that calls the model to make the predictions it was trained for. The model and the scoring script, along with all of its dependencies, form an image that is ultimately deployed as a web service in Azure. Typically, Python dependencies are gathered in the form of a Conda file for the specific environment.

Note Conda is a popular Python package management system to some extent similar to .NET Nuget or NodeJS NPM. In addition, it can also be used to manage and configure the runtime environment.

Having a structured ML model lifecycle, and a model registry and versioning, is probably the most important feature offered by the Azure ML Service. A tighter integration between the Azure ML team and ML.NET is in the works, so at some point in the future ML.NET code could be integrated in the script and ML.NET models stored in the registry. While .NET developers will understandably prefer to have full control of the model in production (e.g., to avoid latency issues), a structured ML model lifecycle and model registry and versioning would be greatly helpful.

ML Learning can create two types of images for the model: one is targeted to an Azure field-programming gate array (FPGA), and the other is targeted to a Docker file going to an Azure Container Instance or Kubernetes. Note that an FPGA is a computationally intensive hardware platform that is slated to outperform GPU for deep learning applications also in terms of reduced power consumption.

ML Service can be leveraged through the Azure portal as well as through a number of other rich environments. One is ML for Visual Studio Code, and another one is Azure Notebooks—a host environment for Jupyter Notebooks.

Note In this context, a *notebook* is a document produced by the Jupyter Notebook App (https://jupyter.org) made of computer code (Python, C++, R, Julia) as well as rich text elements (markdown, tables, equations, charts, links). A notebook is human-readable because it may contain a description of the machine learning experiment. At the same time, it is an executable document that can be run to perform data analysis.

Note Machine learning development in Python is definitely possible through the Azure portal as well as the ML Service extension for Visual Studio Code. Which other options exist? A short list includes Anaconda (www.anaconda.com), PyCharm (www.jetbrains.com/pycharm), PyDev (www.pydev.org), Sublime Text 3 (www.sublimetext.com/3), and Vim (www.vim.org).

Data Science Virtual Machines

Yet another option for machine learning on the Azure platform is getting a data science virtual machine (DSVM). A DSVM is a preconfigured virtual machine full of pre-installed goodies for data analysis, model development, and deployment. It is available on Windows Server and Linux, specifically Windows Server 2016, Windows Server 2012, Ubuntu, and CentOS. The main purpose of a DSVM is saving time and making you immediately ready to go with machine learning experiments.

A data science virtual machine ensures that all the data scientists on a team, as well as all the students in a class, can collaboratively work in the same environment with shared settings. The virtual machine is also the fastest way to evaluate machine learning tools that can be later used on-premise, such as SQL Server ML Services, Visual Studio tools, Jupyter, and a variety of learning toolkits.

In a DSVM, you will also find pre-installed tools like Anaconda, ML Server, R Studio, PyCharm, Vim, Power BI Desktop, Azure CLI, and a number of learning and deep learning frameworks. (See https://docs.microsoft.com/en-us/azure/machine-learning/data-science-virtual-machine.)

On-Premises Services

Some machine learning options are also available on-premises. In particular, you can have a special SQL Server machine learning add-on and a Windows server. Note that on-premises products can also run in a virtual machine hosted in the cloud.

SQL Server Machine Learning Services

SQL Server Machine Learning Services (SSMLS) is a machine learning engine that extends the relational capabilities of SQL Server 2016 and SQL Server 2017. It allows you to build, train, and run models in R and Python on top of the relational data stored in your SQL Server databases. The package also includes Anaconda to help build Python solutions and R Client for R solutions.

Interestingly, you can mix T-SQL and R and Python in your queries. The scripts you write (whether in R or Python) can be injected into stored procedures, and built models can be stored in a SQL Server table. The execution of the scripts takes place within the boundaries of the canonical data security model. In other words, a user who runs the script needs permission to access any relational database of choice. The user is not limited to read and write permissions, but an additional permission also is required to run external scripts. The most common approach for in-database machine learning is to use the *sp_execute_external_script* command passing R or Python script as an input parameter.

Another approach for using SSMLS is from a client workstation that runs Microsoft R Client or a Python IDE. From there, you write code that makes remote calls in much the same way that Windows applications push SQL commands.

Machine Learning Server

Machine Learning Server (ML Server) is a server platform that runs on top of a few operating systems such as Windows (from Windows 7 onward), Linux (Ubuntu, CentOS, Suse), and Hadoop Spark. You install it when you need to build and operationalize models built with R and Python on a server. Another scenario is when you need to distribute R and a Python model at scale on a Hadoop or Spark cluster.

The server comes with a bunch of development tools for both R and Python as well as a number of pretrained models.

Microsoft Data Processing Services

Before companies can unleash the power of machine learning, they need to get valuable analytics from their big data. Here are a few options available on Microsoft Azure.

Azure Data Lake

The term *data lake* commonly refers to a fairly large and growable repository where data (well, big data) is kept in its original, unfiltered format—timelines, emails, social network messages, plain files of any type, databases. In a way, a data lake works like a piggybank: as a user, you just throw data at it without a specific immediate purpose and without a clear duration.

As a result, the content of a data lake is fairly generic and unclassified because the purpose of the data is not defined yet. The moment the purpose of (some of) the data becomes clear, in fact, data is usually fetched and copied elsewhere in a more structured format. Items in a data lake have a minimal indexing layer. Each item is assigned a unique identifier and labeled with a set of tags—that's all of it, no hierarchies, and no pages. Internally, data is only moderately organized based on the declared frequency of access—hot, semi-hot, and cold data. Cold data, of course, is cheaper but slower to get back. On Azure, a single instance of a data lake uses a storage blob account and can store trillions of files and even individual files larger than one petabyte.

The term *data lake* is sometimes used interchangeably with the term *data warehouse*. There's a neat difference between the two. A data warehouse, in fact, is a repository for structured, filtered data that has already been processed for a specific goal. In Azure, you also have the Azure SQL Data Warehouse service for the purpose.

Any content in an instance of the Azure Data Lake can be consumed using Azure Databricks or Azure HDInsight.

Azure Databricks

Databricks (https://databricks.com) was founded by the original creators of Apache Spark as an alternative to the Map-Reduce paradigm. The purpose was to parcel out work through the nodes of a cluster and to ease the machine learning pipeline, from the preparation of data to the deployment of the model.

Today, Databricks is thought to be way faster than the open-source Apache Spark in querying data and is offered as an integrated Azure service. You use Azure Databricks by following these steps:

- Create a workspace to keep all of your things together.

- Configure a cluster based on a runtime environment that contains Spark and the Java virtual machine.

- Create a collection of cells that will run computations on the Spark cluster. The collection of cells is called a notebook. In doing so, you also set the primary language of the computation (e.g., SQL, R, Python).

- Connect a data source.

The list of supported data sources is fairly long and includes anything connected through a JDBC driver, Microsoft SQL Server, Azure SQL Database with Spark connector, Azure blob storage, Azure data lake, Cosmos DB, Cassandra, ElasticSearch, MongoDB, Neo4j, Redis, and a number of sparse JSON CSV and ZIP files.

Azure Databricks also provides a runtime for machine learning, which includes most popular libraries such as TensorFlow, PyTorch, Keras, and XGBoost. The runtime also supports distributed training using Horovod. The main differentiator between Azure Databricks and other machine learning environments is that it is ready to go and frees you from installing and configuring these libraries on the cluster. The machine learning runtime allows you to define models using Python, R, or even Scala and export them into an external system.

The end-to-end machine learning lifecycle is managed through MLflow (www.mlflow.org), an open-source platform to handle machine learning workflows.

Azure HDInsight

Azure HDInsight is a full-spectrum analytics service for enterprises. It can be populated with frameworks such as Hadoop, Apache Spark, Apache Hive, LLAP, Apache Kafka, Apache Storm, R, and more. All together, these frameworks enable a broad range of scenarios related to distributed processing of large datasets across clusters of computers.

Azure HDInsight is designed to scale up from single servers to thousands of machines to support application scenarios such as IoT, data warehousing, Extract-Transform-Load (ETL) and, last but not least, machine learning.

.NET for Apache Spark

Apache Spark is a general-purpose distributed engine for getting analytics over large datasets, typically in the order of terabytes or even petabytes, whether in batch or real-time mode and primarily for statistical and machine learning purposes. The power of Apache Spark is in its distributed nature, which includes a cluster of nodes and large chunks of memory to reduce computation time.

.NET for Apache Spark gives you a dedicated API for using Apache Spark from C# and F# applications, which is ideal for Microsoft-focused development teams. The .NET API allows you to access nearly all aspects of Apache Spark, including Spark SQL, for working with structured data, and Spark Streaming, for stream processing.

The .NET bindings for Spark are written on the Spark interop layer and compare in performance with Scala and Python bindings. It comes as a .NET Standard library and can be used from applications running on a variety of platforms.

.NET for Apache Spark is available by default in Azure HDInsight but can be installed in Azure Databricks and other services such as Azure Kubernetes Service and AWS Databricks. (See https://dotnet.microsoft.com/apps/data/spark.)

Azure Data Share

The latest baby to arrive in the Microsoft Azure family is Data Share. The service addresses a problem that many companies are facing—transferring and/or sharing large quantities of data. Uploading or downloading petabytes of data is enormously costly and time consuming. In addition, it may raise potential security concerns.

Azure Data Share provides a simple and safe solution for sharing large quantities of data between customers. Companies using the service leverage the entire layer of Azure security (authentication, encryption, instant access revocation) and can compose datasets from a variety of Azure sources. A number of customers and partners can be invited to access the data with different levels of access and permissions.

Azure Data Factory

Azure Data Factory is a service to generally address the problem of integrating and manipulating data from multiple silos into a shared and more structured environment, such as a data warehouse. A visual and code-free environment allows you to define and execute Extract-Load-Transform (ELT) and Extract-Transform-Load (ETL) pipelines. Needless to say, the same processes can be defined and executed with code in Python or .NET.

Azure Data Factory comes with more than 80 different built-in connectors for popular data sources and a growing library of templates for common tasks such as building pipelines, defining triggers, copying from a database, and executing SQL Server Integration Services packages in Azure.

Summary

In a nutshell, a machine learning solution is a software solution that hosts some specific form of artificial intelligence somewhere in the business layer. Sometimes, the intelligence is coded manually, implementing tasks around the core services of some frameworks and languages (ML.NET, *scikit-learn*), and sometimes the same task is achieved by combining and connecting cloud services. It is worth noting, though, that ML.NET is going to be more and more integrated into Azure, while providing offline support so you can run it wherever you want the way you want.

In this chapter, we briefly described the major AI-oriented services available on the Microsoft Azure platform. Note that similar services are offered by other cloud platforms such as Amazon Web Services and Google Cloud. In the end, though, our vision is that you don't use machine learning (and, in general, artificial intelligence) as a solution to reverse-engineer into some kind of a problem. We refer to brainstorming meetings along the lines of "What can we do here at *XXX* with computer vision?" or "What can we propose to *YYY* to make them use speech analysis?"

You should use machine learning (and, in general, artificial intelligence) to solve a problem in a possibly more intelligent way. In doing so, most of the time you need to envision, plan, and build an end-to-end solution that encompasses some algorithms and learning steps. In this context, cloud services are just another valuable tool to use. However, in our opinion, the most that you can get from cloud services is data processing capabilities and computational power.

## CHAPTER 21

The Business Perception of AI

There are lots of examples of routine, middle-skilled jobs that involve relatively structured tasks, and those are the jobs that are being eliminated the fastest.
—Erik Brynjolfsson, Director of MIT's Initiative on the Digital Economy

Everyone in the industry is using artificial intelligence as a bullhorn to reach and impress the widest possible audience. Everyone is emphasizing artificial intelligence as a powerful tool that could solve any IT issues and streamline any convoluted processes. But, at its core, AI is not magic but only data crunching, elbow grease, and software acumen.

Beyond hype and promises, companies need to seek end-to-end solutions to concrete business problems and measurable results for their efforts. Machine learning and the various forms in which AI manifests are quite powerful and reliable tools we have today to provide a new generation of end-to-end, tailor-made solutions at a reasonable cost.

That's all of it. Just software, possibly more intelligent than in the past.

Perception of AI in the Industry

Many times, we've heard sales directors glossing over complex business scenarios and promising their teams would deliver magic results just after training an algorithm. Algorithms (and related computing and cloud services) seem to be the new formidable tool capable of turning blurred dreams into sharp reality.

Most strategy meetings revolve around the shape and substance of some killer app to propose to some large customer and the buzzwords to put in the final list of takeaways. It is as if part of the industry waits for AI to show up at the reception to deliver its magic like an ordered pizza while the other part is willing to advertise as deliverable any types of goodies they can think of.

Realizing the Potential

Undoubtedly, the ability to implement forms of artificial intelligence will have a major impact on the efficiency of any organization and will make any software products richer and likely closer to the customers. Having said that, though, consider that none of this is free, and nothing is free of issues.

The hardest part is realizing the potential.

According to a 2019 Gartner survey, less than 10 percent of the companies had already deployed some AI-based solutions with all the others sitting at some planning stage. On the other hand, realizing the potential that a company can materialize through artificial intelligence is not a trivial task. And it is for the simple reason that realizing the AI potential is—no more, no less—the culmination of the digital transformation process.

If your organization is steadily facing the challenges of the market, then in some way you're already using intelligent tools to make decisions. Intelligence is already in the software you use—though not in the more effective ways that go under the name of *machine learning*, *deep learning*, or just generically, *artificial intelligence*.

The key step in realizing the potential of artificial intelligence for your company is not so much listening to what others are doing or what vendors suggest you may be doing. The key step is understanding yourself what artificial intelligence is, how it really works, and how things could work in a more digitally transformed space.

Learn about artificial intelligence and then look at your business unbiased, without mental restrictions. Devise your objectives and strategy and make plans. Artificial intelligence is only a (quite powerful) tool you can use along the way. The point, however, is realizing the potential—not deploying artificial intelligence.

What Artificial Intelligence Can Do for You

In general, more intelligent systems can automate a great amount of work, thus reducing the risk of human errors and speeding up processes. Note, though, that automating tasks is just what plain software has been doing for decades. Artificial intelligence (and machine learning in particular) adds on top the unique ability to be trained to be smart.

Training an algorithm is much like training a new employee. You don't typically expect magic from a new employee, but you expect she has learned enough to deliver good service in the context of the organization. It's the same for machine learning algorithms. You can ultimately get better outcomes, but you actually get that if the employee has the skills and attitude for the role, is well trained, and once at work is assigned appropriate tasks.

As a recap, there are five main areas where artificial intelligence (primarily in the form of machine learning) can be a game changer: prediction, cognition, classification, human emulation, and creation.

Prediction

Predictive modeling leverages the power of statistics to make forecasts in a number of domains. Often associated with meteorology, predictive modeling has, in reality, many applications in business. For example, it is employed in online advertising and marketing where data scientists use historical web data to determine what kinds of products users are likely to click on.

Predictions are extremely helpful in capacity planning, industrial maintenance, scheduling of activities, and customer relationship management to target customers who are most likely to make a purchase. Predictions are crucial in the economy for guessing the future prices of goods and in energy for predicting amount of production in renewable power plants.

Last but not least, predictive models are great at detecting fraudulent behavior by spotting anomalies and outliers in a large dataset of business transactions.

Cognition

Cognitive modeling brings the capability to simulate human mental processes to software. It can be used to achieve human-like performance on tasks that are hard for traditional computers but easy for the human brain. Popular examples of cognition are computer vision (recognizing objects and movement) and speech recognition to lay the foundation of a true conversation.

Chatbots are a great example of applied computer cognition, but detecting obstacles through cameras in the automotive industry is another great example. However, the coolest application (at this stage, only a prototype) of computer cognition is the demo of a computer-based doctor's assistant that records doctor/patient conversation and extracts and selects relevant pieces of information for later analysis.

Classification

Classification is a common technique that allows the grouping of items based on some observed (or reported) characteristics. Classification is related to the detection of trends and patterns and association—namely, the technique that discovers relationships between observed behaviors.

Classification is able to tell how likely it is that certain data match certain known characteristics. Such a generic schema finds a lot of concrete applications in business. For example, it may help determine which of many sales channels will have the highest return based on historical customer behavior so that you can optimize the marketing budget.

Human Emulation

That computers behave like humans is an old dream and probably the area of computer science with the greatest (and largely unexpressed) potential. Artificial intelligence can enable software applications to sustain and comprehend a conversation via natural language, make business decisions autonomously, and perform tasks in an automatic way.

Emulating humans requires implementing a set of capabilities strictly related to understanding. This includes sentiment analysis, word and concept extraction from text, and planning of full recommendation systems.

Creation

Curation of content is an emerging area of artificial intelligence mostly related to classification. However, machine learning can do much more and reach the peak of creating brand new content—whether narrative text, custom images, or even code.

Challenges Around the Corner

The list of results that can be realistically achieved with artificial intelligence is longer than the list of results effectively (and reliably) achieved so far. A great example of the hype around artificial intelligence can be found in the manufacturing industry around the theme of intelligent maintenance of assets. The hot question is: can a computer predict the remaining useful life of devices and machines?

Nearly everyone sees business value in getting a reliable answer to this question. So, investments are being made, and some solutions are even in place somewhere, but the general sentiment is that no universally valid solution has been found yet.

And here's the biggest challenge: developing artificial intelligence in the real world is much more frustrating than most people think.

Problems and Algorithms

The one-problem-one-algorithm equation is good only for sales and marketing gimmicks. The class of problems that the industry wishes to address with machine learning—in some cases, the class of problems that the industry discovered thanks to machine learning—contains both problems for which a solution is known and problems for which no solution is known.

In the former case, it means that you know the business, the important variables, and its dynamics. In the latter case, instead, it means that you're not sure how the business works, but you still need to find a way to reproduce and automate it to the extent that doing so is possible.

How would you solve a problem that you don't know how to solve?

The capable umbrella of machine learning includes techniques borrowed from statistics and computer science that design algorithms to process data, make predictions, and subsequently help make decisions. Unlike pure statistics, machine learning is mostly about reliable predictions and classification, whether those outcomes come from a representative model or the combination of various algorithms applied in a pipeline until it sufficiently works.

To solve a problem that you don't know much about, you can only use sophisticated neural networks such as a convolutional or recurrent neural network. The hard work is to find, in some way, the best combination of parameters to use to drive the network to an acceptable solution.

Trial and Error

Whether you know how to solve a problem and look for some software to do it quickly and reliably, or you don't know how to solve the problem and are just taking a stab in the dark with learning algorithms, to successfully address a business problem, you need patience and commitment.

To successfully employ artificial intelligence, you must be ready to tolerate some level of inaccuracy in the response. If you want it all, and want it right and right away, you're not going to be happy with artificial intelligence.

In addition, you should keep in mind that artificial intelligence doesn't solve a general problem, but only a problem in a specific context. You want to use artificial intelligence to alleviate repetitive tasks and to speed up known tasks. For example, you can have software look at the numbers that generate a chart and raise an alarm instead of painting sophisticated charts and letting humans guess what is possibly going wrong. Another example is having software look into images—say medical images—and make a diagnosis quickly and effectively.

As with humans, there's a lot of training to go through, but it's never a one-step training phase. It's continuous training instead.

Sitting by the River Long Enough

Overall, a crucial mistake in business aspects related to artificial intelligence is sitting by the river and just waiting for the body of your enemy to float by. Here, we're paraphrasing the popular quote from Sun Tzu—the Chinese general and philosopher who lived in the sixth century BCE.

Frustrated by the lack of reliable answers, most managers find it easier to spend money only in front of a working and battlefield-tested product: "Show me the product, and I'll spend my money." The problem is that this is not the ideal way to approach artificial intelligence from a business standpoint.

AI is not a product you can buy at a full or discounted price.

AI is just software to build.

Hence, it needs a plan, a project, and resources in terms of data, people, and money. Worse yet, it needs strong commitment. The best we can suggest to managers and executives is understanding the idea behind artificial intelligence and learning the mechanics of machine learning.

End-to-End Solutions

Whatever your current idea of artificial intelligence is, turning it into reality probably requires a trained model, but that is surely not sufficient.

You need an end-to-end solution. The model you lovingly craft and train needs to be integrated into a software product with a user interface, a user experience, modules of business logic, a database, and networking. From an architectural perspective, a machine learning model is just a domain service.

> **Note** You don't necessarily need machine learning to have some intelligent software. A line of JavaScript code in a web page that offers to copy content across different fields or complete a partially typed date is undoubtedly perceived as "intelligent" by users, not to mention the results of any analysis conducted autonomously on data that become suggestions. No supercomputer is required for this, yet it induces a positive mood about the solution. A nice user experience is a form of artificial intelligence.

Let's Just Call It Consulting

Although AI seems to be a major advancement of these modern times, in the end it is something that nearly everybody, in some form, is already doing and experiencing—except that they call it *optimization* or, more generically, *consulting*.

Is artificial intelligence really different?

Cheap computing power today makes computable things that weren't realistically computable before. In addition, there's a wide availability of processable data that was accumulated in the past decade—not coincidentally in the years that saw the success of social networks. Both factors, though, wouldn't have been enough if it weren't for a third one: the cloud.

The cloud made it easy and affordable to build and sell services of nearly any computational complexity. The cloud allowed some big IT players like Microsoft, Google, and Amazon to build and package a few cognitive and intelligent services for public use. And, all of a sudden, building a web front end that, paired with a camera, can identify in real time all the people passing by has become doable—even in the short time of a hackathon.

However, using a cognitive service is one thing; it is quite another to integrate machine learning models in an end-to-end solution for the real world, such as predicting the price of energy for the day-ahead and intraday markets, scanning financial transactions for fraud, classifying visitors of an e-commerce site from the type of device they're using, and more.

> **Note** In Chapter 7, "Implementing the ML.NET Pipeline," we used a trivial prediction model for the cost of a taxi ride. The model was trivial to build and train and fairly usable in a low-precision scenario. But it's a kind of pointless component if not hosted in the context of broader and focused solution such as, for example, an online taxi platform.

The Borderline Between Software and Data Science

In today's common perception, machine learning is predominantly a data science effort and therefore requires data science and advanced statistics skills. Software development is just another activity.

Data Science Teams

Most companies hire a team of data science geeks, put some vague problems on the table, and leave them free to scan the universe of available historical data repositories (e.g., OSIsoft PI, various manufacturer historians, RDBMS) to capture data and Spark and Azure to store and manipulate it.

The data science team at some point delivers the trained model, signs off on the project, and looks for some other cool challenge to seize. The model is left in the hands of some development team to figure out how to integrate it in some client application (see Figure 21-1). The message is: the algorithm has the highest score; any other problem is necessarily software-related.

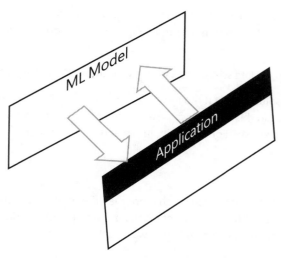

FIGURE 21-1 Machine learning model and application working together

Even the most common selection of tools in a data science space denotes the will to stay away from pure software development. Python, in fact, has the reputation of being a programming language for nonprogrammers.

We wonder if there's any good value in merging data science and software development both in a new professional figure and the practical implementation of projects and composition of teams. We don't much believe in a neat separation between data science teams and software development teams. We believe in teams composed of data scientists, domain experts, and developers, in which they all contribute the best of their expertise but know more than just the basics of other areas.

In other words, we envision machine learning as possibly yet another highly specialistic area for software developers.

> **Important** On the way to merging data science and software development, as .NET is a crucial platform for running user-facing applications, ML.NET is central. ML.NET makes it possible to do native machine learning, but it also allows for the (re)training of TensorFlow models and even addresses the needs of those companies that have data scientists who work only on Python. NimbusML, in fact, is a ML.NET binding for Python and is shaped to be very similar to *scikit-learn*, so data scientists can generate native ML.NET models that can be directly used and scored in any .NET application. For more information, see https://docs.microsoft.com/en-us/nimbusml/overview.

Data Science versus Software

Data scientists write code as a necessary means to a well-known business end. Software developers, instead, write code to the well-known end of building line-of-business applications. Data science and software development are inherently different, however. Data science, for example, is an analytic activity that software development, for the most part, is not. Data scientists tackle business problems such as detecting possibly fraudulent credit card transactions or predicting the price of goods in a given temporal horizon.

The point is, should we consider the output of data science as a business solution? Definitely not.

A trained model is a necessary part of the solution, but it is barely usable without a solid and user-friendly software façade. Can data scientists build this software façade? Possibly, but likely not. Can some smart software developers act as data scientists? For relatively simple and common problems, definitely yes.

Is there any trend we can envision?

Yes, software developers will invade the data science space much more than the other way around. We believe in software developers who know about the internals of machine learning and algorithms. The borderline between software development and machine learning will get thinner and thinner in the context of artificial intelligence projects.

This is nothing more than our opinion, fallible as many human things. However, as a matter of fact, Microsoft is investing money in a framework like ML.NET that trains models using .NET languages. It may not work in a (small? large?) number of cases, but there's no reason why data science can't be done in .NET and by (a subset of highly specialized) software developers.

Agile AI

As you can guess from Figure 21-1, data science and software development teams are commonly viewed as operating at two distinct phases of a waterfall-like process, as in Figure 21-2.

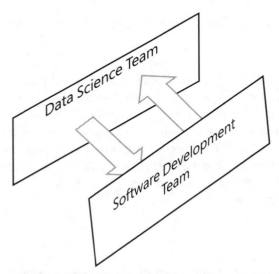

FIGURE 21-2 Waterfall-style separation between a data science team and software development team

Evolving from the Natural Waterfall-style Method

According to the waterfall methodology of project development, model training and model deployment and integration in a client application are distinct stages of the same project, and the data science work finishes before integration can begin. Some stages in between can also be imagined between training and deployment; for example, to get approval from the customer after presenting some numbers about the score of the algorithm.

In general, there's also third phase to take into account at the beginning of the pipeline that can also be viewed as a stage of a waterfall process—data preparation. (See Figure 21-3.)

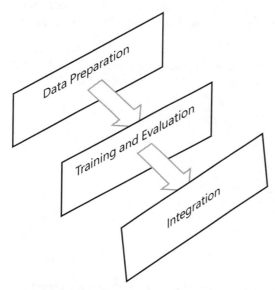

FIGURE 21-3 Three waterfall phases for a machine learning project

Data preparation is functional to training, and evaluation is tightly related to training. In our full example discussed in Chapter 7, we had three distinct projects for each of the steps.

Impact of Rigidity

The most reported issue of machine learning projects is also the major problem of waterfall solutions. In waterfall, the issue is that stakeholders may not see what is going to be delivered until it's nearly done, and by that time, changes can be difficult and costly to implement. In machine learning, it is even worse. The actual outcome of the model can only be evaluated in production and often over relatively long trial periods. In addition, there's not much that can be fixed on the fly.

You can fix an underperforming algorithm in a number of ways: First, you can fine-tune some of the hyperparameters. It is an approach that still requires retraining of the model but not much other work. If not enough, you can consider changing the algorithm. This is much more intrusive work because it may not be obvious which different algorithm to use. And if it's a neural network, the situation is even worse. If a neural network misbehaves in production, changing its parameters for retraining can be like taking a stab in the dark. Finally, the algorithm might be good, but the problem is the data.

In any of these cases, the data science team must be recomposed and work out another trained model from scratch. It's a loss of money, indeed.

Adding Agility

To mitigate these project management problems, we suggest adding agility to the whole machine learning pipeline. The data science team and the development team should then work side by side and develop a host environment and model at nearly the same time so that ensuring the production usage is clear helps in figuring out if all necessary data is on board and how to optimize it for the expected results.

Not having temporally separated phases of work prevents management problems, such as replacing missing people and, in general, turnover. Figure 21-4 revisits the classic Agile DevOps infographic for a machine learning scenario.

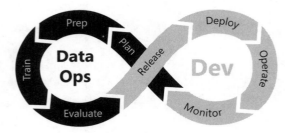

FIGURE 21-4 The Dev DataOps Agile cycle

For data science and development teams to work together (and along with domain experts), it is necessary that skills tend to merge: data scientists learning about programming aspects and user experience and, more importantly, developers learning about the intricacies and internal mechanics of machine learning.

This is the ultimate message of the book.

 Note In Azure ML, the model registry and model versioning with MLOps and MLFlow are key features to take of the entire model lifecycle. See https://docs.microsoft.com/en-us/azure/machine-learning/service/how-to-use-mlflow.

Those are the main reasons why we want ML.NET support in Azure ML.

Summary

The foundation of any artificial forms of intelligence is making programmatic decisions timelier and more reliably. However, this is not what people commonly identify with AI. Like it or not, these days artificial intelligence is perceived as something that can go beyond reality and transcend it. The perspective of AI offered by the media is nothing more than outliers, whether they evoke a doomsday picture (computers will take humans by storm) or prefigure a paradisiac scenario (computers will make human life wonderful).

As a result, IT managers are under pressure: on one hand, they hear wonders about cloud-based AI services; on the other hand, they face staggering bills when embarking on some concrete projects. Artificial intelligence definitely has the power to exceed expectations, but sometimes the expectations (and the needs) of companies and consumers are much lower than sophisticated artificial intelligence algorithms can address. When thinking of artificial intelligence in a business perspective, we see a lot of hype but also a lot of sincere needs. Overall, a significant driver for the business hype around artificial intelligence is the limited intelligence currently provided by most commercial software, and artificial intelligence today is a more powerful and modern way to solve common business problems.

We don't expect AI to clone humans anytime soon, and we don't expect AI to be the implementor of human dreams either. Instead, we expect AI to help humans through a new generation of software applications—still made of executable files but incorporating trained models to provide "magical" answers to known questions. And even though, at the moment, the focus of machine learning is all on data science, there's a lot of software development skills around any trained models.

Index